JENNY WILLIAMS

More Lives than One

A Biography of Hans Fallada

PENGUIN BOOKS

PENGUIN BOOKS

Published by the Penguin Group
Penguin Books Ltd, 80 Strand, London WC2R ORL, England
Penguin Group (USA) Inc., 375 Hudson Street, New York, New York 10014, USA
Penguin Group (Canada), 90 Eglinton Avenue East, Suite 700, Toronto, Ontario, Canada M4P 2Y3
(a division of Pearson Penguin Canada Inc.)
Penguin Ireland, 25 St Stephen's Green, Dublin 2, Ireland (a division of Penguin Books Ltd)
Penguin Group (Australia), 250 Camberwell Road,
Camberwell, Victoria 3124, Australia (a division of Pearson Australia Group Pty Ltd)
Penguin Books India Pvt Ltd, 11 Community Centre,
Panchsheel Park, New Delhi – 110 017, India
Penguin Group (NZ), 67 Apollo Drive, Rosedale, Auckland 0632, New Zealand
(a division of Pearson New Zealand Ltd)
Penguin Books (South Africa) (Pty) Ltd, 24 Sturdee Avenue,
Rosebank, Johannesburg 2196, South Africa

Penguin Books Ltd, Registered Offices: 80 Strand, London WC2R ORL, England

www.penguin.com

First published in Great Britain by Libris 1998
Published in Penguin Books 2012

1

Copyright © Jenny Williams, 1998, 2012
Map copyright © Hanni Bailey, 2012
All rights reserved
The moral right of the author has been asserted

Set in 9.25/12.5 pt Sabon LT Std
Typeset by Jouve (UK), Milton Keynes
Printed in England by Clays Ltd, St Ives plc

ISBN: 978-0-241-95267-2

www.greenpenguin.co.uk

Penguin Books is committed to a sustainable
future for our business, our readers and our
planet. This book is made from paper certified
by the Forest Stewardship Council.

'For he who lives more lives than one
More deaths than one must die.'

– Oscar Wilde

Contents

List of Illustrations

(Illustrations 1–11, 13–24, 26–32 and 34–6 are taken, with the kind permission of Uli Ditzen, from his private collection; illustration 12 is from *Hans Fallada. Sein Leben in Bildern und Briefen* (p. 73); and illustration 25 is from the private collection of Gunnar Müller-Waldeck.)

Map

NORTH SEA

KIEL
Lütjenburg
Neumünster
LÜBECK
HAMBURG

Uelzen
Celle
Plathe
HANOVER
Elbe

Ems
Weser

Blankenburg
Bad Sachsa
Brehna
HALLE
Bad Berka
Marburg
Schnepfenthal
Weimar
LEIPZIG
Tabarz
Jena
Eichfeld
GERA
Rudolstadt
FRANKFURT/M.
Eisfeld
Main

Rhine
Bad Mergentheim
NUREMBERG

Danube

MUNICH

Author's Note

Eleven of Fallada's works have appeared in English translation to date. They are given in chronological order of their original publication in German.

Short Treatise on the Joys of Morphinism (Sachlicher Bericht über das Glück, ein Morphinist zu sein), translated by Michael Hofmann, 2011 (London: Penguin).

A Small Circus (Bauern, Bonzen und Bomben), translated by Michael Hofmann, 2012 (London: Penguin).

Little Man – What Now? (Kleiner Mann – was nun?), translated by Eric Sutton, 1933 (London: Putnam). New translation by Susan Bennett, 1996 (London: Libris); this translation published in US in 2009 (New York: Melville House).

Who Once Eats out of the Tin Bowl (Wer einmal aus dem Blechnapf frißt), translated by Eric Sutton, 1934 (London: Putnam); US title, The World Outside (New York: Simon and Schuster).

Once We Had a Child (Wir hatten mal ein Kind), translated by Eric Sutton, 1935 (London: Putnam).

Old Heart Goes on a Journey (Altes Herz geht auf die Reise), translated by Eric Sutton, 1936 (London: Putnam); US title, Old Heart Goes A-Journeying (New York: Simon and Schuster).

Sparrow Farm (Das Märchen vom Stadtschreiber, der aufs Land flog), translated by Eric Sutton, 1937 (London: Putnam).

Wolf among Wolves (*Wolf unter Wölfen*), translated by
   Philip Owens, 1938 (London: Putnam); restored and with
   additional translations by Thorsten Carstensen and
   Nicholas Jacobs, 2010 (New York: Melville House).

Iron Gustav (*Der eiserne Gustav*), translated by Philip
   Owens, 1940 (London: Putnam).

The Drinker (*Der Trinker*), translated by Charlotte and
   A.L. Lloyd, 1952 (London: Putnam). New edition of this
   translation, 1989 (London: Libris); published in US
   in 2009 (New York: Melville House).

Alone in Berlin (*Jeder stirbt für sich allein*), translated by
   Michael Hofmann, 2009 (London: Penguin); this transla-
   tion subsequently published in the US under the title *Every
   Man Dies Alone* (New York: Melville House, 2009).

English translations before 1950 were often abbreviated or were
based on unreliable sources; quotations from such editions have
therefore been newly translated and page numbers in the notes refer
to the current German editions listed in the Bibliography. In addition,
I have not felt myself bound to use the existing English titles of works
by Fallada in every case. On its first mention each book is given its
German title, followed by an English title, in italics when it corresponds to the published English translation (*Old Heart Goes on a
Journey*) and in single quotation marks when it does not ('Once a
Jailbird', instead of the rather cumbersome *Who Once Eats out of
the Tin Bowl*); subsequent references use the English title. The same
system has been applied to German works by writers other than Fallada;
in this instance, the titles given in single quotation marks are, again,
my translation of the title.

My thanks to Christine Shuttleworth for compiling the original index;
it has been updated for the current edition.

Introduction

This book is devoted to the life of a remarkable man – among other things an alcoholic, drug addict, womanizer, jailbird and thief, in his time wooed by both the Nazi and the Soviet cultural authorities – who in his novels chronicles the fate of a social class in a period of great upheaval and makes an eloquent plea for ordinary human decency and who, in the words of one of the heroes of his youth, discovered for himself that 'he who lives more lives than one/More deaths than one must die.'[1]

'Hans Fallada' was a best-selling German novelist of the early 1930s. His *Kleiner Mann – was nun?* (*Little Man – What Now?*) rescued the business of his publisher and friend Ernst Rowohlt from bankruptcy in 1932.[2] *Little Man – What Now?* was also a success in Britain and the US, where it was filmed by Universal Pictures. However, Rudolf Ditzen, the man behind the *nom de plume* Hans Fallada, had been largely forgotten in the English-speaking world until 2009, when the phenomenal success of *Alone in Berlin*, the first English translation of his last novel, *Jeder stirbt für sich allein*, brought him again to the attention of English readers.[3]

Fallada's reputation has been as much at the mercy of political developments since his death in 1947 as it was during his lifetime. Yet his output – novels, poems, short stories, letters, translations, reviews and children's stories – was prodigious, his observation of the contemporary scene acute, and his talent as a storyteller unsurpassed in twentieth-century German literature. Now, more than sixty years after his death, it is time to undertake a reassessment of a writer who lived a turbulent life in turbulent times and through it all maintained a belief in universal human values.

Hans Fallada was the pseudonym of Rudolf Ditzen, who published his first novel at the age of twenty-six under an assumed name ostensibly in order to spare his parents' feelings. Ditzen relates that his pen name derived from characters in two of Grimms' *Fairy Tales*: 'Hans', the happy-go-lucky simpleton in 'Lucky Hans' and 'Fal(l)ada', the horse in 'The Goose Girl', who, even after he has been beheaded, continues to bear witness to the truth.

The adoption of a pen name had an additional and more complex significance: it permitted Rudolf Ditzen through the persona of Hans Fallada to create a world in which the conflicts and tensions of his life could be resolved. The pseudonym was thus cause and effect of the artistic process. In a radio broadcast in 1946 Ditzen declared: 'Everything in my life ends up in my books.'[4]

The strongly autobiographical dimension which is a striking feature of Ditzen's writing is a further indication that the pseudonym Hans Fallada was not a mere stratagem to protect his family from publicity but was central to his artistic impulse. As we shall see, everything written under the name Hans Fallada was fiction – even ostensibly autobiographical pieces. This biography, which views its subject not only as a writer but also as farmer, white-collar worker, husband and father, will therefore refer to him as Rudolf Ditzen since this is the name which he used in everyday life and by which he was known both inside and outside his immediate family circle.

Born on 21 July 1893, the son of a member of the Prussian judiciary who was later appointed to the German Imperial Supreme Court in Leipzig, Rudolf Ditzen was committed to a psychiatric hospital at the age of eighteen after killing a close friend in a duel. This was the first of many periods spent in psychiatric care. In the 1920s he served two prison sentences for theft and embezzlement; in 1933 he was arrested and held in custody by the SA, the Nazi Party's private army, or storm troop (*Sturmabteilung*); eleven years later he was imprisoned once again, on this occasion for the attempted murder of his first wife.

Ditzen chose to remain in Germany during the Nazi period. He never joined the Nazi Party, indeed he loathed all the strutting and posing, the corruption and the denunciations. However, he accommodated himself to the authorities to the extent that he rewrote the conclusion to one of his novels at Goebbels's behest, and as a major in the *Reichsarbeitsdienst* he undertook three officially sponsored tours to the Front in 1943 to gather material for the Nazi propaganda machine. Yet, when the Soviet army arrived in Mecklenburg in the spring of 1945, it installed him as mayor of Feldberg, his local town, where his duties included supervising the denazification effort.

Is this the life-story of a moral coward or a political opportunist or, even, a schizophrenic? Or is it representative of thousands upon thousands of Germans in the first half of the twentieth century? Momentous decisions, such as Rudolf Ditzen's decision not to emigrate to England in 1938, were made without the benefit of hindsight. Should this make the judgement of posterity less harsh? Bertolt Brecht, in his poem 'To Those Born Later', begs future generations to remember him and his contemporaries 'with forbearance'. Does this apply to Ditzen, too? Or was Thomas Mann right when he stated: '. . . any books which could be printed at all in Germany between 1933 and 1945 are worse than useless . . . A stench of blood and shame attaches to them; they should all be pulped.'⁵ To what extent can Ditzen's lack of resistance to National Socialism be read as support? These are all questions which a biographer is obliged to address. Indeed, these are the very questions that make Rudolf Ditzen such a fascinating and challenging subject.

After the war, in the Soviet zone of occupation, Ditzen enjoyed the patronage of Johannes R. Becher, the senior literary figure among those German Communists who returned from exile in the USSR, and there in 1946 he wrote the first anti-fascist novel of the post-war period, *Alone in Berlin*. Rudolf Ditzen died on 5 February 1947 in East Berlin, a physical and psychological wreck – amid praise in the East for his contribution to the German humanist tradition and opprobrium in the West for his opportunism and capitulation to fascism.

The story of Hans Fallada does not end with Rudolf Ditzen's death. His second wife, Ulla Ditzen, was named his sole and legitimate heir in September 1949 and she remarried a month later. The chaos of the immediate post-war period, combined with her drug dependency, her ignorance of literary matters and her apparently rather unscrupulous third husband resulted in a number of Ditzen's manuscripts being sold and/or lost. The Hey family bought what remained in 1955 and

Ditzen's letters, reviews, manuscripts and other writings lay in a cellar in Braunschweig until they were acquired by the Academy of the Arts in East Berlin in the late 1970s at the instigation of Tom Crepon, the then Director of the Writers' Centre in Neubrandenburg.

The view of Ditzen/Fallada in what was then, and remained until 1990, the German Democratic Republic (GDR/East Germany), had been moulded by Becher, who in his graveside oration expressed the view that: 'Fallada the writer was no profound thinker ... It was everyday life and ordinary people he loved ... He knew the lives of these ordinary men and women better than almost anybody else and he reflected their joys and their sorrows in a realistic manner. This was his strength and at the same time it was his weakness as both man and artist.'[6] This view was taken up and developed by Alfred Geßler, who produced the first comprehensive East German assessment of Fallada's work in 1972, placing him, in Marxist terms, in the petit bourgeois, democratic tradition. Geßler saw Ditzen as an outsider with a tendency to run away from problems, who observed and chronicled people and events but did not understand the forces at work in society. According to Geßler, Ditzen's critical realism and humanism enabled him to portray the plight of the 'little man', the white-collar worker with his working-class income and middle-class aspirations, with sympathy and understanding, thereby ensuring the success of his novels. Geßler's study, entitled *Hans Fallada. Sein Leben und Werk* ('Hans Fallada. His Life and Work'), views the writer through the filter of his work, with the result, for example, that the first thirty-three years of Ditzen's life are covered in a mere twelve pages.[7] Geßler and subsequent East German critics discounted Ditzen's first two novels, *Der junge Goedeschal* ('Young Goedeschal') and *Anton und Gerda* ('Anton and Gerda'), on the grounds that they were immature 'puberty novels' and not representative of Ditzen the critical realist.

The second East German biography, by Tom Crepon, appeared in 1978. In the foreword the author describes his *Leben und Tode des Hans Fallada* ('The Lives and Deaths of Hans Fallada') as 'not a scholarly monograph' but 'a largely authentic report', an attempt 'to follow Rudolf Ditzen's path through life and to reconstruct situations, places and conversations along the way'.[8] Crepon, who acknowledges the influence of Anna ('Suse') Ditzen, the author's first wife, on his study, chronicles Rudolf Ditzen's life in a largely non-judgemental and sympathetic manner, filling gaps in the record with imaginative 'reconstructions'.

In 1981, Ditzen's papers and manuscripts were returned to Feldberg and housed in an archive in a refurbished villa on the wooded slopes of the Haussee lake. Across the lake lived Anna Ditzen, widely acclaimed as the 'model' for the heroine of *Little Man – What Now?*, and her house, too, soon became a place of pilgrimage for students and scholars interested in her husband's work. The year 1981 also saw the publication of a third East German biography – *Hans Fallada. Sein großes kleines Leben* ('Hans Fallada. His Great and Little Life') by Werner Liersch.[9] Liersch views Rudolf Ditzen as the product of a particular socio-historical situation and draws parallels with other male writers of his generation and class. He argues that Ditzen's illnesses and addictions were determined primarily by social and historical factors rather than genetic or psychological ones.

However, the East German scholar who made the greatest contribution to ensuring the success of Fallada's work is Günter Caspar, who was responsible for the ten volumes of *Ausgewählte Werke* ('Selected Works') published by Aufbau between 1962 and 1987. Caspar not only produced meticulous editions but wrote detailed and extremely well-researched commentaries for eight of the volumes.[10]

Following the opening of the archive, a Friends of Hans Fallada society (Fallada Freundeskreis) was formed in Feldberg in 1983. This band of enthusiasts collected rare editions, celebrated the author's life and work and carried out and published valuable research, such as Manfred Kuhnke's work on Ditzen's last period in Berlin. The existence of such a society is testimony to the special place that Ditzen/Fallada continued to enjoy in the hearts and minds of his readers in East Germany.

East German television contributed to the popularity of Fallada's work by commissioning a regular supply of films: *Wolf unter Wölfen* (*Wolf among Wolves*) in 1964, *Little Man – What Now?* in 1967, *Alone in Berlin* in 1970 and *Altes Herz geht auf die Reise* (*Old Heart Goes on a Journey*) in 1987. There were also a number of films based on Fallada's stories for children.[11]

In the Federal Republic of Germany (FRG/West Germany), Rowohlt began publishing again in 1946. *Little Man – What Now?* was the first volume to appear (in 1950) in the popular *rororo* paperback series. This novel found a steady readership in the 1950s in West Germany, as did the 'unpolitical' books. In 1963 a biography by Jürgen Manthey appeared in the Rowohlt Picture Monograph series.[12] Manthey regards Ditzen as the victim of an authoritarian, repressive upbringing which engendered guilt and a desire for self-destruction. He draws on Wilhelm Reich's psychoanalytic analysis of the petit bourgeois personality in his assessment of Ditzen's psycho-sexual development, concluding that Ditzen suffered from acute identity problems and a dual personality, which he attempted to resolve through writing and the excessive use of alcohol and other addictive substances. Manthey lays particular emphasis on Ditzen's relationship with his father, noting that nowhere in Fallada's work is a positive father figure to be found, and he characterizes his literary output as 'the work of an author with a clear mother fixation'.[13]

Television in West Germany commissioned Fallada films, too. The first post-war Fallada film, *Wer einmal aus dem Blechnapf frißt* ('Once a Jailbird') was made in 1962 for the West German Broadcasting Company (WDR), which also produced a film of *Alone in Berlin* in the same year. *Der Trinker* (*The Drinker*) followed in 1967, *Bauern, Bonzen und Bomben* (*A Small Circus*) in 1973, a second film of *Alone in Berlin* in 1975, and *Der eiserne Gustav* (*Iron Gustav*) in 1979.

It was not until the late 1960s that the prison novel 'Once a Jailbird' and the political novels *Wolf among Wolves* and *A Small Circus* began to sell in significant numbers in West Germany. In 1972, Peter Zadek produced a musical based on *Little Man – What Now?* which was adapted for the stage by Tankred Dorst, and by the late 1970s in West Germany the status of *Little Man – What Now?* as a twentieth-century German 'classic' was confirmed when extracts began appearing in school textbooks. Two publishers included studies of the novel in their 'Teachers'/Students' Notes' series in 1978 and 1983.[14] By the mid-1980s in England *Little Man – What Now?* was a set text for the German A-Level examination and in 1987 Methuen published a schools edition.[15]

The popularity of the novel on its publication was not confined to Germany. In England, where *Little Man – What Now?* was published by Putnam, *The Times Literary Supplement* review of 11 May 1933 concluded: 'How the little family survive the pressure of the dole, how they cling to each other with the clutch of the drowning, all this is revealed with an insight and sympathy that makes the book no mere series of photographs but rather a formidable picture.' In the United States the Simon and Schuster edition was equally successful.[16] Universal Pictures acquired the film rights and the film *Little Man – What Now?*, starring Margaret Sullavan and Douglas Montgomery, was premiered on 31 May 1934 in New York.

Putnam published seven Fallada novels between 1933 and 1940. While *Little Man – What Now?* was the most popular, with sales of over 22,000 by the beginning of 1939, *Who Once Eats out of the Tin Bowl*[17] sold over 11,000 and *Once We Had a Child* over 7,000 copies in Great Britain during the period. Fallada short stories were sold to the *Evening Standard* and the *News Chronicle* as well as to *Esquire*, *The Argosy* and Hutchinson's *Golden Book*. After the war, Putnam published *The Drinker* in 1952. While some of the 1930s translations were reissued by Howard Baker in the 1960s and 1970s, it was not until 1989 that a new Fallada edition appeared in England, when Libris published *The Drinker* with an introduction by John Willett. This was followed in 1996 by a new translation of *Little Man – What Now?* introduced by Philip Brady.[18]

The continued success of *Little Man – What Now?* is something Rudolf Ditzen would have found perplexing. While he warmly welcomed the recognition and the financial security the novel brought him in 1932, he never really understood the applause which greeted 'that wimp Pinneberg who would be nothing without his wife' and the film 'which, thank God, I've never seen'.[19]

The English translation of *Jeder stirbt für sich allein* by Michael Hofmann, published first by Penguin in the UK as *Alone in Berlin* in 2009 and later in the same year by Melville House in the US as *Every Man Dies Alone*, was a publishing sensation in the English-speaking world. A reviewer in the *Observer* on 23 May 2010 described the novel as 'taking bestseller lists by storm on both sides of the Atlantic', and by the summer of 2011 almost 400,000 copies had been sold. The impact of the English translation resulted in the sale of translation rights in more than twenty languages, with the Hebrew translation topping the Israeli bestseller list in August 2010. The success of *Alone in Berlin* has ushered in a new era of Fallada translations which will reconnect him with an English readership after a gap of more than seventy years.

A comprehensive assessment of the life and work of this German writer has been hampered by the development of divergent views of Rudolf Ditzen in East and West Germany. In addition, his status as a popular writer has resulted in a reluctance in academic circles to take his work seriously. The unevenness of Ditzen's work, which ranges from masterpieces of narrative technique to works of little, if any, literary value, also makes it difficult to assign him an appropriate position in the history of German literature. A further factor contributing to his relative neglect has been that his name has not been associated with any particular literary movement. His early works, with their intense subjectivity and fantastic, dream-like sequences are decidedly Expressionist, his novels of the early 1930s belong, if anywhere, to the 'New Sobriety' movement; after that, some of his work could be classified loosely as 'Realist' but this epithet would have to be modified in turn, depending on the novel in question. Fallada has therefore all too often been seen as unique, a loner, an exception – which is largely how Rudolf Ditzen, whose favourite book as a child was *Robinson Crusoe*, viewed himself.

However, as the narrator of *The Magic Mountain* said of Hans Castorp, Ditzen, too, lived 'not only his personal life, as an individual, but also, consciously or unconsciously, the life of his epoch and his contemporaries'. He was born in the same year as the radical dramatist Ernst Toller and in the same decade as Johannes R. Becher, Bertolt Brecht, Erich Kästner, Kurt Tucholsky, Walter Benjamin, Gertrud Kolmar and Carl Zuckmayer. He belonged to a generation of German writers born into an authoritarian German Reich who attained adulthood at the time of its disintegration in the First World War, and who experienced a mere fourteen years of parliamentary democracy before the advent of fascism and a second world war. This generation was moulded by Wilhelmine Germany and irrevocably changed by fascism, and it was their response to fascism which determined the course of the rest of their lives. This is no less true of Brecht, who went into exile, or of Benjamin and Toller, who both committed suicide, or of Kolmar, who died in a concentration camp, than it is of Ditzen, who retreated into a rural idyll in the hope that by maintaining a low profile he could weather the storm.

The end of the Cold War and the unification of Germany have witnessed a revival of interest in Rudolf Ditzen's life and work. This process was set in motion by the foundation of the Hans Fallada Society (Hans Fallada Gesellschaft) in Germany in 1991 and continued during the centenary celebrations in 1993 when a recurring theme was the timeless and universal appeal of Ditzen's work, as well as its contemporary relevance in a world where the 'little man' is facing unemployment and social upheaval once more. The centenary year saw a new, largely unchanged, edition of Liersch's 'Hans Fallada. His Great and Little Life',[20] as well as a popular and rather sensationalist biography by Klaus Farin, *Hans Fallada. 'Welche sind, die haben kein Glück'* ('Hans Fallada. "Some People Have No Luck at All"'), which relies almost entirely on secondary sources.[21] In 1993 Aufbau also published a new edition of Ditzen's first two novels for the first time since the early 1920s, as well as hitherto unpublished early prose works.[22]

Since the unification of Germany, the University of Greifswald has hosted two conferences on Ditzen's life and work. Further conferences have been organized by the Fallada Society in Carwitz and by the Fallada Forum in Berlin, Canada, the US and the UK.[23] The federchen publishing house in Neubrandenburg has produced a number of monographs[24] and, in addition to the *Hans Fallada Jahrbuch* (Hans Fallada Yearbook),[25] the Fallada Society publishes a regular newsletter which carries not only Society news but short pieces on ongoing research.

In the 1990s, the Writers' Centre in Neubrandenburg acquired and set about renovating the smallholding in the remote village of Carwitz which Ditzen bought in 1933 and where he lived with his family until 1944. The house and grounds are now open to the public and copies of most of Ditzen's papers are housed here, while the archive itself is located in Neubrandenburg.

The fiftieth anniversary of Ditzen's death, in February 1997, was marked by two new publications. *Hans Fallada. Sein Leben in Bildern und Briefen* ('Hans Fallada. His Life in Pictures and Letters') is a handsome volume from Aufbau of over two hundred photographs and extracts from letters, diaries, articles and reviews which present a kaleidoscopic overview of the complexity of Ditzen's life and work.[26] This compilation not only made a significant amount of archival material available for the first time but also, as the reviewer of the *Süddeutsche Zeitung* remarked on 7 February 1997, it 'whets the reader's appetite for the enormous treasure-trove of correspondence'.

Ditzen was an enthusiastic letter-writer and his correspondence consists of over six thousand letters to friends, family, publishers and readers spanning the years 1912 to 1947. These documents provide valuable insights into his life and creative processes as well as into the times in which he lived. Since 1997, a small proportion of Ditzen's letters have been published: excerpts from his correspondence with Anne Marie Seyerlen, an early muse, spanning the years 1917 to 1921; a selection of the 2,371 letters which passed between Ditzen and his publisher Ernst Rowohlt from 1919 to 1946; around a third of the letters which he exchanged with his first wife, Anna Ditzen, between 1928 and 1946, and part of Ditzen's correspondence with his elder son Uli during the years 1940 to 1946.[27]

The second publication in 1997 was a new biography by Cecilia von Studnitz, *Es war wie ein Rausch. Fallada und sein Leben* ('It was like Intoxication. Fallada and His Life').[28] The author takes as her starting point the fact that Ditzen's 'autobiographical manuscripts are not free from fiction nor are his fictional characters and plots free from autobiography' and goes on to base her account of Ditzen's life largely on quotations from his work and the existing German biographies.

In contrast, the present biography is based on both published and unpublished primary sources. The latter category includes correspondence and other writings by Ditzen himself as well as new material donated to the archive in recent years. In addition, members of the former Friends of Hans Fallada society have generously made available archival material in their private possession. Finally, the author was fortunate to have met and talked at length on three occasions with Anna Ditzen, Rudolf Ditzen's wife for fifteen crucial years.

Ditzen's own 'autobiographical' writings, *Damals bei uns daheim* ('Our Home in Days Gone by') and *Heute bei uns zu Haus* ('Our Home Today'), are not sufficiently reliable to provide a sound basis for biography.[29] Ditzen wrote 'Our Home in Days Gone by' in 1941 at a time when he needed money and when trivial, escapist literature was all he could hope to have published. In his letters to his sister Elisabeth, who provided a substantial amount of material for the work, he freely admitted, 'I invent stories – about parents, siblings, relatives – I steal childhood memories shamelessly from other people.'[30] He confided to a friend, 'I'm turning my worthy parents, who I couldn't stand in my youth and who I only came to appreciate as I grew older, into two angelic figures.'[31] In 'Our Home in Days Gone by', Ditzen deliberately omits any reference to one of the most important influences during his youth – his aunt, Adelaide Ditzen, who encouraged his early literary efforts, because 'I would have to adopt a more faithful and serious approach to give the kind of approximately accurate account which I owe her.'[32] In a subsequent letter to his sister he also admitted that the conclusion to the book, which depicts a smooth transition from boyhood to manhood, is a complete invention.

'Our Home in Days Gone by' is therefore of very little use to a biographer. Its rosy glow of nostalgia, however, ensured its success on publication in March 1942 and encouraged Ditzen to write a sequel, 'Our Home Today'. This work's subtitle – '*Erlebtes, Erfahrenes und Erfundenes*' (literally: 'Things Experienced, Heard and Invented') – indicates its unreliability. A preface contains the further warning that 'no one is portrayed here as they really are, not even the author.' Thus Ditzen gave himself a licence to conjure up an idyllic rural existence with no marital disharmony, no extra-marital affairs, no village gossips, Nazi denunciations, unsympathetic publishers, no alcoholism or depression.

Ditzen's 'autobiographical' works, tellingly published under the name Hans Fallada, are, arguably, greater works of fiction than some of his novels and will be treated as such.

It is intended that this biography, which aims primarily to (re)-introduce a neglected German writer to an English-speaking readership, will also make a serious contribution to the reassessment of his life and work wherever he is read.

1 1893–1912
The Search for Self

> To [Dorian Gray], man was a being with myriad lives and
> myriad sensations, a complex multiform creature that bore
> within itself strange legacies of thought and passion, and
> whose very flesh was tainted with the monstrous maladies
> of the dead.
>
> – Oscar Wilde[1]

The birth of Rudolf Ditzen on 21 July 1893 made a lasting impression on his eldest sister, Elisabeth, for it came the day after her fifth birthday, which seemed to her to have passed largely unnoticed in the family. All became clear, however, the next morning, when she peeped into the cot to inspect her 'belated birthday present'.[2] Ditzen's relationship with his sister Elisabeth was closer and more lasting than with his second sister, Margarete, who was three years his senior, or any other member of his immediate family.

The Ditzens had moved to Greifswald, a university town on the Baltic seaboard, four months before Rudolf was born and were to stay there six years. Rudolf's father, Wilhelm Ditzen, was a magistrate in the county court and destined for a distinguished career in the legal profession. His mother, Elisabeth Ditzen (*née* Lorenz), had grown up in the home of an uncle who had a thriving legal practice in the town of Uelzen near Hanover, where she enjoyed a typical middle-class upbringing which, in addition to school lessons, included needlework and music, and culminated in a year spent with relatives in Frankfurt to finish her education. While in Greifswald the Ditzens moved house twice, each time to a more central address.

Both of Rudolf's parents were interested in literature and there was even evidence of some literary talent in the family: a distant relative, Luise Westkirch, was a moderately successful regional novelist who was famous for travelling fourth class on the railway in order to listen to the language of the ordinary people, which she then reproduced in her work.[3] However, it was not primarily their shared love of literature, or indeed considerations of social class, which drew Rudolf Ditzen's parents to each other. According to his father, 'our mutual love of music and that alone was what awakened my interest and determined my choice.' Wilhelm and Elisabeth Ditzen played the piano together as often as they could from the day they were married in September 1887 until she fell seriously ill in May 1930, an indication in itself of what both considered a happy marriage.

During Rudolf's childhood the Ditzens could afford a four-week family holiday every summer, usually on the Baltic coast, and often his parents, or his father alone, had an additional three- to four-week vacation in Switzerland, Austria or Italy. Rudolf and his two elder sisters and younger brother also spent a number of childhood holidays with his mother's relatives in Uelzen, Celle and Hanover, where no doubt he heard many of the tales of comedy and tragedy, of eccentricity and banality which his mother recalls in her memoirs.

His father's work provided another source of fascinating tales. Contemporary newspaper reports record Wilhelm Ditzen presiding over cases of arson, perjury, intent to deceive, assault, rape, attempted rape and infanticide. The accused were workers, farm labourers, young women in service and tradesmen of various sorts. Their defence frequently contained rather transparent pleas of faulty memory, poor eyesight and impaired hearing. During his childhood and adolescence Rudolf took a keen interest in the cases which came before his father. Wilhelm Ditzen encouraged this interest in the hope that his eldest son would follow in his footsteps and enter the legal profession. However, it was the human rather than the legal aspects of these cases that primarily interested the young Rudolf.

Rudolf spent the two summers following his second and third

birthdays with his sisters and parents in the resort of Zinnowitz on the Baltic island of Usedom. The following December (1896), his brother Ulrich was born, and the next summer the four children were entrusted to the care of the aunts and maternal grandmother in Uelzen while Elisabeth and Wilhelm Ditzen went on a three-and-a-half-week vacation to the Tyrol. On their return in August 1897 Wilhelm Ditzen, Prussian and patriot, fulfilled a long-standing ambition when he came face to face with Bismarck and looked into his eyes 'for an unforgettable moment'.

In 1898, Wilhelm Ditzen was unable to join his family on holiday in Zinnowitz because he had been called to Berlin to work from June to September on the new Civil Code. He and his wife made up for this with a five-week holiday in Italy in the autumn. For Wilhelm Ditzen trips to Italy offered an opportunity to keep in touch with his unmarried sister Adelaide, known in the family as Tante (Aunt) Ada. She was one of many independent-minded young German women attracted to Rome in the last quarter of the nineteenth century by Malwida von Meysenbug, a champion of women's emancipation. Von Meysenbug educated these young women 'to a sense of self-regard, to economic independence by way of education, in order to help them promote the goal of full civil, legal and political rights for women'. Von Meysenbug, who had fled Germany after the failure of the 1848 revolution, was acquainted with the leading revolutionaries, philosophers and artists of the day.[4] She had a particularly strong influence on the French writer Romain Rolland, whom Adelaide Ditzen met during his stay in Rome from 1889 to 1891, a meeting from which her nephew Rudolf was later to profit.

Rudolf's father's three-month period in Berlin led to career advancement when, early in 1899, he was promoted to the position of Counsellor in the *Kammergericht* in Berlin, the highest court in the state of Prussia. This marked another milestone on Wilhelm Ditzen's path to the Imperial Supreme Court in Leipzig, a goal which he had set himself in 1878, when he took up his first appointment at the District Court in Kloster Wennigsen. Offers of positions on the Railways Board (in 1882) and in the law department of Greifswald University (in 1895) had not deflected him from his chosen path. Rudolf Ditzen in later life expressed admiration for his father's single-mindedness in terms which suggest that such dedication was alien to him. However, father and son had more in common than either, especially the son, cared to admit. Singleness of purpose was one such shared characteristic.

Wilhelm Ditzen took up his appointment in Berlin on 25 March 1899, and his family moved to join him a few weeks later. The Ditzens' residence in Berlin coincided with a period of accelerated urban expansion and imperial aggrandizement which was manifest in the architecture and atmosphere of the capital city. In 1900, Berlin was the first European city to introduce trolley buses. In 1902, the first city railway (S-Bahn) came into service, and in 1905 the first omnibuses made their appearance. It was during these years that a new concept in shopping, the department store, arrived in the German capital, with the opening of Wertheim in the Leipziger Strasse in 1904 and, three years later, the KaDeWe at Wittenbergplatz. At the same time, new buildings, statues and monuments were enhancing the city's grandeur, and the Kaiser missed no opportunity to demonstrate in public the pomp and circumstance of the imperial court. Rudolf's sister Elisabeth recalls in her memoirs that her school class was taken to cheer visiting royalty such as England's Edward VII. On another occasion, she records that the Tiergarten park in the city centre was left in a state of devastation after a very large crowd had turned out to see the Crown Princess Cecilie. It was an exciting time to be growing up in Berlin.

The Ditzens' fashionable address and spacious accommodation in the Luitpold Strasse was indicative of Rudolf's father's advancement in the legal profession, as was the fact that, in 1900, they could take two servants with them on holiday. Both Rudolf and Elisabeth recall in their memoirs the carefree holidays of their youth: the packing, the excitement at the station, the endless sunny days of cowboys and Indians in the woods, the berry-picking and the games on the beach.

In Berlin, Wilhelm Ditzen was able to pursue his musical interests, often in the company of Fritz Danneel, with whom he had shared rooms in Prussia's top public school at Pforta, south of Naumburg on the river Saale. It was Danneel who had introduced Wilhelm Ditzen to Beethoven's piano music. Now, in Berlin, they shared an enthusiasm for Brahms.

Every evening after dinner – social engagements permitting – Wilhelm and Elisabeth Ditzen played the piano together and the children sat and listened to the music of Wagner, Weber, Schubert and Schumann. If this exercise was intended to transmit a love of music and an interest in playing an instrument, it failed miserably. Rudolf and Elisabeth both took the view that piano lessons were wasted on them. However, both appreciated the fact that the music was followed by readings from German and English literature – including Schiller, Raabe, Stifter and Shakespeare – as well as from history books. Their parents frequently took them on day trips into the surrounding woods and forests, as well as to museums and the zoo. Many a boring journey was enlivened by their father's readings. Once a year, the whole family went for a meal in one of Berlin's most expensive restaurants.

Rudolf Ditzen therefore spent the first seven years of his life in a materially secure and caring environment, with the rough and tumble associated with four children who one minute would be playing peaceably with toy soldiers on the dining-room table and the next engaged in pillow-fights in the bedrooms. Both Rudolf Ditzen's parents, and particularly his mother, had had rather lonely and emotionally deprived childhoods: Elisabeth Ditzen in the extremely strict and forbidding household of her relatives, the Seyfarths, and Wilhelm Ditzen in boarding school in Pforta. They obviously tried to create a genuine family environment for their own children. In the case of their daughters, they appear to have succeeded; in the case of their elder son they did not.

The writings of Wilhelm and Elisabeth Ditzen provide some clues to the values of those responsible for Rudolf Ditzen's upbringing. In her memoirs Rudolf's mother describes the sort of person she admired when she writes about a certain Frau Hobel, the wife of an architect: 'a quite splendid woman. She never thought of herself, she never stopped working, hardly went out at all, helped her husband with his intricate drawings and accompanied his violin playing on the piano. She was a first-class housekeeper.'[5] Self-sacrifice, indefatigability and a capacity for hard work – the ideals espoused by Elisabeth Ditzen – were also the qualities which her son was to seek, and find, in his first wife. Rudolf's father, looking back on his own schooldays, believes that in Pforta he acquired an 'ability to work quietly and consistently and a feeling of responsibility for the consequences of each and every one of my actions, a feeling which has determined the way I have lived my life since.'[6]

Wilhelm Ditzen was not only a judge by profession, he also had a very strong sense of justice in his everyday life. On one occasion, he recommended a particular company to a friend who wanted to buy a piano. After the sale, the company sent him a percentage of the money received as an 'agent's fee'. This he refused to accept and returned with the following note: 'I see you can sell pianos more cheaply. Please let the customer be the one to benefit from this.'[7] While the Ditzen household subscribed to the values of middle-class Wilhelmine Germany, Wilhelm Ditzen, with his love of literature and music, did not conform entirely to the stereotypical authoritarian father of the period. He certainly spent more time with his children than most of his contemporaries.

There are four accounts of Rudolf's childhood, all written a number of years later. Elisabeth notes nothing remarkable in her account except the family's concern when he had appendicitis, a concern which was not unrelated to the other children's dismay at having to eat dry meatballs so that Rudolf could have beef tea.[8] His Tante Ada formed a very positive view of her nephew when she joined the family on holiday in the Baltic resort of Graal, east of Rostock, in 1906.[9] Rudolf's mother has a different view: 'Our Rudolf developed much more slowly than the other children. His long periods of illness took their toll. In any case boys in my experience don't develop as quickly as girls. He was much older when he began to walk, and to talk, too . . .'

As we have seen, Ditzen's 'memoirs', 'Our Home in Days Gone by', provide a highly fictionalized account. In them, he claims: 'All through my childhood and youth I was dogged by exceptional bad luck.' His German biographers Manthey, Crepon and Liersch accept this assessment of their subject. Rudolf Ditzen used the word 'Pechvogel' to describe himself. English has no one expression for this common German term, which refers to someone who is accident prone or dogged by bad luck – a walking disaster-area. 'Pechvogel' is a convenient label; it assigns a person to a recognizable 'type', thereby precluding further discussion. It reveals, however, very little about the human being concerned and, moreover, absolves everyone from any responsibility in the matter.

Close examination of the instances of 'bad luck' reveals that the incidents in question were often the result of an adventurous spirit or an unwillingness to obey the 'rules' (or a failure to understand them). Ditzen's German biographers make much of his many childhood illnesses, which were scarcely the result of bad luck but of specific physical, biological and genetic factors. It is, after all, not uncommon for infants and young children to suffer an apparently interminable series of illnesses in their early years. This is not to underplay the seriousness of the illnesses or the concern they caused Rudolf's parents. It is merely to suggest that this type of early medical history does not, in itself, predispose to literary greatness.

Rudolf Ditzen started school in the summer term of 1901 and, according to Manthey, 'here he ran into more bad luck'.[10] A closer look at the facts, however, indicates that it was not so much a case of the child's bad luck as the parents' bad judgement. The school chosen by his parents was the Prinz Heinrich Gymnasium in the nearby Grunewald Strasse, a single-sex grammar school where the sons of Prussia's military and civil-service elite were educated. It was hardly a congenial environment for a boy who had until then led a rather sheltered existence. In addition to suffering from the excesses of the authoritarian school regime, Rudolf was the butt of his schoolmates' humour: they poked fun at the grey patches on his navy trousers (a result of his mother's somewhat unnecessary thrift) and made jokes about his long hair.

His parents' lack of understanding for Rudolf's problems at school can be explained to some extent by their own experience. Elisabeth Ditzen had loved school; she had been an eager scholar who frequently came first in her class. She took leading parts in school concerts and often read 'patriotic poems' on special occasions such as the anniversary of the Battle of Sedan. Wilhelm Ditzen, too, enjoyed his schooldays. He recalls acting in school plays and on one occasion in 1871 reciting a patriotic poem which he had composed himself at a school concert. Rudolf did not share this enthusiasm. Indeed, he sometimes found school so intolerable that he made himself ill to avoid going.

The summer holidays continued to provide a welcome break, and in 1903 the Ditzens spent five weeks in Neu-Globsow in the Mecklenburg lake district. The accommodation, which they shared with the local fieldmice, was rather primitive and the landlady deaf to all protests. Nonetheless, Ditzen's sister Elisabeth recalled Neu-Globsow thirty years later as 'a childhood paradise'.[11]

After Neu-Globsow, Wilhelm Ditzen travelled on to Switzerland, where he was joined by Tante Ada for a few weeks. The year 1903 was another important one in Wilhelm Ditzen's career for he was transferred from the civil to the criminal division to replace a colleague deemed to be too hostile to the police. He was initially very reluctant to move, since he enjoyed dealing with the civil appeals which came through the lower courts. However, as a civil servant, he had to accept the transfer and, no doubt, consoled himself with the thought that this appointment brought him another step nearer his goal of the Imperial Supreme Court in Leipzig.

Meanwhile, Rudolf sought an escape from the trials and tribulations of the classroom and playground and found it in the world of books. Both Rudolf and his sister Elisabeth particularly enjoyed those which their parents considered unsuitable and which were officially not available to the children. These included books by not only the popular adventure writer Karl May but Flaubert and Zola, Dumas and Stevenson, Dickens and Dostoyevsky.

In 1906, Rudolf's problems came to a head. According to 'Our Home in Days Gone by', the twelve-year-old Rudolf and one of his friends, no doubt inspired by their hero Robinson Crusoe, decided to undertake a real-life adventure by running away to sea. Unfortunately for Rudolf, his plans were uncovered on the eve of his departure, and 'I stood before my parents as the accused.' The account in 'Our Home in Days Gone by' goes on to relate in dramatic fashion Wilhelm Ditzen's conviction that his son was a liar and a thief, and Elisabeth Ditzen's feeling that her son had betrayed her trust and was henceforth untrustworthy. However that may be, Rudolf's parents were sufficiently concerned to investigate the matter further. A visit to the Prinz Heinrich Gymnasium persuaded Wilhelm Ditzen that the school was partly to blame for what had happened, so Rudolf was moved in 1906 to another, more suitable school. He did not break all his ties with his old school, for he remained in touch with his friend Walter Simmichen, who was, indirectly, to play a fateful role in his life. At the end of his first year in the Bismarck Gymnasium in the Wilmersdorf district of Berlin, Rudolf came sixth out of thirty-two pupils, which indicates that his previous educational difficulties were due primarily to the school and not to him.

The year 1906 saw other changes in the Ditzen family. After the family's summer holiday in Graal, Rudolf's sister Margarete set out for finishing school in Lausanne. In October, Wilhelm Ditzen was appointed a member of the commission set up to revise the Reich Criminal Code – he was the only member of the Prussian judiciary to receive such an invitation. The importance of the task with which he was being entrusted, coupled with his strong sense of public duty, enabled him to overcome his initial misgivings that the work might become 'political'.

In 1907, the Ditzens returned to Graal on holiday, and afterwards Rudolf set out on his own to spend three weeks with his father's sister and brother-in-law in Blankenburg in the Harz mountains. Rudolf was now fourteen years old and was soon to begin confirmation classes. His maternal grandfather, Emil Lorenz, had been a Protestant minister and prison chaplain, and his grandmother Lorenz was a very devout woman noted for her acts of charity. The Ditzen household, however, was a nominally Christian but not overtly religious one. Rudolf had simply accepted his parents' conventional religious beliefs. It was not until he began to attend confirmation classes that he thought about religion in any conscious way. The classes began with the tutor presenting four proofs of the existence of God. Rudolf immediately wondered why proof was necessary. As a well-read, intelligent young man, he started to ask questions and, when no satisfactory answers were provided, he began to doubt. He continued to attend, however, and was confirmed in Berlin Cathedral in March 1909.

Wilhelm Ditzen's career continued to progress, and at the end of

1908 he was appointed to the Imperial Supreme Court in Leipzig. As soon as the Christmas celebrations were over, Elisabeth and Wilhelm went house-hunting, and on 28 January 1909 Wilhelm Ditzen moved to Leipzig. He was followed by his wife and his two sons at the end of March.

Thus, Rudolf Ditzen's first period of residence in Berlin coincided with his formative years, between the age of six and fifteen. It was here that he experienced his first difficulties in conforming to the norms and expectations of two institutions central to Wilhelmine Germany: the Prussian education system and the Church. It was here, too, that in the psychological and emotional disorientation of early adolescence he found his parents lacking in understanding and sympathy. And it was in Berlin that he became addicted to reading, to the world of the imagination, which offered not only an escape but also an alternative and more attractive version of reality. His abortive attempt to run away to sea had been the first sign that this son of the legal establishment was not going to conform.

It was also, not surprisingly, in Berlin that Rudolf Ditzen became aware of social class, as he explored the north inner city and discovered that not everyone lived, as he did, in a comfortable seven-room apartment in fashionable Charlottenburg. By 1905, Berlin was the most densely populated city in Europe, with some three quarters of a million people living in one-room accommodation.

Rudolf's reaction to the announcement in December 1908 that his father had been appointed to the Imperial Supreme Court in Leipzig is not recorded. His father had achieved the ambition of a lifetime. His mother, who later described her years in Berlin as 'the most difficult of all',[12] had no regrets in moving to Leipzig, where she had a number of relatives and where she could look forward to a livelier social life. Rudolf's sisters were old enough to pursue their own lives. Rudolf's case was slightly different: to leave a school where he had been reasonably happy, to say good-bye to his friends and turn his back on a city where he had spent ten such important years cannot have been easy for a fifteen-year-old. An added difficulty arose from the different organization of the school year in Leipzig, which started in April rather than September. Rudolf was therefore faced with the choice of either repeating six months or sitting a special examination and moving into the next year after Easter. His ambitious and diligent father persuaded him to work hard for the examination and arranged private tuition during the last months in Berlin. It is therefore hardly likely that Rudolf looked forward eagerly to the move to Leipzig.

Some three weeks after arriving, and less than a month after his confirmation, Rudolf Ditzen was involved in a road accident which, as he wrote in 'Gedanken über den Glauben' ('Reflections on Faith'), 'was to have such a decisive effect on my life and completely turned my world upside down'.[13] On Sunday 17 April 1909, the day before he was due to sit the examination for which he had been cramming, he set out on a bicycle trip into the country. Having forgotten something, he turned back, and on his way home collided with a horse-drawn butcher's cart. He was kicked in the face by the horse, knocked to the ground and run over by the wheels of the cart. One foot, too, was broken. On admission to hospital, he was placed on the critical list and not expected to survive the night. Among the wild thoughts that raced through his mind as he lay there expecting to die before dawn was the one recurring question: Why me? He could not understand what he had done to deserve such a fate. After all, he had sacrificed everything over the last few months to concentrate on his school-work. The doubts which Rudolf Ditzen had experienced during the confirmation classes in Berlin now turned into certainty: 'If you are God then I now know what sort of God you are. Leave me alone for I cannot stand the sight of you.'[14]

Recovery from the accident was slow, and Rudolf continued to suffer dizzy spells and severe headaches for some months afterwards. His foot injury, too, took a long time to heal. He was, however, well enough to accompany his parents and younger brother Uli on holiday to Tabarz in Thüringen in July and to travel on alone to visit his mother's brother, Friedrich Lorenz, in Börry. After his return to Leipzig in mid-August he was able to start his new school.

The Königin Carola Gymnasium, a grammar school which had some four to five hundred boys on its roll, catered for the sons of Leipzig's middle class. In Rudolf Ditzen's year there were four other boys whose fathers were members of the judiciary, one of whom, Willi Burlage, became a life-long friend. Five pupils had fathers in the civil service, three had fathers who were teachers and, reflecting the importance of Leipzig as a centre of trade and industry, the fathers of five boys were merchants. The school had a strong sense of national pride and events such as the birthdays of the King of Saxony (on 25 May) and the German Kaiser (on 27 January) were celebrated with suitable readings and music.

Rudolf did not cut his ties completely with Berlin, for he returned in March 1910 to visit Walter Simmichen. This friend from his days at the Prinz Heinrich Gymnasium put him in contact with a young man in Rudolstadt, Hanns Dietrich von Necker, with whom Rudolf began to correspond. They discovered a number of interests in common, including literature, and their correspondence developed in the course of 1910 into a close friendship.

In Leipzig, Wilhelm Ditzen attempted to interest his elder son in music by taking him to listen to the famous choir in St Thomas's Church on Friday evenings. Rudolf did not enjoy the experience and, as he became increasingly inventive in his excuses, his father finally admitted defeat and took his younger son, Ulrich, instead. Ulrich turned out to be the only Ditzen child to have any aptitude for music.

In April 1910, Rudolf moved into the 'Obersekunda', the lower sixth, where the curriculum included seven periods of Latin, seven periods of Greek and two periods of Hebrew per week, in addition to Religion, German, French, English, Maths, Physics and History. The beginning of the new school year on 25 April was overshadowed by the suicide of Friedrich Hammer, a pupil in his final year. The school principal believed that 'unsuitable reading material' had affected 'the balance of his mind'.[15]

The school marked the king's birthday in May by a lecture entitled 'Military Security and Education Yesterday and Today'. Four weeks later, the Literary Society, of which Rudolf Ditzen was an active member, staged an event around the theme of the Renaissance which included works by Dante, Ronsard, Shakespeare and Wilde. To what extent Rudolf was responsible for the inclusion of one of Wilde's *Poems in Prose* is not recorded. What is recorded is his enthusiasm for Wilde's work, especially his poetry and *The Picture of Dorian Gray*, in which Wilde explores the nature of art and beauty and chronicles the disastrous consequences of extreme aestheticism. So impressed was Rudolf by Wilde's story that he called himself 'Harry' Ditzen after Lord Henry (Harry) Wotton.

It is not difficult to understand how a young man who had rejected Christianity and was questioning the values of the society in which he found himself should be attracted to Oscar Wilde, who not only in his work but also in his life challenged conventional mores. Wilde's Lord Henry is clever, witty, amoral and detached. A chain-smoking cynic and covert homosexual, he 'adopts' the beautiful youth Dorian Gray and is, at least indirectly, responsible for his degradation and suicide. Rudolf Ditzen's assumption of the name was indicative not only of his literary tastes and his political preferences but also of his adolescent struggle to establish an identity.

He, too, replaced his Christian faith with a love of beauty. In his 'Reflections on Faith', probably written in 1910, he declares: 'Whenever I have done something really good and great, I will not say, as the Christians do, "I thank you, God, for giving me the strength" but rather: "Ah, you beautiful, beautiful world, I thank you that your beauty was strong enough to enable me to develop the beauty that is in me."' He dedicated his poem '*Dank der Schönheit*' ('Thanks to Beauty'), appended to the 'Reflections on Faith', to his classmate Willi Burlage. This poem, the earliest surviving literary document by Rudolf Ditzen, is composed in rhyming couplets and tells of the poet's blind and aimless wanderings until he encounters the 'Beauty of Life', to which he has now devoted himself.

The Literary Society was also where Rudolf Ditzen gave a speech on modern educational methods which ended in the declaration, 'Modern schools can only produce criminals or madmen.'[16] The programme of the student-run Literary Society with its espousal of foreign writers and promotion of anti-establishment attitudes stands in stark contrast to the 'official' literary events of the school year, which included a celebration of the centenary of the north German novelist Fritz Reuter and a reading from the ballads of the nationalist writer Ernst von Wildenbruch.

In the summer of 1910, at the age of seventeen, Rudolf Ditzen spent his first summer holiday apart from his family when he went on a trip with the Wandervogel youth group to Holland. He later based an incident in his novel *Wir hatten mal ein Kind* (*Once We Had a Child*) of 1934 on this trip, and he also refers to it in his memoirs. However, the importance of this holiday lies not so much in the trip itself as in its consequences, for on his return to Leipzig at the end of August he was diagnosed as having contracted typhoid.

This illness marked a turning point in Rudolf Ditzen's life. His mother recalled that 'from then on he was very strange, extremely uncommunicative and shut himself off from us as much as possible'. Adelaide Ditzen, who visited Leipzig in October and December 1910 and again in January 1911, noticed that her nephew 'was strangely changed, had a restless, nervous look in his face and was brutal and inconsiderate, especially towards his mother'. His heavy smoking and drinking, and his staying out late, led to quarrels with his parents. He paid no attention to his father's warnings and advice. Indeed, he seemed to have developed an intense dislike of his parents. Around this time, he began to talk to his Tante Ada about his ambition to become a writer.

It was in the autumn of 1910, while recovering from typhoid, that Rudolf Ditzen first contemplated suicide. He wrote about his intentions to Hanns Dietrich von Necker, who came to Leipzig during the Christmas holidays. Although this was the first time the two young men had met, their relationship was obviously very well established, for Necker brought his friend 'Harry' Ditzen poison to assist him in his suicide plans. This attempt was not successful, nor was a subsequent one to cut his throat.

Rudolf Ditzen's attempts to end his life were not an isolated phenomenon but part of a much broader wave of suicides and suicide attempts that swept through Germany in the years before the First World War. Germany's imperialist ambitions and the rigid, authoritarian nature of German society induced feelings of hopelessness and despair in the younger generation. It is perhaps not coincidental that the son of a Supreme Court judge whose task it was to uphold the status quo should feel the general malaise so acutely. Another son of the judiciary and contemporary of Rudolf Ditzen who also rejected the values of his parents' generation during his teenage years was the poet and, later, Communist Johannes R. Becher. The largely autobiographical hero of Becher's novel *Farewell* calls his father, the public prosecutor, a 'hangman'. Becher himself was involved in a suicide pact with a young woman, Fanny Fuß, in 1910 which was modelled on the joint suicide of Heinrich von Kleist and Henriette Vogel. Fanny Fuß died; Becher survived but suffered the consequences, physical and psychological, for many years after. Becher's brother, Ernst, died by his own hand at the age of eighteen.

The new year, 1911, began with another suicide at Rudolf's school. The principal of the Königin Carola Gymnasium described the victim as 'one of the most gifted pupils the school has ever had'. This young man declared in a suicide note that he no longer had 'the strength and courage to go on living'.

Meanwhile, the school year continued in Leipzig with the annual ball in the middle of January, in which Rudolf was unable to participate fully because of his foot injury. At that time, the significance of dancing extended far beyond the activity itself, for dancing classes and dances provided one of the few opportunities in a single-sex education system for young men and women to make contact with each other, both socially and physically. Here, again, was an area of social convention with which Rudolf felt ill at ease.

The school celebrated the Kaiser's birthday on 27 January with a lecture entitled 'Germans and German Culture Overseas', given by one of the teachers. This was followed by readings of a suitably patriotic nature such as Freiligrath's *The Trumpet of Vionville* and a performance of Wagner's *Kaisermarsch*. Rudolf's reaction to these celebrations is not recorded, but – given his taste in literature – can hardly have been enthusiastic.

Four days later, on 31 January, another final-year pupil, Erich Pöschmann, committed suicide. Like the previous two victims, he was a very talented young man with a bright future. According to his father, he had 'lost the courage to go on living'. The Pöschmann family clearly felt that the school was at least partly to blame for their son's death, for they requested that no school representative attend the funeral. The incidence of three suicides in one class within the space of ten months alarmed the school authorities, and a meeting of the parents of final-year pupils was held at the beginning of February.

By now, Rudolf Ditzen was facing a serious crisis. He had rejected Christianity, he was out of sympathy with the values of Wilhelmine society, and out of tune with the world of his parents, who obviously did not understand him. The adoption of the persona 'Harry' was a clear indication of just how difficult it was for him to construct an adolescent identity.

Rudolf Ditzen instinctively felt that writing, especially the composition of poetry, offered a solution to his problems, not only in the sense of providing an outlet for the torment of adolescent emotions but also as a means of forging an identity for himself. His inexperience and the lack of support in his environment made him doubt his talent – in which case there did not seem to be much point in living. Those three final-year pupils had taken the only logical step! Poison had not worked for him, nor had a knife; perhaps a gun was the answer?

The crisis came to a head in March 1911. The catalyst was his friendship with a young woman. According to his own account in 'Our Home in Days Gone by', Rudolf Ditzen's rite of passage from boyhood to manhood was accomplished at the instigation of a sexually experienced housemaid one evening when his parents were at the theatre. Nothing could be further from the truth. On the contrary, his first relationships with women were accompanied, as we shall see, by obsessive behaviour and a death wish.

Rudolf Ditzen grew up in the age of Wedekind's *Spring Awakening* when children were given no sex education, either at school or at home and, beyond the strictures of religious instruction, received little guidance in dealing with the emotional turmoil of adolescence. Given Rudolf's state of mind and the sexual taboos of the era, it is perhaps not surprising that his first attempts to establish contact with young women of his own age should be accompanied by mildly obscene letters. He persuaded someone to write these 'anonymous' letters on his behalf so that his handwriting would not be recognized. The object of his affections was Käthe Matzdorf, a young woman who belonged to his circle. He even showed his parents one of these 'anonymous' letters, which warned the Matzdorfs to protect their daughter from 'bad' Rudolf Ditzen. He later told the family doctor, Dr Eggebrecht, that he was obsessed with a compulsion to hurt people he loved and that he preferred committing suicide to hurting Käthe. The actual reason for his decision to kill himself was rather different. One of the letters contained a reference to something that only Ditzen or his friend Willi Burlage could have known. When suspicion fell on Burlage, Ditzen could not let his friend take the blame, nor could he find the courage to admit his own guilt: suicide seemed the only option. He therefore told Burlage that he was planning to cycle out of town and drown himself in a lake on the heath.[17]

Willi, in despair, told his own mother, who rushed round to the Ditzens' with her son to find Rudolf sitting at his desk writing a suicide note. Wilhelm Ditzen was sent for and Rudolf had to be physically restrained from leaving the house. He sat, motionless and silent, for several hours and then, in a written note which he gave to his sister Elisabeth, he told his parents he wanted to leave Leipzig. In view of the scandal already brewing, his parents readily acceded to his request, and his mother accompanied him shortly afterwards to Kloster Mariensee near Hanover, where he spent four weeks with her relatives, the Kettlers. In going through her son's papers she subsequently found some poetry and a short piece expressing his despair of ever becoming a writer.

While contemporaries, such as Johannes R. Becher, were able to find soul mates in the Bohemian cafés of Munich and Berlin where the young Expressionist poets gathered to discuss their anger, despair and revolt, Rudolf Ditzen found no such forum for his ideas or support for his literary endeavours. Such isolation was to become a characteristic feature of his creative life.

While the Expressionist movement at this time was centred largely on Berlin and Munich, Leipzig was not without its cultural avant garde. A literary circle met regularly in Wilhelms Weinstube near the city hall and was presided over by 'a colossal figure with enormously broad shoulders; beneath a tuft of ginger hair beamed the reddish face with the excessively short, pointed nose'.[18] This was Ernst Rowohlt, printer and bookseller, who had opened his 'publishing house' in one room in Leipzig's König Strasse in 1909. It was in November of the same year that Kurt Wolff offered to invest in Rowohlt's publishing business, and together they set out to discover new writers such as

Georg Heym, whose *Der ewige Tag* (*The Eternal Day*) they published in April 1911. Ernst Rowohlt received no indication that a new literary talent who would one day become one of his most famous authors was living within walking distance of his first publishing house.

Rudolf Ditzen left his parents' home on 11 March 1911 never to return to live there again. He ends 'Our Home in Days Gone by' after the 'housemaid episode' with the words: 'And now the world of childhood was really closed to me, but I was not sorry. And I was no longer at home in my parents' house, I had departed from them and I was glad.' This statement applies equally to both Rudolf Ditzen's life and the one which Hans Fallada constructs for himself in his memoirs.

Rudolf continued to be plagued by headaches in Mariensee, and Dr Eggebrecht recommended a sanatorium in Berka not far from Weimar. Elisabeth Ditzen persuaded her son to take the doctor's advice, and she accompanied him there in April. When they arrived in Berka, Rudolf, realizing that he was in a psychiatric clinic, became very angry and accused his parents of wanting to lock him up in a lunatic asylum. His instinctive aversion to the sanatorium was borne out by subsequent events. Dr Starcke observed in his patient 'a pathological belief in the value of his own personality which has no doubt been fuelled by unsuitable reading material. He has, in addition, a very inflated view of his talent as a poet and a writer; the pieces of his work which I have seen were of little literary value.' This was hardly a doctor who could be expected to understand or sympathize with Rudolf Ditzen's plight. Dr Starcke described his patient's physical condition as 'undernourished' and 'anaemic' with 'slight trembling in his hands' and his mood as 'depressed and uncommunicative'.

While his son was undergoing treatment in Berka, Wilhelm Ditzen was making plans for his future. Rudolf had to continue his education, but could not do so in Leipzig, even if he had so wished. In any case, he had made it patently obvious that he no longer wished to live under his parents' roof. Wilhelm Ditzen was only too aware that his wife's health had been suffering under the strain of Rudolf's accident, illness and suicide attempts. His own experience of boarding school led him to conclude that day-school was the best form of education for young people, so he began to look around for a suitable school not too far from Leipzig where Rudolf could be expected to be happy. The most obvious choice was Rudolstadt, where Rudolf's friend Hanns Dietrich von Necker lived. Walter Simmichen had also spent two and a half years there. Closer enquiries revealed that Simmichen had lodged with a Protestant minister, Dr Braune. Wilhelm Ditzen approached Dr Braune in April, and he agreed to take in Rudolf on condition that he would comply with the 'rules of a Christian household'. This arrangement must have seemed very satisfactory to Wilhelm Ditzen, for it combined his son's wish for independence with the parents' desire that Rudolf should not be entirely alone. Hanns Dietrich seemed a lively, outgoing young man, a very suitable companion, and the school, the Fürstliches Gymnasium, was quite acceptable.

Rudolf was discharged from Dr Starcke's care in early June and, after a short stay with relatives in Schnepfenthal in southern Thüringen, moved into the Braunes' on 15 July 1911, a week before his eighteenth birthday. While their son was settling into Rudolstadt, Wilhelm and Elisabeth Ditzen spent their four weeks' summer holiday in the Erzgebirge, where they were joined by their elder daughter Elisabeth, now a student in Berlin. Margarete had set out at the beginning of July on a three-month tour of England, Scotland and Wales.

During August and September, Rudolf continued to suffer dizzy spells, vomiting and headaches and as a result was frequently absent from school. Dr Braune became concerned and called in a doctor, who diagnosed nicotine poisoning. Apart from his health problems, Rudolf seems to have settled quickly into the Braune household. Dr Braune shared his lodger's literary interests, and during July and early August Rudolf would read aloud passages from Dante to the couple in the evenings. Rudolf also showed his poetry to Dr Braune, who appears not to have paid it much attention. He did not approve of Rudolf's enthusiasm for Oscar Wilde, especially not *Dorian Gray*. Dr Braune described his lodger as 'a very clever and articulate young man who was outwardly very much in control of himself but who was inwardly weak in combating his instincts and passions'.

In Rudolstadt, freed from the constraints of his parental home, Rudolf cultivated the persona of 'Harry Ditzen', a world-weary, amoral poet. One of his poems of the period is entitled '*Von der großen Müdigkeit*' ('The Great Weariness'). In Rudolstadt he began reading Hugo von Hofmannsthal and Nietzsche, and 'the indifference towards life which they engendered fitted my mood completely and it all developed into an unwillingness to go on living'. He often confided these feelings of hopelessness and suicidal despair to Hanns Dietrich, who was his constant companion during July and early August.

Rudolf threw himself into the literary life of his new school in Rudolstadt. The Literaria Club decided to stage a performance of Ernst von Wildenbruch's *Der Mennonit* (*The Mennonite*) of 1881, set in a Mennonite community near Danzig during the Napoleonic occupation. The hero, Reinhold, rejects their pacifism, espouses the cause of German nationalism and dies a hero's death at the hands of the French. Although initially unenthusiastic about this chauvinist, anti-pacifist play, Rudolf ('Harry') Ditzen soon found himself taking the leading role, as indeed his father had done before him in school productions in Pforta. Hanns Dietrich, too, had a small part in the play.

The teaching staff at Rudolstadt was not impressed by the new boy. His form master, Dr Rübesamen, while recognizing that his pupil's 'contributions in literature classes were surprisingly good' and that he 'translated Horace and Homer tastefully and competently', described him as 'a decadent person who seemed almost weary of life, who felt himself to be above the law'. Furthermore, Rudolf acted as if 'the normal rules of society did not apply to him'. Dr Nagy, the principal, noted that 'Harry' Ditzen made a big impression on his fellow pupils because of his experience of city life and his knowledge of literature.

The performance of *Der Mennonit* on 30 September was a huge success. Rudolf, having first consumed considerable quantities of cognac and smoked a large number of cigarettes, played the part of the hero, according to the review in the local newspaper, with 'youthful enthusiasm'. Hanns Dietrich's mother described Rudolf's performance as 'passionate'.

Shortly afterwards, Rudolf decided to change his lodgings. He appears to have grown tired of the restrictions of the Braune household. Having been reprimanded for throwing a cork at a neighbour's window to attract a young woman's attention, Rudolf told the Braunes:

'It was a mistake to take lodgings in your home. I was not brought up in a religious household and I've simply been putting on an act by joining in your prayers and religious devotions and going to church with you on Sundays.' Dr Braune later recalled that they parted on good terms and that 'Ditzen always behaved impeccably.' Rudolf moved into the Busse household on 3 October. Oskar von Busse, a retired colonel, described Rudolf in the following terms: 'He gave the impression of being a very talented and well-behaved young man who fitted well into our family and even took part in our evening prayers.' Rudolf did not mention his literary ambitions to the Busses, possibly because of Oskar von Busse's reaction to a book 'by a certain "Mann"' which Rudolf had shown him – possibly, Heinrich Mann's *Professor Unrat* of 1905 (later filmed as *The Blue Angel*) – and which the colonel considered 'not suitable for a young person'.

Rudolf changed his lodgings without first obtaining the permission of Dr Nagy, which resulted in two interviews in the principal's office. At the end of the second interview, Rudolf promised to give up smoking and concentrate on his schoolwork. The principal later recalled: 'On that occasion Ditzen did not make a very positive impression on me. I was struck by his enormous self-confidence.'

Soon afterwards came the October mid-term break. Rudolf did not go home to Leipzig for the holidays. He told the Busses that he 'wasn't one for families'. The explanation he gave Dr Nagy, namely that 'there had been a tragedy in the family', was nearer the truth, for his uncle by marriage (his mother's sister's husband) had committed suicide. To what extent this event influenced Rudolf is uncertain. What is certain is that his own existential crisis came to a climax in October 1911.

By the autumn of 1911, Rudolf's attempt to find a place for himself in Wilhelmine Germany had failed. His literary efforts – his one hope of salvation – had received no recognition. He was in poor health, exacerbated by excessive smoking and drinking. Once again, like so many young men of his generation, he saw no point in continuing and he decided to put an end to his life.

He went to his friend Hanns Dietrich to borrow a revolver, whereupon the latter suggested a suicide pact. Hanns Dietrich von Necker's interest in suicide is well documented. Their mutual friend Walter Simmichen stated that Necker had lost his peace of mind (*Seelenfrieden*). Necker himself had composed a short piece of prose on committing suicide; he had also drawn up a contract with Rudolf Ditzen under which both agreed to write a piece of literature and the one whose piece was judged inferior by a neutral third party would be shot. During early October, Rudolf had on one occasion hidden Hanns Dietrich's revolver because of Necker's suicide threats.

According to Rudolf, it was his friend's idea to stage their deaths as a duel fought over the honour of a young woman. They then engineered a scene in which Hanns Dietrich insulted the fifteen-year-old sister of a classmate, Erna Simon, in public and Rudolf demanded satisfaction. This no doubt appealed to their theatrical talent and literary inclinations, for had not Dorian Gray's grandfather engineered a 'duel' based on a staged 'public insult' to rid himself of an unsuitable son-in-law? Reinhold, the Mennonite, had also challenged a French soldier to a duel after he had dared to kiss Reinhold's beloved Maria in von Wildenbruch's play. A duel also presented the two young men with a way of ending their lives that was socially acceptable in Germany in 1911 and would, they hoped, spare their families a scandal. The date was set for 17 October.

Hanns Dietrich obtained a revolver, which had probably belonged to his late father. On 16 October, Rudolf borrowed his landlord's small-bore rifle, ostensibly to shoot sparrows in the garden. He burnt all his papers, including his letters and poems. At lunchtime he announced that he and his friend were planning a walking tour the next day and would make an early start. The two young men spent the afternoon 'shooting sparrows' in the Busses' garden.

Rudolf did not in fact destroy all his poems. One was later found in the Busses' garden, which, while not of great literary merit, gives some insight into a young man's suicidal state of mind at the time.[19]

On the evening of 16 October, Hanns Dietrich composed a suicide letter to his mother, in which he wrote:

> I love my friend Harry Ditzen very much. He exercised a strange power
> over me, he was able to subject me completely to his will. The mistake

I made, which is responsible for all the terrible things which have happened, is that I was too weak to break off our friendship when that was still possible. Once I had fallen under his spell, it was too late.

One day, a lovely day, when I was once more under his influence, I gave him my word, I gave it freely, to help him carry out his plans.

This word of honour refers to the promise made by Hanns Dietrich on 27 September to give Rudolf a revolver when he required it.

Echoes of Dorian Gray are to be heard in Hanns Dietrich's name for his friend and in the themes of domination and the death of the dominated. *The Picture of Dorian Gray* explores the power one man can exert over another. Lord Henry, contemplating Dorian, thinks:

To a large extent the lad was his own creation. He had made him premature. That was something. Ordinary people waited until life disclosed to them its secrets, but to the few, the elect, the mysteries of life were revealed before the veil was drawn away. Sometimes this was the effect of art, and chiefly the art of literature . . .

The painter, Basil Hallward, tells Dorian: 'From the moment I met you, your personality had the most extraordinary influence over me. I was dominated soul, brain and power by you.' Dorian's pursuit of beauty leaves a trail of suicide and murder in its wake which anticipates the words of Wilde's 'Ballad of Reading Gaol': 'And all men kill the thing they love.'

Hanns Dietrich went on to explain to his mother how 'Harry's' plans later turned to death and, given his inability to commit suicide, to his demand that Hanns Dietrich kill him. When Hanns Dietrich refused, they dreamt up a 'duel' and engineered a public insult to stop gossip about a double suicide or murder. Hanns Dietrich tells his mother: 'And Harry can't help the way things have turned out. Please don't be angry with him. I do not go willingly to my death, I was so happy.' The suicide letter concludes with the words: 'My word of honour, given so carelessly, is to blame for everything. I beg you, dearest mother, forgive me.' Rudolf later claimed that Hanns Dietrich had chosen to use the 'honour' motive because it was the only one his mother, the widow of a military man, would understand and accept.

Very early on the morning of Tuesday 17 October, Hanns Dietrich von Necker and Rudolf Ditzen set out on foot from Rudolstadt to climb up to a local beauty spot, the Uhufelsen. There, in a clearing among the pine trees near the top, they took up their positions, each wearing a red ribbon to mark the location of his heart. Hanns Dietrich drew his revolver; Rudolf cocked his rifle. In the first exchange of fire, both shot wide of the mark. They paused to reload Rudolf's rifle – a task which Hanns Dietrich had to perform because Rudolf had no idea how to do it. The second time they fired, Hanns Dietrich missed Rudolf again but was himself wounded in the heart. Rudolf ran over to his friend, who begged to be shot dead. Rudolf lifted Hanns Dietrich's revolver and administered a third shot. Rudolf Ditzen used the two remaining bullets in the revolver to shoot himself.

Some time later a forester came across the bleeding figure of Rudolf Ditzen staggering down the hill from the Uhufelsen. He helped him into an inn in the nearby village of Eichfeld, from where he was transported to Rudolstadt hospital. On admission it was found that a bullet had injured his lungs and passed close to his heart. He was not expected to survive, and his parents were summoned from Leipzig to his bedside.

The report in the next morning's edition of the *Rudolstädter Zeitung*, a local newspaper, saw the incident in the light of 'the significant number of schoolboy suicides in recent times'. Another local newspaper, the *Schwarzburg–Rudolstädter Landeszeitung*, prophesied that 'even if [Rudolf Ditzen] recovers, he will face a severe sentence and his life will be in ruins'. By 21 October the newspapers were reporting that Rudolf's condition was improving every day and that his recovery seemed assured. Three days later a warrant was issued for his arrest on a charge of murder, based on paragraphs 205, 206 and 208 of the Reich Criminal Code of 1871.[20]

When Wilhelm Ditzen returned to Leipzig on 22 October, his wife and Margarete remained in Rudolstadt. Elisabeth reported that her son could not understand why he had survived since 'he had had so little practice in shooting while Necker was a first-class shot'. The answer to this puzzle emerged in the evidence of Friedrich Wolf, a weapons expert. Rudolf's rifle could kill at a distance of eighty yards while Hanns Dietrich's revolver was unlikely to hit a target at more than thirty paces, and even then the outcome would depend largely on luck. Wolf concluded his statement by claiming that the two young men must have known about the unequal nature of the weapons.

Adelaide Ditzen, who arrived in Rudolstadt on 8 November, remarked on her nephew's apparent lack of remorse for the murder of his friend. She thought him much too frivolous and reported that he was happiest when reciting from his enormous store of lyric poetry. Was this a Wildean performance? Was it the exhilaration of a young man who had narrowly escaped death? Was it the reaction of a man who knew that his friend had wanted to die? The events of 17 October 1911 remain – as often in such cases – unclear and cannot be satisfactorily explained. All that can be said with certainty is that Ditzen's life was changed irrevocably. He was unable to finish his schooling; there could be no question of attending university and following in his father's footsteps into the legal, or indeed any other, profession.

Elisabeth and Margarete Ditzen returned to Leipzig on 10 November. Five days later, Rudolf was admitted to the psychiatric hospital in Jena for a period of observation. On arrival he was uncommunicative and seemed resigned to a prison sentence, comparing his situation with that of Oscar Wilde in Reading Gaol. In some ways, a prison sentence was not unwelcome, for he thought it would allow him to escape from a society which he had rejected, a world which had no place for him. His Tante Ada, who had accompanied him to Jena, visited him frequently in hospital, and her visits often included French and English lessons.

In Jena he wrote some poetry which, according to the director of the hospital, Professor Otto Binswanger, 'revealed a fantasizing and melancholy mood'. Rudolf Ditzen was not the only young poet to be treated by Professor Binswanger. A subsequent patient, Johannes R. Becher, dedicated a poem to 'Geheimrat B.' as a mark of gratitude after a period of treatment for drug addiction in 1917.

Professor Binswanger completed his report on Rudolf Ditzen on 13 December 1911. He concluded that 'at the time when the deed was committed the balance of his mind was disturbed, such as to preclude the free exercise of his will.' He added that, given his patient's current mental state, arrest and detention were not advisable. He offered to keep Rudolf in Jena if the family were willing to pay.

Professor Binswanger's view that Rudolf Ditzen's mental state on 17 October 1911 was unbalanced to the point where he could no longer be said to be acting on the basis of free will was crucial to the case, because the Criminal Code was based on the assumption of free will. If it could be demonstrated that Rudolf Ditzen had been unable to exercise free will at the time of what Wilhelm Ditzen preferred to call the 'accident', then paragraph 51 could be invoked and the defendant declared unfit to plead.

And so, on 12 January 1912, the murder charge was dropped against the accused. Wilhelm Ditzen no doubt breathed a sigh of relief. While his son's future prospects did not look particularly good, Rudolf had at least been spared a criminal record. Margarete was probably equally relieved, for now her marriage to the eminently suitable and promising young lawyer Fritz Bechert could go ahead: a brother in psychiatric care was, socially, infinitely more acceptable than one behind bars. The court declared that Rudolf Ditzen was still mentally ill, and he remained in Dr Binswanger's care until 3 February, when he was moved to Tannenfeld sanatorium.

2 1912–1920
Rudolf Ditzen and Hans Fallada

A stranger to himself, inside him grew a tree
On its own soil – he did not know its name,
As a distant dream his life appeared to be
While near as in a dream was the unknown ...

Then this he felt he could no longer bear,
And set out one morn at break of day;
He saw dark clouds towering in the air
Night still hung feather-light along the way.

He saw the horizon redden in a glow,
The sun brought death to dark and gloom,
The ice exploded, out of his distress there flowed
The first word from his heart: 'the dawn'.

– Rudolf Ditzen[1]

Tannenfeld sanatorium was housed in an eighteenth-century villa set in extensive parkland some forty miles east of Jena. It had been opened in 1899 by Dr Artur Tecklenburg, a former student of Professor Binswanger, as 'a care and treatment centre for the mentally ill', specializing not only in mental illness but also drug and alcohol addiction; treatments included special diets, hydrotherapy, electrotherapy, massage and medication.

Dr Tecklenburg placed particular emphasis on the importance of physical work for the process of recovery, and the Tannenfeld estate offered opportunities for work in horticulture, agriculture, carpentry and fishing. Recreational facilities included a games room, a photographic room, a small library and tennis courts. Each patient had a comfortably furnished room which, apart from the secured windows, was designed to resemble their home environment as closely as possible. There was, in addition, a secure ward for dangerous or suicidal patients, where Rudolf Ditzen spent his first few nights and to which, periodically, he had to return.

Tannenfeld cost between 210 and 450 marks per month, depending on the size of the room. Wilhelm Ditzen paid a small additional fee to secure the services of a male nurse for his son. There was also accommodation for relatives and friends, and Adelaide Ditzen accompanied her nephew to Tannenfeld, where she undertook to further his education. He was fortunate to have such a cultured and enlightened teacher who was willing to leave her work and friends in Italy to devote herself to him. Tannenfeld sanatorium must have seemed a satisfactory solution not only to Wilhelm and Elisabeth Ditzen but also to their son, for he had been granted his wish to be cut off from the world.

The world, indeed, was not a very congenial place in the spring of 1912. Germany and England were arming, the Balkan countries were preparing for war against Turkey and, on the home front, the prominent German Social Democrat August Bebel was prophesying 'the twilight of the gods of the bourgeois world'. The seclusion of Tannenfeld provided a refuge from the stormclouds gathering over Germany.

Seclusion, however, also meant isolation and separation from like-minded spirits. Rebellion, despair and – as we have seen – suicide attempts were not unique to Rudolf Ditzen. Expressionism, characterized by Max Krell as a revolt against 'the fathers',[2] produced countless images of death, decay and revolt in the four years before the outbreak of the First World War. Young, angry and disillusioned poets such as Franz Werfel, Georg Heym, Walter Hasenclever, Alfred Lichtenstein, Johannes R. Becher and Georg Trakl had their work published in *Die Aktion*, *Der Sturm* and the many other literary journals which mushroomed all over Germany during these years.

In Tannenfeld, Rudolf Ditzen had no contact with other poets nor could he experience, for example, the sensation caused by the publication of Gottfried Benn's *Morgue* cycle in March 1912. The solitude in which Rudolf Ditzen began his literary career remained a feature of his life as a writer. He did not become associated with any literary movement, nor did he seek the company of fellow writers.

In Dr Tecklenburg's care, he continued to write poetry. One poem of this period he entitled 'Tannenfeld':

> Perhaps here park means nothing more than sorrow,
> Perhaps here tree's a swallowed sobbing cry,
> And every leaf is clothed in melancholy,
> And joy and sorrow choke and putrefy.
>
> Perhaps each path here leads the way to madness,
> Perhaps the pond's a deeply poured out pain,
> And every building stands eternally in darkness,
> Within my walls dead heartbeats remain.
>
> That may well all be true – but death is not
> So stupid, still and silent in this world,
> It screams and writhes and bleeds a lot
> And nothing falls silent till it's dead.
>
> Only things are dead and perhaps not even these.
> They, too, resist and scream their deepest pain,
> Men also scream and suffer all their days
> Until at last dark wreaths are woven them.[3]

Thoughts of suicide and death overshadowed the first few months in Tannenfeld, during which Rudolf Ditzen experienced violent mood swings which affected his relationship with his aunt. One day he would be enjoying his French and English lessons with her, the next he would accuse her of conspiring with Dr Tecklenburg behind his back. An infatuation with Fräulein Busch, a member of the Tannenfeld staff, plunged him into a crisis in June 1912 which was accompanied by nightmares and phantasies of Hanns Dietrich von Necker's older brother exacting revenge on him. Adelaide Ditzen happened to be away from Tannenfeld at the time, seeking relief from an allergy on the North Sea coast, and it is a measure of her nephew's dependence on her that he longed for her return. By the time of his nineteenth birthday in July, however, she was able to take him out on a day trip, and by the beginning of August his condition was improving.

Rudolf remained in contact with his parents by letter and his father visited him in May, though there is no evidence that his mother ever visited Tannenfeld. Rudolf was anxious to maintain relations with Leipzig but was careful not to worry his parents by telling them anything that might upset them. Wilhelm and Elisabeth Ditzen had some cause for celebration in September 1912 when their daughter Margarete married the promising young lawyer Dr Fritz Bechert.

Adelaide Ditzen based her lessons in Tannenfeld on the European humanist literary tradition. Encouraged by his aunt, Rudolf wrote in October and again in November 1912 to her acquaintance Romain Rolland requesting permission to translate his *Vie de Michel-Ange* (1905) and *Vie de Beethoven* (1903). Unfortunately, Rolland had already given the translation rights to the socialist playwright Wilhelm Herzog and this project came to nothing.[4] In December, Rudolf offered Eugen Diederichs Verlag in Jena a book about Tolstoy, which the publisher rejected on the grounds that there was currently no market for Tolstoy in Germany.[5] Rudolf Ditzen's enthusiasm for Rolland and Tolstoy was ill timed. Germany's relations with France had been strained since the Agadir crisis of 1911, and Germany's support of the Austro-Hungarian Empire in November 1912 against a Russian-backed Serbia very nearly erupted into full-scale war. Xenophobia was widespread in the German press. A highly tendentious article in the *Tägliche Rundschau* claimed that French literature presented Germans in a universally negative light. Rudolf Ditzen was so incensed by this distortion that he wrote an article in reply entitled '*Deutschland in der heutigen französischen Litteratur* [sic]' ('Germany in Contemporary French Literature') in which he recommended Romain Rolland's novel *Jean-Christophe*: 'Anyone who has read this book will think differently of our neighbours across the Rhine and, irrespective of all the current disagreements, will shake hands as one decent man with another.'[6] In this article, the first he submitted to a newspaper, Rudolf Ditzen quotes with approval Romain Rolland's words: '. . . *les braves gens de tous les pays se ressemblent. Je me trouve chez moi partout en Europe.*' ('. . . decent people are alike all over the world. I feel at home anywhere in Europe.') This enthusiastic endorsement of French literature and of a French humanist writer, which was never published, provides an important insight into the nineteen-year-old's thinking. Ditzen was attracted by Rolland's espousal of universal humanist values. Rolland's theme of *les braves gens* anticipates Rudolf Ditzen's belief in *die Anständigen* ('decent people'), a constant motif in his subsequent work.

In early 1913, Ditzen offered a translation of Alphonse de Chateaubriant's *Monsieur des Lourdines*, which had won the Prix Goncourt in 1911, to nine publishers in Germany. The hand of Adelaide Ditzen can be seen behind his attempt to become a translator. Perhaps she regarded translation as a literary activity less likely to upset her nephew's delicate nervous balance, or as a preparation for becoming a writer, or simply as a language-learning exercise. In any case, the xenophobic climate of Germany at the time was not receptive to the work of French or Russian authors. Ironically, Rudolf Ditzen might have had more success finding a publisher for his Expressionist poetry than for his translations of foreign literature.

In March, the local military authorities enquired about Rudolf Ditzen's fitness for military service. Dr Tecklenburg, who was opposed to the enlistment of his patient, stated that Rudolf Ditzen was still mentally ill and would remain so for the foreseeable future. As a result, he was declared 'permanently unfit for military service' and exempted from conscription.[7] In fact, Rudolf Ditzen was making good progress. He received visits from his father, his brother Uli and his friend Willi Burlage in March 1913, and when Wilhelm Ditzen returned in June plans were made for his son's future. Adelaide Ditzen's presence was now no longer required full time in Tannenfeld and she could begin to pick up the threads of her life in Italy again.

In the course of the previous months, Rudolf's periods of depression had become both less frequent and less serious; he had learned to 'recognize his limitations, control himself, deal rationally with his emotions, live an ordered life and devote himself to a practical activity'.[8] Dr Tecklenburg was convinced that fresh air and hard physical work were what his patient required, so he approached the Herrmann family who owned the nearby estate of Posterstein about employing Rudolf Ditzen as assistant to their chief steward, Herr Schönekerl.

A shadow was cast over the happiness of the Ditzen family in June 1913 with the death of the Becherts' twin babies. Rudolf's great-uncle, who had been the terror of his mother's childhood and who was known in the family only by his surname – Onkel Seyfarth – died, too, at the end of July.

On 15 September 1913, Rudolf was officially discharged from Tannenfeld sanatorium to begin work under the supervision of Herr Schönekerl in Posterstein. Schönekerl had a reputation for strictness and toughness, and his protégé soon learned the meaning of hard work, for he was expected to rise at three in the morning to supervise the milking of over 120 cows. Rudolf Ditzen's twelve-line poem 'Erwachen' ('Awakening') describes a day's work on the land when the poet is up before dawn, exhausted by noon and then revived by a jug of beer in the shade which enables him to face the rest of the day with renewed vigour.[9]

Rudolf Ditzen was just settling into his first job when, quite unexpectedly, his past caught up with him. One Sunday in October 1913, when he was attending Church with the Herrmann family and the other estate workers, the usual clergyman was unable to attend and was replaced by a Pastor Schultze, who turned out to be the son-in-law of Pastor Braune, Rudolf's former landlord in Rudolstadt. Pastor Schultze publicly refused Rudolf Holy Communion on the grounds that he had blood on his hands. Dr Tecklenburg was able to calm the ensuing storm by assuring the authorities that Rudolf Ditzen did not pose a danger to the public and that this was the case of a young person who was over-coming the problems of puberty as he grew older and more mature and who would become 'a respectable and useful member of society'. The affair did not adversely affect Rudolf, who soon became a popular member of the Posterstein community, known for his flirting with the young women, his heavy smoking and for the light-hearted poems he wrote for Christmas and other special occasions.

By Christmas 1913, Rudolf Ditzen had begun to put the nightmare of puberty behind him. He had learned to cope with his nervous disposition, he had found a job which suited him and he was beginning to enjoy the independence of adult life. The Herrmanns provided board and lodging for their apprentice and Wilhelm Ditzen supplemented this with a monthly allowance.

Rudolf Ditzen had not abandoned his ambition to become a writer and, in January 1914, he offered a novel to Xenien Verlag in Leipzig, along with some sketches and a translation of poems by Dante Gabriel Rossetti. Although Xenien Verlag was initially enthusiastic, this publishing project, like the previous ones, came to nothing.

The tensions and rivalries which had been growing between the European imperial powers since the end of the nineteenth century came to a head in June 1914 with the assassination in Sarajevo of the heir to the Austro-Hungarian throne. Within a month, the Austro-Hungarian Empire had declared war on Serbia, and the other European powers began to take sides for the conflict to come.

Wilhelm Ditzen's schoolfriend Theobald von Bethmann-Hollweg, now Imperial Chancellor, wired his ambassador in Vienna on 29 July: 'It is solely a question of finding a means of making the realization of Austria-Hungary's aims possible . . . without at the same time unleashing a world war, and if this is in the end not to be avoided, to bring about the best possible conditions under which we may wage it.'[10]

The enthusiasm for war in Germany was almost universal, with all the political parties, the trade unions and the Churches in favour. The military victories on the Western Front in early August only served to fan the flames of national fervour. It seemed as if every able-bodied young man was volunteering for active service. In August, Rudolf Ditzen's brother-in-law, Fritz Bechert, joined up, leaving Margarete and their three-month-old son in the care of the Ditzens in Leipzig. Rudolf's younger brother, Uli, volunteered too.

In this atmosphere of euphoria it is not surprising that Rudolf Ditzen also wanted to be part of the national effort. His father accompanied him to a number of recruitment centres near Posterstein in August, but without success. Wilhelm Ditzen then requested Dr Tecklenburg to certify that his son was fit for active service. This Dr Tecklenburg refused to do, pointing out that, on his recommendation, the military authorities had already declared Rudolf Ditzen permanently unfit. He advised most strongly against Rudolf's enlistment, not least because people could easily draw the conclusion that his patient's alleged mental illness had only been a pretext used by a senior judge to have the murder charges dropped against his son. Wilhelm Ditzen ignored this advice and supported his son's attempts to join the army. These efforts were eventually successful in September 1914 in Leipzig, where Rudolf enlisted in the 19th Ordnance Corps.

Many writers, artists and intellectuals supported the war effort. Thomas Mann declared in September 1914: 'War! It was purification, it was liberation, that we felt and enormous hope.'[11] A group of ninety-three leading intellectuals declared their support for Germany's war effort, which they insisted was not expansionist in intent. Voices of opposition, such as Hermann Hesse and Wilhelm Herzog, were few and far between. One other such voice was that of Romain Rolland, who, in his *Au-dessus de la mêlée* (1915), appealed to intellectuals across Europe to work together to overcome hatred and injustice and to bring about reconciliation.

Meanwhile, Rudolf Ditzen's career in the army had come to an abrupt end: he was declared unfit for any kind of military service and discharged on 22 September. He was greatly relieved to have escaped the 'scolding and bullying',[12] and after a short stay with his parents in Leipzig he returned to Posterstein. Uli had left to join his regiment two days after his brother's discharge. Ernst Rowohlt also joined up in Leipzig, and found himself in the same regiment as Uli Ditzen, whom he came to know quite well in the course of the war. In a letter to his parents in October 1931 Ditzen mentions that Rowohlt still talked with affection of Uli. There is no indication that Uli mentioned this friendship to Rudolf, whom he saw at only infrequent intervals between 1914 and 1918.

As the German advance was halted on the Western Front in the autumn of 1914, the war began to take its toll. Among the fallen in September were the Expressionist painter August Macke and the poet Ernst Wilhelm Lotz. Fritz Bechert was wounded in Flanders in October and returned to Leipzig to convalesce. The death of Ernst Stadler, poet, translator and former Rhodes scholar at Oxford, was recorded on the front page of *Die Aktion* on 21 November 1914. In the same month the poet Georg Trakl, a medical orderly on the Eastern Front, committed suicide, unable to face the horrors of the battlefield.

Rudolf Ditzen continued his apprenticeship at Posterstein under Herr Schönekerl. His working day was long and hard. After putting the milk on the first train to Gera, he had a quick breakfast before being sent out to the fields to supervise ploughing or planting, or into the woods to check up on the woodcutters. When the day's work was done and the animals had been fed, it was Schönekerl's habit to lecture his apprentice on the business of the estate, a ritual which required the apprentice to remain standing and which lasted for some considerable time after the other farm workers had gone.

Rudolf's sister Elisabeth, clearly anxious not to lose touch with her brother, brought her fiancé, Heinz Hörig, to meet him in Posterstein at the beginning of January 1915.

Rudolf Ditzen's years in Posterstein and on other estates not only taught him about agriculture, horticulture and forestry but:

> ... all this time – and I only discovered this decades later – I was learning, learning to become what I was going to be one day: a writer. For I spent nearly all my time with other people, I stood behind the endless rows of chattering women weeding beet or lifting potatoes and I heard these women and young girls chatting away all day. Then at the end of the day the boss chatted to me and the dairymen chatted over their cows and the labourers over their animal feed in the barn. I could not help listening and I learnt how they talked, what they talked about, what their worries were, what sort of problems they had ...[13]

Although nominally in charge, Rudolf Ditzen's status as an apprentice made him one of the workers. Here, at last, he escaped the isolation and self-absorption of his teenage years and learned to live and work with a wide range of people, sharing their joys and sorrows.

By the autumn of 1915, Dr Tecklenburg was satisfied that his patient no longer required supervision. So, having completed his apprenticeship in Posterstein, Rudolf obtained a position as second (deputy) steward on the Heydebreck estate near Plathe in Pomerania. Heydebreck, which belonged to the Bismarck family, was much bigger than Posterstein, with large forests and extensive hunting. Rudolf, writing to Dr Tecklenburg on 7 November 1915, expressed enthusiasm for his new job: 'While the war has brought much unhappiness to many people, it has done me nothing but good, for in peacetime nobody would ever have considered entrusting me with such a responsible job.' He was optimistic about his prospects in Heydebreck and hoped to become the chief steward on the estate at the beginning of 1916.

Other young men who did not join the army were less fortunate. Johannes R. Becher, who refused to do military service, led a very precarious existence during the war years in Germany when, apart from a period of employment by Kurt Wolff in his publishing business in Leipzig, he had to depend largely on patrons. Becher continued to write poetry and, in *Die Aktion* at the end of 1915, announced a new collection entitled *An Europa* ('To Europe'). In 1915, *Die Aktion*, under the editorship of its founder Franz Pfemfert, began a regular feature entitled '*Verse vom Schlachtfeld*' ('Poems from the Battlefield') which included poetry by Erwin Piscator and Kurd Adler, among others. Other opponents of the war such as Hugo Ball, Frank Wedekind, Franz Werfel, Hermann Hesse and Ernst Bloch found their way to Switzerland, where Romain Rolland spent the war years, too, working for the International Red Cross.

In Heydebreck, Rudolf Ditzen had little time for literary activities. The war must have seemed quite remote, for the German front had moved eastwards across most of Lithuania and Poland in the course of 1915. The Ditzens, like most German families, were not unaffected by the war; the entry of Italy on the side of the Entente powers in May had forced Adelaide Ditzen to leave Rome and take up residence with her sister and brother-in-law in Blankenburg.

Rudolf Ditzen's enthusiasm for Heydebreck did not last long. The onerous workload and inadequate diet had a bad effect on his health. On medical advice and with the blessing of his employer, he left Plathe in March 1916 to take up an office job with the *Landwirtschaftskammer* (Chamber of Agriculture) in Stettin, the capital of Pomerania and Germany's third largest commercial port after Hamburg and Bremerhaven. There he worked as assistant to a Dr Strömer and dealt with correspondence in relation to seeds and fertilizers. It was through his work here that he met Johannes Kagelmacher, a colourful and unconventional character who was then farm manager of the Strellin estate near Greifswald, and who was to become a lifelong friend. In his new job, Rudolf Ditzen became involved in a vital part of the war effort: the organization of food production.

Ditzen's experience of the poor diet in Heydebreck was not unique in Germany during the winter of 1915–16. The economic blockade by the Entente powers, begun in November 1914, meant that foreign imports had come almost to a standstill. In addition, agricultural production had dropped considerably as a result of conscription, the requisitioning of animals and the reduced availability of fertilizers. The rationing of bread and flour had been introduced and, in order to prevent speculation, the government had set fixed low prices for potatoes. While the potato crop in 1915 had been good, many farmers, seeing very low profit margins in selling them, preferred to feed them to their pigs and then sell the pigs at inflated prices, thereby causing a shortage of potatoes that winter. The poor harvest in 1916 exacerbated the situation.

On the military front, 1916 was a turning-point in the war. The failure to take Verdun and the slaughter at the Battle of the Somme demonstrated that Germany could not win the war on the Western Front. Among the casualties at the Battle of the Somme was Uli Ditzen, who was wounded, although not seriously enough to be sent home. His friend and comrade-in-arms, a Major Schauer, later told Elisabeth Ditzen that, as they lay in the trenches, he and Uli decided that 'they did not want their bodies to be taken home nor did they want their graves to be tended, if they fell.'[14]

The outcome of the Battle of Jutland in May only served to emphasize the efficacy of the blockade and the impotence of the German navy to break out of the North Sea. The Baltic was thus turned into a naval and commercial backwater. Stettin, described in the *Encyclopedia Britannica* of 1911 as 'comparatively an uninteresting city', undoubtedly became even less attractive, which is perhaps one reason why Rudolf Ditzen wanted to leave it at the first opportunity. Twenty-six years later, in May 1941, when Ernst Rowohlt was stationed in Stettin during the Second World War, Ditzen wrote him a sympathetic letter: 'I know from experience how very boring Stettin can be in the long term. ... Always in that café in Parade Street, or whatever it was called, and then across the street was a bar you went into when you had money (which wasn't often).'

Little Man – What Now? contains an echo of Ditzen's disdain for Stettin when the urbane Mia Pinneberg comments to her new daughter-in-law who has just arrived in Berlin: 'I hear you're all supposed to be still in flannel underwear in Pomerania.' For her, Pomerania was clearly a byword for backwardness.

Ditzen's opportunity to escape Stettin came in the guise of a seed potato company set up in Berlin in October 1916 to improve the production and supply of potatoes. In November, Rudolf found himself in Berlin, employed to promote the potato: 'I became an expert in growing potatoes. At the peak of my powers I was able to distinguish 1,200 varieties of potato, and not only by name but also by their appearance, eyes, the shape and colour of the tuber.'[15]

Rudolf Ditzen was delighted to return to Berlin, 'which is my only home, although I wasn't born there'. However, the Berlin Rudolf Ditzen returned to in November 1916 was very different from the Berlin he had left in 1909. This was the first 'Kohlrübenwinter' (turnip winter), where turnips replaced potatoes as the staple diet. Rationing now included meat, butter, eggs and sugar. The Dadaist poet Richard Huelsenbeck, who arrived in Berlin from Zürich around the same time, wrote:

> Shortages had increased dramatically, the German Empire was tottering and the loudest victory announcements could not banish the expressions of worry and hidden fear from the people's faces. In Zürich, where there was no rationing, art became of necessity a game, an idyll. In Zürich you could rage in beautiful trochees and well formed novels against the war. In Berlin fear grabbed your heart, the horizon became darker, there were too many people dressed in black . . .[16]

War-weariness had started to make itself felt. May Day 1917 had been marked by a demonstration for peace on the Potsdamer Platz. The Social Democrats were beginning to split into pro- and anti-war factions. Writers, such as Wieland Herzfelde, who had been sent home from the Western Front in 1915 as 'unworthy to wear the Kaiser's uniform', and artists, such as Oskar Kokoschka, who had been wounded in action, were attracted to Berlin. Herzfelde published a new journal in July 1916 entitled *Neue Jugend* which featured drawings by George Grosz and had on its first page a poem by Becher. The poet Sylvia von

Harden, who first met Becher in 1916, later recalled: 'Wild and talented, this morphine addict wrote like a man possessed ... He was as much obsessed with his poetry as with his politics.'[17] In Berlin, Rudolf Ditzen, too, turned to writing again. From his new lodgings in Berlin-Schöneberg he wrote to Xenien Verlag in December 1916 demanding the return of the Rossetti translations he had submitted in early 1914.

The year ended with the marriage of Rudolf's older sister Elisabeth to Heinz Hörig. Wilhelm and Elisabeth Ditzen now had their home to themselves again. Their joy in their daughters' marriages and their two grandchildren (Margarete had given birth to a daughter in June) was overshadowed by fear for Uli's safety at the Front and concern that the temptations of city life might prove too much for Rudolf.

Despite the demanding nature of Rudolf Ditzen's job, which required him to travel extensively throughout Germany encouraging farmers to plant potatoes and advising on the different varieties, he still found time to seek out the company of women; he wrote to his Tante Ada that he believed women held the key to human understanding, and women certainly played an important role in his life and work.

Early in 1917, he announced his engagement to a woman of humble origins who earned her living as an accounts clerk. This caused much consternation in the family. Adelaide Ditzen tried to dissuade him from marriage to this or any young woman because of 'his quickly changing moods and his quite unfounded acts of hostility towards those close to him', as she wrote to Dr Tecklenburg on 3 July 1917. Wilhelm and Elisabeth Ditzen shared these reservations and agreed with her that a woman from a lower social background would not be able to satisfy her nephew intellectually. Rudolf Ditzen chose his first fiancée from the ranks of that social class, '*die kleinen Leute*', the petit bourgeoisie, which he came to immortalize in his writings.

Rudolf Ditzen's fiancée was the 'Jagusch' he would recall in 1924 in his Prison Diary. In the entry for 30 June he explains that he is keeping a diary of his dreams:

> ... in order to conjure up that glorious dream I had after I broke off
> my engagement to Jagusch.
>
> Jagusch! – strange, it seems such a long time since I thought about

her. And now her name flows from my pen, but it brings back nothing
of the happiness of being in love which we must once have shared, only
the excruciating helplessness and tearfulness of parting.

The importance of Jagusch is underlined by a poem dedicated to her
in his collection 'Shapes and Images'.

In April 1917, Rudolf offered this collection to four publishers.
A few weeks later, Willi Burlage sent a copy of the manuscript to the
Kurt Wolff Verlag in Leipzig. It exists in an (unpublished) typed manuscript of 103 pages containing some 70 poems. They mostly consist of
three to six four-line verses with a simple '*ABAB*' rhyme scheme.
Death (including suicide), alienation and the search for meaning are
the major themes, and many of the poems are clearly autobiographical. Besides the titles already mentioned, there is '*An W. B.*' ('To W. B.')
and a poem entitled '*Sehnsüchte*' ('Yearnings') which sees the potato
as a symbol of longing in its yearning for light and blossom and concludes that fulfilment of that longing brings death. There are love
poems, erotic poems and what Adelaide Ditzen called 'quite perverse
literary efforts'.

There are also quite sophisticated poems, such as '*Wanderung*'
('Wandering'), in which the poet spends his life walking through the
sand dunes, searching in vain for the sea.[18] In '*Büro*' ('Office'), the poet
observes young women typists in an office, whose hands fly across the
keys while their thoughts are elsewhere, namely, with their lovers.[19]

Rudolf Ditzen's failure to find a publisher in 1917 may have been
partly due to the war. The overthrow of the Tsar in March and the
entry of the USA into the conflict at the beginning of April had fuelled
the general unrest. In addition, Ditzen's poetry was very much a product of early, pre-war Expressionism, whereas the experience of the
battlefield, or exile, or the privations of wartime Germany had altered
the perspective of many poets. Yvan Goll's '*Appell an die Kunst*'
('Appeal to Art') in *Die Aktion* in 1917 declared: 'The subjective lyri-
cist who cuts himself off from humanity and daubs his imagined pain
with rose oil is telling lies . . .' The development of Becher's poetry, for
example, illustrates this turning away from introspection to a more
socially aware approach.

Besides seeking a publisher for his poetry, Rudolf Ditzen had taken up translation again. He began work on Gabriele d'Annunzio's *La Gioconda*, and in August 1917 he offered Insel Verlag a German translation of the *Rubáiyát of Omar Khayyám*. He based his translation on the famous English version of 1859 by Edward FitzGerald, who made no secret of the fact that this was a very free adaptation. Ditzen's claim in a letter to his prospective publisher on the twenty-ninth of that month that his translation was 'of all the translations I am familiar with, the only one to adhere completely to the Persian metre' seems rather disingenuous. It met with as little success as his previous translation projects, which may be less a comment on his translation skills than on the difficulty of publishing translations in a period of nationalist fervour.

By the end of June, Rudolf's engagement was off. Perhaps the Ditzens' disapproval played a part in this. It is also likely that an accounts clerk would have had difficulty adapting to the society in which Rudolf Ditzen now moved and which his aunt referred to as 'evil circles ... Futurists, Cubists, Expressionists'.[20] However, the main reason for the end of Rudolf Ditzen's engagement was his relationship with Anne Marie ('Annia') Seyerlen, whom he met through his friend the sculptor Lotte Fröhlich in the spring of 1917.[21] Annia took a personal interest in Rudolf's writing and encouraged him in his literary ambitions. Her husband, Egmont Seyerlen, had published a sensational book about his adolescence, *Die schmerzliche Scham; Geschichte eines Knaben um das Jahr 1900* ('The Painful Shame: Story of a Young Boy around the Year 1900'), which had appeared in 1913. Rudolf Ditzen devoted his first novel to the same topic and gave it the working title '*Leiden eines jungen Mannes in der Pubertät*' ('Sufferings of a Young Man in Puberty').

The sophisticated and urbane Annia Seyerlen was very different from the farm workers, rural nobility and lower-middle-class women whom Rudolf Ditzen had met since he left Tannenfeld. With Egmont Seyerlen absent at the Front, Ditzen fell head over heels in love with Annia, and by the end of the year they had a 'secret' flat in Berlin where they could meet without attracting attention.

Adelaide Ditzen, who was kept informed by her nephew of the

progress of his novel, was concerned about the effect of a book 'which deals with every sexual perversity'[22] on her brother and sister-in-law. Wilhelm Ditzen's health was deteriorating. He was coming to the end of a career which had absorbed his energies for forty years; the Germany which his generation had built was disintegrating in the chaos of war. His schoolfriend Theobald von Bethmann-Hollweg had been forced to resign in July because he was regarded as too liberal by the military command.

While the Russian Revolution in November 1917 brought about a cessation of war in the East, it also lent support to the opponents of the war in Germany. The clamouring for peace intensified, as did the militancy of the labour movement, so that by the end of 1917 the Social Democrats had split into a moderate and a revolutionary wing.

In the hunger and privation of the second 'turnip winter', Rudolf Ditzen travelled the country in his expensive fur coat and could spend 1,500 marks on three months' supply of cigarettes. His aunt, whom he visited on 28 December, reported his poor physical shape and his chain-smoking to Dr Tecklenburg on 6 January 1918: 'His face has remained small and childlike, but there are times when he looks like an old man.'

His haggard appearance was undoubtedly due to his lifestyle – constant travelling, heavy smoking and excessive drinking. A young man with money in his pocket had access to all the pleasures and temptations Berlin had to offer in 1917.

He read excerpts from his novel to Adelaide Ditzen, and her comments, while largely negative, reveal why he was interested in her judgement: 'Some parts are undeniably well written but they are interspersed with quite weird, incoherent words and senseless abominations.'[23] While Adelaide Ditzen had no time for modern Expressionist writing – for reasons of both taste and family considerations – she was able to recognize good writing when she saw it. She also shared her nephew's genuine love of literature.

At the end of January 1918, Rudolf, fearing a recurrence of his nervous illness, considered going back to Tannenfeld for treatment. However, his health improved sufficiently to enable him to continue working on his novel. In February, he wrote to Ernst Rowohlt for the first time, and towards the end of the month he took leave from his job and devoted himself to what his aunt was now calling 'the dreadful, so-called novel'. Uli was now on leave in Leipzig and working for his School Leaving Certificate. After three and a half years on the Western Front he was suffering from heart disease and agoraphobia, and his aunt described him as a 'nervous wreck'.[24]

Wilhelm Ditzen retired on 1 March 1918, as the Germany which he had helped to shape and uphold was falling apart, both internally and externally. Peace demonstrations, mass strikes and the formation of workers' councils were evidence of the growing social disaffection at home. The victories embodied in the peace treaties with Russia and Rumania in the East could not mask the failure of the German High Command to advance on the Western Front.

Rudolf finished the first draft of 'The Sufferings of a Young Man in Puberty' on 10 March and set about reworking it four days later under the new title of *Der junge Goedeschal* ('Young Goedeschal'). As he became absorbed in his literary activities he found his 'purely mechanical job' increasingly irksome and began to cast around for a means of escaping the drudgery of 'wage labour' to devote himself full time to writing.[25] His father, who was unwilling to see his son give up a good job for a very uncertain future, suggested that Rudolf should have an expert look at his work before taking such a drastic step. Rudolf replied that his work to date was not good enough, that he needed time to produce more and better pieces, and he asked his father to support him for a trial period of one year, a 'literary year'. Wilhelm Ditzen, anxious – as ever – to do the best for his son and – yet again – at a loss as to what that might be, consulted Dr Tecklenburg, an authority whom both father and son respected.

Dr Tecklenburg advised his former patient in a letter of 15 May: 'I am still of the opinion that it would be better, from the point of view of your health, if you had a practical job which provided material security rather than engaging in such an uncertain activity as literature which will adversely affect your nervous system and may possibly cause your psychopathic predisposition to assert itself again.' Having expressed his reservations, Dr Tecklenburg left the decision to Rudolf. His only word of warning was to stop 'that stupid smoking'.

Rudolf read this reply as support for his plans and brushed aside his father's suggestion that, instead of devoting himself to literature for a year, he should devote himself to 'potatoes'. His father reluctantly agreed to his son's 'literary year', but made two conditions. For the sake of his health, Rudolf should leave Berlin and spend the year in the country. His second condition was that Rudolf should publish his novel under another name. He explained the reasons for this in a letter to Dr Tecklenburg on 19 May: 'I am making this stipulation primarily in his own interest. The Rudolstadt events are still too recent.'

And so, on 1 July 1918, Rudolf Ditzen, with the support of his father, became a full-time writer. Wilhelm Ditzen drew up a contract at the beginning of August in which he undertook to pay his son 3,600 marks in addition to his standard annual allowance of 1,200 marks for the period from 1 July 1918 until 30 June 1919. Rudolf Ditzen undertook to find a job from 1 July 1919 if his literary year was not successful. His father concluded the letter accompanying their contract by wishing his son every success.

The next day, 8 August 1918, the Entente counter-offensive began east of Amiens and in the ensuing battle six German divisions were destroyed. Among the fallen on 12 August was the twenty-one-year-old Ulrich Ditzen. He was buried two days later. It was another six days before the news reached Leipzig. A death at the Front was a death without a funeral, without an opportunity to mourn.

The death of Uli, the 'baby' of the family, who had planned to study medicine after the war, had a shattering effect on Wilhelm and Elisabeth Ditzen. It also had a much greater effect on Rudolf Ditzen than has hitherto been recognized. Not only did he name his firstborn son twelve years later after his dead brother but he made frequent reference to Uli in his letters to family and friends. The fact that Ulrich Ditzen's memory remained very much alive is shown not only by the references to his birthday in December which remained a regular feature of family letters but also by gestures such as the present of Ulrich's sketchbook which Ditzen received from his parents at Christmas 1936 and reminiscences such as Elisabeth Hörig's remark in July 1937 that her husband's calculations always made her think of 'our Uli who could only tell the difference between right and left by

44

the mole on his left hand'. In the 1930s, Ditzen and his wife made a habit of sending two bunches of dried flowers to his mother on 12 August. In March 1941, he referred in a letter to Rowohlt to Uli's former commanding officer, Kratzert, 'whom my brother Uli couldn't bear because he forced him to drink alcohol'. In 1942, he was still in correspondence with Uli's closest friend and comrade-in-arms, Major Schauer. Uli also featured prominently in Rudolf's last letter to his mother, in December 1946.

The presence of Uli can also be discerned in Ditzen's writing, where the motif of a son who dies in battle occurs in two major novels: in the figure of Otto Hackendahl, the gentle, earnest son of the tyrannical Gustav Hackendahl in *Iron Gustav*; and in Otto Quangel, the son of Anna and Otto Quangel in *Alone in Berlin*. Both young men are peace-loving and kind individuals who go reluctantly to war and leave a grieving wife/fiancée behind. In the case of *Alone in Berlin*, it is the death of their son which leads to the Quangels' decision actively to oppose fascism.

The immediate effect of Ulrich Ditzen's death on his older brother can be seen in the turn which his life took in the autumn and winter of 1918–19. Rudolf had now given up his job and was working full time revising his novel, as well as writing short stories. Berlin, where, despite his father's wishes, he remained until June 1919, was hardly conducive to literary composition: the collapse of the war effort, the promise of reform by a newly appointed civil government under Prince Max von Baden , the resignation of General Ludendorff, who, with General Paul von Hindenburg had been in charge of the war effort, the mutiny of the German fleet at the end of October: all paved the way for the November Revolution in 1918. While sailors, soldiers and workers were forming their revolutionary councils, writers, too, were involving themselves in the Revolution. Ernst Toller was elected chairman of the short-lived Munich Soviet. The poet Erich Mühsam was also active in Munich, Friedrich Wolf in Dresden and, in Berlin, Kurt Hiller set up a 'Council of Intellectual Workers'. Karl Jakob Hirsch later recalled the atmosphere in Berlin at that time:

> The revolution surprised nobody in Germany ... At that time we all believed in a better, a new future ... On 9 November at 8 p.m. the

'Council of Intellectual Workers' was formed. I was a member. The first meeting was held in the Reichstag and demands were made which did not seem so revolutionary to us, for example: the abolition of the Academies, public ownership of all theatres ... the immediate establishment of a world parliament ... The word 'radical' played a large role in all these meetings ... People should not laugh about a time when young people seriously wanted to build a new world.[26]

Rudolf Ditzen was one of those young people. His antipathy to the old order in Germany, which not only had had no place for him but which had also murdered his brother, made him a natural supporter of social change. Adelaide Ditzen, however, was scathing about her nephew's revolutionary fervour. In a letter to Dr Tecklenburg in December 1918 she declared: 'That's all we needed – for Rudolf to discover his love for the revolution. Needless to say it's another case of 'cherchez la femme'. I wonder whether he's playing his new role in the elegant fur coat he dazzled me with last year or in a sailor's cap?' Tante Ada clearly did not approve of her nephew's relationship with Annia Seyerlen.

It was around this time that Ditzen began to seek solace from outer and inner turmoil in morphine. He had first encountered it while in hospital undergoing treatment for stomach ulcers in the winter of 1918–19. In fact, in a letter to Dr Tecklenburg on 15 August 1919, he drew a direct link between his brother's death, the stomach ulcers and his morphine addiction. A likely source was Wolfgang Parsenow, the son of Lotte Fröhlich, who may well have brought a supply home from the Front. Parsenow, a returning soldier, showed Rudolf Ditzen how to inject. He had the contacts to supply the drug, and Rudolf Ditzen sold his not inconsiderable library (which he estimated at three thousand volumes) and stole 1,800 marks from Annia to finance his habit. Some eleven years later, Ditzen's experience of morphine addiction was to find expression in the highly original autobiographical monologue 'Sachlicher Bericht über das Glück, ein Morphinist zu sein' (Short Treatise on the Joys of Morphinism), in which the addicts 'Hans' and 'Wolf' search desperately for morphine (and cocaine) in Berlin.[27]

The death of his brother, the November Revolution and his first period of drug addiction – these were the circumstances of the first half of Rudolf Ditzen's 'literary year' and the completion of his first novel.

He witnessed the strikes, demonstrations and street battles which shook Berlin during and after November 1918 but, unlike other writers such as Becher or Toller, Ditzen does not appear to have joined any revolutionary party or grouping. On the one occasion when he attempted an artistic depiction of the November Revolution, in Chapter 4 of *Iron Gustav* twenty years later, a very general and confused picture emerges, not the account of someone closely involved.

Evidence of Ditzen's general support for the Revolution emerges from his father's 'deep regret that your views are so very different from ours'. In the same letter, of 2 April 1919, his father continues: 'But we regret even more deeply that you appear to have no inkling at all that by drawing attention to the differences which exist between us you are erecting the kind of barriers which could destroy our relationship.' Notwithstanding these political differences, and his serious doubts about his son's ability to earn a living by writing, Wilhelm Ditzen offered to extend his son's 'literary year' by six months, to 1 January 1920. As his reason for making this offer he wrote: 'Your literary year was full of illness which meant that you could not work for long periods.' What his parents did not know was that their son had attempted suicide on 30 January 1919. He was in despair about his first novel and himself doubted his literary talent; he knew that his relationship with Annia was coming to an end because her husband would soon be returning from the war; he was also ashamed that he had stolen money from Annia and had no prospect of repaying her in the near future. In a letter to Annia on 3 February 1919 he described his attempt to inject oxygen into his veins:

> And then a terrible thing happened: it didn't work. No matter where I injected, thick black blood came out but no air would go into my veins, they were all rusted up. And that was fate again, for it was clear that I wasn't allowed to die, but had to live, to keep on living, on and on, to start all over again . . . So I put down the needle and embraced life once again, dear life.

One of the results of Rudolf Ditzen's renewed espousal of life was the completion of 'Young Goedeschal' on 19 April 1919. He gave one copy each to the Seyerlens, and Egmont Seyerlen passed a copy on to his friend and former comrade-in-arms Ernst Rowohlt. Rudolf was present at the Seyerlens' on 29 April when Egmont Seyerlen phoned Rowohlt and was told that 'Young Goedeschal' had been accepted for publication. Thus Rudolf Ditzen's ambition to become a writer, first announced in 1910 and never abandoned, came to fruition. He dedicated 'Young Goedeschal' to Annia Seyerlen in acknowledgement of her support and encouragement. By the time she received her copy, their relationship had come to an end.

Rudolf Ditzen's next step was to acquire a pen name. This time he did not seek his literary persona in the pages of Oscar Wilde but in the world of Grimms' *Fairy Tales*: Hans, from the protagonist of 'Lucky Hans', an easily duped but happy-go-lucky young man, and Fallada from the horse called Falada in 'The Goose Girl' who, even at the cost of his own life, and after death, always told the truth and ensured that justice was done. Rudolf Ditzen was informed by the authorities that he did not require special permission to use a pen name as long as it was restricted to his literary activities.

And so, on 14 May 1919, the new author, with his new name, went to meet Ernst Rowohlt and his chief editor Paul Mayer. The publisher appears to have shared Adelaide Ditzen's view that the novel was too long, and Rudolf Ditzen promised to cut fifty pages. In the event, he found this impossible and Rowohlt agreed to publish the manuscript uncut, which is perhaps why the contract which Rudolf Ditzen signed on 19 June was less favourable than the one discussed on 14 May. Rowohlt consoled him with the prospect of better terms for future books.

Meanwhile, the conditions which the Allies imposed on the German government in the same month in the Treaty of Versailles were even more draconian than had been feared. In addition to the loss of territory in Europe and overseas, most of the German fleet was to be surrendered, the German army substantially reduced, large-scale reparations were to be paid and Germany, in the 'war guilt' clause, was held responsible for causing the war. Patriotic citizens like Wilhelm

Ditzen, who had invested considerable sums in war loans, lost a lot of money. Indignation and dismay at the provisions of the Treaty along with disappointment that the Revolution had failed to remove the military, land-owning and industrial elites ensured that parliamentary democracy got off to a shaky start in Germany in the summer of 1919. The Weimar Republic was, in the words of one historian, 'little more than the defeated empire minus the Kaiser'.[28]

Immediately after signing the contract Rudolf Ditzen set off for the Baumgarten estate near Dramburg in Pomerania to stay with his friend Johannes Kagelmacher, who had taken up a post as estate manager there in 1919. Bee-keeping was one of Kagelmacher's responsibilities, and it was in Dramburg in the summer of 1919 that Ditzen first discovered the fascination of bees, which led to the establishment of a beehive on his smallholding in Carwitz, near Feldberg, some twenty years later.

Ditzen eventually sent his amended manuscript to Berlin on 10 July, ten days behind schedule. Author and publisher agreed on a typeface, and setting began in August. But when proofs arrived in Dramburg towards the end of that month, Rudolf Ditzen was no longer there.

The move to Dramburg had been an attempt to escape the temptations of city life and cure his morphine addiction in particular. After six weeks it became clear that country air and the ministrations of the sympathetic Kagelmacher were not enough. On 15 August, Dr Tecklenburg received a telegram from his former patient requesting admission to Tannenfeld 'to cure my morphine addiction'.

On returning from their summer holiday in Bad Sachsa, Wilhelm and Elisabeth Ditzen learned that their son had suffered 'a slight nervous breakdown'. Rudolf, aware of his parents' advancing years and poor health, did not want to cause them anxiety.

The proofs of 'Young Goedeschal' that had been dispatched to Dramburg were now redirected to Tannenfeld, where Rudolf continued to work on them. On 7 September 1919, Dr Tecklenburg informed Wilhelm Ditzen of his son's drug addiction and advised him that the treatment would last another few weeks. Perhaps this breach of patient–doctor confidentiality was the reason why Rudolf left Tannenfeld ten days later, before his treatment was completed. Rudolf spent a few days in Leipzig before being admitted to Carlsfeld sanatorium in Brehna near Halle.

In Leipzig, Dr Eggebrecht, the family doctor, suggested that Rudolf Ditzen should be certified feeble-minded as a result of his morphine addiction and permanently locked up. Wilhelm Ditzen was not prepared to initiate such proceedings 'lest all the bridges between us and Rudolf be destroyed', as he confided to Dr Tecklenburg. The picture of Wilhelm Ditzen that emerges from his letters is that of a man frequently at a loss but determined to do the best for his son.

Rudolf Ditzen owed much to his father, who first kindled a love of literature in him, who refused to abandon him in his difficult adolescent years, who supported him financially while he was writing his first novel and who was always at pains to keep the channels of communication open. Although father and son had much in common – a love of literature, an almost obsessively meticulous approach to work, the tenacity with which they achieved their life's ambition and the cost of that achievement to their health – their relationship was a very uneasy one until shortly before Wilhelm Ditzen's death in 1937. These difficulties are reflected in Rudolf Ditzen's novels, where few positive father figures may be found. To his son, Wilhelm Ditzen remained the judge who pronounced death sentences and the representative of a social order which he rejected. As we have seen, the truth was somewhat more complex.

Another set of proofs arrived in Tannenfeld after Rudolf Ditzen's sudden departure, and had to be redirected to Carlsfeld. The delay in submitting the manuscript and the subsequent delays in finishing the proof-reading meant that 'Young Goedeschal' could not appear in the autumn, as originally planned. At the end of October, Rudolf Ditzen had second thoughts about the book because of its 'artistic shortcomings', but Paul Mayer was able to reassure him and at the beginning of December told Rowohlt's newest author that his first book would appear early in the New Year.

By 15 January 1920, 'Young Goedeschal' was ready.[29] Its publication brought Rudolf Ditzen and Becher together for the first time, although the encounter was a purely literary one: the dust jacket of 'Young Goedeschal' carried a notice about the publication of Becher's new anthology *Ewig im Aufruhr* ('Always in Revolt'); it was to be another twenty-five years before they would meet in person. Ernst Rowohlt sent Rudolf Ditzen, still undergoing treatment in Carlsfeld, an advance of 500 marks on his 'new opus, the volume of short stories'. As his 'literary year' had come to an end on 1 January, this payment was particularly welcome.

'Young Goedeschal' had been written in Berlin during a period of enormous social and political upheaval. When it appeared in the shops its author was in a sanatorium trying to recover from an illness at least partly induced by the momentous events he had witnessed and lived through. Yet according to the publisher's promotional material, the novel, subtitled '*Ein Pubertätsroman*' ('A Novel about Puberty'), had little to do with these events: 'The writer of this captivating book describes the tragic fate of a young man who, assailed by premonitions of budding sexuality, lurches from one bewildering experience to the next. Not since Wedekind's *Spring Awakening* have the erotic longings of adolescence been depicted in such a stirring manner.'

In his first novel, Rudolf Ditzen captures the bewilderment of a young man confronted with the physical and emotional changes of adolescence, for which he is ill prepared. On a first reading, the most striking aspect of 'Young Goedeschal' is its strongly autobiographical dimension: events and characters are based on the author's experiences in Leipzig and Rudolstadt. Kai Goedeschal writes anonymous and mildly obscene letters to his girlfriend's family (whose name, Lorenz, was the maiden name of Rudolf Ditzen's mother). When he is exposed, he decides to ride out of town and hang himself, and is only prevented from doing so by the intervention of his friend Arne Schütt and Frau Schütt, Arne's mother. The parallels to Willi Burlage and Willi's mother and the suicide threat in 1911 are striking. There are references in the book to Oscar Wilde and Omar Khayyám, including a quotation in English from FitzGerald's version of the *Rubáiyát*, as well as to *Robinson Crusoe*. There is a Wandervogel trip which ends badly for Kai, a well-meaning family doctor and a housemaid who tries to seduce the young master. Descriptions of Kai's difficulties in school are reminiscent of the author's, as is his love of beauty above everything else. Kai, like Rudolf, procured a revolver from a friend.

The autobiographical dimension of the novel extends to the choice of words: Ilse's assertion 'Everything happened as it had to happen' reproduces the words Rudolf Ditzen used in describing the duel to Professor Binswanger. Kai's claim that 'The only evil that exists is what I feel to be evil' echoes Rudolf Ditzen's comment to his classmate Bernhard Hübner in Rudolstadt.[30]

Kai Goedeschal, like Rudolf Ditzen, regarded himself as an outsider who was universally misunderstood and who did not belong. Yet Kai has recognizable literary antecedents. Like his creator, he was unable to take dancing lessons, but while the ball scene has autobiographical resonances, it also recalls the dance scenes in Thomas Mann's *Tonio Kröger*, where the artist remains an onlooker while his friend Hans Hansen dances with Inge Holm. Indeed, Kai's feelings when a schoolmate interrupts his talk with Arne have a parallel in Tonio's disappointment and resentment when Jimmerthal joins in his walk with Hans.[31]

'Young Goedeschal' was written with great passion. Kai's turbulent emotional life is depicted in breathless Expressionist prose characterized by verbal nouns, adjectival nouns, nouns without articles, sentences without verbs, fractured syntax and inner monologues sometimes indistinguishable from dialogue. Towards the end of the novel, the syntax reflects the state of near collapse in which the author completed the work.

'Young Goedeschal' is autobiographical on two levels: on one level, it reflects events and characters from the author's adolescence. On another level, it registers the author's reaction to a war which robbed him of his brother and a revolution with which he probably sympathized and which ended in defeat. The scream emitted by Kai at the end can be read as an expression of the author's despair in 1919:

> And he felt in this scream that nothing had ended, everything remained the same: love, hate, loneliness, torture; starting all over again ...
>
> And wept. And wept.

The society in which Kai has grown up is a hierarchical one based on the values of obedience, duty, order and punctuality. At home he feels misunderstood and distances himself as much as possible from his parents. His mother, frequently portrayed weeping, is determined that her son should remain 'innocent'. His father believes that Kai is too young for sex education, which is, in any case, not the responsibility of the parents but of the school authorities and which, according to the Ministry of Education, should not take place until the final year of schooling. Kai's comment – 'The fathers were too old' – characterizes a whole generation as not only physically old but politically and socially anachronistic. At the end of the novel Kai recognizes that his father does love him but that his love is of the sort 'which goes the wrong way about things, which misses the mark'. One wonders whether Wilhelm Ditzen was able to draw any comfort from these words of grudging recognition.

Images of death, war and decay pervade the novel. On the one occasion when Kai receives praise in school it is for an essay on Sallust's *Bellum Catilinae* in which he describes his favourite scene: the discovery of Catilina's body on the battlefield among the corpses of the enemy. Kai imagines himself kneeling by the dead body, 'and his dead lips smile at me'. Kai's view of Catilina is mingled with Rudolf Ditzen's view of his brother.

'Young Goedeschal' is very much a first novel and the work of an angry young man. It is, as both Adelaide Ditzen and Ernst Rowohlt recognized, too long; the author is also emotionally entangled in the characters and events he portrays. This is no Heinrich Mann surveying the Wilhelmine era in the magisterial sweep of *Der Untertan* (1918; *The Man of Straw*), but a writer whose opposition to the world of the 'fathers' was instinctive and emotional. The teacher who cannot understand why Goedeschal finds Sallust's battle scene so vivid criticizes Kai for his emotional approach to Catilina and urges him to 'think' rather than 'feel' – a comment which could equally well be applied to 'Young Goedeschal' in which the author reproduces Kai's frustration and despair in torrents of emotion. Indeed, while Rudolf Ditzen's style as a novelist later developed away from such Expressionist excesses, his relationship to his characters remained essentially an emotional one.

'Young Goedeschal' anticipates the later novels in other ways, too. All Ditzen's work had a strongly autobiographical dimension, although this is nowhere so overt as in the first novel. In the discussion between Kai's father and the family doctor in Chapter 28 there are flashes of that talent for dialogue which was later developed to such good effect; there is also clear evidence of Ditzen's ability to sketch credible characters.

'Young Goedeschal' received mixed reviews, ranging from the damning comments in the *Deutsches Tageblatt* – 'I have never in my whole life read a book which left such a bad taste. A bowl of soap and water is the first thing that is required after putting this book down' (8 May 1920) – to the very positive review in the *Saale Zeitung* in Halle: '... the first work of a new artistic direction ... Expressionist psychology which will scarcely ever be surpassed' (9 April 1920).

The reviews varied according to the political stance of the publication. Reviewers in favour of a public discussion of puberty and sex education welcomed the novel. Those who considered such issues unsuitable literary material did not. On the whole, however, the reception of the novel was low key but positive – no doubt, a source of some satisfaction to the author. Rowohlt was confident enough to encourage Ditzen to submit a volume of short stories and, in early June 1920, Paul Mayer broached the subject of a second novel.

3 1920–1928
'That Little Tent of Blue'

*The strange, mysterious, perhaps dangerous, perhaps sav-
ing comfort that there is in writing: it is a leap out of murderers' row; it is a seeing of what is really taking place.*
                                        – Franz Kafka[1]

For Rudolf Ditzen, as for many Germans, the third decade of the
twentieth century brought hardship and insecurity. Although he was
discharged from Carlsfeld sanatorium in June 1920, it took him
another eight years to extricate himself from the alcoholism and drug
addiction into which the events of 1918–19 had plunged him.

The year 1920 was one of despair for those who had embraced the
ideals of the November Revolution. The coalition led by the Social
Democrats, which had established the first democratic republic in
German history, was defeated in the elections in June and remained
out of office for eight years. Ernst Toller wrote from his prison cell to
Romain Rolland: 'My German homeland is not on the way to spiritual and intellectual recovery. Military barbarism, the plague of
corruption, the scourge of subservience are devouring its body . . .'[2]
Johannes R. Becher declared: 'I am in despair about the Germans.
Things are going downhill and I see no trace of hope anywhere.'[3]
After the failure of the revolution, Becher withdrew from active political involvement for nearly four years, during which time he wrote
mystical, quasi-religious poetry.

The myth of the Golden Twenties was a phenomenon none of
these writers would have recognized. For Ditzen, the 1920s signified

not glamour but poverty, imprisonment and very little recognition of his talents as a writer. When he emerged from Carlsfeld in June 1920 his most pressing problem was financial. His father, whose capital had been eroded by the war and the instability which followed, could no longer support him to the same extent, nor did the twenty-six-year-old seek his father's help. He asked Ernst Rowohlt for a second advance on the projected short stories but, having received no response by mid-June, he set out once more for Dramburg in Pomerania, where he could be sure of a warm welcome from Johannes Kagelmacher. There, just over a week after his arrival, he received 500 marks from Rowohlt.

Kagelmacher and Ditzen had much in common. Kagelmacher shared Ditzen's contempt for bourgeois hypocrisy and chose to mix with the outcast and the dispossessed. Among his many eccentricities was a life-long interest in astrology and the occult; he frequently provided horoscopes for friends and acquaintances facing important decisions. Kagelmacher was a sympathetic, non-judgemental companion and a true friend, providing a home for Ditzen and taking a genuine interest in his problems. In his ignorance, he thought the best way to cure his friend of his drug addiction was to introduce him to a socially more acceptable drug: alcohol. While Kagelmacher's motives may have been above reproach, the effect of his actions was disastrous. By the autumn, Ditzen was back in Carlsfeld sanatorium for another course of treatment.

On being discharged in November 1920, he went to work on the Marzdorf estate near Deutsch Krone in West Prussia (now Wałcz in north-west Poland). Meanwhile, Kagelmacher had moved from Dramburg to the Baltic island of Rügen, where he fulfilled his ambition to run his own farm. Ditzen moved to work there in early 1921, and it was from Kagelmacher's farm in Gudderitz, near Altkirchen, that he sent his new work, *Die Kuh, der Schuh, dann du* (literally: 'The Cow, the Shoe, then You'), to Paul Mayer, on 23 February.[4]

The title of this short novel, unpublished during Ditzen's lifetime, refers to the three primary first-person narrators in the work: the 'Cow' is Muhtsche, whose calf Muh tells his story before and after birth; the 'Shoe' belongs to a shoe fetishist who kills the object of his desire, the prostitute and cocaine addict Coccola; the 'You' is a fifty-year-old inmate of a psychiatric hospital who after several unsuccessful attempts succeeds in hanging himself.

'The Cow, the Shoe, then You' is an experimental novel in which Ditzen explores different narrative identities and attempts to shape a coherent story out of elements, both fantastic and sordid, which appear to have little in common. Like 'Young Goedeschal', it has strong autobiographical resonances: there is a broken-off engagement, an appearance by the author's sister Elisabeth under her nickname Itzenplitz, and a father who sets his son legal puzzles, as Wilhelm Ditzen used to do. Two narrators have difficult childhoods and stormy adolescences; one narrator kills the woman he loves. 'The Cow, the Shoe, then You' even includes a reference to the origin of Ditzen's pen name in the Grimms' 'The Goose Girl'.

This short novel provides an insight into the author's experience of life in mental institutions and also charts his experimentation with narrative perspective and dialogue. However, it is a very uneven work. Ditzen is much too preoccupied by his own troubles to have any distance to his narrative. Only in the narrative of Muh and Muhtsche can we catch a glimpse of his potential story-telling and imaginative talent, for instance, in his ability to relate the life of a calf inside and outside the womb.

Three weeks after submitting his new manuscript, Ditzen felt he could approach Rowohlt for an advance on his next novel. Since he assumed from a recent copy of 'Young Goedeschal' that it had been reprinted, he asked for an advance of 1,000–1,500 marks. Paul Mayer replied that the information '3,000–4,000 copies' on the inside cover did not indicate the number of copies sold, which in fact stood at only 1,283, and that he could send only 500 marks at Easter.

Ditzen spent the spring and early summer of 1921 working on Kagelmacher's farm and writing his new novel. He grew very fond of Gudderitz and took particular delight in Kagelmacher's garden, which 'became home to me' and which provided the opening scene in his new book, as well as featuring in several subsequent stories. In the summer of 1921, Ditzen left Gudderitz to take up a post on the Bollhagen estate near Doberan in Mecklenburg. It was not until

7 September that Rowohlt wrote to inform him of his decision not to publish 'The Cow, the Shoe, then You'. The reasons for the delay in contacting Ditzen are unclear; one factor may have been Rowohlt's marriage on 1 April to Hildegard Pangust. The rejection letter cited commercial reasons for the decision but went on to encourage Ditzen to submit his next novel and call into the office next time he was in Berlin.

January 1922 found him in Gudderitz once more, where Kagel-macher pursued a policy of employing ex-offenders and other social misfits in an idealistic attempt to assist in their rehabilitation. It was around this time that Ditzen and Kagelmacher took a trip to Munich 'and travelled back in a fourth-class compartment, with no dinner jackets, no gold watches and not a penny to our names'.[5]

At the end of June 1922, Ditzen took up employment on the Neu-schönfeld estate near Bunzlau in Silesia (now Bolesławiec in western Poland). Here he observed the right-wing paramilitary activity which had its origins in opposition to the new Republic, condemned for having stabbed the army in the back and accepted the humiliating provisions of the Versailles Treaty. Originally recruited from disaf-fected sections of the army, these terrorist groupings were particularly active in Silesia, where they became involved in the border disputes with Poland over Upper Silesia, and in Bavaria, where they attracted Adolf Hitler to their cause. They had been the instigators of the attempted coup d'état by Wolfgang Kapp in March 1920 and had been responsible both for the assassination in August 1921 of Matthias Erzberger, a signatory to the armistice and the peace treaty, and for the murder of Walther Rathenau, the foreign minister, in June 1922.

Ernst von Salomon (1902–72), who, like Ditzen, was to become one of Rowohlt's authors, served a five-year prison sentence for his involvement in Rathenau's murder. The son of a senior police officer, he, too, had rebelled against the strictures of an authoritarian upbring-ing. While Ditzen sought salvation in drugs and Becher in Marxism, von Salomon took up arms to defend the German nation against the 'traitors' of the Weimar Republic.

Ditzen completed his new work in Neuschönfeld and dispatched it to Paul Mayer, who reacted very positively, describing 'Anton and Gerda' as 'a significant artistic achievement ... a book which is assured of success', and proposed a publication date in the spring of 1923.[6] Mayer showed it to the writer and editor Franz Hessel, whose *Der Kramladen des Glücks* ('The Junkshop of Happiness') was also due to be published by Rowohlt in 1923; he was equally enthusiastic. Rowohlt's confidence in Ditzen's talent and potential as a writer can be seen in the contract he signed for 'Anton and Gerda' in December 1922, which committed Ditzen to giving Rowohlt first refusal on any books he would write in the next three years.

Ditzen's use of third-person narration in 'Anton and Gerda' marks a shift away from the self-absorption of the first two prose works; yet the figure of Anton Färber, a penniless, short-sighted author of about thirty, indicates that this novel, too, has an autobiographical aspect. Ditzen was later to disown the book because of the influence of Annia Seyerlen on its composition, and there is much to suggest that the relationship between Anton and Gerda was modelled on the author's relationship with Seyerlen. In the novel, Anton, a seventeen-year-old schoolboy from a sheltered, conventional middle-class home imbued with the values of duty, work and piety, falls in love with Gerda, an older, experienced woman who earns a living from prostitution. His love is reciprocated, and they run away together to a Baltic island, where they play out their love against a background of sun, sea and forest until Anton's family tracks them down. At the end of the novel they determine to stay together and live off Gerda's earnings.

Gerda is the first in a series of strong, independent women in Ditzen's work who provide emotional and, often, financial support for their weak and ineffectual men, the most famous example being Lämmchen in *Little Man – What Now?* Like Lämmchen, Gerda has a motherly dimension to her character: she calls Anton '*Junge*' (sonny) and frequently refers to him as 'child'. Ditzen uses the figure of Gerda, the outsider and sinner, to expose the hypocrisy, moral cowardice and duplicity of Church and state.

The ghost of Ditzen's schoolfriend Hanns Dietrich von Necker appears in one of Anton's dreams in the pale, emaciated figure with three black-edged holes in his left breast, which evokes 'a dawning memory' in the dreamer:

> I bend down. The gaunt figure lies groaning on the ground, the three bullet holes gleaming phosphorescently which I once . . . Oh, it's lunacy. That was all so long ago!
>
> . . . I bend down and lift my friend who has been shot dead.

In his dream, Anton carries the body to the cemetery but when he goes to place it in the grave the corpse is already there, leering maliciously at him. At this point the dream takes a particularly spine-chilling turn: Anton discovers he is carrying his own heart in his hand.

There are other autobiographical references in the use of the name of another schoolfriend, Burlage, as well as in the night which Anton spends on the ward for the terminally insane in a mental hospital. The unspecified Baltic island owes much to Ditzen's experience of Rügen, and Kagelmacher's interest in astrology and the occult is shared by Gerda. The account of Anton's sexual initiation and the love-making scenes are intense and suggest a basis in personal experience. Echoes of Oscar Wilde can be heard in Anton's words to his cousin Inge: 'Since then I've lived a thousand lives. I've died a thousand deaths.'

The use of dialogue in 'Anton and Gerda' demonstrates Ditzen's development as a novelist. The exchanges between Professor Färber and the doctor, between Anton and the hotel receptionist in Leipzig, between Gerda and the client who buys her a dress, as well as a row between Anton and Gerda in a Leipzig hotel, are realistic and convincing and anticipate the role of dialogue in the later novels. Ditzen's ability to establish an immediate rapport with the reader by appealing to a common human experience can be seen in the opening paragraph, where Anton's attempts to have an afternoon sleep are constantly frustrated by the barking of a dog. A number of lyrical and erotic passages reveal the development of Ditzen's descriptive powers.

With 'Anton and Gerda', Ditzen can be seen maturing as a writer, gaining mastery of his material, developing techniques of dialogue and description, and translating his close observation of human life into literature.

In a letter to Paul Mayer in the autumn of 1922, Ditzen reported that he was in good spirits and was about 'to fulfil [his] dearest dream' by acquiring a farm of his own. This plan came to nothing. While spiralling inflation may have been partly responsible, the major reason Ditzen could not realize his dream was his arrest in October 1922 for trading large amounts of Neuschönfeld grain on the black market.

It was Ditzen's drug habit that had driven him to swindle his employer: 'For I cannot go without, I am trapped by this luxury and the days are gone when I thought of living simply in a house in the woods ... and I'll most likely not be spared the worst: stealing and being punished.' These words, spoken by Anton at the end of the novel as he contemplates his future as Gerda's pimp, could equally well be applied to Ditzen's relationship with morphine and cocaine at the time. Not being an experienced criminal but an addict desperate for a fix, it is hardly surprising that he was caught and dismissed from his job in Neuschönfeld.

He moved back to Marzdorf, some 150 miles to the north, where his former employers knew nothing of his crime, and found casual work there without any difficulty. He remained in Marzdorf until the end of the year and spent part of January 1923 in Gudderitz. Here he received a cheque from Rowohlt for 25,000 marks, an indication of the currency devaluation which had already begun before French and Belgian troops occupied the Ruhr on 11 January in retaliation for Germany's non-payment of reparations. The political and economic turmoil unleashed by this crisis engulfed Germany in social, industrial and political unrest for most of 1923 and further undermined the attempts to establish a democratic society.

In February, Rudolf Ditzen returned to Leipzig, where he spent a few months with his parents working on his next novel, *Ria. Ein kleiner Roman* ('Ria. A Short Novel') and awaiting the outcome of the legal proceedings against him. Helped by Kagelmacher, he managed to keep his arrest, his court appearance and subsequent jail sentence from his infirm and ageing parents. Wilhelm and Elisabeth Ditzen shared the fate of many middle-class Germans in 1923, watching helplessly as their pensions and savings were eroded by inflation. Wilhelm Ditzen described a journey in the summer of 1923 to Blankenburg in the Harz mountains, when 'the fourth-class railway-ticket cost 58,000 marks on the way there and 580,000 marks on the way back. The next day the price would have been 2,320,000 marks.' His sister Ada, who had remained in Germany after the war, also lost her savings as a result of inflation, and earned a living teaching languages and translating until her appointment as a lecturer at the University of Marburg.

Ditzen had now become a member of the German Writers' Union (*Schutzverband Deutscher Schriftsteller*), which had been founded in 1919 as a trade union to protect writers' economic interests and provide legal advice. He enjoyed good working relations with Ernst Rowohlt, Franz Hessel and Paul Mayer. All three frequently ended their letters to him with an invitation to drop in to see them in Berlin. Paul Mayer, in particular, had become a close friend, and his letters to Ditzen often strike a personal note. On 26 June 1923, for example, he recalled a recent night on the town together: 'There we were – absolutely determined to indulge in the vice of gambling and not a game to be had anywhere! One of us must indeed have a guardian angel.' Ditzen was clearly good company and, despite – or because of – his many problems, knew how to enjoy himself.

Rowohlt had sent him a cheque for 50,000 marks in early March. When this ran out he needed to find a job – no easy task in view of the pending criminal proceedings and the soaring levels of unemployment. Kagelmacher came to the rescue by providing references which papered over the cracks in Ditzen's employment record and helped him obtain a position as book-keeper on the Radach estate near Drossen (now Radachów in Poland). Towards the end of June he received the first proofs of 'Anton and Gerda' in Radach, with an entreaty to return them as quickly as possible, since devaluation was adding daily to the costs of production.

On 13 July 1923, Rudolf Ditzen appeared before the magistrates court in Bunzlau and was sentenced to six months' imprisonment for embezzlement, which would not take effect until the following year. At the end of the month, Franz Hessel approached him to contribute to the new literary journal Rowohlt was planning entitled *Vers und Prosa*. In a letter of the twenty-eighth, Hessel explained the complicated arrangements Rowohlt had put in place for paying authors to protect them against unprecedented levels of inflation. By the end of July, three hundred paper mills were working full time in Germany to provide enough paper for the one hundred and fifty printing companies that were operating twenty-four-hour shifts producing banknotes. Matters came to a head in a general strike which began on 10 August and toppled Wilhelm Cuno's government. The formation of a coalition government, involving the Social Democrats for the first time since 1920 and headed by Gustav Stresemann, provided a temporary respite, although inflation continued.

Rudolf Ditzen recommended his new work 'Ria. A Short Novel' to Hessel, who preferred, however, to publish some extracts from 'The Cow, the Shoe, then You'. Hessel criticized the narrative form of 'Ria' with 'its monologues and dream-like dialogues', which he found inappropriate to the content. Unfortunately, this is all that is known about 'Ria' for the manuscript has not survived, although the name 'Ria' recurs throughout Ditzen's fiction. By September, Hessel was expressing concern that 'world history [might] sabotage our little journal.'

The autumn of 1923 saw a number of armed uprisings in Germany. On 1 October, from the relative safety of Radach, Ditzen observed the attempted putsch by the right-wing paramilitary organization the *Schwarze Reichswehr* in Küstrin (now Kostrzyn on the Polish side of the Polish–German border) some twenty-five miles to the north-west. He later incorporated this incident in *Wolf among Wolves*.

Ditzen was not only an avid writer, he was also an avid reader and frequently requested Ernst Rowohlt to supply him with books. At the end of October, Ditzen received six volumes of Balzac, which cost Rowohlt 116,760 million marks to post. Rowohlt's decision to publish a Balzac edition marked a general trend away from Expressionism in German publishing during the 1920s. Kurt Wolff embarked on a major edition of Zola around the same time, and Herzfelde's radical Malik Publishing House turned from Dadaism to progressive foreign writers such as Upton Sinclair and Maxim Gorki.

Ditzen left his job on the Radach estate and moved to the nearby town of Drossen, where he began working as an accounts clerk in Georg Kippferling's grain, potato and feed merchants on 1 November 1923.[7] Drossen provides the model for Ducherow, the small town in

Part One of *Little Man – What Now?*, and Ditzen's experiences in Kippferling's business would find literary expression in the description of Pinneberg's period of employment by Emil Kleinholz in the same novel.

An attempted Communist uprising in Hamburg in October and Hitler's 'beer-hall' putsch in Munich on 9 November precipitated the collapse of the Stresemann government. A new regime was installed under a new chancellor, Wilhelm Marx, which implemented emergency legislation and brought inflation under control. 'Anton and Gerda' was published in the first week of December. Ten days later, Rudolf Ditzen received 100 Goldmarks from Rowohlt, an indication that the currency had been stabilized.

Meanwhile, Franz Hessel was still trying to publish Ditzen's work in *Vers und Prosa*. He sent the manuscript of 'The Cow, the Shoe, then You' to Ditzen in March, requesting him to select ten to twelve pages for publication. Ditzen seems to have lost interest in this project, for he left the selection to Hessel. In the end, no extracts from 'The Cow, the Shoe, then You' ever appeared in *Vers und Prosa*, which folded in December 1924.

In the spring of 1924, Rudolf Ditzen had other matters on his mind, for he knew that his term of imprisonment was imminent. After he left Kippferling's in mid-April he spent some time with his parents in Leipzig before going to Gudderitz, his 'official' address, as far as the authorities were concerned, where he received notification on 10 June that he was to report to Greifswald prison by 6 p.m. on the twentieth.

The prospect of prison does not seem to have held particular terrors for Rudolf Ditzen. He had, after all, grown up in a household where crime and the law were topics of everyday conversation. The thought of serving his sentence in Greifswald prison, to which his father had dispatched a number of criminals during Ditzen's own childhood, may well have made him curious. He had, in addition, experienced the secure wards of two mental hospitals, which could scarcely be worse. A number of his literary heroes, including Dostoyevsky and Wilde, had served prison sentences. Moreover, sentences were not such a rarity in Germany in the years after the First World War. As a result of the widespread social and political unrest, as well as the draconian provisions of several rafts of emergency legislation, twenty-four additional 'special' courts were established between 1919 and 1923. The left-wing writers and activists Ernst Toller and Erich Mühsam each spent five years in Bavarian jails, the right-wing Adolf Hitler considerably less. This was in addition to the general rise in criminal activity associated with periods of great economic instability. Ditzen himself experienced the increase in the prison population during his time in Greifswald, when more and more individual cells were turned into communal ones to accommodate it. He was also part of a work gang which moved additional furniture into the courthouse. Against this background, a six-month prison sentence did not seem too onerous, especially to a person with Ditzen's curiosity about life in all its aspects.

He prepared for prison in typical fashion. As a bibliophile, he learned Rilke's poem 'The Prisoner' by heart, leafed through Wilde's 'Ballad of Reading Gaol' and then read a piece by Wilde on children in prison. As a scarcely reformed alcoholic, he set off with Kagel-macher on 19 June for a night on the town, then caught the steamer to Stralsund, where he flirted with 'three crazy Saxon women in a cabin', picked up a young woman in Stralsund, took her to a café and then left her standing in the street. On the train to Greifswald he 'brushed knees with a young girl', Hedwig Hanson, and told her of his destination. She was extremely sympathetic, as Ditzen later noted in his Prison Diary: 'These women of the people feel only sympathy in such situations. They don't think a prison sentence is a disgrace but just the kind of misfortune that can happen to anyone . . .'[8] He took Hedwig Hanson into a café, '. . . and there she allowed me to do everything that can be done in a café whose only other occupant is dozing fitfully at the next table.' Ditzen reported to Greifswald prison just before 3 p.m. on 20 June 1924, not quite sober.

He kept a Prison Diary from 22 June until 2 September, when his 'promotion' within the prison to the position of trustee (a prisoner who is given jobs of responsibility within the prison because of good behaviour) and his removal to a communal cell made writing impossible. The Diary records Ditzen's initial difficulties in dealing with the cockroaches in his cell and adjusting to the work regime of sawing and chopping wood in the timber yard, as well as pulling the cart which made deliveries to various locations in Greifswald, including on one occasion to a house in the street where he had lived as a child. The prisoners also formed work gangs for local farms and market gardens. Ditzen's thoughts often strayed to Gudderitz and the potato harvest, the slaughtering of the pigs and the other summer routines on Kagelmacher's farm. He shared the major preoccupations of the prison population: how to supplement the inadequate prison diet, how to collect the materials (paper, tobacco, matches) for a smoke, how to treat feet bruised and bleeding from the regulation wooden clogs.

Ditzen's Diary chronicles his dreams, which feature women from his past: Kagelmacher's wife, Lotte Fröhlich, Annia Seyerlen, as well as a certain Ria, whom he describes as 'in terms of purely physical eroticism, the happiest, most liberated of my experiences' (5 July 1924). Dreaming, according to Ditzen, was 'much better even than morphine' (26 June 1924). His sister Elisabeth and his brother both figure in his dreams, as does his mother, whose appearances induce feelings of guilt. He also dreams of Kagelmacher shooting him in the company of a third, unspecified man and notes: 'And yet I remember very well the gentle green meadow and a willow tree with hanging branches to the left of the man shooting at me.' (10 July 1924). Necker's death clearly continued to haunt Ditzen. After four days in prison he concluded: 'I have never been treated so decently in any sanatorium or mental hospital as I am here. As long as I do my work, no one bothers me. I'm in my cell, I can read, sleep, write, sing, walk up and down: no one interferes. And the wonderful peace here . . .' (24 June 1924). Ernst von Salomon, who was serving a prison sentence at the same time in Striegau (now Strzegom in Poland), shared Ditzen's views on the advantages of prison life: 'For anyone who loves order, prison is a very attractive place.'[9]

Ditzen turned out to be a model prisoner. He was rewarded not only by being promoted to the rank of a trustee but also by being released over a month early. One of the reasons for his success in prison was his willingness to 'squeal' on his fellow inmates. He is commendably honest in assessing his actions and admits to being ashamed: 'But that's life. I have to survive. Let stronger men be heroes and martyrs, I have only enough talent to be a small-scale coward' (4 July 1924). On 6 August he provided the prison authorities with crucial information about the plans of two escapees and concluded:

> Despite all my books, despite all my opinions: I am a born bourgeois, I always side with authority. But that isn't the whole truth either: I think I do it because I enjoy doing it, and because it makes me feel important. I'm a born spy, who acts in a mean way not for the sake of my own advantage but for the sake of the meanness itself.

At the age of thirty-one, Ditzen had clearly shed the sexual taboos of his upbringing and rejected the prevailing religious and social mores of the day. However, the authoritarianism in which he had grown up had left its mark in a tendency to identify with those in positions of power, especially where that power was absolute. This authoritarian character trait was common to many of Ditzen's contemporaries. Unlike most of them, however, he recognized it in himself and felt sufficiently ashamed to seek to justify his behaviour. It would take him many more years to overcome it.

The most fascinating aspect of the Prison Diary lies in the insights it provides into its author's relationship to literature. No sooner had he been admitted to prison than Rudolf Ditzen requested permission to write. This was granted on 22 June. Two days later he remarked: 'It would be hard if I didn't have this joy in the evenings of being able to write. It is almost as if I lived only for this.' Writing had always been a way of coping with his situation – puberty, adolescence, war and revolution, the death of a brother, drug addiction, alcoholism – and now it served a similar function in prison.

Ditzen's determination to be ruthlessly honest in his Diary and the consequent necessity of concealing it from the prison staff indicates that writing was also a way in which he asserted himself against the prison regime. Writing thus became a form of protest, albeit a very personal one.

In prison, literature provided a source of strength, despite the inadequacy of the prison library, which finally drove Ditzen to read the Bible – he particularly enjoyed the Old Testament stories. His ability to recite poetry in the timber yard lifted his spirits and he found parallels between Greifswald prison and Reading gaol and between his own situation and that of Dostoyevsky's Raskolnikov in *Crime and Punishment*.

On 12 July, the tone of the Diary began to change, as he describes the garden in Gudderitz where 'Anton and Gerda' began. Then he thinks of Omar Khayyám and tries to improve on his previous translation. These exercises were in preparation for the decision he took a week later when he was sitting in his cell, enjoying the luxuries of Saturday evening in prison – clean clothes, a cigarette and a freshly made bed: 'Suddenly I scent the whiff of the first chapter of the new novel which I shall start tomorrow.' Part of his motivation was financial, for Rowohlt represented his only source of money, his parents' income having now shrunk to his father's pension.

He spent the whole of the next day writing and remarked at the end of the day:

> It's all very strange. When I wrote in my diary yesterday evening about the novel which I wanted to start today, I had quite a different story in mind. How the brain must work while we're asleep! When I awoke this morning the plan for this new novel . . . was complete . . . While I slept! It is indeed the most incomprehensible and thrilling experience I have ever had.

This novel, provisionally entitled '*Mörder, Liebe und die Einsamkeit*' ('Murderers, Love and Loneliness'), begins with a description of the Gudderitz garden and is written alongside the diary entries.

On 2 August, Ditzen had an idea for another novel, about an ex-convict's rehabilitation in society 'with the help of a simple young woman'. He had in mind someone like the woman he had met in the train on his way to Greifswald – Hedwig Hanson, a '*Mädel aus dem Volk*' (a woman of the people). In fact, he made the connection between Hedwig Hanson and his writing explicit the next day, when he noted in his diary: 'I really ought to find out more about ordinary people ['*das Volk*']. There must be more to them than their smutty jokes and obsession with eating. But I know nothing about it.'

Ditzen was released on 3 November 1924 and set out for home,

1. Rudolf Ditzen's parents, Elisabeth and Wilhelm Ditzen, *c.* 1900.

2. With his sisters Elisabeth (left) and Margarete, *c.* 1896.

. As a schoolboy in Berlin, *c.* 1906.

4. His mother, Elisabeth Ditzen, 1910.

. Before setting out on the Wandervogel trip to Holland in 1910.

6. Adelaide Ditzen, Rudolf's Aunt Ada, 1911.

7. As a sixth-former in Rudolstadt, *c.* 1911.

8. A postcard entitled 'Duke's Visit to Posterstein' sent to his father in August 1914.

9. Stable hand with horses on the Heydebreck estate in Eastern Pomerania, 1915.

10. Brothers Rudolf (left) and Uli Ditzen in Leipzig.

11. Brother Uli, shortly before his death in 1918.

12. Neumünster Prison.

13. Neumünster 1929. Note on the reverse: 'In my office at the Association for Tourism and Commerce. Background: Posters!'

14. Anna Ditzen (Suse) with son Uli in Neuenhagen, Berlin, September 1930.

15. Suse, October 1931.

16. After the success of *Little Man – What Now?*, August 1933.

which meant Gudderitz, with the manuscript of 'Murderers, Love and Loneliness' in his suitcase. When he emerged from prison the state of emergency had been completely lifted and, thanks to the Dawes Plan – adopted by the Reichstag on 29 August of that year – the economic situation in Germany was improving. The Weimar Republic was entering a period of stability which was to last until the New York Stock Exchange collapse in the autumn of 1929.

In prison, Ditzen had often imagined his homecoming: '. . . the journey home, first of all a decent piece of meat, then Kagelmacher will fetch a bottle of Moselle from his cellar' (29 July 1924). After the initial celebrations, Ditzen settled down to complete work on his new manuscript, which he sent to Franz Hessel in December under the new title of *Im Blinzeln der großen Katze* ('In a Wink of the Big Cat's Eye').[10]

Friedrich Lütt, the first-person narrator in the novel, tells his story in a prison cell, where he is on remand awaiting trial on two charges of murder. The novel starts off as a 'confession' to his brother Erich, who has lost everything as a result of Friedrich's actions. However, writing, for Friedrich, increasingly becomes a means of explaining his 'crimes' and clarifying his future plans.

The ghosts of Ditzen's adolescence continued to haunt him, for they reappear in Lütt's alleged victims. The first of these is a certain Erna, whom he wishes he had murdered but in fact has not; Erna Simon, the young woman who had provided the pretext for the duel in Rudolstadt, comes immediately to mind. The second charge arises from a suicide pact which misfires. The doctors and prison guards suspect Lütt of planning to escape conviction by invoking Section 51 of the Criminal Code, an allegation which he initially denies. At the end of the novel, however, he undergoes a change of heart and declares, in words echoing Ditzen's Prison Diary: 'But I have to survive . . .'

The name 'Friedrich Lütt' belonged to a twenty-nine-year-old inmate whom Ditzen met in Greifswald prison and whose overweening conviction of the rightness of his own views was a source of irritation to the other prisoners. There are other echoes of Ditzen's prison experiences in the description of Lütt's cell and also in biblical references in the book.

The bank clerk Friedrich Lütt is the first of Ditzen's 'little men' – indeed, the word '*lütt*' is a northern German dialect word for 'little'. In 'In a Wink of the Big Cat's Eye', Ditzen demonstrates his ability to enter into the persona of and depict the petit bourgeois male, a man who describes himself at the beginning of the novel as 'timid' ('*ängstlich*'). His description of Lütt's tortuous thought processes anticipates other institutionalized male characters like Erwin Sommer in *The Drinker* and Willi Kufalt in 'Once a Jailbird' (one of the criminals in 'In a Wink of the Big Cat's Eye' is also called Willi). The dialogues in the novel indicate Ditzen's growing confidence in handling a wider range of themes, including the law, the criminal underworld and prison life.

On the whole, however, this novel is a work of little literary merit. The big cat of the title is mentioned only once, and its significance is not elaborated. Ditzen's attempt to develop a symbolic dimension out of two types of garden, the domestic and the enchanted, is full of possibilities but abandoned before it can be properly explored. The juxtaposition of the sadomasochistic Pübe, who appeals to Lütt's 'base instinct', and the 'pure' Ria, Lütt's pregnant wife, is not only banal but corresponds to the mother-whore antithesis of a prevailing morality which Ditzen did not endorse. Pübe's murder of Erna is also poorly motivated.

Ditzen's description of the two gardens provides an instructive insight into his state of mind at the end of 1924. The first garden is a vegetable, fruit and herb garden: 'Not an exciting garden, nothing lovely about it, no, a cultivated kitchen garden, in which a farmer might sit for half an hour in the evening before going to bed.' The garden which the narrator prefers is: '. . . the other garden, the flower garden, the scented garden of enchantment, one step off the straight and narrow. I lived a long time in the cultivated garden, years and years, but I spent only one day in the garden of intoxication [*Rausch*].' '*Rausch*' is the German word for the exhilaration induced by alcohol or other addictive substances. Lütt experiences his 'criminal' existence as a *Rausch*. In one chapter, he contrasts his 'quiet, bourgeois, orderly life' as a bank clerk with the exhilaration (*Rausch*) he feels after outwitting a policeman.

Crime is thus another means of rejecting and escaping from society.

Like alcohol, morphine and cocaine, it, too, leads to an institution for society's outcasts. In Greifswald in 1924, Ditzen discovered that prison provided a very effective cure for his alcoholism and drug addiction; he found the strict routine and orderly existence of prison life therapeutic.

However, the tone of 'In a Wink of the Big Cat's Eye' suggests that, in his search for *Rausch*, Ditzen might well find himself in prison again soon. What is particularly uncanny, as we shall see, is that Friedrich Lütt, in forging his boss's signature and then giving himself up and making a full confession, anticipated Ditzen's actions.

In the Diary entry for 13 July 1924, Ditzen had recorded the receipt of a letter from Johannes Kagelmacher. He commented: 'It's a pity that he has such unfavourable things to report about his wife. She will now take up the cudgels against him with every ugly act of vileness imaginable and, as is the way with women, not tire of taunting him.' Kagelmacher's marital difficulties find literary expression in Ditzen's story '*Die große Liebe*' ('The Great Love'), which tells of the ill-matched couple Fritz and Thilde Dohrmann.[11] Fritz is interested in farming, books, philosophy and everything life has to offer. Before his wedding he wonders: 'What woman could he talk to about the things that mattered to him? Really talk, not a monologue? Books, paintings – they all considered such things to be decorative, trifling, purely ornamental.'

Thilde believes in the 'great love' outlined in St Paul's First Letter to the Corinthians (verse 13) and devotes herself totally to Fritz. He feels increasingly stifled by a woman who is small-minded, jealous and his intellectual inferior. Their relationship ends in bitterness, hatred and divorce. 'The Great Love', which was not published in Ditzen's lifetime, may be seen as a preliminary study for his later work, *Once We Had a Child*, where the relationship between Johannes and Elise Gäntschow runs a similar course. The name of the boatman, Tredup, also anticipates the protagonist in *A Small Circus*.

Tredup reappears in *Der Apparat der Liebe* ('The Machinery of Love'), which dates from 'before the summer of 1925',[12] in the figure of the bank official and would-be poet whom Marie (Mie) Lauterbach adopts as a protégé.[13] Ditzen frequently recycled names. 'Mia' recurs in Mia Pinneberg in *Little Man – What Now?*, in which 'Lauterbach' is also recycled as the name of a Nazi colleague of Pinneberg's. Ditzen, as we have seen, also drew on the names of friends, lovers and acquaintances. In 'The Machinery of Love', Mie Lauterbach's maiden name is Schildt, the surname of Ditzen's former lover Ria. In 'The Great Love' one of Thilde Dohrmann's fellow students is an extremely clever young woman called Ada.

In 'The Machinery of Love', the first-person narrator Marie Lauterbach, now in her early forties, looks back over her life: the rape, pregnancy and suicide of her sister Violet (a name which recurs in *Wolf among Wolves*); her years at school and college; her jobs as governess in Mecklenburg and Eastern Pomerania; her marriage to Hans Lauterbach, and their three children; and her extra-marital affairs. The innovative aspect of this story lies in Ditzen's attempt to create a female first-person narrator. His interest in and experience of women enabled him to construct a female narrative voice which is mostly credible, although it falters from time to time in its description of domestic responsibilities and child-bearing. Like his previous prose fiction, this story has no specific historical setting. It has also a strong autobiographical dimension: Ditzen may have based the description of Marie's sexual liberation through Heinz and Sepherl Delbrück on his own experience with Annia Seyerlen: 'The past fell away, I no longer felt horror and disgust. I was free.' Marie Lauterbach's view of the shy and tongue-tied artist, Tredup, probably reflects Annia Seyerlen's assessment of the young Rudolf Ditzen: '... a man who only knew life out of books created his own world. It was young and gentle, but I was very struck by how this shy and retiring person could see into people's hearts and by how much this man who ran away from women knew about them.'

While Ditzen's fiction was located in an ahistorical Germany unaffected by war, social upheaval and inflation, this did not mean that Ditzen had no interest in such matters, for towards the end of 1924 he turned his hand to essay-writing. Franz Hessel sent Ditzen's essay on prison life, '*Stimme aus den Gefängnissen*' ('A Voice from the Prisons') to Stefan Grossmann, editor of the liberal weekly *Das Tage-Buch*, who published it on 3 January 1925. Ditzen begins this piece by stating that he had just served a short prison sentence and felt like 'a traveller returning from an unknown part of the world'. He goes on to tackle three aspects of prison policy he believes to be in need of reform: the excessively harsh treatment of prisoners on remand, the absence of a coherent education and rehabilitation strategy for prisoners serving sentences and the lack of transparency in the remission system. Grossmann published a second essay by Ditzen on 11 April, about the famous Tscheka court case, in which the Communist Party was charged with running a military wing. Ditzen viewed these proceedings as a prime example of a show trial and commented: 'It would be interesting to write a book about how to stage political trials.' A third essay appeared in *Das Tage-Buch* on 15 August, which dealt with the paramilitary activities Ditzen had witnessed while working in Radach in the autumn of 1923. Entitled '*Stahlhelm-Nachtübung*' ('War Veterans' Night Exercises'), it criticized the local landowners for inciting unrest at no risk to themselves. The writer and theatre director Heinrich Fischer approached Ditzen for book reviews or other contributions to Rowohlt's new literary journal *Die literarische Welt* and published his essay '*Was liest man so eigentlich in Hinterpommern?*' ('What are People Actually Reading in Eastern Pomerania?') in October.

Ditzen's *Tage-Buch* essays of 1925 show his interest in the contemporary social and political scene. In each case, he instinctively sides with the helpless and powerless, the victims of an unfair system. His stance is not party-political. What moves this son of a high-court judge to put pen to paper is a profound sense of justice and a desire to focus public attention on cases where society has failed to guarantee individuals their social or political rights.

Journal editors also showed an interest in Ditzen's short stories. In August 1925, Max Krell published '*Der Trauring*' ('The Wedding Ring') in *Die große Welt*, for which the author received 125 marks. This story features a hard-up estate foreman who steals a ring to pay off his debts and looks enviously at the steward who can 'organize the disappearance of a few hundredweights of rye from the granary without anybody noticing' – a theme with which Ditzen was familiar. Krell encouraged him to submit more stories. *Die neue Rundschau*, turning down 'The Cow, the Shoe, then You' on account of its length, asked Ditzen to send in other, shorter pieces.

Ditzen moved from Gudderitz to Leipzig at the end of January, where he received a cheque for 400 marks from Rowohlt with the promise of a further 500 marks on 1 April and 1,000 marks on 1 October. Rowohlt had assured Ditzen in January that he would publish either 'In a Wink of the Big Cat's Eye' or a projected volume of short stories by the summer. Paul Mayer received the stories, *Liebesgeschichten mit Tieren* ('Love Stories with Animals'), in the third week in March. Shortly afterwards, Ditzen went to work as a bookkeeper on the Lübgust estate near Neustettin in Pomerania (now Szczecinek in northern Poland).

By early July, it became clear that Rowohlt was not going to publish 'In a Wink of the Big Cat's Eye' in the immediate future. In fact, Ditzen's fiction no longer fitted into Rowohlt's programme, nor did it correspond to the concerns of the emerging '*Neue Sachlichkeit*' ('New Sobriety') movement. Ditzen's lack of involvement in the many and diverse literary endeavours of the twenties is all the more remarkable in one who was not only a writer but a '*Büchernarr*', someone mad about books. Unlike Becher, Brecht or Toller, he did not involve himself in radical literary experiments. He took no part in the debates in the Writers' Union or the Prussian Academy of Arts, and appears to have had no contacts with other writers apart from Paul Mayer, Franz Hessel and Rowohlt's immediate circle.

His alcoholism and drug dependency, the legacy of his troubled past as well as his rootless existence, resulted in a preoccupation with his own concerns which produced strongly autobiographical works. As we have seen, these provide important insights into Ditzen's development as a writer; however, they were hardly publishable in the context of the period. In addition, Ditzen spent most of these years, when not in prison, on estates remote from the urban centres of Weimar culture and in the company of people who, with the possible exception of Kagelmacher, were not interested in ideas.

By 1925, however, Ditzen was no longer totally dependent on Rowohlt. He had established contact with another publisher. Heinz Stroh, the chief literary editor of Spaeth Verlag, had asked Rowohlt in December of the previous year for permission to include an extract from 'Young Goedeschal' in a volume about childhood. As a result,

Ditzen entered into correspondence with Stroh and, on 7 July, asked if he would be interested in publishing the manuscripts in Rowohlt's possession or indeed any other of his books. Relations between Ditzen and Ernst Rowohlt seem to have deteriorated during that summer of 1925. Ditzen, who was still trying to fulfil his dream of owning his own farm, approached Rowohlt for money in June and was turned down. He then twice requested the return of 'In a Wink of the Big Cat's Eye' in July, so that he could give it to Spaeth Verlag. Rowohlt refused to return the novel and showed no inclination to publish the short stories.

On 14 July, Ditzen sent Stroh his 'child' – a term which he used from this time onwards to describe his works of fiction – the short story, *'Länge der Leidenschaft'* ('A Lasting Passion'), which describes the life-long love affair between Ria, daughter of a prosperous land-owner, and Martens, a clerk and con man. Ria comes to the realization that 'running away, embezzlement, theft, these were external things, their real life was their love.' Again, the autobiographical dimension needs little elaboration.

On 1 July, Ditzen had left Lübgust and moved to Schleswig-Holstein, to a job as senior book-keeper on the Neuhaus estate in Lütjenburg, some twenty miles east of Kiel. In a letter to Heinz Stroh on the twentieth of that month he confessed that he had left his heart behind in Lübgust but concluded, in words which echo Fritz Dohrmann's musings on the eve of his wedding in 'The Great Love', that it was all for the best: 'It's another world, my dear Stroh. It's nice, but it's not enough. People who have never learned to read – you know what I mean – are simply out of the question for people like you and me.'

In the same letter, Ditzen pronounced himself happy in the beautiful surroundings of Lütjenburg. He had every reason to be so. His essays were being published, his short stories were in demand and he was working on a new novel, *Robinson im Gefängnis* ('Robinson in Prison'). In addition to his salary of 200 marks per month (plus free board and lodging), his writing was also bringing in some money. By contemporary standards, this was sufficient to sustain a reasonable standard of living. However, it was not sufficient to sustain the requirements of a man addicted to nicotine, alcohol, morphine and cocaine. It was only a matter of time before the bubble burst.

On 12 September, Ditzen sent a postcard, describing a holiday trip around Schleswig-Holstein to his father, who had remained in Leipzig in the care of a nurse while Elisabeth Ditzen went to visit her mother and sister in Celle. The next communication from Lütjenburg, posted four days later, was addressed to her and must have come as a great shock.

It was a letter from Herr Hoffmann, the estate manager, in which he enquired whether she knew the whereabouts of her son, who had set off for Kiel on estate business with 14,000 marks of his employer's money the previous Saturday and had not returned. Hoffmann wrote again the next day, confirming the Ditzens' worst fears: Rudolf had forged a cheque for 10,000 marks and cashed it; Hoffmann had searched his book-keeper's room and found the certificate of release from Greifswald prison and the references which Kagelmacher had provided to cover the period from when Ditzen started work in Neuschönfeld until he left prison.

The news that their son had already served one prison sentence and was now facing another dealt a severe blow to Wilhelm and Elisabeth Ditzen. Wilhelm, seventy-two years old and in poor health, was no longer able to deal with his son's misdemeanours. He sent to Zittau for his son-in-law, the lawyer Fritz Bechert, who came directly to Leipzig, arriving late on the evening of the nineteenth. Bechert took charge of the case and proved most conscientious in representing both the Ditzens' interests and those of their wayward son. Bechert was on his way back to Zittau when the news arrived that Rudolf had given himself up in Berlin and made a full confession. And what a confession it was! Not only had he embezzled 14,000 marks in Neuhaus, he claimed to have stolen 5,000 marks from Lübgust and to have committed a further seven crimes of embezzlement 'before I became addicted to morphine'.

After Ditzen had spent the 14,000 marks on all the pleasures which Kiel had to offer in the way of wine, women, song, cocaine and morphine, and the initial intoxication began to wear off, he was faced with a sobering prospect. With his medical history and criminal record, he would most probably be sentenced under Section 51 of the Criminal Code, as he had been in 1912 – only this time he could expect a very long, if not life-long, stay in a mental hospital. This he wanted to avoid at all costs. He was convinced that prison would provide a better cure for his alcoholism and drug dependency than any mental hospital, where drugs were always available and the company of the other inmates was likely to drive him properly insane.

Determined, therefore, to prove what a hardened criminal he was, Ditzen greatly exaggerated the extent of his criminal activities and entered a plea of guilty to all charges. He knew that the courts were overworked and would not be able to check instances of embezzlement going back as far as his period in Posterstein before the First World War. His tactic worked, and he was sentenced to two and a half years in prison. The court decided that Section 51 was not applicable, that Rudolf Ditzen was of sound mind and body, although 'a thoroughly degenerate psychopath'.

After the trial in Kiel on 26 March 1926, Ditzen was taken immediately to Neumünster prison, twenty miles to the south and, in view of the time he had spent on remand, the sentence was reduced to two years.

Bechert negotiated the return of his brother-in-law's belongings, ensured that his social insurance contributions were kept up to date and wrote to Rowohlt on Ditzen's behalf. Despite the apparent deterioration in the relationship between author and publisher, Paul Mayer visited Ditzen when he was on remand in Berlin and Ernst Rowohlt offered to pay for defence counsel. As Ditzen pleaded guilty to all charges, he did not take up Rowohlt's offer.

Ditzen was hopeful that he could begin to repay his debts by authorizing the payment to his creditors of the 1,000 marks which Rowohlt had promised to pay him on 1 October and by holding Rowohlt to his other promise of publishing one of the manuscripts. He hoped to sell the second manuscript to Spaeth Verlag. Rowohlt, however, produced records to show that it was Ditzen who actually owed *him* money and refused to hand over the manuscripts. By August 1927, Ditzen instructed Bechert to drop the Rowohlt affair, since he was not writing anyway. In October, Hoffmann confirmed that the amount outstanding was 10,248 marks and 36 pfennigs. Georg von Rohr, owner of the Lübgust estate, was owed a further 1,000 marks.

In January 1928, Ditzen submitted an application for a review of his case. Having now recovered from alcoholism and drug addiction, he wanted to set the record straight. He applied to have the verdict changed to one of temporary insanity (by invoking Section 51 of the Criminal Code) on the grounds that he was not a criminal and had only been driven to crime by alcohol and drug addiction. In attempting to expunge his criminal record, he was thinking not only of himself and his future prospects but also of his parents. His application was rejected.

During the two and a half years Ditzen spent in prison, Germany experienced economic prosperity. Thanks to the injection of American capital, German industry was able to regain its strong position in Europe. The threat from the political Right, evident in the early years of the Weimar Republic, appeared to have receded, too. The 1928 elections, in which the National Socialists won only 2.6 per cent of the total vote, saw the Social Democrats emerge as the largest single party. On the international scene, the Treaty of Locarno (1925) had confirmed Germany's western borders and began the process whereby Entente troops began to leave German soil. A treaty of neutrality was signed with the Soviet Union in April 1926, and in September that year Germany became a member of the League of Nations.

Adelaide Ditzen was offered a job as bilingual secretary with the League in Geneva but turned it down, preferring to continue her teaching in Marburg. Her nephew kept in sporadic touch with her and, interestingly, wrote to her while he was on remand, describing himself as '*ein Ausgelieferter*', i.e. a man at the mercy of his alcohol and drug addiction and no longer in control of his life.

Apart from Ditzen's correspondence with Fritz Bechert, there is very little evidence to suggest what the inmate of cell 284 on C Wing thought, felt or did during his sentence. Meanwhile, outside the prison walls, cultural and political trends were emerging which would shape the future of German literature into the Third Reich and beyond, and determine the arena to which Ditzen the writer would return.

Hans Grimm's *Volk ohne Raum* ('Nation without Space') of 1926 belonged to the *Blut und Boden* (blood and soil) tradition and anticipated fascist literary practice in its chauvinist and expansionist tone. The publisher's note described it as 'more than a novel, more than literature, it is The German Book, the novel of our destiny'. The popularity of this book, which sold 250,000 copies in ten years, was an ominous sign of the attractiveness of this kind of literature to the German reading public.

On the other hand, the Weimar era celebrated the scientific and technological advances of the 1920s in film, radio and photography. Eisenstein's *Battleship Potemkin* caused a sensation when it was shown in Berlin in the spring of 1926. The next year, Erwin Piscator, in his new, radical theatre on Berlin's Nollendorf Platz, used film in his production of Ernst Toller's *Hoppla, Wir Leben* ('Hoppla, Such is Life'). Another radical of the period, Bertolt Brecht, published an anthology of poetry in 1927 entitled *Bertolt Brechts Hauspostille* (*Bertolt Brecht's Manual of Piety*), which displayed a fascination with the macabre and grotesque as well as an uncompromising rejection of religion. The final poem, '*Gegen Verführung*' ('Against Temptation') would have been very much to Ditzen's taste:

> Do not let them gyp you
> Life's not very big.
> Drink it! And go on drinking
> And when at last you're sinking
> You'll want another swig.[14]

By the time Rudolf Ditzen was beginning his second prison sentence, his fellow writer Johannes R. Becher had overcome his morphine addiction, recovered from his disappointment at the failure of the 1918 revolution and was redirecting his energies into radical politics. Becher was now a committed Marxist and a leading exponent of the Communist Party's cultural policy, which encouraged working-class talent through the Worker Correspondents Movement and would go on to establish the League of Proletarian Revolutionary Writers in 1928. Becher's anti-war novel *Levisite* of 1926 resulted in a charge of high treason being brought against him in October of the following year, which turned the whole affair into an international *cause célèbre* with writers like Gorki and Rolland rallying to Becher's support. All charges were subsequently dropped in the general amnesty which followed the Social Democrats' success in the 1928 elections.

It would be misleading to suggest that the cultural achievements of the middle years of the Weimar Republic belonged solely to the left. For example, 1927 saw the publication of Hermann Hesse's *Steppenwolf*, representative of a more conservative strand in German literature, which began to 'emigrate inwards' before the National Socialists came to power.

Humanist writers such as Heinrich Mann, Alfred Döblin and Erich Kästner remained committed to democracy in Germany, as did a number of others, such as Erich Maria Remarque, whose *Im Westen nichts Neues* (*All Quiet on the Western Front*), serialized in the *Voßische Zeitung* at the end of 1928, sold two and a half million copies in twenty-five languages within eighteen months.

In 1928, there was little to indicate that Germany's next best-seller, *Little Man – What Now?*, would be written by Rudolf Ditzen. There were, however, signs that he had overcome the self-absorption of the past. Towards the end of his time in prison he sent two articles about prison life to a number of newspapers, although neither was ever published. He also involved himself in prison welfare and prepared a talk on the release of prisoners for a meeting of the German Association for the Care and Resettlement of Offenders, in which he advised:

> Prisoners who have served long sentences should not be released without adequate preparation. A man who has not been allowed to move without permission, who for years and years has had to suppress every independent thought or action, cannot cope with the onslaught of feelings, worries, impressions on the outside. Make transitional arrangements ... so that the prisoner, regardless of his status, can learn to feel free, to move freely and to handle money.[15]

Ditzen's articles and other journalistic pieces in the 1920s indicate his interest in the social and political issues of the day. They also testify to his humanist approach, which, as we have seen, was formed by his own experiences as well as by the influence of his aunt Adelaide

Ditzen and writers such as Romain Rolland. The next step in his development as a writer would be to integrate the social commitment evident in his non-fiction with the literary talent evident in his novels.

Rudolf Ditzen was released from Neumünster prison on 10 May 1928, having put his alcoholism and drug addiction behind him. Through the prisoners' welfare organization he had secured accommodation and the possibility of employment in Hamburg. A new beginning, a new life, beckoned.

4 1928–1931
Breakthrough

To Berlin, to Berlin,
To move to Berlin
From the dreariest town on earth –
How divine! – So long numb
And supine and humdrum,
I turn cartwheels for all that I'm worth.

– Joachim Ringelnatz[1]

When Ditzen arrived in Hamburg in the spring of 1928, he took two steps which indicated his determination to make a fresh start. He joined a total abstinence organization, the Order of the Good Templar, and he became a member of the Social Democratic Party (SPD). On 3 November 1929, he wrote to his mother that he had chosen this political party because its policies were 'closest to my own views'. Ditzen's membership of the Social Democratic Party and the Order of the Good Templar had a significance beyond the immediate aims of these organizations: it demonstrated his desire to find a place for himself inside society rather than to continue his previous existence on the edges.

Nothing is known about the level of Ditzen's activity within the SPD or, for example, his views on German rearmament, an issue which split the party in August 1928 when the Social Democrats, who had opposed naval reconstruction in opposition, performed a U-turn and enthusiastically embraced it in office. Ditzen was probably too preoccupied by the difficulty of scraping a living to concern himself with the major political issues of the day. His parents, after consultation with Hans Bithorn, governor of Neumünster Prison, agreed to pay their wayward son a monthly allowance of 150 marks. In return, he undertook to write to his mother on a regular basis, keep her informed of his activities and provide her with a detailed monthly account of his expenditure. Only when he had proved to his parents that he really had turned over a new leaf would he be allowed to visit them in Leipzig. In the event, this probation period lasted over five years.

An allowance of 150 marks was, of course, better than nothing. It was not, however, enough to live on. Ditzen acquired a second-hand typewriter with money provided by his sister and brother-in-law, Margarete and Fritz Bechert, and during the spring and summer of 1928 he eked out a very meagre existence addressing envelopes and undertaking other typing work.

On 8 August, from his lodgings in Hamburg's Hasselbrook Strasse, he wrote to Ernst Rowohlt in Berlin: 'I'm pretty much at the end of my tether and don't know where to turn.'[2] He begged Rowohlt for a job, however menial, and assured his former publisher that he was cured of alcoholism and drug addiction. Ditzen's decision to resume contact with Rowohlt was indicative not only of his desperation to find work but also of his determination to continue writing. In prison he had collected the material for three short stories about petty criminals which he began around this time: '*Mein Freund, der Ganove*' ('My Friend the Crook'), '*Besuch bei Tändel-Maxe*' ('Visit to Casanova Maxe') and '*Liebe Lotte Zielesch*' ('Dear Lotte Zielesch').[3] Rowohlt took two months to reply and, by then, Ditzen's circumstances had changed.

Ditzen had joined the Phoenix Lodge of the Good Templar Order in Hamburg, and it was here that he met Anna Issel, known as Suse, a tall, fresh-faced, fair-haired 27-year-old. The exact circumstances in which Rudolf Ditzen first met Suse Issel are somewhat unclear. In conversation with the present author in September 1983, Frau Ditzen stated that she had met her husband through the Good Templar Order. In the letter which Rudolf Ditzen wrote to his future wife on 10 February 1929, however, he referred to '13' as their lucky number, since they had met on 13 October 1928. This tallies with the account given by Hans Fallada in the otherwise unreliable 'Our Home Today', in which he recalls meeting his wife on that date, the day he left Hamburg for Neumünster. Descending the stairs from the Issels' flat, he ran into her in the hall and: ' . . . whether it was love at first sight or something else mysterious I don't know. In any case I travelled to the town which we shall call "Altholm" in a completely transformed state of mind . . .' It seems likely that he first came into contact with Hans Issel through the SPD and the Good Templar Order and subsequently made the acquaintance of his sister.

Suse Issel, a 'woman of the people', worked in the wholesale millinery business and was involved in the trade union movement. Ditzen was attracted to this working-class girl, with her lack of sophistication and uncomplicated attitude to life. He may also have sensed the inner strength and caring approach which underpinned her commitment to total abstinence. Suse Issel was attracted to this man eight years her senior who made no secret of his history of petty crime and substance abuse and who had now forsworn alcohol and even practically given up coffee in his determination to exorcize the ghosts of the past. Her membership of the Good Templar Order showed a willingness to help reformed alcoholics; it was not surprising that she should fall in love with one.

Suse lived with her mother, two sisters and brother at 259 Eiffe Strasse. Her father was an insurance clerk who had separated from his wife and family some fifteen years previously. The Issels 'adopted' Ditzen and, at the end of September, he gave up his lodgings in Hasselbrook Strasse and moved into their home, taking over Suse's room while she was away undergoing treatment for a persistent kidney complaint.

By this time, Ditzen had received no reply from Rowohlt in Berlin and had concluded that he had no hope of finding employment in Hamburg. With a heavy heart, he decided to return to Neumünster, where the prison governor Hans Bithorn had promised his support. Ditzen was also hopeful that his contacts among the prison staff might be helpful. In any case, it would be cheaper to spend the winter in the provincial town of Neumünster than in Hamburg.

On 21 October, Ditzen confided in Kagelmacher: 'Since I left Hamburg I know for certain that I have succumbed once more to fair Eros and this time in a very sweet and tormenting way.' At Ditzen's request, Kagelmacher consulted his astrological charts to determine the suitability of the couple. He produced a horoscope for Rudolf Ditzen and Suse Issel, which he described as 'quite excellent'.

Theirs was a whirlwind romance. He travelled to Hamburg as often as he could and they wrote to each other frequently, sometimes daily. This unexpected happiness provided some joy and consolation in the bleak days of October and November 1928 in the depressing surroundings of Neumünster, which Ditzen described in a letter to Kagelmacher as 'really dreadful. It's such a narrow-minded backwater, full of factory workers thrown together from all over the place ... horrific.'

Ditzen lamented the absence of attractive female company in the temperance meetings. Even in adversity he retained his sense of humour, commenting in a letter to Kagelmacher on the 'lumpy' stockings which seemed to be a feature of female attire in Neumünster: 'I really ought to set up in business here to teach young women how to put on stockings smoothly, but I fear there would be no demand for such unimaginable luxury.'[4]

Finding employment in Neumünster, where yet another factory closed down shortly after Ditzen's arrival, proved difficult. In November 1928, a wave of strikes in the iron and steel industry, continuing into the New Year, heralded the end of economic and political stability in the Weimar Republic. It was not a propitious climate for an ex-prisoner seeking work. Indeed, Ditzen was nearly evicted from his lodgings in Schützen Strasse, just round the corner from Neumünster Prison, when his landlady learned of his criminal record.

Rowohlt's reply to Ditzen's letter, which arrived in mid-October, contained a general offer of help, but nothing definite. At the beginning of November, Hans Bithorn was able to give Ditzen 30 marks out of a local charitable fund, and his parents agreed to increase his allowance for the month by 25 marks to cover the additional expense incurred in moving to Neumünster and making job applications. After four weeks of leading a hand-to-mouth existence Ditzen was summoned to the office of Herr Berthold, secretary of Neumünster's Association for Tourism and Commerce, who also edited the *Schleswig-Holsteinische*

Verkehrszeitung, the association's newspaper-cum-information sheet, which was distributed free of charge. Berthold, in addition, sold subscriptions and advertising space for the *General Anzeiger*, a local newspaper with a decidedly nationalist and anti-Semitic orientation. Thanks to the influence of Hans Bithorn, Berthold offered Ditzen a part-time job assisting him in his work for the *General Anzeiger*. Anxious to avoid situations where alcohol might be on offer, Ditzen came to an arrangement whereby he had no dealings with publicans or restaurant owners in the course of his work. He was paid on commission which, in view of the paper's falling circulation, was not a lucrative way to earn a living.

Impressed by the conscientiousness as well as the organizational and literary talent of his new colleague, Berthold offered Ditzen the prospect of becoming director of the new office which the Association for Tourism and Commerce was due to open in the New Year and in which the owner of the *General Anzeiger*, Karl Wachholtz, also had a major interest. Berthold, however, required Ditzen to invest 2,000 marks in the new undertaking. Wilhelm Ditzen, on Hans Bithorn's advice, agreed to make this payment. The contract was signed on 13 December and the money paid six days later.

On 20 December, Ditzen wrote to thank his parents for making this new job possible, and promising 'that I will do my best to get on, to make up for the past, that I will seize the opportunity you have offered me'.[5] On the same day, he also wrote to his two sisters expressing a desire to re-establish relations with them and their families.

When Ditzen set out for Hamburg two days later to spend Christmas with the Issels, he was a man with prospects. His new job would bring in 150 marks per month; he could count on some support from his parents; there was the possibility of earning some money from journalism in Neumünster; and, for the first time in over three years, he had some of his work published: two short stories, in December 1928. His affairs at last in some order, his foot 'on the bottom rung of the ladder again', Rudolf Ditzen was now in a position to ask Suse Issel to marry him. She accepted, and they became engaged at 3.30 a.m. on 26 December 1928. 'I have never been so happy in my whole life,' Ditzen wrote to Kagelmacher three days later.

He anticipated that his parents would oppose any plans he had to marry, partly for the same reason they had opposed his first engagement and partly because they would consider Suse, as his social inferior, unsuitable. Yet, if he was to enjoy their continued financial support, he was obliged to keep them informed; however, he waited several weeks before announcing his engagement. Meanwhile, he assured Wilhelm and Elisabeth Ditzen that he was a changed man and added (not entirely truthfully) that he had no plans to get married in the near future.

The office of the Association for Tourism and Commerce was housed in the same building as the *General Anzeiger*, for which Ditzen was still obliged to work. As more and more businesses closed their doors, it became increasingly difficult to sell advertising space, especially in a conservative newspaper with a dwindling circulation in a largely Social Democratic town. However, Ditzen's working day, which began at 8 a.m. and continued with a two-hour lunch break until 7 p.m., offered other, more interesting challenges. He began to review films and report on lectures and shows, which extended his working day until nearly midnight. The *General Anzeiger* of 25 January 1929 carried a report by Ditzen on a lecture against the death penalty given by a Dr Schmidt, a lawyer in Neumünster. While Ditzen agreed with the speaker's sentiments, he criticized the way in which he presented his argument. This attracted the attention of Wachholtz, who turned out to be a friend of Dr Schmidt, and resulted in a request that Ditzen should not be so polemical. 'Neumünster is a dump. The slightest thing causes offence, you have to take so many interests into consideration,' Ditzen wrote to his parents.[6]

Ditzen's job gave him a unique insight into the workings of a small town: into the print media where one man, Karl Wachholtz, owned both the conservative *General Anzeiger* and the more liberal *Holsteinischer Courier*; into the machinations in the town hall; into the effects of the severest economic crisis in world history, not only on the industrial and commercial life of the town but also on the surrounding countryside, where the fall in world food prices accompanied by the steep rises in interest rates and taxes imposed intolerable burdens on the farming community.

Ditzen's own position was anything but secure, and in Neumünster he experienced 'how nowadays millionaires exploit the difficult situation of white-collar workers to depress salaries as much as possible. Work unlimited, salary barely visible.'[7]

In January he discovered that 150 marks per month gross represented a mere 135 marks net. A begging letter to his parents elicited the promise of an allowance of 65 marks per month. And on the basis of the princely income of 200 marks per month, he moved out of his room in Schützen Strasse into two rooms (a living-room and bedroom) in Johannis Strasse, which was closer to the office. Here he was able to have his books and pictures around him for the first time since 1925. He wrote to thank his sister Margarete for obtaining his belongings from Hoffmann in Neuhaus and storing them while he was in prison, and described his surroundings as the 'sign of a new order, the symbol of a new beginning in my life'.[8]

In the course of January and February 1929, Ditzen had become suspicious of his immediate boss, Berthold. He had suspected for some time that the 2,000 marks deposit had found its way into Berthold's pocket rather than into the coffers of the Association for Tourism and Commerce. Then he stumbled on incontrovertible evidence that Berthold had embezzled monies donated to a local political party. When Berthold claimed he was unable to pay Ditzen's salary at the end of February, Ditzen went straight to the Chairman of the Association, the Social Democratic Mayor of Neumünster, Herrmann Lindemann, with his evidence, and Berthold was relieved of his duties.

Wachholtz was impressed by Ditzen's acumen and appointed him from 1 March to the staff of the *General Anzeiger*, put him in charge of the Association for Tourism and Commerce and made him editor of the association's newspaper, the *Schleswig-Holsteinische Verkehrszeitung*. Ditzen's rise in salary to 225 marks per month was very much against the general trend of falling wages. Indeed, Germany's deteriorating economic position had led to the establishment in February 1929 of a new commission under the American banker Owen D. Young to renegotiate the Dawes Plan and reschedule Germany's reparation payments.

Meanwhile, Ditzen and his fiancée managed to see each other most weekends, either in Hamburg or Neumünster. After his salary had been raised in March they decided to wait no longer and set the wedding for 5 April. Kagelmacher reported that the day was 'an unusually good choice for both parties'. He went on to predict that 1929 was Ditzen's year, 'especially in intellectual matters', and urged his friend to take up his literary pursuits again.[9]

Rudolf Ditzen and Suse Issel were married on Friday 5 April 1929 in Hamburg and spent their four-day honeymoon in Berlin. Here, Ditzen introduced his wife to some of his old friends, in particular Lore Soldin, whom he had met during the war years and who was to become a close friend of Suse's. In Berlin, Ditzen also made contact with Rowohlt again and wrote to him immediately on his return to Neumünster to tell him that he had resumed work on 'Love Stories with Animals'.

The Ditzens' married life got off to a disappointing start when Suse contracted suspected diphtheria and a kidney infection which initially looked like a repetition of her lengthy illness of the previous year. In the event, she recovered sufficiently to be discharged from hospital in the middle of May and move to Neumünster, where Ditzen had found a furnished flat comprising two rooms and a kitchen on the 'Kuhberg', the town's main thoroughfare.

The reaction of Ditzen's family to his marriage was not as negative as he had feared. His parents increased his allowance immediately to 85 marks per month and then to 100 marks from July. They also gave him the 2,000 marks deposit, which had been retrieved from Berthold, as a 'nest egg'. His mother also began to send monthly food parcels to her son and daughter-in-law. However, Wilhelm and Elisabeth Ditzen did not express any desire to meet Suse, and their continued financial support was dependent on detailed accounts being submitted at the end of each month.

Tante Ada sent her congratulations and a small sum of money; she took a lively interest in her nephew's household and sent money as often as she could. Margarete sent a cookery book for Suse, who was an enthusiastic but inexperienced cook. His other sister, Elisabeth Hörig, sent 20 marks, with an apology that she could not send more because of difficulties facing her husband's piano business.

The fate of Heinz Hörig's business was typical of many small and medium-sized enterprises which went bankrupt as the industrial and commercial landscape of the Weimar Republic became increasingly dominated by trusts, cartels and monopolies. The consequent pauperization of the middle classes and the apparent helplessness of the coalition government in the face of rising unemployment were reflected in an increase in the National Socialist Party's vote in the regional elections in Saxony and Mecklenburg that spring.

It was in the course of 1929 that the National Socialist Party made the leap from the periphery into mainstream politics, when the media magnate Alfred Hugenberg drew Hitler, along with other nationalist groupings, into his campaign against the Young Plan, which, among other things, finally fixed the level of German reparations and set a 59-year schedule for repayment.

The May Day celebrations provided a catalyst for the general unrest. As a result of the wave of strikes and demonstrations earlier in the year, all public rallies and a number of publications were banned. Karl Zörgiebel, the Social Democratic chief of police in Berlin, refused to lift the ban for the May Day march, and the ensuing disorder left thirty-five people dead.

Meanwhile, in Neumünster, the readership of the *General Anzeiger* continued to decline; Ditzen, after his trip to Berlin in April, began to think seriously about moving to the capital. When one of Suse's sisters moved there in July, Berlin became even more attractive. Lore Soldin approached several newspapers on Ditzen's behalf, all to no avail. Rowohlt was encouraging about 'Love Stories with Animals' but was not in a position to offer Ditzen a job.

By mid-June, Suse was fully recovered; she no longer required bedrest or a strict diet and the Ditzens could settle down to married life together. Money was extremely tight and he had to work long hours for the two newspapers and in the Tourism and Commerce office. They could not even afford to take up Kagelmacher's invitation to spend their summer holiday on Rügen, let alone help to finance his latest project, the establishment of an artists' centre on the island. Despite their straitened circumstances, the early months and years of the Ditzens' marriage were extremely happy. Suse took charge of the household budget and quickly improved her cooking skills, especially after they moved to a flat with a bigger kitchen in Kieler Strasse on 1 August. Ditzen, now thirty-five, had a home, regular meals, love and companionship.

From Rudolf's letters there emerge scenes of domestic harmony, with Suse sitting on the sofa, sewing and darning, while he 'assumed Papa's habit of reading aloud to my wife in the evenings'.[10] Indeed, this was not the only similarity between the marriages of father and son. In 'Our Home in Days Gone by' Hans Fallada was to write of his parents' marriage: 'Father took Mother and led her out of the narrow confines of her existence into the big wide world. She, who had never had anything to call her own, developed as a human being under his tuition.'

A somewhat exaggerated tribute paid by Ditzen to his wife in 1933 suggests a similar pattern to the early days of his own marriage: 'She was a proper little Cinderella in a miserable old working-class family and nobody wanted anything to do with her. There I found her and took her away from all this trivia, pettiness and family squabbling.'[11] While Elisabeth and Suse Ditzen had little in common in terms of social class or accomplishments, Rudolf Ditzen's wife shared his mother's belief in thrift, cleanliness, orderliness and good housekeeping.

On the day the Ditzens moved house to Kieler Strasse, Neumünster witnessed an event which had lasting consequences not only for the town but also for their own future. The summer of 1929 saw the high point of the *Landvolk* movement, a loose association of small farmers who combined forces to protest about the effects of the economic crisis on their livelihoods. As the Fallada scholar Günter Caspar has shown, the small farmers of Schleswig-Holstein were particularly adversely affected by the drop in demand and consequently by the falling price of meat, butter, milk and vegetables.[12] The farmers fell further and further into debt and were increasingly unable to pay their taxes. As a result, the government impounded their cattle and auctioned off their farms. The *Landvolk* association reacted with acts of passive resistance and occasionally more radical tactics, involving the bombing of government buildings. One of their leaders, Wilhelm

Hamkens, was sentenced to one month's imprisonment for incitement to civil disobedience and was due to be released from Neumünster prison on 1 August. Feelings were running high, and a crowd of supporters gathered to greet their hero on his release and escort him out of town. When it was announced that Hamkens had been taken to Flensburg for his release, the crowd decided to march through the town anyway. The police objected to their flag, which had a scythe protruding from its shaft, and used force to seize it. In the ensuing mêlée a number of farmers were injured. The event received nationwide coverage, and the farmers reacted by announcing a boycott of Neumünster. A number of events, including the annual Agricultural Show, had to be cancelled and the boycott, which lasted until July 1930, badly affected the town's commercial life.

On 14 August, two weeks after the *Landvolk* demonstration, Ditzen wrote to Rowohlt announcing his new novel, 'the story of an ailing newspaper in a provincial town'. He added that Suse was planning to type it for him. Before Rowohlt received the letter, however, he met the Ditzens in person. They had received complimentary tickets for a special Sunday excursion to Sylt on 18 August and ran into Rowohlt, who was on holiday there.

This meeting was later mythologized by both Rowohlt and Ditzen. In '*Die Geschichte einer Wieder-Entdeckung*' ('The Story of a Rediscovery'; 1930) Rowohlt claimed that he had had no contact with his former author since the publication of 'Anton and Gerda'.[13] Ditzen made similar claims in *Lebensabriss von Hans Fallada* ('The Life Story of Hans Fallada'), a piece written for publicity purposes in 1932,[14] and, later, in 'Our Home Today', he described this chance meeting as 'the turning-point in our lives'. As we have seen, the truth was rather more mundane.

Ditzen no doubt told Rowohlt about his new novel, provisionally titled *Ein kleiner Zirkus namens Belli* ('A Small Circus by the Name of Belli') and repeated his desire to move to Berlin. Rowohlt thought there might be the possibility of a job with *Tempo* magazine and said he would look into it.

The next surprise in the eventful month of August 1929 was the discovery that Suse was pregnant. Given Ditzen's past history of substance abuse, they had simply assumed that conception was out of the question. After they had recovered from the initial shock, Ditzen once again wrote to Kagelmacher: 'I am happier and more contented now than I have ever been in my whole life.'[15]

Meanwhile, Ditzen's working conditions were becoming increasingly difficult. The conservative *General Anzeiger* supported the farming lobby, while the chairman of the Association for Tourism and Commerce, Herr Lindemann, was the chief of police. Thus Ditzen found himself working 'in the mornings against the police and for the townspeople and farmers, and in the afternoons the other way round'.[16] As a Social Democrat, he was 'not at all in sympathy with "Landvolk" and right-wing groups'.[17] However, he was critical of the police chief for having 'lost his nerve and acted with unnecessary force'.[18] So not only were his two employers on opposite sides of the argument, as a party member he was also critical of the actions of the Social Democratic mayor and the chief of police.

On the day before the Wall Street Crash, Ditzen took his seat in the courtroom in Neumünster to report on the *Landvolk* case. Just over two weeks later, on 12 November 1929, the court ruled in favour of the farmers and was highly critical of the police. Ditzen's reporting of the case inevitably earned him the wrath of one of his employers: Mayor Lindemann refused to speak to him.

Ditzen's attempts to secure a foothold in Berlin met with some success in September with the publication of an article on the *Landvolk* case in *Das Tage-Buch*.[19] A second article appeared in *Das Tage-Buch* on 23 November. Less successful had been his contacts with the *Berliner-Zeitung-am-Mittag*, which had set him a test piece in October. As his position in Neumünster became more precarious, he wrote to Rowohlt again at the beginning of November, enclosing the first section of his prison memoirs and informing him that he was facing unemployment on 1 January (which, while not strictly accurate, was a real possibility), and that they were expecting a baby in March. It was the news of the baby which decided Rowohlt 'that now something must be done'. He wrote to Ditzen on 14 November offering him a part-time job, which would leave the afternoons free for writing, and enquiring how much he would need to earn. Ditzen replied by return of post that their total income in Neumünster was 250 marks per month and that they would need more in Berlin. He went on to state that he no longer received an allowance from his parents and that he had no prospect of ever receiving such an allowance if he moved to Berlin. This was a tough negotiating stance, based on Ditzen's assessment of his prospective employer and on his own calculation that, if needs be, he and Suse could survive on the same income in Berlin as they had in Neumünster – in itself a measure of their desperation. Would Rowohlt respond favourably? At first, it looked as if he was not going to respond at all.

Ditzen's income in November was augmented by one of Tante Ada's regular donations, an additional grant from his parents towards the cost of the baby and, for the first time in over four years, fees from journalism (amounting to 60 marks) from *Das Tage-Buch*. He also had an article on the *Landvolk* case accepted for publication in the respected left-wing journal *Die Weltbühne*.[20] However, the end of the *General Anzeiger* seemed in sight and the Association for Tourism and Commerce was suffering from the hostility of the business community towards Lindemann, who was generally held responsible for the action of the police which had precipitated the boycott.

The Ditzens' flat in Kieler Strasse turned out to be very draughty in the winter and not at all suitable for a newborn baby. Ditzen had applied for a council flat but, given his uneasy relations with Lindemann, did not rate his chances highly.

A referendum in November produced a majority in favour of the Young Plan, although that 5.8 million voted against it was an indication of the growing influence of the nationalist Hugenberg press, Hitler and the extreme Right. The long-term effect of the *Landvolk* movement was to prepare a breeding-ground for fascism in the farming community. In Schleswig-Holstein, the National Socialist vote increased from 4 per cent in 1928 to 27 per cent in 1930. The Wall Street Crash led to unprecedented levels of bankruptcy in small businesses, rural and urban. Industrial production and agricultural output began to fall, and unemployment, already at 14.6 per cent in 1929, began to rise steeply. By 1932, only one in three of all workers in Germany would be in full-time employment.

As Christmas approached, Ditzen faced yet again the unpleasant prospect of trying to sell advertising space to a dwindling number of businesses in a newspaper whose official circulation figures bore no relationship to reality and which was viewed as hostile to the business community. Ditzen continued to work long hours, reporting on births, marriages, wedding anniversaries and the other bread-and-butter issues of provincial journalism. He also sold bus tickets, published pocket timetables, provided tourist information (on Schleswig-Holstein, as well as tourist destinations farther afield) and advised on special events. His evenings were often spent working, too. Only a man determined to make good and buoyed up by personal happiness could have maintained this pace for so long.

As the birth of their first child drew nearer, the Ditzens began to consider names. In the case of a baby girl, they would call her Lore after their good friend Lore Soldin. If the baby was a boy, they wanted to call him Ulrich (Uli) after Rudolf's younger brother, who had died in the closing months of the First World War. Given the sensitive nature of this choice, Ditzen wrote to his parents on 15 December, his brother's birthday, seeking their permission, a request which they duly granted.

Just when the Ditzens had given up all hope of ever hearing from Rowohlt again, a letter arrived on 20 December offering Rudolf 250 marks a month for a job in charge of the reviews department. He would be required to work in the office from 9 a.m. until 2 p.m. from Monday to Saturday; his job would consist of sending out review copies of new books and collecting and filing all reviews published. Rowohlt's choice of Ditzen was inspired, for Ditzen combined a love of books with an almost obsessive tidiness as far as paperwork and correspondence were concerned. Rowohlt was later to remark that Ditzen was the best reviews editor he had ever employed.

A job in Berlin, working with books; time to write his new novel and earn the same salary for fewer hours' work – what a Christmas present! The Ditzens lost no time in shaking the dust of Neumünster from their feet. Suse's sister found them lodgings in the Moabit district of Berlin and they moved to the capital soon after Christmas. It was a very happy man who walked down Calvin Strasse on the morning of Thursday 16 January 1930 and crossed the footbridge over the river Spree into Bellevue station, from where he travelled two stops on the train, got out at Zoo station and walked to the Rowohlt offices in Passauer Strasse.

The spring in Ditzen's step was not only due to his new job. He was a happily married man – an increase of 20lb in weight was ample proof of this. His wife was expecting their first child. The ghosts of the past had been exorcized; he had not touched alcohol, morphine or cocaine for over four years, nor did he feel any desire to do so.

The move to Berlin and the job in the Rowohlt offices marked the end of Ditzen's literary isolation. He worked on a day-to-day basis with Rowohlt's editors, Paul Mayer and Franz Hessel, both authors in their own right. He had contact with writers as diverse as the prolific biographer Emil Ludwig, whose *Lincoln* and *Michelangelo* both appeared in 1930, the Austrian humanist Robert Musil, whose *Der Mann ohne Eigenschaften* (*The Man without Qualities*) was also published during Ditzen's first year in Passauer Strasse, and the left-wing publicist and satirical poet Kurt Tucholsky, whose poem *Deutschland, erwache!* ('Germany, Awake!') of 1930 warned of the growing danger of fascism. Tucholsky was also a frequent contributor to the *Weltbühne* and a close friend of its editor, Carl von Ossietzky. Another frequent and popular visitor was the cabaret artist Joachim Ringelnatz, who brought all work in the company to a standstill with his highly entertaining political sketches.

It was here that the paths of Rudolf Ditzen and Ernst von Salomon crossed for the first time, for Rowohlt had just offered a contract to von Salomon for his novel *Die Geächteten* ('The Outcasts'), a fictionalized account of his paramilitary involvement in Upper Silesia in the aftermath of the First World War. Ditzen, who had witnessed the activities of such paramilitary groups during his time in Radach, took a keen interest in the project. Von Salomon, on the other hand, had been arrested in the autumn of 1929 on suspicion of supporting terrorist activities in association with the farmers' movement in Schleswig-Holstein, which formed the background to Ditzen's new novel. The two men had therefore much to talk about.

The most impressive literary figure in Passauer Strasse, however, was Ernst Rowohlt himself. 'He was a delightful man, of giant blond Aryan stature and complexion. He had a positively cherubic face, with innocent blue eyes, round, ruddy, plump cheeks and an irrepressible and spluttering humour,' according to Martha Dodd, the daughter of the US ambassador to Berlin in the early 1930s. She continues:

> Rowohlt was a tremendous drinker and also a very serious and vital man. He loved life and freedom passionately, was tremendously proud of his past record and spoke bluntly and honestly about any subject that arose . . . He was the type of man who aroused and held the devotion and unswerving loyalty of his subordinates and who could attract anyone by his tremendous energy and intelligence.[21]

Thomas Wolfe, in *You Can't Go Home Again*, draws a more subtle portrait of Ernst Rowohlt in the figure of Lewald. Wolfe contrasts Lewald's ebullient manner with the real man behind it:

> That bluff and hearty openness was just a mask which Lewald used against the world with all the deceptive grace and subtlety of a great matador preparing to give the finishing stroke to a charging bull. Behind that mask was concealed the true image of the man's soul, which was sly, dexterous, crafty and cunning . . .
>
> The eyes were little, blue, and twinkled with crafty merriment. One felt that they saw everything – that they were not only secretly and agreeably aware of the whole human comedy, but were also slyly amused at the bluff and ingenuous part that their owner was playing.[22]

Rowohlt's patronage meant security and support, although Ditzen did not see much of his employer during his first few weeks at work. Nor does he seem to have sampled the cultural delights of the German capital, which included experimental and revolutionary theatre pioneered by Erwin Piscator, Friedrich Wolf and Bertolt Brecht and contemporary music under Otto Klemperer, as well as the shabby glamour of Berlin's nightlife, epitomized in Erich Kästner's *Fabian* and Christopher Isherwood's *Goodbye to Berlin*.

The Ditzens spent the first few weeks settling into Calvin Strasse, where they occupied two rooms and a kitchen in a flat belonging to a retired couple called Nothmann. Preparations were also made for the impending birth of their first child. Suse was booked into the local hospital in Moabit; they acquired a cot from a friend in Neumünster and bedding from Lore Soldin. Ditzen's family showed their support by sending money: 100 marks from Wilhelm Ditzen's sister and brother-in-law, Luise and Arthur Nostitz, 40 marks from Wilhelm and Elisabeth Ditzen and 20 marks from Tante Ada.

The stresses and strains of the two years since Ditzen had left prison were beginning to tell: at the end of 1929 he had developed serious eczema, which spread all over his body and took five months to clear. A nagging toothache turned out to be a gum abscess which, apart from being excruciatingly painful, required extensive (and expensive) dental treatment lasting six months.

Mindful of his obligation to Rowohlt, Ditzen resumed work on 'A Small Circus by the Name of Belli' on 4 February. He wrote to his parents on 2 March: 'The book has not the slightest similarity with my previous books; it has nothing to do with my personal life. It's purely a man's novel.'

While Ditzen's new book was not autobiographical in the same way as his previous novels, with their first-person narration and self-absorption, it did have its origins in his life and work in Neumünster. Ditzen drew on his own experience in the creation of the character of Tredup, who leads a precarious existence selling advertising space and writing local news items for an ailing, right-wing newspaper, the *Pommersche Chronik*, in the provincial town of Altholm. Tredup addresses envelopes in the evenings, lives in fear of losing his job, joins the SPD and dreams of becoming an editor. Many minor characters in the novel bear the names of Ditzen's friends and neighbours: Soldin, Parsenow, Nothmann, Frerksen (the married name of Suse's sister); the name of one of Ditzen's landladies in Neumünster resurfaces in the figure of Frau Gehl, who keeps house for the president of the regional government, Temborius.[23] It is possible that the rather unusual name of Gareis, which Ditzen gives to the Social Democrat mayor of Altholm, is based on that of a Munich socialist who was murdered in 1921.[24]

What makes this novel different from Ditzen's previous work is its profoundly political content. Ditzen, who knew the SPD from the inside, lays bare both the weaknesses of the party and of the Republic.

He exposes the canker at the heart of the first German democracy and the forces that threaten it from many directions.

Another striking feature of this novel is the almost total absence of a 'love interest'. It is indeed a man's world which Ditzen portrays. He suggested a reason for this in a letter to his sister Margarete on 2 May 1930: 'Now that I'm happily married, love has stopped being a problem for me.' However, the absence of a 'love story' in the novel was partly due to the nature of the material itself: the business, farming and political life of a small town in Germany in 1929–30 was largely a male affair. Women in the novel are wives, to be ignored or abused at will, prostitutes, to be used as required, or hysterical spinsters, to be ridiculed and mocked.

With the prospect of a novel being published again, Ditzen (re)-joined the German Writers' Union on 1 March. His motives, however, were not purely professional, for he was hopeful that he might qualify for a flat in one of the union's housing cooperatives. Yet again, for the fourth time within a year, the Ditzens were planning to move house. Their landlord, Herr Nothmann, had turned out to be quarrelsome: he insisted they pay rent for a telephone they did not use; there were constant disputes about the payment of bills. In addition, the rent of 100 marks per month was too high for someone with an income of 350 marks gross. The couple had acquired some furniture from Frau Aldendorff, a wealthy friend of Lore Soldin, and, tired of living in furnished accommodation, felt ready to set up house on their own.

Moving house, the new novel and all other plans came to a halt on 14 March 1930 with the arrival of Ulrich Ditzen (Uli) who was born at ten minutes to midnight after a long and difficult labour. 'The boy . . . is terribly like me. He has quite the Ditzen nose and thick fair hair,' Ditzen wrote to his parents the next day. 'I feel like a millionaire.'

The arrival of the new baby brought chaos to the Ditzen household, and the proud father found himself exiled to the kitchen whenever he wanted a cigarette. Suse took some time to recover from the birth, and first her sister and then her mother came to stay and help out. Ditzen's letters in March and April are full of the joys and tribulations of new parents. Is the baby getting enough milk? When will his navel heal? How do we persuade him to sleep through the night? From the beginning, Ditzen himself was closely involved in his son's upbringing and took enormous delight in Uli's progress.

It was not until 31 March that he was able to concentrate on his novel again. By then, Germany had ceased to be a working democracy. When the cabinet had refused to sanction Chancellor Müller's proposed increases in social insurance contributions on 27 March, the government collapsed and President Hindenburg invoked Article 48 of the Weimar Constitution to appoint Heinrich Brüning, chairman of the conservative Centre party, as the new Chancellor. On 30 March, Chancellor Brüning found himself in charge of a government without a parliamentary majority. The prerequisites for parliamentary democracy – economic stability, the consent of the majority to the system, the reconcilability of different interest groups – were no longer present in Germany. Ditzen's new novel, which would ponder the malaise of German democracy, was indeed very different from his previous work. Two and half years in prison, unemployment, his experience of the commercial and political life of a provincial town, his inside view of the SPD – all contributed to an acute awareness of the political landscape of a democracy in decline.

Ditzen's family continued to support their newest member. Margarete Bechert sent clothes, Wilhelm and Elisabeth Ditzen money – Elisabeth even sent 10 marks to Suse, although she expressed no wish to meet either her daughter-in-law or her grandson.

Ditzen made good progress with his novel, despite a painful and recurring toothache, and was able to submit the Prelude and Part 1 to Rowohlt on 27 May. Both Rowohlt and Mayer were enthusiastic, and Ditzen was given Saturdays off to enable him to finish. The contract, made officially with Suse so that Ditzen's creditors could be kept at bay, specified a deadline of 31 October that year.

In order to save some money, at the beginning of May, Ditzen began walking to work; however, it became increasingly clear that his family could not stay in Calvin Strasse, for the Nothmanns had now begun to complain about Uli crying. They decided to move somewhere cheaper, away from the city centre, where they would no longer be at the mercy of a landlord's whim and found a brand-new, unfurnished, two-bedroom terrace house in a small housing estate in the eastern suburb of Neuenhagen. This cost 65 marks per month and, as well as a cellar, had a patio and small garden at the rear. The Ditzens had Frau Aldendorff's furniture, Lore Soldin gave them two beds, and they used up most of their savings for the deposit, which was returnable with interest, and to equip the house. They moved to Neuenhagen on 12 June, and Rowohlt gave Ditzen three days' leave to get the house in order.

Just before they moved they received news that Elisabeth Ditzen had fallen ill while on holiday with Wilhelm at the Nostitzes' in Blankenburg. She had had two operations there and then been transported back to Leipzig by car in considerable pain. This turned out to be the last holiday Wilhelm and Elisabeth Ditzen would spend together. Her illness also meant a temporary halt to the food parcels for her son and daughter-in-law, which were replaced by a monthly donation of 10 marks.

The economic and political crisis continued over the summer. The free-market orthodoxy, embraced by Brüning, prescribed cuts in wages and public expenditure along with rises in taxes as the cure for the Depression. This resulted in strikes by those who still had jobs and, ultimately, mass unemployment. When the Social Democrats opposed Brüning's economic programme on 16 July, he in turn used Article 48 of the Constitution to push his legislation through and then dissolved parliament, calling a general election for 14 September. Recourse to emergency decrees would become a frequent feature of German political life over the next two and a half years as parliament and the democratic process became increasingly irrelevant.

Ditzen celebrated his thirty-seventh birthday on 21 July 1930. Five days later, he completed the second part of his novel and took a week off work to put the finishing touches to it. Then he turned his attention to the garden. It had been five years since he had last worked on the land, but he had not abandoned his dream of one day owning his own farm: 'If I had the money, I would buy a farm right away,' he wrote on 27 July in a letter to his parents. Suse had inherited her mother's green fingers and was also a keen gardener.

The bad weather at the beginning of August, which undid most of the Ditzens' work in their garden, had a disastrous effect on the harvest. Ditzen, for example, noted a number of crops on a neighbouring farm rotting in the fields. The resultant price rises only exacerbated an already difficult economic situation. He wrote to his mother on 17 August urging her to make sure to buy in enough coal to last the winter: 'I'm a bit fearful of the winter. I think there will be trouble, especially as the general election is not expected to produce a working majority and people are talking in terms of a dictatorship.'

Despite his concerns about the future, Ditzen was delighted to have a place of his own, with no interfering landlord, and thought the ninety-minute journey to the office a small price to pay for a house to themselves, with a garden, and removed from the turmoil of Berlin, where the election campaign now under way was marked by street battles between Communists and fascists. Any connection the German National Socialist Party might have had with socialism had been irrevocably severed by the expulsion of the Otto Strasser faction from the party at the end of June. Hitler and his party were now aligned with extreme right-wing nationalism.

In the peacefulness of Neuenhagen, Ditzen took pleasure in the development of his son and the success of his marriage. He wrote to Kagelmacher on 8 August: '. . . if I have ever loved another human being on God's earth, then Suse is the one . . . I have a wonderful wife. She is goodness, tranquillity, gentleness, calmness in person. There can be no better, more loyal, more courageous partner in the world.'

Ditzen completed his novel in September, ahead of schedule, and Rowohlt sent a secretary to Neuenhagen to type the last part. Erwin Piscator's radical People's Theatre in Berlin expressed an interest in staging a dramatized version and negotiations were under way for a pre-launch serialization in a newspaper or illustrated magazine.

The Social Democrats emerged from the general election on 14 September 1930 as the largest single party, albeit with a reduced number of seats (143). The second-largest party was the National Socialist Party, which increased its share of the vote from 2.6 per cent to 18.3 per cent and which now had 107 seats. The Communist Party, too, increased its vote and became the third largest, with 77 seats. Brüning's Centre coalition, comprising ten parties, had 209. The extreme right (the National Socialists and the German People's Party) had a total of 148. The Comintern policy pursued by the Communists, which identified the Social Democrats as the main enemy, made a coalition of the two parties on the left impossible, so the Social Democrats decided to support Brüning, since he seemed to offer the best chance of upholding the Republic.

Ditzen wrote to his parents on election day: 'Who knows whether things will get better? It all looks so dismal and everyone I know, office workers like myself, trembles at the thought of the day each month when we can be issued with notice of dismissal.' Brüning's programme for economic recovery, presented to parliament on 1 October, which contained more cuts in wages, pensions and benefits, and corresponding increases in taxation, elicited the following response from Ditzen in a letter to his parents four days later: 'And then people wonder why the National Socialists get so many votes! (Not from us!)' He urged his parents again to ensure that they had enough coal to last the winter: 'The whole place here is buzzing with rumours. First one dictatorship, then the other; first a coup with the army, then a coup without the army. It's going to be a terrible winter.'

While Ditzen was putting the final touches to a book which would expose some of the fatal weaknesses of Weimar democracy, other writers were turning their attention to the rise and nature of fascism. Lion Feuchtwanger's *Success* examined the sociological roots of National Socialism in Bavaria, while Thomas Mann in his short story 'Mario and the Magician' (1929) had explored the psychological processes by which fascism operated.

Rowohlt's business received a very welcome boost in 1930 when one of his American authors, Sinclair Lewis, won the Nobel Prize for Literature. In the office, Ditzen found himself caught up in the annual autumn frenzy as one new book was launched after another. Rowohlt's autumn list, compiled no doubt with an eye to the current trend to the political right, included *Rossbach* by Arnolt Bronnen, which celebrated Hitler's attempted putsch in Munich in 1923, and 'The Outcasts' by Ernst von Salomon. Given Ditzen's and von Salomon's experience of Upper Silesia, the criminal justice system and the *Landvolk* movement in Schleswig-Holstein, it is not surprising that a friendship developed between them which, as we shall see, was later to land Ditzen in trouble with the Nazi regime.

The Ditzens had a visit in late October from Kagelmacher, who had been forced to give up his farm on Rügen and was passing through Berlin on his way to Leipzig, where he planned to pursue his astrological interests. Kagelmacher, another victim of the Depression, cut a very sorry figure, and Ditzen, mindful of how often his friend had helped him in the past, promised to send him money as often as he could. He also tried, unsuccessfully, to persuade him to write his memoirs, and undertook to help him find a publisher.

October also saw the death of Ditzen's uncle, Arthur Nostitz. When his widowed aunt decided to sell up and move to live with her sister Ada in Marburg, the Ditzens in Neuenhagen 'inherited' some furniture and clothing, which was packed and dispatched by Margarete Bechert. In his letter of thanks to his sister, Ditzen described the harmonious evenings in Neuenhagen when Uli had been tucked up in bed and he had resumed his habit of reading aloud to his wife while she sat sewing and darning.

Rowohlt negotiated the serialization of Ditzen's new novel in the *Kölnische Illustrierte* magazine and the author then had to cut it substantially. The magazine also introduced another change, crucial to the reception of the work: the editor decided that the title 'A Small Circus by the Name of Belli' was not sufficiently sensational, and it was changed to the much more effective *Bauern, Bonzen und Bomben*, literally, 'Farmers, Functionaries and Fireworks'. The positioning of the farmers as the first item in the title and the linking of the farmers to the functionaries and the fireworks completely shifted the emphasis to the farming community, which actually plays a secondary role in the work. The original title, retained in the new Penguin translation (*A Small Circus*), drew attention to the corruption endemic in the newspaper world, for it is the circus's failure to advertise in the *Chronik* newspaper at the beginning of the novel that results in an extremely negative review and provides an introduction to the more widespread corruption and political intriguing in the town itself. Ditzen merely uses the farmers' demonstration and subsequent boycott as a means of highlighting this skulduggery. The change in the title shifted the spotlight to the farmers – and the novel was examined for the author's view of the *Landvolk* movement.

Ditzen lamented that the abridged version 'has little in common with my novel, it has been terribly reworked'.[25] However, the main attraction of the serialization, apart from the advance publicity, was the fee of 4,000 marks, the equivalent of sixteen months' salary. Here, at last, was an opportunity to start repaying his creditors; he also needed a new typewriter, Suse needed new clothes and dental treatment; items were required for the house. Although exhausted from the effort of finishing the novel as well as from the pressure of work in the office, Ditzen completed the serialization in record time and dispatched the manuscript on 7 November.

He then announced his intention of having a rest before starting on the next novel, which was already taking shape in his mind. A break was very much overdue, for he was 'so irritable and always cross'. He told Kagelmacher at the beginning of November: 'Too much work and too much coffee have turned me into a bundle of nerves.'[26]

The speed with which Ditzen wrote *A Small Circus* was to become typical of much of his later work. This has been widely ascribed to his obsessive nature and linked with his other obsessions: coffee, tobacco, alcohol – and even women. While there is no doubt some truth in this, there were often very material reasons for his speed. In the case of *A Small Circus*, money was a major motivating factor. He told Kagelmacher that the novel could have been much better if he had spent more time on it, but that he had needed the money. In addition, his upbringing had instilled a strong sense of duty. Once he had signed a contract or even set himself a goal, he would commit himself 100 per cent. His parents wanted monthly accounts? Very well, they would have them – in detail and on time. Rowohlt had given him the afternoons free to write? Very well, he would start writing within three weeks of moving to Berlin. The deadline for the novel was 31 October? Very well, it would be ready on time, earlier if it could be managed. In this respect, too, he was his father's son.

On 20 November, he wrote to his brother-in-law Fritz Bechert to set in motion the process of repaying his debts. The first problem was to ascertain the exact amount he owed. Ditzen's tactic in 1925, of exaggerating the sums of money involved, looked as if it would rebound on him when Count von Rohr in Lübgust demanded the sum which

Ditzen claimed to have stolen (5,000 marks) rather than the actual and much lower amount. Despite incomplete court records, the sums were eventually agreed as 10,000 marks to Count von Hahn in Neuhaus (who generously made no demands for payment of interest) and 1,100 marks plus interest to Count von Rohr in Lübgust. Ditzen arranged to have the first instalments paid directly from his Rowohlt account.

While Ditzen's financial position had improved considerably, he could not help becoming aware on his daily journey into the city centre that the lot of many Berliners had deteriorated noticeably. Lore Soldin, a frequent visitor to Neuenhagen, was a social worker and she often spoke of 'the widespread misery nowadays which we are helpless to combat'.[27]

The Ditzens were planning to spend a quiet family Christmas in Neuenhagen with their son, whose constant good humour had earned him the nickname Sonnenkind ('sun-child'), but these plans were dashed when Suse became ill at the beginning of December. The doctor diagnosed another kidney infection and prescribed bed-rest and a strict diet. Suse's sister was able to take Uli to live with her and Ditzen organized some domestic help. By Christmas Eve, Suse was sufficiently recovered for Ditzen to bring Uli home.

The strain of the pre-Christmas rush at Rowohlt, the worry about Suse (and their son), as well as the burden of the Christmas preparations, which had fallen solely on his shoulders, exhausted Ditzen and contributed to the recurrence of a minor heart problem that had been diagnosed in prison. The news that the People's Theatre had decided not to stage *A Small Circus* because the novel was considered too much weighted in favour of the farmers, most probably came as a relief.

On 29 December, Elisabeth Ditzen addressed one of her regular letters to Neuenhagen for the first time to both her son and her daughter-in-law: 'Dear Rudolf, dear Suse'. The tone of the correspondence was gradually becoming warmer. Ditzen had made a point of writing to his parents at Leipzig on Friday the twelfth, three days before the anniversary of his brother Ulrich's birthday: 'I'll be thinking about you both on Monday. That is one day which I'll never forget. One of the few days.' Despite their reservations, Wilhelm and Elisabeth Ditzen were beginning to believe in their son's rehabilitation. They still judged it too soon, however, to arrange a meeting.

The pleasures of a quiet family Christmas came to an abrupt end on 30 December when Suse collapsed while bathing Uli. This time, the doctor recommended a stay in a sanatorium, and the family reluctantly decided temporarily to leave their house in Neuenhagen: Uli would go back to Suse's sister; Suse would go to a small hotel in Weimar to rest while awaiting approval from the Health Insurance Scheme for her sanatorium treatment; and Ditzen would move into Frau Aldendorff's spacious apartment in Berlin, where he would have a room (and a typewriter) to himself.

He used the opportunity of being based in central Berlin to catch up on his work in the office. He stayed there every day until 5 or 5.30 p.m. and then spent the evenings working on the dramatization of *A Small Circus*. While the Aldendorffs made him very welcome, he did not feel comfortable surrounded by such affluence: 'These people live here as if there was no misery, no unemployment, no struggle being waged in Germany. Pleasure, theatre, dancing – that's all they are interested in. And such a lack of understanding about social issues – oh, I'd rather not talk about it, it makes me so angry.'[28]

He wrote every day to Suse, who made a good recovery in Weimar, although the Health Insurance Scheme refused to approve her application for sanatorium treatment. The doctors also strongly advised her against becoming pregnant again in the near future because of the risk of a recurrence of her kidney complaint. While his parents were writing to each other every day and missing each other very much, Uli was having a great time in the company of his cousins. Indeed, he had some difficulty adjusting to the relative peace and quiet when the family was finally reunited in Neuenhagen after seven weeks apart.

Ditzen continued to work a full day at Rowohlt's until the end of February. After they returned to Neuenhagen this meant getting up at five in the morning to spend some time on the dramatization of *A Small Circus* before setting off for the office, and then not returning until after six in the evening. In view of the difficult economic climate, Rowohlt could not afford to pay Ditzen for this 'overtime' but gave him 100 marks' worth of books each month instead. Rowohlt's economic difficulties, compounded by poor financial control, also caused a delay in the repayment of Ditzen's debts. By the end of February,

Count von Rohr had received 500 marks, but nothing had been sent to Count von Hahn.

As the economic situation continued to deteriorate in Germany, the political situation became more precarious. Brüning, with the support of the SPD, prorogued parliament for eight months: the Reichstag met on only forty-one occasions in 1931. Unemployment continued to soar and membership of the National Socialist Party doubled within twelve months. Brüning ruled by emergency decree, passing forty-four decrees in 1931, an increase of thirty-nine on 1930. One such measure, the *Osthilfegesetz* (Act governing Aid for the East) of 26 March, provided 2,500 million marks for the Junker, landed gentry and large-scale farmers east of the River Elbe – a very controversial piece of legislation which was widely seen as Brüning using public money to help his party's friends and supporters.

The publication of Ditzen's new novel, with its 'sensational' title and its depiction of urban and rural malaise, was bound to be a political event in March 1931. The right-wing press praised the novel for what was seen as an espousal of the farmers' cause. Goebbels' *Der Angriff* described it as 'masterly'. Ditzen himself was taken aback at such adulation: 'I reject the notion that I have written a novel about farmers and I certainly don't want to be identified with the extreme right . . .'[29]

If a perceived espousal of the farmers' cause won the support of the political right, it also ensured the novel's rejection by most of the left. The majority of left-wing journals read the novel as an attack on the SPD, despite the fact that the most sympathetic character in *A Small Circus* is Gareis, the Social Democratic mayor of Altholm. Given the split in the international labour movement at the time, any attack on the SPD could expect a warm welcome from the Communist press: *Die Rote Fahne* described the novel as 'a great piece of reporting'. On the other hand, Karl Wittfogel, in the Communist *Linkskurve*, edited by Becher, among others, went so far as to describe the author of *A Small Circus* as 'fascist'. Tucholsky's review in the *Weltbühne* represented one of the very few positive reviews from the non-Communist political left. He called the novel 'a political textbook on the fauna Germanica that could not be bettered', and went on: 'Fallada's book is the best description of a German provincial town in recent years ... No, it is no great work of art but it is genuine ... so terribly genuine that it's frightening.' Tucholsky praised Ditzen's exposure of the failure of democracy in Germany and warned, with reference to the Grimms' 'The Goose Girl': 'If they get their hands on you, Hans Fallada, if they get their hands on you: take care that you don't hang!'

Ditzen's literary colleagues praised the realism of the novel; they admired Ditzen's humour and narrative style. Axel Eggebrecht, son of the Ditzens' family doctor in Leipzig and himself a journalist, declared that Ditzen's story-telling talent was superior to that of Erik Reger, who had been awarded the Kleist Prize in 1931 for his *Union der festen Hand* ('Union of the Firm Hand').[30] Hermann Hesse praised the novel's 'genuine love and genuine humanity' in a review in the *Bücherwurm* journal, and Robert Musil in a letter to Rowohlt on 22 April described it as 'uncommonly vivid and original'.

A number of critics remarked, with justification, that the scenes involving the farmers and the events in the farming community were not quite so well drawn as their counterparts in the town of Altholm. Tucholsky was also no doubt correct in his assessment of the work's dubious artistic merit. Indeed, *A Small Circus* would have benefited from more editorial refining, as Ditzen himself admitted to Kagelmacher. It is a novel brimming over with characters and plots, which tells the story of the town of Altholm, its two newspapers, and the political intrigues in the town hall, as well as in the regional and national administrations. The novel charts the events which precede the farmers' demonstration, the scuffles that take place during the event, the farmers' boycott of the town and the ensuing court case. There are many villains and few heroes, but the real subject of the novel is the fate of the first German democracy, a subject on which Ditzen is not 'neutral' and 'objective', as Peter Suhrkamp and, latterly, Günter Caspar have claimed.[31] Ditzen described his own view of the novel in a letter to Fritz Bechert on 26 November 1930: 'Ernst von Salomon ... said his impression after reading the novel was: poor Germany. That was my aim, not the impression: poor farmers.' By revealing the corruption endemic in every aspect of life in Altholm,

Ditzen criticizes a political culture which was unable to develop truly democratic structures. Even the admirable Gareis is forced to resort to dubious means to achieve his laudable ends. Ditzen's friend, Heinz Dietrich Kenter, who was involved in the novel's dramatization, wrote in *Die Literatur* in July 1931 that Ditzen:

> ... tackles the political problem of Germany at the present time when it has reached a critical stage. [He shows h]ow the concept of Germany which ought to have been rethought and rebuilt by the new state after 1918, how this concept has become flesh and blood in feeble party politics, a partisan press, a St Vitus dance of private, sectional interests.

Ditzen's close observation and attention to detail should not be confused with objectivity. Nor should his criticism of all sections of Altholm society be read as 'neutrality'.

Whatever its literary shortcomings, *A Small Circus* established Hans Fallada's name as a promising literary talent as well as an author not afraid to tackle controversial issues. His next project, which he began once he had reverted to his normal office hours at the beginning of March 1931, was based on his experience of prison and his views on the rehabilitation of offenders. This was an equally controversial topic, although more likely to endear him to the political left than the political right.

As the economic situation worsened, foreign investors began to withdraw their capital from Germany, which resulted in more business failures. At the end of March, the closure of a papermill resulted in Rowohlt being presented with a bill for 80,000 marks. Bankruptcies in the book trade caused further losses of 105,000 marks in April. Rowohlt responded by bringing in a new financial controller, who, to Ditzen's surprise, turned out to be none other than Egmont Seyerlen, the former husband of Ditzen's first love and erstwhile muse, Annia Seyerlen. Following his return from the war and his divorce from Annia in 1919, Seyerlen had established a successful consultancy business, specializing in rescue plans for companies in financial difficulties.

The critical success of *A Small Circus* did not translate into high sales figures: by the beginning of June, only 3,200 copies had been sold. It did, however, mean that the author Hans Fallada was in demand for reviews, articles and short stories, which provided a very welcome source of income. Between May and December 1931, Ditzen had some twelve short stories published. Farming, social problems in the big cities and prison life were his three major themes. These stories demonstrate his ability to understand and portray the motivations of characters as different as the farmer's son in *'Blanka, eine geraubte Prinzessin'* ('Blanka, a Stolen Princess'), the pensioner neglected by her family in *'Mutter lebt von der Rente'* ('Mother Lives on Her Pension') and the petty criminal in *'Einbrecher träumt von der Zelle'* ('Burglar Dreams of a Prison Cell'). *'Wie Herr Tiedemann einem das Mausen abgewöhnte'* ('How Herr Tiedemann Put an End to Pilfering') reveals Ditzen's sense of fun: a young farmhand is cured of stealing by having *Omar Khayyám* read aloud to him in English while his employer, modelled no doubt on Kagelmacher, 'x-rays' his brain with a telescope! Ditzen himself thought that he had 'no real talent' for this sort of prose and in May he even turned down a commission for a short story worth 1,000 marks because he was 'no good at these things which need to be run off quickly'.[32] He recognized these short pieces as a stop-gap and a useful way to earn money but regarded them as a waste of his talent.

Besides his work at Rowohlt's, Ditzen's stories, reviews and his new novel, *A Small Circus* continued to occupy him. A new serialization for the *Fränkischer Kurier* required the original serialized version to be cut by two thirds; he was still working on a stage version, this time for a different theatre – the Barnowskybühnen. At the beginning of June, Ditzen shelved his prison novel, which, as he wrote to his parents (on 21 June) was 'too bleak for these summer days', and turned to a more light-hearted project with the provisional title *'Pinneberg und sein Murkel'* ('Pinneberg and His Shrimp').

June 1931 was indeed a bleak month, both for the Ditzens and for Germany. An emergency decree on the fifth introduced more cuts in salaries, pensions and benefits and imposed a 'crisis tax' on workers and employers. In addition, Brüning appealed for an end to reparations, which eventually came a month later when President Hoover proposed a general moratorium on all inter-Allied debts and reparations – a moratorium which soon became permanent.

Ditzen eventually finished the dramatization of *A Small Circus* in mid-June, only to be told that his version was not suitable and would need to be considerably revised. The financial crisis facing Rowohlt made it imperative for Ditzen to continue writing for newspapers and journals. To meet all his commitments, he started working a very long day: he would get up at four in the morning and work before setting out for the office shortly after seven o'clock. On his return, after three in the afternoon, he would have a rest before sitting down to his type-writer again. This lifestyle required large quantities of coffee and tobacco, both of which the doctor who had examined his heart in April had advised him to avoid.

The next blow came on the twenty-second, when Rowohlt was forced to suspend payment of his debts. Besides his salary, Ditzen was owed fees and royalties from two serializations of *A Small Circus* and from the novel itself. He did not receive his June salary until 5 July and then he received only 100 marks. Even more worrying was the fact that Rowohlt, despite repeated promises, had not yet paid any money to Ditzen's creditor Count von Hahn in Neuhaus.

Then, on the thirtieth, all Rowohlt's employees were given three months' protective notice. Ditzen was not unsympathetic to Rowohlt, whom he regarded as a victim of 'the times we live in, bad debtors, bankruptcies of related companies . . . poor sales'.[33]

Ditzen's frenetic working day made it impossible for him to get down to work on 'Pinneberg and His Shrimp', which he described as 'a story about a marriage and children, with a social background, the fate of a white-collar worker. Not very long, 300 pages at the most. Intended as a rest.' The original idea of basing a novel on a white-collar worker 'was recommended to me years ago by Heinz' (his brother-in-law, Heinz Hörig).[34]

Hörig, too, had become a victim of the economic recession which left very few Germans unscathed. On 13 July, the Darmstädter und Nationalbank, which provided much of the finance for Lore Soldin's welfare organization, declared itself insolvent. A further five banks closed their doors over the next few days. Only the intervention of the German government, which used public funds to support the banks, defused the situation.

In the parliamentary vacuum and in the face of an unprecedented economic crisis, new alliances were being sought. In the summer of 1931, Hitler approached some of Germany's leading industrialists with his party's programme. One of them, Edmund Hugo Stinnes, told Hitler in July 1931 that he shared his aim of 'expanding the German space towards eastern and south-eastern Europe' and 'giving living-space, land and employment to our nation which is intolerably overcrowded'.[35] A group of businesspeople in Frankfurt am Main wrote to President Hindenburg on 27 July declaring their support for the National Socialists, the German People's Party and the Stahlhelm veterans organization, which they described as the 'national opposition'. The right-wing coalition which had come together to oppose the Young Plan initiated another (unsuccessful) referendum in August 1931 to have the SPD-dominated Prussian regional parliament dissolved.

By the middle of August, the stage version of A Small Circus was finally completed; however, Ditzen was not optimistic about it ever being performed, despite Kenter's enthusiasm. It made the rounds of the drama publishers and, eventually, Ditzen put Kenter in charge of negotiations and swore never to become involved in a dramatization again. In the event, A Small Circus was never staged but was published in 1932 as a theatre text by the Reichard publishing house in Freiburg.

Kenter, who knew about Ditzen's dream of owning a farm, invited him to join a scheme to buy an estate in Bavaria, but Ditzen declined, largely for financial reasons. By this stage, he needed a break, although any break now meant a reduction in income. He took two weeks off in the second half of August, and although the beginning of his holiday was overshadowed by a recurrence of the gum abscess and resultant dental treatment, he was soon able to relax with his family and in his garden. He wrote to his parents at the end of the month that the two years since his marriage had been 'the best time of my life'. Uli, despite his teething, continued to be a source of great pleasure, and Ditzen enjoyed playing with him and 'Hoppelpoppel', a pull-along toy dog which Elisabeth Ditzen had sent. The Ditzens had rented some land adjoining their garden and had begun to grow fruit and vegetables, not only as a means of saving money but also with a view to surviving possible food shortages in the future.

By now, Ditzen had received his full salary for June and July. However, the future of Rowohlt's business was still unclear; all salaries were going to be cut by 15 per cent, and a new company had been founded on 28 August to start publishing Rowohlt's new books. The fate of the old company, which owed Ditzen over 2,000 marks, had not yet been decided.

Ditzen was now no longer a suppliant, begging for crumbs from Rowohlt's table, but an author in his own right. On 12 September, he wrote to Rowohlt about the contract for his next novel and setting out his proposals for dealing with the monies owed to him in connection with *A Small Circus*. Rowohlt did not want to lose such a promising author, one whom he had begun to address in August 1931 as '*Lieber Meister Ditzen*', '*Meister*' in this context meaning 'master craftsman'. However, Rowohlt's hands were tied by the accountants who had been called in to oversee his business, so it took some weeks before he could offer Ditzen acceptable terms. Finally, they agreed that Rowohlt would pay Count von Hahn 2,000 marks immediately, that Ditzen would receive 200 marks salary for the months of September and October and leave Rowohlt's employment officially at the end of that month. Ditzen undertook furthermore to sign the contract for 'Pinneberg and His Shrimp' with Rowohlt's new company. The contract stipulated an advance of 1,500 marks, payable in six monthly instalments, and a submission date of 31 March 1932. Ditzen took two weeks' leave owing to him and, on 18 October 1931, he fulfilled the ambition of a lifetime by becoming a freelance writer. He was never to enter paid employment again.

5 1931–1933
Success

Reality is in no way contained in the more or less fortuitous sequence of observations that make up reportage, rather it resides exclusively in the mosaic which gathers together discrete observations by grasping their real meaning. Reportage photographs life, a mosaic of this kind produces a picture of it.

– Siegfried Kracauer[1]

Ditzen began his career as a full-time writer in October 1931 with 'Pinneberg and His Shrimp', the book which was to become *Little Man – What Now?* In the original outline of the novel, submitted to Rowohlt on 12 September, he planned a light-hearted piece which would portray the world of the 'little man', the petit bourgeois, and which would include a father-in-law who, thanks to his SPD connections, has landed himself an office job, a Communist brother-in-law and colleagues who join the Nazi party. The novel would expose the shortcomings of the Health Insurance Scheme (which Ditzen had experienced after Uli's birth and in connection with Suse's illness), depict the reality of unemployment and the housing shortage (topics with which Ditzen was familiar) and describe the social welfare system (which Ditzen knew from his friend Lore Soldin and her daughter Eva). In the course of writing, however, the focus of the novel changed. He explained in a letter to a reader: 'Perhaps I did once – at the very beginning – I really cannot remember now – want to write a novel about unemployment, but gradually and imperceptibly this book became a tribute to a woman.'[2] He wrote to another reader that 'this book is a mark of gratitude to a woman, a small part of a large feeling of gratitude.'[3] He told his mother, who had still not yet met Suse: '"What others can do, we can do, too" – this sentence of Lämmchen's in my new novel comes from my wife."[4]

There is no doubt that Ditzen's relationship with Suse Issel, their marriage and the birth of their son had a major influence on the final version of the novel. Suse began calling him *Junge* ('Sonny') in January 1929, shortly after their engagement, and he addressed her as *Schäfchen, schönes weisses Bählamm* ('Little sheep, lovely white baalamb') later the same month, terms of endearment which feature prominently in *Little Man – What Now?* Pinneberg's view of Lämmchen ('Lambkin') as a mother-figure is anticipated in Ditzen's letter to Suse Issel on 17 February 1929 when he declared: 'I want to be able to tell you everything for you are not only the woman whom I love but also my mother. And I am your child.'[5] As we have seen, Ditzen was extremely happy during the first three years of his marriage and was, understandably, grateful to his wife.

Lämmchen is the most attractive figure in the novel and the one who accounted largely for its success. She is totally devoted to her husband and son, full of compassion, practical and able to cope in every situation. It is Lämmchen's love and firm moral principles that support and sustain Johannes Pinneberg, the little man of the title. An indication of Lämmchen's popularity was the competition run by a Stuttgart newspaper in 1932 offering fifteen prizes for entries on the topic 'Your View of Lämmchen'. Perusal of the winning entries reveals the attractiveness of this character, who appealed not only to men's ideals of womanhood but also to women's desire to fulfil those ideals.

Ditzen himself encouraged the identification between Lämmchen and Suse, much to his wife's annoyance. In conversation in 1984 she described her husband's angry reaction when she criticized Lämmchen as an entirely unrealistic character and rejected any connection between herself and what one reviewer called 'a modern Madonna'.[6] However, she eventually acquiesced in what was to become an accepted view in Fallada research.

Little Man – What Now? is divided into a Prologue ('Blithe Spirits'),

Part One ('The Small Town'), Part Two ('Berlin') and an Epilogue ('Life Goes On'). The novel tells the tale of the accounts clerk Johannes Pinneberg and his girlfriend, the shop assistant Emma Morschel (known as Lämmchen) from the day they discover that Lämmchen is pregnant, through the ups and downs of married life, flat-hunting, the birth of a baby, job insecurity and, finally, long-term unemployment.

Ditzen's own experience of office work, and the insights he gained into the labour movement through his membership of the SPD, inform his portrayal of the gap between Pinneberg's aspirations and his income. The theme of the white-collar worker in a period of economic crisis is introduced in the Prologue when Pinneberg meets his father-in-law, who has nothing but contempt for non-unionized labour: 'Because you do unpaid overtime, because you take less than the agreed wage, because you never strike, because you're always the blacklegs.' Pinneberg replies indignantly: 'It's not just to do with money . . . We think differently from most working men. We have different needs.' This response is met with ridicule as Mr Morschel, referring to his daughter's pregnancy, comments: 'Not very nice, sir. And a very proletarian habit.' The exchange which follows between Lämmchen's Social Democratic father and Communist brother reflects the split in the international labour movement at the time and was familiar to Ditzen from his SPD days.

Johannes Pinneberg is a representative figure: 'He was one of millions. Ministers made speeches to him, enjoined him to tighten his belt, to make sacrifices, to feel German, to put his money in the savings-bank and to vote for the constitutional party.' The Pinnebergs discuss politics. They consider voting Communist but cannot bring themselves to do so in the end. Faced – like 6 million others in 1932 – with the question of unemployment, Pinneberg's response is to retreat into the bosom of his family. And so the novel, which begins with a trenchant critique of German political and economic life in 1930 and charts Pinneberg's transformation from a respectable office worker to a social outcast, symbolized in the discarding of his starched white collar, concludes with a romantic idyll in which Pinneberg seeks refuge from a cruel world with Lämmchen and their son.

The ending of the novel, which borders on the sentimental, is based on Ditzen's concept of *Anständigkeit* ('decency'). He wrote to one of his readers: 'What we need and what we will eventually achieve, is – above and beyond all parties and ideologies – a Front of "decent people" [*Anständigen*], a Front of people who think in a humane way.'[7] He took the view: ... 'that it helps a little to say to people: act decently towards each other ... I think, for example, that the clerk in the Health Insurance office who deals with my Pinneberg and who has read the book will be just a little bit nicer to him.'[8] It is Lämmchen who embodies this ideal in the novel. It is she who insists that Pinneberg does not join the other unemployed men on their wood-stealing expeditions and that he accept only legitimate employment.

Ditzen's solution to the question 'What now?' in 1932 was therefore a private, individual one. The fact that he considered other endings to the novel is shown by the short story '*Fröhlichkeit und Traurigkeit*' ('Happiness and Sadness'), published on 2 February 1932 in the *Frankfurter Zeitung*. Here, the protagonist, unlike Pinneberg, joins the wood-stealing expeditions; he also befriends a prostitute on one of his weekly visits to the employment exchange; he brings her home in the naive desire to show her his family, and his wife makes her coffee and gives her five marks. Such an ending would have required a very different novel, for stealing and any kind of relations with prostitutes, however innocent, were not in keeping with Pinneberg's character.

Ditzen made good progress with his novel, which he wrote by hand and then typed; he was able to deliver the first part to Rowohlt in person on 16 November 1931. His other reason for calling into Passauer Strasse was to attempt to retrieve his social insurance, tax and other documents from Rowohlt's rather chaotic bureaucracy.

Working at home brought a change in routine: Ditzen still rose early and worked for an hour or so on his correspondence before waking Suse and Uli at 7 a.m. After breakfast, their daily help arrived and Ditzen took his son for a long walk and played with him until around eleven thirty. He spent the rest of the morning on book reviews and other routine matters. Dinner was at twelve thirty, followed by a rest. He devoted the time between afternoon tea and supper mostly to Uli and, from 8 p.m., with Uli in bed, worked on his novel for three to four hours.

October 1931 also marked a change in fortune for Adolf Hitler. After meeting President Hindenburg for the first time on the tenth, he took part in the foundation of the Harzburg Front on 11 and 12 October. This was a further development of the 'national opposition', which brought right-wing and nationalist political parties together with representatives of industry, the banks, the Junker and the military. The Harzburg Front declared itself determined 'to preserve our country from the chaos of Bolshevism, to rescue our political life from the whirlpool of economic bankruptcy by means of effective self-help', and willing 'to assume responsibility through nationally led governments in Prussia and the Reich'.

The members of the Harzburg Front demanded national sovereignty in military affairs and the right to rearm, promised to support every individual and group 'who answered the call of the German nation' and refused 'to shed one drop of blood in support of the current government and the current ruling system'. They appealed to President Hindenburg to appoint 'a truly national government' which would 'bring about a change of course to remedy the situation'.[9] In other words, they wanted the president to use his powers to install a right-wing nationalist government. Ditzen, who learned about the effects of nationalism in Italy through his Aunt Ada, concluded that 'the apparent affluence and prestige which Mussolini has brought to that country is costing the people of Italy dear, especially those who do not belong to the wealth-owning classes.'[10]

On 23 November, a week after receiving Ditzen's manuscript, Paul Mayer responded enthusiastically to what was now called 'The Little Man'. As Ditzen was gradually establishing himself as a writer, those forces were gathering strength which would make literature, especially the socio-critical, humanist literature he was developing, a hazardous occupation. On the same day that Mayer conveyed his enthusiasm about 'The Little Man' to Ditzen, Carl von Ossietzky, editor of *Die Weltbühne*, was sentenced to eighteen months' imprisonment for revealing Germany's secret rearmament in violation of the Treaty of Versailles.

Ditzen's research for 'The Little Man' took him to the local employment exchange, where he was shocked at what he learned: '. . . it's appalling, the husband of our daily help gets 16 marks 50 a week for himself, his wife and their two children. They do not mention the fact that she works for us, because then they would get even less.'[11] Although Ditzen counted himself very fortunate as he watched a number of their neighbours moving out of Neuenhagen into cheaper accommodation, he was aware that his own future was only secure until the end of March 1932. He therefore agreed to every request for short stories, articles and book reviews. In the last week of November alone, he had some fifteen to twenty reviews to write. The pressure of work and the sheer difficulty of working in a two-bedroom terraced house with a teething child all became too much, and he took himself off to the Baltic island of Hiddensee for two weeks at the beginning of December. There he was able to take long walks in the fresh air and work on his novel without any distractions. He returned on 17 December with 150 pages in his briefcase.

Sales of *A Small Circus* had continued slowly but steadily and were now approaching five thousand, which meant that Ditzen could soon expect royalties. He was hopeful that, when the first edition (i.e. six thousand copies) was sold, he would be able to negotiate a new contract with Rowohlt's new company.

The Ditzens spent a quiet Christmas in Neuenhagen. Their daily help and her family came on Christmas Eve; Lore and Eva Soldin visited them on 27 December. Ditzen received three Feuchtwanger novels, and Suse a gardening book as well as *Jettchen Gebert*, a popular novel by Georg Herrmann about Jewish life in old Berlin which 'Kai Goedeschal' had once recommended to 'Ilse Lorenz'.

Now that he was working at home full time, Ditzen needed a room to himself, which was impossible in the house in Neuenhagen. They began to consider moving to somewhere bigger, 'if Pinneberg turns out to be a success'.[12]

Work on 'The Little Man' was interrupted in January 1932 by a visitor with an attractive proposal: a Herr Falkenheim from Bavaria, who thought, 'like most Berliners that there will be a revolution in February or March and probably very bloody clashes between National Socialists and Communists',[13] wanted to invest his money in a large farm, and offered Ditzen the position of farm manager. Rudolf found much to recommend this project: it would guarantee food and shelter, and it would mean that he would not be entirely dependent on writing. This was important, because he reckoned that 'if the Nazis come to power, the newspapers I write for will be finished and I will have no income.'[14] Furthermore, the offer was a means of fulfilling his dream of becoming a farmer.

As Kagelmacher was staying in Neuenhagen at the time, Ditzen sent him out to view likely properties. This erstwhile farmer, however, was so engrossed in his mysticism and astrology that he was incapable of carrying out what should have been for him a rather simple task. Ditzen concluded 'with regret that he is in certain respects mentally ill',[15] and went himself to look at farms for sale in Mecklenburg, where he discovered that only farmers, and not businessmen like Falkenheim, were allowed to purchase them. Falkenheim subsequently found a suitable farm in Bavaria; however, Ditzen was not interested in moving so far away.

Falkenheim's fears were not without foundation. The forces of the 'national opposition' continued to gather momentum in the course of 1932. On 27 January, Hitler was invited to address a three hundred-strong audience in Düsseldorf's Industrieclub. In his speech, he stressed his commitment to private property, his belief in the superiority of the white race and concluded: 'I see two diametrically opposed principles: the principle of democracy, which in its practical implications is the principle of destruction, and the principle of the authority of the personality, which I would term the principle of achievement.[16]

These were the ideas that appealed to the 'little men in a society that crushed them between the rock of big business on one side and the hard place of rising mass labour movements on the other. Or which, at the very least, deprived them of the respectable position they had occupied in the social order, and believed to be their due, or the social status in a dynamic society to which they felt they had a right to aspire.'[17] Siegfried Kracauer's study *Die Angestellten* ('The Salaried Employees') of 1930 had analysed the position of this new sub-class of white-collar workers whose ranks had swollen as a result of industrialization and the introduction of American business methods in the post-war period. Kracauer summed up their position in the following terms: 'The mass of white-collar workers differs from the industrial proletariat in that they are spiritually and politically homeless. They cannot identify with their proletarian comrades and the bedrock of bourgeois feelings and ideas on which they had constructed their world has collapsed as a result of economic developments which have shattered its foundations.'[18] Ernst Bloch, reviewing Kracauer, identified this section of the petit bourgeoisie as a potential breeding-ground for fascism.[19] In 'The Little Man', Ditzen had chosen a topic which touched the nerve of the age.

He sent the second part of the manuscript to Paul Mayer on 11 February and submitted the finished book some ten days ahead of schedule. The plot owes much to Ditzen's experience of office work, marriage, parenthood and unemployment. However, he himself cautioned against too close a biographical interpretation: 'Of course . . . my own recollections often provide the raw material, but everything always turns out differently than in reality. Suse says that everything could almost be true but that nothing is.'[20]

As soon as he had completed 'The Little Man', Ditzen, despite another abscess on his gum, turned to work on a radio play, *Der Klatsch* ('Gossip'), which he co-authored with Heinz Dietrich Kenter, his collaborator on the dramatization of *A Small Circus*. He also agreed to work on a manuscript he received from Hans-Joachim Geyer, an old friend from his days in Radach who had fallen on hard times. He continued to write short stories, some eighteen of which appeared in the course of 1932. One of these, '*Die geistesgegenwärtige Großmutter*' ('The Alert Grandmother'), which appeared in the *B.-Z.-am-Mittag* in August, was based on an incident in the life of his maternal grandmother, Charlotte Lorenz, who had died in January 1932 at the age of ninety-three. Reviewing books also attracted the bibliophile in Ditzen, for each review added another volume to his rapidly increasing library. One review he wrote in 1932 was of *Frauen* by Dr Else Kienle, who had been imprisoned for breaking the abortion law, had gone on hunger strike in defence of her beliefs and was subsequently released. Although critical of some aspects of her feminism, he admired her commitment and her conviction '. . . that this world must be changed. It must be. And if we come to this realization (and then fight for it), it does not really matter how we come to it. As long as we fight for it.'

Ditzen also admired Erich Kästner, whose work he reviewed in an essay in *Die Literatur* in April 1932. He viewed Kästner as a man 'who gives tens of thousands of people the courage to keep going in a humane way . . . What he gives his readers is a slice of their daily lives: exact, sober, without any illusions . . . And also a guiding principle: if you're having a tough time, don't give other people a tough time. Let everyone do what they can.' He summarized the moral of Kästner's stories as follows: 'be decent [*anständig*] to each other, help each other, through thick and thin.' He particularly liked Kästner's *Fabian* (1931), which tells the story of an outsider who rejects the society he lives in and – a non-swimmer – dies in an attempt to save a drowning child. As we have seen, the concept of *Anständigkeit* plays a large role in *Little Man – What Now?* Ditzen's response to the problems of his times was, like Kästner's, one of individual morality.

One day during the last week in March, Ditzen and his wife called into Rowohlt's office after a shopping expedition in Berlin to enquire about the progress of 'The Little Man'. One matter still to be finalized was the title. Peter Zingler, who dealt with foreign publishers and placing the work of Rowohlt authors with magazines, newspapers and journals, joined in the discussion, and it was he and Suse who simultaneously hit on the idea of adding 'What Now?' to 'Little Man'. So the new title was born.

On this occasion, Ditzen pressed Rowohlt yet again to pay Count von Hahn the money promised over a year previously, which Rowohlt, as usual, promised to do. They all spent such an enjoyable evening together that the Ditzens missed the last train and had to take a taxi home to Neuenhagen.

On 8 April, Ditzen received a telegram from Rowohlt with the good news that the prestigious *Voßische Zeitung* had been signed up for the serialization of *Little Man – What Now?* Even more important to Ditzen than the prestige was the fee of 2,000 marks. This meant he could afford to have the gum abscess which had been plaguing him since the middle of March treated. The family could also afford its first summer holiday and begin to think about moving house.

On the eighteenth of that month, the Ditzens were in Berlin again and Rowohlt invited them, with Mayer, Zingler and Hessel, 'to a merry little gathering to "wet the novel's head"'. He assured Ditzen that they would be able to catch the last train home and would not have to incur the expense of a taxi 'which might upset your wife'.

Rowohlt's capacity for food and drink was legendary. Ernst von Salomon described Rowohlt's drinking habits: 'Rowohlt enjoyed drinking and drank a lot without ever being a drinker. Even if he had drunk the night away, he would stagger into a cold shower, emerge completely fresh and sober and appear at his desk at 8 o'clock in the morning. None of his colleagues ever knew him to arrive late or in a drunken state.[21] Rowohlt was therefore not the ideal companion for a man with a history of alcoholism like Ditzen. Since giving up his job with Rowohlt in October, Ditzen would drop into the office around the middle of each month to pick up his fees, discuss his current projects and then spend the evening with his former colleagues. The fact that Suse began accompanying him on these trips in March suggests that she was concerned about his drinking. She had, of course, other reasons, too. Having just finished correcting the manuscript of *Little Man – What Now?*, she was naturally interested in its fate. She was also in charge of the household accounts and therefore needed to keep track of income and expenditure.

Apart from the temptations of city life, Berlin became an increasingly uncongenial place in the course of 1932. In the presidential election in April, Hitler, an Austrian who had speedily acquired German citizenship, attracted 37 per cent of the vote. In the elections for the Prussian regional parliament a fortnight later, the National Socialist Party vote rose from half a million in 1928 to 8 million, making it the single largest party in Germany's biggest and most important state. The Ditzens therefore had a number of personal and political reasons for wanting to move house farther away from the capital. They were attracted to the lakeland and forests east of Berlin where Rowohlt lived, and used a visit there on 23 April to view possible properties. Ditzen also began negotiations on the contract for his prison novel. This developed into a general contract covering all his literary production and guaranteed him a measure of security to the

end of 1932 and, if *Little Man – What Now?* sold well, for the following two years.

Ditzen finished work on 'Gossip' in April, and it was broadcast on
2 May. He was rather disappointed with the outcome; his manuscript
had been considerably abridged and the critical response was mixed.
By the beginning of May he was feeling in need of a holiday; he had
been working since Christmas without a break and the long course of
dental treatment had been painful and wearing. In a letter to his parents on 5 May he expressed his 'feeling that things can't go on like this
much longer without me collapsing'.

Suse and Uli left on 12 May to spend two weeks with Suse's mother
in Hamburg and Ditzen wrote to Rowohlt five days later: 'It will do
me good to lead an ordered life for the next while – I've been having
some problems with my heart.' Rowohlt replied by return of post,
inviting him over the next weekend and promising him that there
would be no alcohol – another indication that Ditzen's drink problem
had resurfaced. By the time Rowohlt's invitation reached Neuenhagen, however, Ditzen had already left for Hamburg, where he joined
Suse and Uli for the remainder of their stay. He asked Rowohlt not to
contact him unless he had good news: 'I don't feel much like work at
the moment, I'm rather down.' Again, Rowohlt replied by return of
post, assuring him that his literary and financial prospects were good
and that he had no reason to be depressed. Ditzen wrote back that his
depression had nothing to do with literature or finance: 'It seems as if
happiness always has a swollen cheek: if it smiles on one side of its
face, the other side is twisted'[22] – an allusion perhaps not just to his
dental but also to his drinking problems. The political situation gave
little cause for rejoicing either. May 1932 witnessed the enforced resignation of both the Minister of Defence, General Groener, the only
senior member of the army wholeheartedly loyal to the Weimar
Republic, and Heinrich Brüning, the last chancellor committed to parliamentary democracy.

The Ditzens had now organized a long summer holiday on the Baltic coast and hoped to be able to leave Neuenhagen by 4 or 6 June.
They had booked accommodation in a guest house in Kölpinsee on
the island of Usedom recommended by Rowohlt, who had recently

stayed there with Seyerlen. Ditzen planned to clear his desk so that he could go on holiday and have a complete break. However, an appointment with Erich Engel of the Ufa film company on 2 June led to negotiations about filming *Little Man – What Now?*, which was already arousing interest in the *Voßische Zeitung*. This delayed the Ditzens' departure until the thirteenth, by which time a film contract had been signed and detailed discussions on the filmscript had been concluded. Ditzen agreed to submit an outline filmscript within a week and took it with him on holiday. Also in his briefcase was Geyer's novel, which he had promised to revise, as well as a veritable avalanche of letters from enthusiastic readers of the *Little Man – What Now?* serialization, each of which he insisted on answering individually (despite Rowohlt's advice to the contrary).

By now it was becoming clear that *Little Man – What Now?* was going to be a huge success: the predicament of the white-collar worker and the impoverishment of the middle class were topics with which many Germans could identify in 1932. The story of the Pinnebergs' romance, their marriage and the birth of their first child had a universal appeal. In addition, Ditzen's narrative style, with its well-observed dialogue and sympathetic narrator made the book immediately and widely accessible. Using the technique he first employed in 'Anton and Gerda', Ditzen opens the story with a description of an everyday situation: a young man waits impatiently for his girlfriend, who is late for their date. The novel contains many such episodes: Pinneberg's embarrassment when he asks the gynaecologist for advice on contraception, Lämmchen's failures in the kitchen in the early days of their marriage, Pinneberg's terror of losing his job at the end of each month, the heavily pregnant Lämmchen's flat-hunting, Pinneberg's feelings when Lämmchen goes into labour, the Shrimp's first tooth, to mention but a few. The success of the novel's serialization was a foretaste of things to come.

Rowohlt provided Ditzen with a typist, Dora Isbrandt, to accompany him and his family to Kölpinsee. Hardly had they arrived at Frau Voß's guest house than the two-year-old Uli fell ill with a lung infection and was admitted on 16 June to Swinemünde hospital, where he underwent treatment for three weeks.

Little Man – What Now? was launched on 18 June 1932, as the number of 'little men' was increasing by the day. President Hindenburg had appointed Franz von Papen, a right-wing member of the Prussian parliament but not of the Reichstag, to replace Brüning as chancellor. Papen proceeded to dissolve the Reichstag on 4 June and the Prussian parliament, the last outpost of Weimar democracy, on 14 June. He introduced an economic programme which cut unemployment benefit by 23 per cent and other welfare benefits by between 15 per cent and 25 per cent and imposed an additional crisis tax. These measures led to mounting unrest in the cities and street battles which left 183 people dead by the beginning of August. Kölpinsee, with its beach, sea, lakes and woods was a good place to spend the summer of 1932.

Ditzen sent off the outline filmscript on 14 June and started work on the first half of Geyer's novel, which he dispatched to Rowohlt on the twenty-fourth. Dora Isbrandt then returned to Berlin, no longer merely a typist but a firm family friend known as 'Tante Huschbahn' as a result of Uli's unsuccessful attempts to pronounce her name.

Rowohlt's optimism about the success of *Little Man – What Now?* was confirmed as sales boomed and one positive review appeared after another. Hermann Hesse and Carl Zuckmayer declared it their favourite book of 1932. For Lion Feuchtwanger it came second only to Joseph Roth's *Radetzkymarsch*.

Peter Suhrkamp declared Lämmchen 'a completely new literary figure',[23] while Hans Reimann of the Munich journal *Die Volkswirte* saw her as a worthy successor to Gretchen in Goethe's *Faust*. The novelist Clara Viebig, on the other hand, took the view that Lämmchen was 'no poetic and ethereal Gretchen'.[24]

The very few dissenting voices came from the extremes of the political spectrum. The *Hamburger Tageblatt* criticized the novel from a Nazi point of view, attributing the love scenes to Jewish influence and rejecting the portrayal of the SA in the figure of Lauterbach. The Communist *Rote Fahne*, on the other hand, while acknowledging the realism of the novel, criticized the novelist for providing no answer to the question 'What now?'

Ditzen himself commented in a letter to his parents: 'The Nazis and Communists are both tearing my work to shreds. That will do no harm, for I don't want to write party-political books.'[25] By the end of June, over two thousand copies had been sold, much to Ditzen's bewilderment. He commented to Peter Zingler: 'I can't understand why, for *A Small Circus* is much better.'[26] Four months later, when the sales figures had topped twenty-one thousand, Ditzen still remained unconvinced of the novel's literary value and described it in a letter to Kagelmacher on 17 October as 'one of my weaker books'.

Zingler sent Ditzen the final film contract at the beginning of July. As he was already committed to this project, he agreed to complete it but, in view of his recent experience, he told Rowohlt that he wanted nothing more to do with stage versions, film versions, radio versions, essays, and so on: 'I'm a novelist, that's all!'

Now that Uli was discharged from hospital and the film project, worth between 5,000 and 6,000 marks, was secured, the Ditzens could relax: 'We are so very happy, we need not worry about being able to afford a bigger house; we can furnish it nicely, pay off the debts and, above all, prolong our summer holiday.'[27] A long summer holiday was very desirable. Ditzen was still not sleeping well, always an indication of health problems in his case, and his dental treatment was still not completed.

He wrote to Kagelmacher on 26 July to thank him for his birthday greetings and offered his old friend the prospect of coming to stay with them once they had moved house. He commented on the state of his marriage: 'You know how things are with Suse and me; we have our ups and downs, for I shall probably never be a really noble human being, but there is nothing seriously wrong and it is as lovely as ever and Suse makes everything easy, even the making amends for my stupid and thoughtless behaviour.' Although Suse had not completely recovered from the gynaecological problems following Uli's birth, they both felt it was time to have another baby, so Ditzen requested a prediction for 'Uli's sister' from Kagelmacher.

In the last week in July they visited nearby Zinnowitz, where Ditzen had spent his summer holiday as a five-year-old. Thirty-four years later, he was not impressed: 'Zinnowitz ... is dreadful, Nazis everywhere. The band played a song called "Anyone Approaching from Manasse's Tribe." No, not our scene at all.'[28]

The Nazis continued to grow in number and influence under Papen's chancellorship. On 20 July, he invoked Article 48 to declare a state of emergency in Berlin and had himself declared state commissioner for Prussia. In an action little short of a coup d'état, Papen removed the SPD premier of Prussia, the SPD chief of police in Berlin and many officials loyal to the Republic. His minister of defence, General Kurt von Schleicher, announced a 'restructuring of the army', which marked the official beginning of German rearmament. The Reichstag elections on 31 July 1932 saw the National Socialists returned as the largest party, with 37.4 per cent of the vote and 230 seats out of a total of 608. Papen invited Hitler to join his cabinet, but Hitler's conditions – that the Nazi Party should have the chancellorship, the Prussian premier's position, the ministries of the interior at national level and in Prussia – were considered unacceptable. It is not surprising that Ditzen considered leaving Germany at this point. He wrote to his parents on 25 July: 'I am a little afraid of the long dark winter; the book I am writing is also very melancholy, the times are miserable – I don't know if I want to remain here.' He appears to have had the offer of a house in the south of France and was attracted by the prospect of 'a bit of sunshine'. The house in question was probably Seyerlen's villa in St Jean-de-Luz, where Rowohlt often sent authors who needed a break. Ernst von Salomon, for example, had stayed there from June 1931 to October 1932. In the end, the Ditzens decided, however, not to take up the offer.

They spent August enjoying the Baltic summer, receiving visitors from Berlin and dispatching eels and other local delicacies to Rowohlt. Uli was in the care of a local girl, thirteen-year-old Lieschen Behn, who featured in Ditzen's short story 'Lieschen's Sieg' ('Lieschen Wins the Day'), which appeared in the Frankfurter Illustrierte on 28 July. Ditzen did some background reading for his prison novel and answered the mountain of post which the status of a best-selling novelist brings. That Little Man – What Now? was a best-seller was now no longer in doubt. Some 150 to 200 copies were sold every day, ten newspapers had bought the serialization rights, and translation rights had been negotiated with seven foreign publishers by the end of August. The only aspect of the book consistently criticized was the illustration of Lämmchen by Georg Grosz on the cover. Ditzen himself had suggested Grosz as a suitable illustrator and both Rowohlt and Ditzen were happy with Grosz's work. The major objection to his depiction of Lämmchen was that she was not pretty enough – a view which Rowohlt did not share: 'Whenever I think of Lämmchen taking care of the Shrimp I have in my mind's eye a picture just like Grosz's.'[29] Rowohlt suggested a compromise for the next print run: the cover would simply have the title on it and the Grosz illustration would appear on the dust-jacket, so that any one who did not like it could discard it. However, this proved impossible, because Rowohlt had lost Grosz's original. He therefore gave in to popular demand and commissioned a new cover from Walter Müller of Worpswede for the fifth edition of the novel. The Grosz story did not end there, however. Grosz had made a present of his original illustration to Ditzen, who was understandably upset to discover that Rowohlt had lost it. When he offered to make amends, Ditzen requested a drawing of Suse to be done by Grosz, whom they were both very fond of. This was one of the last commissions Grosz carried out before emigrating to the United States in January 1933.

The Ditzens returned to Neuenhagen at the end of August 1932. Ditzen had planned to spend September working on the filmscript for *Little Man – What Now?*, but the film company had got into difficulties and the project was postponed. By now fourteen thousand copies of the novel had been sold and Ditzen was inundated with requests from magazines and journals as well as from enthusiastic readers.

The question 'What now?' was becoming more acute at all levels in German society. Papen's response was to announce measures to revitalize the economy which included wage and salary reductions of up to 27 per cent as well as the abolition of collective bargaining. This unleashed a wave of strikes and, when the Reichstag refused to sanction Papen's proposals, he dissolved it and called elections on 6 November.

Ditzen continued work on his prison novel, which was now provisionally entitled '*Kippe oder Lampen*', an example of underworld slang which he 'translated' for his sister Elisabeth as 'share the loot or I'll grass on you'. On 16 September he made his regular trip into

Berlin, where, with Zingler and Rowohlt, he celebrated the continuing success of *Little Man – What Now?*, which had not only made Ditzen a rich man but had also given Rowohlt's business a much-needed boost.

By the end of September the Ditzens had found a new home in Berkenbrück on the river Spree, to the east of Rowohlt's house in Grünheide. There they had arranged to rent the first floor of a villa belonging to an elderly couple who had fallen on hard times and needed to let part of their house. Ditzen described their new landlord and landlady, the Sponars, as 'quite ordinary old people'. The new accommodation comprised two bedrooms, a bathroom, dining-room (with balcony overlooking the river), living-room, maid's room, kitchen and study. There was a separate entrance to the first floor, central heating, a jetty and a huge garden. They decided to employ a maid to do the housework so that Suse would have time for Uli and the garden, as well as typing Ditzen's manuscripts. They chose Hildegard Biedenweg, whom they had met in Kölpinsee. They also planned to have a phone installed so that Ditzen would not have to travel so often into Berlin. The removal date was set for 15 November.

The film project was reactivated in mid-October, which meant that Suse had to take charge of the preparations for the move. Ditzen, furthermore, had a recurrence of his dental trouble, which meant another extraction and a few days' bed-rest at the end of the month. By 19 November, however, he was able to write to Zingler from his new home: 'The sun is shining today and when I look up from my typewriter I can see two arms of the River Spree, boats passing noiselessly by and forest, forest ...' The Reichstag elections of 6 November brought losses for the Nazis and Social Democrats and slight gains for the Communists. The resultant deadlock led to Papen's resignation on 17 November, followed by a period of negotiations about the appointment of a new chancellor. Ditzen felt that the outcome of the election was partly to blame for the decrease in the sales of *Little Man – What Now?* Rowohlt initiated a new advertising campaign in a bid to push sales up to thirty thousand by Christmas. Ditzen was not so optimistic in view of the widespread unrest, but commented that 'Herr von Papen's return [might help] to restore order.' Rowohlt responded wryly,

'Don't mention Papen in case he turns up again, for God's sake. I much prefer Schleicher. At least he doesn't look as thick and stupid as Papen.' In fact, Hindenburg offered the chancellorship once more to Hitler, who, once more, declined to accept when his conditions were not met. On 2 December, Schleicher was appointed instead.

Ditzen was fully aware of his good luck in his personal and professional life and did not forget the widespread misery around him. He sent money regularly to Kagelmacher and to his sister Elisabeth Hörig, whose health was beginning to suffer as a result of her husband's unemployment. At the end of 1931, he had even proposed co-authoring a science-fiction novel with the Hörigs, who were both unemployed scientists. He also tried to help Geyer to have his manuscript published and recommended other would-be writers to Rowohlt. On 3 December, he asked Zingler to assist a Herr Bösser, 'who's down on his luck' and who wanted some material on the serialization of Ditzen's novels for an article in an SPD journal.

The weekend Schleicher was appointed chancellor, the Ditzens had a house full of guests in Berkenbrück. Lore Soldin, Peter and Joie Zingler, Ernst Rowohlt and his fiancée, Elli Engelhardt, as well as some press photographers, came to inspect their new home and were suitably impressed. While the rent was 20 marks a month more than the house in Neuenhagen, they had much more room and were well over an hour's journey away from Berlin, in the heart of the countryside. Towards the end of December, the Sponars, whom Ditzen described as 'genuinely good people', agreed to lease the entire garden, an area of 8,000 square metres, to the Ditzens for a period of three years. Now they could grow their own fruit and vegetables and become more self-sufficient, a great relief in troubled times.

At last Ditzen could afford a house in the country. For the first time, he had a study of his own, overlooking the river and the forest. Suse, now expecting their second child, could indulge her love of gardening. Their new maid, Marie Wendland, was a great improvement on her predecessor, whom they had sacked at the end of the year. She was particularly good with Uli, who missed his friends in Neuenhagen but enjoyed the walks with his father in the forest. There were also indications that the Ditzen family were preparing to welcome back their black sheep: Ditzen's sister Margarete had announced her intention to visit Berkenbrück in February 1933 and a visit was planned to the Hörigs in Braunschweig in the New Year. Rudolf now no longer needed an allowance from his parents and was in a position to repay all his debts.

There were, however, some indications that all was not well with him. Although he had earned over 12,000 marks in 1932, he had also spent large sums of money. Rowohlt was concerned enough about his author's apparent profligacy to urge him to 'keep the good old lolly together' ('*die liebe, gute Pinke zusammenhalten*'). Ditzen also requested his January payment from Rowohlt in cash, which suggests that none of it was destined for the bank account in his wife's name. That he was drinking again is evident from a sentence in Rowohlt's letter of 20 December in which he hopes that Ditzen 'has recovered from Tuesday evening'. The frequent moves, the insecurity, the overwork, the sudden fame and fortune, the political instability all around, were beginning to take their toll.

Ditzen continued to write short stories but was fairly dismissive of their literary merit because they 'are written in a rush, on demand and without much enthusiasm'.[30] In January 1933, he was able to turn his attention again to '*Kippe oder Lampen*'. By writing this novel from the point of view of a released prisoner, he wanted 'to improve the situation of these unfortunate human beings, 90 per cent of whom revert to crime'.[31] The submission date had been set for 1 October 1933 to give him plenty of time and to avoid the last-minute rush of the previous two novels.

Although Ditzen had withdrawn from Berlin, he could not escape the turmoil which resulted in Schleicher's resignation and the appointment of Hitler as chancellor on 30 January. The battles inside the Writers' Union had resulted in a flood of protest mail from the group that had been on the losing side and letters of justification from the right-wing group that had taken control. Ditzen, irritated by this conflict, parted from the organization. In his letter of resignation he expressed his dismay at 'the way in which the opposition has been excluded'.[32]

His general irritation is evident in his refusal to accept any invitations to give lectures and readings; the only exception he made was the radio, 'where I don't need to show myself to the gawking and admiring crowd'. He had to remind Rowohlt once again, in a letter bristling with indignation on 22 January, of his promise to repay his debts to Count von Hahn. Then someone told him that she had searched six bookshops in vain for a copy of *Little Man – What Now?*, which led to another irritated exchange with his publisher.

On 23 January, the filming of *Little Man – What Now?* began and Ditzen moved to Berlin to fulfil his commitment to be involved. The Europa film company, which had now acquired the rights, had assembled a prestigious team for what Kurt Weill, who had been engaged as composer, described as a 'big-budget, first-class movie'.[33] Berthold Viertel arrived in Berlin on 31 January to direct, and Caspar Neher, who had collaborated with Brecht and Weill on *The Threepenny Opera*, *Happy End* and *Mahagonny*, was employed to design the sets. Ditzen wrote positively about his work in 'the very nice collective'. The collaboration, however, was to be short-lived.

The new regime, which had dissolved the Reichstag and called elections for 5 March, was using every means available to remove opposition. Heinrich Mann was forced to resign the chairmanship of the literary section of the Prussian Academy of Arts on 15 February after signing 'An Urgent Appeal' for unity between Social Democrats and Communists. Alfred Kerr, President of the German PEN (Poets, Essayists and Novelists) Centre, fled to Czechoslovakia on the same day. Viertel and Weill were Jews, and Ditzen cannot but have been aware of the tensions in the air.

The pressures of the film studio, in addition to the atmosphere of intimidation and uncertainty in Berlin, did little to improve Ditzen's already irritable state. Suse, whose second pregnancy was proving more difficult than her first, was dividing her time between Berkenbrück and Berlin in an effort to support her husband and keep his drinking within limits. His sister Margarete saw him for an evening in Berlin on her way to Berkenbrück in February and he felt it necessary to apologize to her afterwards for his behaviour. Otherwise, her visit was a huge success and she congratulated him on Suse, whom she described as 'the most splendid woman I have ever met'.

Other sources of irritation were the blurb for the English edition of *Little Man – What Now?* and the derisory fee for an article in *Die Literatur*. However, much more serious dangers were looming. The Ditzens and Rowohlts were having an evening out in one of Berlin's premier wine bars on 27 February when the news arrived that the Reichstag building was burning. The two women managed to persuade their husbands not to go and view the spectacle and got them safely home. The Reichstag fire was used as a pretext to round up and intern opponents of the new regime and pass the draconian Decree for the Protection of the People and the State which suspended the freedom of the press, and legalized internment, the interception of mail, telephone tapping and house searches, as well as introducing the death penalty for acts of sabotage. The state governments were replaced by *Statthalter*, governors appointed by the Nazi minister of the interior. Eighty-three Communist MPs were arrested and interned. Ditzen, who was neither a Communist nor an outspoken opponent of the new government, was not directly affected. Among the intellectuals who managed to escape after the Reichstag fire were Berthold Viertel and Kurt Weill.[34] The scriptwriter Fritz Wendhausen took over directing the film.

With the support of Rowohlt and a good solicitor, Ditzen managed to extricate himself from the film project on 4 March, leave Berlin, 'which is full of panic rumours', and return to the peace of Berkenbrück. From here, he wrote reassuringly to his parents on 6 March that 'the new government has no adverse effects for me.'

The same could not be said for Käthe Kollwitz, Ernst Barlach and Ricarda Huch, who were forced out of the Prussian Academy of the Arts at the beginning of March. Again, Ditzen held no public office, so the witch hunt against opponents of the Nazi Party in prominent public positions did not affect him personally.

The National Socialists obtained 43.9 per cent of the vote in the March elections, which, with the imprisonment and exile of many opposition MPs, was enough to secure a majority. They celebrated their greatest electoral triumph by passing the Enabling Law of 23 March, which made both parliament and the presidency largely irrelevant. The process of *Gleichschaltung* ('enforced integration') had begun.

Back in Berkenbrück, Ditzen settled down to working on his novel and refused all requests for short stories and articles. His decision to 'reduce these trips into Berlin to an absolute minimum' is indicative of an attempt to avoid anything that might upset his fragile equilibrium. And yet, a Robinson-like existence was difficult to sustain. The SA, enlisted by Göring as an unofficial Nazi police force, raided the offices of the *Neue Leipziger Zeitung*, a newspaper which numbered Ditzen among its contributors, in early March. Ditzen received a final demand from Count von Hahn in the third week in March, which resulted in another indignant letter to Rowohlt, who, on this occasion, could prove that payment had in fact been made.

One piece of good news on the business front was the continued success of *Little Man – What Now?* By the beginning of March 1933 over forty-two thousand copies had been sold in Germany. Later in the month, it appeared in London, published by Putnam. The reviews in England were very positive, with the *Manchester Guardian* praising the novel's 'unsentimental realism' and *The Times Literary Supplement* describing it as 'a formidable picture'. Its success can be gauged by the fact that Putnam reprinted it four times before the end of the year.

In Germany, the Nazi terror continued unabated. On 30 March, the new regime announced 'The Instructions of the National Socialist Party Leadership on the Introduction of Anti-Semitic Measures' which came into effect on 1 April. Victor Klemperer, Professor of French at the University of Dresden, compared the atmosphere to that 'before a pogrom in the darkest Middle Ages or in deepest Tsarist Russia'.[35] Ditzen was not a Jew and, although he was no doubt concerned for his Jewish friends – Lore Soldin, Paul Mayer and Franz Hessel – he was not personally affected by the campaign against the Jews.

Rowohlt, who had published many Jewish authors, began to make arrangements for them, and his Jewish friends, as well as others at risk, to leave Germany. His son, Heinrich Maria Ledig (-Rowohlt), who had taken over Ditzen's job in the company, used his contacts at the American embassy, particularly the ambassador's daughter, Martha Dodd, to secure US visas. Rowohlt increasingly conducted his business from his home in Grünheide. The Ditzens, too, often had visitors at the weekends who were anxious to escape the turmoil in the city.

The measures against the Jews were followed on 7 April by a law which aimed to purge the civil and public service of 'non-Aryan' and politically 'unreliable' elements. Again, Ditzen was not a public employee, so this did not affect him.

By early April, he seemed to have put the upsets of January and February behind him. As a result of the success of *Little Man – What Now?* he negotiated a new contract with Rowohlt which gave him 28,000 marks immediately and the promise of another 12,000 on 1 July, in addition to his regular monthly payment of 500 marks. At last, he could realize his dream and buy a farm. By now, however, his priorities had changed. The success of *Little Man – What Now?* had confirmed him in his desire to be a writer and not primarily a farmer. There did not seem to be much point in purchasing a farm if it meant employing someone else to run it. After much consideration he decided to make the Sponars an offer for their house and land. They agreed that Ditzen would take over their debts, acquire the property and allow them to live rent-free in part of the ground floor for the rest of their days. This appeared a good deal all round, and Ditzen had all the legal papers drawn up. By 8 April, he had paid off the largest debt on the property, amounting to 15,000 marks, and was now living rent free. The Ditzens were looking forward to spending Easter with their friends in their own house; their money worries were over, their future secure.

This idyll was shattered on 12 April, the Wednesday before Easter, by the arrival of the SA, accompanied by a regular policeman, who searched the house for three hours, in vain, for evidence of anti-government activity. Ditzen had been denounced as a conspirator against Hitler and, although the search produced nothing, he was taken off to prison in the nearby town of Fürstenwalde. In addition, the telephone line had been cut and an SA guard was posted on the door. Ditzen, assuming that this was a mistake of some sort and that he would soon be released, took neither money nor change of clothes with him.

Prison held no terrors for Ditzen, and he soon cleaned his cell and settled in. As he was only being held for questioning, he was able to buy his own food and tobacco, and the guards allowed him to join two Jewish prisoners for card games. However, as time wore on, he became aware of the legal limbo he was in: he was allowed no visitors, not even his solicitor, and was only permitted to write one letter a day.

On 18 April, Suse managed to visit him – in his *In meinem fremden Land. Gefängnistagebuch* 1944 ('In My Foreign Country. 1944 Prison Memoirs') he speculates that the guards took pity on the pregnant woman with the small boy at her side and notes that, in the spring of 1933, qualities such as decency and personal courage had not yet been eradicated in German society.[36] Suse was able to tell him the reason for his imprisonment: the Sponars, members of the Nazi Party, had denounced him.

Ernst von Salomon, who had been arrested on the same day as Ditzen, discovered the background to the denunciation from a former comrade-in-arms who was now a police officer in the notorious police station on Alexanderplatz, where von Salomon had been taken for questioning. Von Salomon had visited the Ditzens in Berkenbrück on 7 April and Ditzen had described him to their housemaid as a rather peculiar fellow and political assassin. She had conveyed this in all innocence to the Sponars, who immediately assumed that Adolf Hitler was the target of an assassination plot. They seized this opportunity to repossess their house which, thanks to Ditzen, was now no longer mortgaged to the hilt.

This incident revealed the true nature of what the new regime liked to call a 'national awakening' which, by suspending the rule of law, encouraged Nazi Party members at all levels to give free rein to their impulses of cruelty, envy and revenge in the certain knowledge that the normal sanctions of civilized society did not apply. It also indicated that the tentacles of the Nazi Party stretched into every village and hamlet in Germany. 'What now?' was becoming an increasingly urgent question.

On 19 April, Ditzen received the good news that the American Book of the Month Club had announced *Little Man – What Now?* as its choice for June 1933, and the next day he (re)commenced work on '*Kippe oder Lampen*', a novel which he had originally conceived in

1925 after his first spell in prison. Now, eight years later and in prison again, he returned to the tale of Willi Kufalt.

Meanwhile, Rowohlt had become worried about his best-selling author, whom he had not been able to contact over the Easter weekend, and when he discovered what had happened, he engaged one of the leading lawyers of the day, Dr Alfons Sack, who had the added advantage of being in favour with the new government. Thanks to Sack's intervention, Ditzen was released on Saturday 22 April.

As soon as he arrived back in Berkenbrück that evening, Ditzen sat down and wrote a letter to the Sponars, giving them notice to quit. 'I left the letter for them on the hall table and took a bath, in which I bathed my body in hot water and my soul in hot feelings of revenge.'[37] Next morning, as he was writing to his sister Elisabeth, outlining their plans to go on holiday until the Sponars had moved out and they could take possession of the house which was rightfully theirs, he had a second visit from the SA. This time, they told him that he had forfeited all rights to the house and that he and his family must leave immediately. When Ditzen protested, he was told that failure to comply would result in his being arrested again. The Ditzens reluctantly packed up and set out for the guest house where they normally stayed in Berlin, the Pension Stössinger at 48 Lietzenburger Strasse in Wilmersdorf, not far from Rowohlt's office in Passauer Strasse. Ditzen was incensed and immediately sought legal advice.

It came as a profound shock to him to discover that the new regime did not share his concept of legality; Dr Sack had some difficulty in persuading him that his return to Berkenbrück was completely out of the question. To a son of the judiciary, the injustice of what had happened was bad enough; the lack of redress was even worse. The stresses and strains of the previous months added to Ditzen's distress and plunged him into a nervous breakdown.

He was therefore oblivious to the attempt by the Nazi Party to take over the May Day celebrations and the move on 2 May to disband the trade unions, occupy their offices, impound their equipment and drag off their officials to prisons and camps. Ditzen was not involved in the trade union movement and had considered it judicious

to leave the white-collar workers' organization, the Deutsche Angestellten Gewerkschaft, heavily criticized in *Little Man – What
Now?*, before the publication of the novel. The official campaign
against the trade unions had thus no immediate implications for him.

He did manage to rouse himself on 3 May to write a letter to Robert Neppach, the producer of *Little Man – What Now?*, in which he
described the screenplay as 'horrific' and took delight in telling Neppach 'the truth' about the film. A quick intervention by Zingler was
sufficient to repair the damage.

Suse was anxious to get Ditzen out of Berlin; despite problems
caused by her pregnancy, she went on 4 May to see a house on the
Fünf-Eichen estate near Neubrandenburg which they had been offered
for the summer. Fünf-Eichen was later to become a German prisoner-
of-war camp and, in 1945, a Soviet internment camp. It proved
unsuitable, and Suse found rooms in a hotel in Buckow in the pictur-
esque Märkische Schweiz, some forty miles north of Berkenbrück. It
was a safe place to be on 10 May, when the books of the German
humanist tradition were publicly burned in university towns throughout the land. The list of banned books included works by Becher,
Brecht, the Mann brothers, Tucholsky, Feuchtwanger, the two Zweigs,
Kästner, Remarque, Ossietzky, Alfred Kerr, and many others. The
number of banned books rose to some four thousand in the next two
years. They included half of Rowohlt's list, and he set about replacing
them with more acceptable topics and employing additional, more
acceptable editors, such as the conservative Ernst von Salomon and
Friedo Lampe, a young writer who, while not a Nazi, was tolerated by
the new regime. Ditzen's books were not on the blacklist on 10 May
1933, nor was the name 'Fallada' among those of the twelve authors
banned by the new official Book Trade Association (Börsenverein der
Deutschen Buchhändler) three days later. This was not surprising,
since he was regarded as a newcomer on the literary scene. Few people
remembered his first two published novels. His third novel, *A Small
Circus*, had been well received by the Nazi press, and *Little Man –
What Now?* was not only too popular but also politically too
inoffensive to be banned in 1933.

In the second week in May, Ditzen suffered a relapse, 'which involves the kind of symptoms I had at the age of twenty after a big event you know about' – as he wrote to Kagelmacher on 6 June. All three Ditzens moved to a private clinic in nearby Waldsieversdorf.

Peter Suhrkamp took over the negotiations in Berkenbrück and by the end of May the affair appeared to be settled, with Ditzen able to extricate himself from the purchase, albeit at a price. Ditzen was keen to put the matter behind him and buy a new place as quickly as possible, before Suse's confinement in July. By now they also knew that Suse was expecting twins, which partly accounted for the difficult pregnancy. The knowledge that Ditzen's sister Margarete had given birth to twins, both of whom had died at birth twenty years before, was no doubt further cause for concern.

At the end of May, Thomas Mann, Ernst Toller and Stefan Zweig, with other members critical of the new government, were excluded from the German PEN Club. Again, Ditzen had not been actively involved and so was not personally affected. There is no doubt, however, that the events of May 1933 contributed to his illness. Ditzen's response to personal and political crises – in 1911 and again in 1918–19 – had been a nervous breakdown. One critic has described Ditzen's work in the post-war period as a 'seismograph of social crises'.[38] The same could be said of his life: it is almost as if he registered physically the earthquakes which rocked German society between 1893 and 1947. At the beginning of June, he suffered yet another relapse and all plans for moving house had to be shelved. Suse, too, fell ill and had to be confined to bed. All three Ditzens and their maid-cum-nanny Marie Wendland moved back to the Pension Stössinger on 20 June to await the arrival of the twins. Ditzen wrote to his parents on the twenty-fifth of the month that the Berkenbrück affair was now resolved: 'we take the view that many people nowadays experience similar and much worse things and that we really have got off lightly.'

On 22 June, the government moved against the SPD, banning it and arresting three thousand officials. The resultant clashes between the SA, SS and Social Democrats and other anti-fascists in the Berlin district of Köpenick left ninety-one dead. Ditzen, who had never been very active in the SPD, had destroyed his membership card early in 1933 and was therefore not directly affected. His brother-in-law,

Hans Issel, had also left the Social Democrats, but in his case it was to join the Communists.

By the end of the month, Ditzen was able to view a farm near the Malchower See in Mecklenburg. Before he came to pick up his 12,000 marks on 3 July, Rowohlt wrote: 'Let me give you some fatherly advice: put this money straight into the bank, so that you don't spend too much of it!' Indeed, Ditzen began to respond to Rowohlt's '*Lieber Meister Ditzen*' by addressing his publisher as '*Liebes Väterchen Rowohlt*' (literally, 'Dear Little Father Rowohlt').

By the beginning of July, Suse had difficulty walking and the Ditzens had resigned themselves to living out of suitcases until after the birth of the twins. However, Rudolf was gradually recovering from his breakdown and had taken up his prison novel again. On 13 July, he received a letter from his father for the first time since he had left Neumünster prison. Wilhelm Ditzen wrote:

> Since the 21 July is your fortieth birthday, let me say a word about the past and the present: we cannot forget, but we can and we want to forgive. Without reservation. Let us draw a line under the past and make a new start. As a first step we ought to see each other again, visit, meet up. That's not practical at the moment. Unfortunately! But I think it is important for now to at least express our wishes.

At last, Ditzen had won his father's approval. But his father was no longer the supreme authority in his life; there was another authority that was much more threatening. The Nazi journal *Der Angriff* published a piece on 3 July about Will Krause's new novel *SA-Kamerad Tonne*, which tells the tale of how a working-class boy finds his way into the SA. In it, Krause explained his reasons for writing his novel:

> I wanted ... to write a book which would overcome the spirit of Remark [*sic*] and Mann and Fallada.
>
> I wanted to replace the pessimistically sick, questioning, negative approach of these people, which is made palatable to the masses by means of a stylistically attractive form and contemporary themes, with the simple, straightforward, affirmative approach to life of young German workers.

While Ditzen had been able to shake off the (very few) negative reviews of *Little Man – What Now?* in the Nazi press in 1932, this was now no longer possible. In future, there would only be a Nazi press. On 14 July 1933, the government passed the Law against the Formation of New Parties, the first section of which declared: 'In Germany there exists only one political party, the National Socialist German Workers' Party.'

On 18 July, Suse gave birth to twin girls: Lore, born at 8.15 p.m. and Edith, born half an hour later. Edith's head was damaged at birth and she lived only three hours. Margarete Bechert, who knew the pain of losing babies at birth, wrote to her brother on 25 July: '. . . time will help you both get over the disappointment; time heals so much and more quickly . . . than we ever believe possible.' Although Edith's death was an accident that could not have been foreseen, Ditzen felt partly responsible. His illness, the worry, their constant moving over the last three months, had left Suse in a very weak state and also made recovery from the birth much slower than usual. He decided to make amends by finding a new home, and enlisted Peter Zingler's assistance. Zingler, who was very fond of Suse, was only too willing to help, and on 20 July they found a smallholding on the edge of the remote hamlet of Carwitz in Mecklenburg: '. . . a proper old farmhouse, very cosy, with electric lighting, stoves, seven rooms and an attic which could be converted to provide two more'. The house was situated on the side of a lake at the entrance to a small, hilly peninsula, the Bohnenwerder, with magnificent views over lakes, forests and hills. There were outhouses and, although the whole property had been somewhat neglected, it had enormous potential for growing fruit and vegetables and keeping livestock.

In 1933, a network of sandy tracks and lakeside paths joined Carwitz to the outside world. The small town of Feldberg, some four miles away, could be reached by horse and cart, bicycle or on foot. A rather sleepy train service connected Feldberg to the main railway network at Neustrelitz. Apart from an inn and a bakery, Carwitz had no shops and was served by a grocer's van and a butcher's van which came once a week from Feldberg. Carwitz offered the Ditzens a place of their own at last, ideal conditions in which to raise a family, remoteness from the temptations of city life as well as from the excesses of the Nazi regime, the possibility of farming on a small scale and the peace which Ditzen needed to write. Zingler and Ditzen had every reason to congratulate themselves on their find.

They returned to Berlin to tell Suse the good news, only to discover that she had developed thrombosis, which quickly spread to both legs. Besides being very painful, this meant that she would have to stay much longer in hospital. Margarete offered to look after Uli, but Ditzen could not bear to let him go, for 'he is the only consolation I have at this worrying time'.[39]

Ditzen was not only worried about his wife, he was worried about his livelihood. If he wanted to publish in Germany he would need to become a member of the new official Writers' Union, the Reichsverband Deutscher Schriftsteller (RDS). The remaining members of the Writers' Union, which Ditzen had left early in the year, were enrolled automatically in the new organization. Ditzen turned for advice to Rowohlt, who enlisted the assistance of Hans Richter, vice-chairman of the RDS, to secure Ditzen's membership.

By the end of July, over twenty-five thousand Germans had been arrested and interned, including the writers Erich Mühsam, Carl von Ossietzky and Joachim Ringelnatz, a particular favourite of Ditzen's. Others, such as Lion Feuchtwanger, Heinrich Mann, Ernst Toller, Kurt Tucholsky, Bertolt Brecht and Johannes R. Becher, had escaped persecution by leaving Germany. Gottfried Benn was one of the few writers of standing who actively embraced National Socialism in 1933. Others, such as Erich Kästner, Ricarda Huch, Günther Weisenborn, Reinhold Schneider, Gertrud Kolmar and Bernhard Kellermann, adopted different strategies to cope with the new situation. Ditzen's response to the question 'What now?' was to withdraw as far as possible from a hostile environment and seek solace and personal happiness in his family. He had admitted in a letter to a reader in November 1932: '... I am very aware that this response – to seek a solution solely in the private sphere – is rather trivial. In Pinneberg's case, this means Lämmchen, but I freely admit that Lämmchen is a stroke of luck.'[40] While Ditzen's fictional solution provides the novel with a happy ending, its translation into Ditzen's life was less likely to produce similar results, not least because the happy ending of *Little Man – What Now?* depends on the figure of Lämmchen, whose saintliness is a rare commodity in real life.

In the summer of 1933, the Ditzens could not know what National Socialism held in store either for them or for Germany. They were instinctively opposed to this new dynamic political movement and found its strutting and posing distasteful. In conversation in 1983, Frau Ditzen recalled her revulsion when she heard the slogan '*Laßt die Köpfe rollen!*' ('Let heads roll!').[41] Ditzen, however, did not belong to any of the groups targeted by the Nazis. The incident with the SA at Easter, while profoundly disturbing, could be viewed as the result of individual malevolence, not political persecution. His natural inclination was to run away from unpleasant situations; he thought that by removing himself and his family to a remote corner of Mecklenburg he could escape the excesses of the Nazi Party. Unlike Pinneberg in *Little Man – What Now?*, however, Ditzen was not prepared to withdraw completely into the private sphere. On the contrary, he was determined to pursue the very public, and in 1933 acutely political, activity of writing.

He fell ill again at the beginning of August, which may have been related to the première of the film version of *Little Man – What Now?* on Friday 3 August in Berlin's Capitol cinema. Lotte Lenya described it in a letter to Kurt Weill as 'awful' and 'a big flop'.[42] Wilhelm Ditzen, who went to see it in Leipzig, enjoyed it, but thought it bore little relationship to his son's book.

Ditzen managed to get himself to Feldberg on 12 August to complete the purchase of his new home. Here he took rooms for Uli, Marie and himself in the Deutsches Haus hotel, from where he supervised the building work in Carwitz. The fresh country air and good cooking did him good, and he wrote to Rowohlt on 17 August that he was feeling much better. His only worry now was financial: the cost of the private clinic where Suse had to stay much longer than expected, the cost of extricating himself from Berkenbrück, his own illness and a recent tax bill, as well as the purchase and renovation of the house in Carwitz, all left him rather short of money. Rowohlt gave him another piece of 'fatherly advice' about saving for a rainy day, and arranged for an advance.

In the course of August, Suse gradually recovered and Lore thrived. Ditzen promised himself and his wife that life would be better in Carwitz. He wrote to his parents on 31 August that Suse was:

> ... the most wonderful woman in the world ... who always helps me and is always patient with me ... I've known for some time now that Suse is the greatest success of my life. Without her I would have collapsed and sunk without trace in that small provincial town. She has given me the strength and courage to go on working. Marriage is, God knows, not easy but Suse has a tranquillity which is the source of all strength.

Part of Ditzen's new resolution was to reduce his drinking; it became a standard joke with Rowohlt that they would have only 'weak beer and spit' when they met for dinner in Berlin. Rowohlt, too, was forbidden to drink alcohol owing to a serious attack of phlebitis at the beginning of September.

By the second week in September, Ditzen was able to fetch Suse, who was still very weak and required a nurse, and the family was reunited in Feldberg. Meanwhile, Peter Suhrkamp was organizing the removal of the Ditzens' furniture from Berkenbrück, where the Sponars, difficult to the last, were now facing bankruptcy as a result of their treatment of Ditzen.

The success story of *Little Man – What Now?* continued, with seven thousand copies sold in August. In Denmark, sales reached twenty thousand within four weeks of publication; the thirteenth foreign publisher had just bought translation rights. This success gave a boost to the sales of *A Small Circus* both at home and abroad, and Ditzen's Italian publisher even requested permission to translate 'Young Goedeschal', which he refused. He was having second thoughts about publishing his prison novel and was already planning another project, entitled *Once We Had a Child*: 'The title says it all,' as he commented in a letter to his sister Margarete on 26 August.

By the end of September, the Berkenbrück affair was finally resolved, Suse was much better, and the house in Carwitz was ready. Ditzen was still worried about his financial position and asked Rowohlt to send the 3,000 marks due on 1 October two days early; he then asked for a further advance immediately and complained that his current contract was a bad deal. Rowohlt, in reply, told him he would receive over 6,000 marks for the US film rights and added: '. . . let's be honest, if – and you cannot deny it – you had not been so careless with your money over the summer months, you would not be bleating about our agreement now.'[43] Rowohlt, however, found the extra money and sent it on 6 October.

Marie Wendland, who had been an invaluable help and support during the previous six months, left the Ditzens' service to get married on 30 September, and Joie Zingler arrived from Berlin to help with the move to Carwitz. Ditzen turned down all demands for short stories and even declined an invitation to go to Hollywood to work on the American film of *Little Man – What Now?*, so determined was he to concentrate on his novel, his family and his new home.[44] The family moved to Carwitz on the first Saturday in October and celebrated with a dinner of a roast goose, which Rowohlt had sent specially for the occasion from Berlin. Ditzen wrote to his friend and publisher on 10 October: 'You have no idea what it means for an obsessively tidy, pedantic person like myself to sit at last in a proper study again.' After six months of living out of suitcases, a nervous breakdown, a difficult pregnancy and the death of a baby, the family had finally found a home. Suse, who was well enough for the nurse to leave a week after they moved in, was determined to support Rudolf's resolution by banning all alcohol from the house. In addition to their radio, they now also had a gramophone and planned to be self-sufficient culturally as well as materially. The telephone would also considerably reduce their need to leave Carwitz. Ditzen first dealt with the mountain of post which had accumulated over the previous weeks, before returning to his prison novel '*Kippe oder Lampen*'.

Among the letters to be answered was one from Friedrich Hermann Küthe, an unemployed librarian and ardent fan who had written an essay marking 'Fallada's' fortieth birthday in the magazine published by the Association of Lending Libraries. In it, Küthe, who had clear Nationalist sympathies, praised *A Small Circus* for its depiction of 'the spineless, worm-eaten Republic' and praised the author's work for its 'Germanness'. Ditzen, as was his custom when writing to readers, as opposed to anyone else, signed his letters to Küthe 'Hans Fallada'. Küthe, who had ambitions to become a writer, asked 'Fallada' for advice. 'Fallada' advised him to join the Nazi party, and added on a personal note: 'Quite honestly, if I knew a way of joining the National Socialist Party at the moment without a lot of fuss I would do it. Because this is my sincere belief: while one can argue about details, this is the party which will save Germany from chaos.'[45] Ditzen had no reason in October 1933 to express such sentiments if he did not hold them sincerely. In conversation in September 1983, Frau Ditzen recalled that many Germans in 1933 thought the Nazi regime, however distasteful, would soon establish order from chaos, and then everything would return to normal. In this respect, too, Ditzen can be seen as a 'seismograph', registering in his life and work what was going on around him. The sentiments expressed in this letter to Küthe are the first indication that his great strength as a writer – his ability to reflect the views and emotions of his fellow-Germans – was, at the same time, a great weakness which could render him incapable of independent thought and action.

On Monday 16 October, Ditzen resumed work on '*Kippe oder Lampen*', which presents in fictional form the ideas he had expressed in his essay on prison life in 1925 and developed in the speech he drafted in 1928 for the conference on the Care and Resettlement of Offenders. He believed that the prison regime brought out the worst in all concerned, that it was often little more than a school of crime, and that insufficient effort was made to help prisoners prepare for life on the outside. The provisional title was dropped in favour of 'Once a Jailbird', which underlined Ditzen's concern with the reasons for the very high rate of re-offending.

The novel tells the tale of Willi Kufalt, who is released after serving a five-year prison sentence for embezzlement and forgery in 'an industrial town in Schleswig-Holstein'. Determined to make a fresh start, he sets out for Hamburg, where the prison chaplain has arranged accommodation in a hostel run by a religious charity which also has a typing bureau where Kufalt is employed. The hostel regime is spartan in the extreme and the wages derisory. Eventually, Kufalt and some of the other workers rebel and set up their own typing business.

The charity, which is singularly lacking in Christian spirit, closes down the enterprise and Kufalt takes up with one of his prison cronies, whom he intimidates into giving him a share of some stolen money. With this, he returns to the 'industrial town in Schleswig-Holstein' where he tries, again, to make a fresh start. After some initial success this, too, comes to an end when his criminal record is discovered. He then goes back to Hamburg, dabbles in petty crime and awaits the inevitable and welcome return to prison, where:

> ... it is great to feel so at home again. No more worries. Almost like it used to be going home again with Father to Mother.
>
> Almost?
>
> Even better. Here there is peace and quiet. Here nobody bothers you. Here you don't have to make any decisions. Here you don't have to make an effort.

The novel ends in a prison cell as 'Willi Kufalt falls gently asleep, smiling peacefully.'

Willi Kufalt, like his companions, is portrayed as 'not a criminal by nature; he had become one, he had learnt crime.' They are the victims of circumstance and the criminal justice system. The novel is an extended plea for a radical reform of the system and, by implication, of society itself.

In 'Once a Jailbird', Ditzen draws heavily on his own experience of prison life and rehabilitation. When he left Neumünster prison he also considered setting up the kind of typing bureau which Kufalt and his companions organize. The description of Kufalt's job with a newspaper owes much to his own experience with the *General Anzeiger*. In this novel he continues his practice of recycling characters' names, in this instance Wrede and Lütt, and interweaving into the narrative the names of friends and acquaintances, such as Wendland (after their maid and nanny Marie Wendland), Behn (after Lieschen Behn from Kölpinsee) and Preisach (after Dora Preisach, who typed part of the manuscript).

Ditzen not only describes Kufalt's return to crime but also charts his gradual slide back into alcoholism – the beer at the station on the day of his release in May, 'although he had forsworn alcohol', the three or four schnaps on the way home from his fiancée's in December 'so that he could get to sleep more quickly', and a binge on New Year's Eve. As we have seen, the period of the novel's composition coincided with a resurgence of Ditzen's own drinking problems.

One of the most striking autobiographical passages in 'Once a Jailbird' is the flashback to Kufalt's youth at the beginning of Chapter 10: the Uhufelsen, the small town, the young Kufalt's relationship with a girl, which results in his expulsion from school, his father's suggestion that he should take up agriculture as a career – all point to Ditzen's teenage years in Leipzig and Rudolstadt. The inclusion of this passage, the first fictional representation of the events in his work, is poorly motivated, and the connection between this and Kufalt's subsequent career in petty crime is unclear. Perhaps Ditzen's recent breakdown, accompanied – as he told Kagelmacher – by the symptoms he had experienced after the events in Rudolstadt, had revived these memories and led to their incorporation in his current work.

In 'Once a Jailbird', Ditzen takes the radical approach he adopted in *A Small Circus*. This time it is the criminal justice system which is exposed to scrutiny and found wanting. He was aware, as he wrote to his parents in November 1933, that he had written 'a very controversial book'. The plea for a more humane approach to crime was bound to attract opprobrium, as was the inclusion of a homosexual relationship, an unmarried mother, and a protagonist who views prison as 'a blessed island in the foggy grey sea of his life'.

He was also aware of the fact 'that nowadays there are not only artistic considerations but a host of other factors to be borne in mind'.[46] He therefore arranged to send the manuscript to Rowohlt before he undertook any corrections. A bicycle accident in late October left him unable to type, so Rowohlt sent Dora Preisach, who was Jewish and had recently lost her job, to Carwitz to type the last section. Ditzen took one day off in the first week in November to entertain his sister Margarete, the first member of the Ditzen family to visit Carwitz, before completing 'Once a Jailbird' on Thursday 9 November. Dora Preisach took the manuscript back to Berlin with her the next day; it had been eagerly awaited by Rowohlt, who read it immediately and rang on Sunday to pronounce it Ditzen's best book to date. The following Tuesday he described his immediate reaction to the novel in a letter to Ditzen: 'I was so excited that I very nearly hit the bottle. Thank goodness Peter Zingler managed to talk me out of it – you, too, have experienced how good he is at that!' Rowohlt spent the next weekend in Carwitz where, as Ditzen warned before his arrival, 'there is no alcohol to be had. You'll plead in vain for your early morning schnaps and at midday you'll have to make do with milk from our good Eri-Cow.'

Unlike the previous two novels, 'Once a Jailbird' was not serialized prior to publication. Monty Jacobs, the editor of the *Voßische Zeitung*, which had published *Little Man – What Now?*, was very enthusiastic about it, but his opinion no longer counted and he was soon to leave Germany for exile in England. Other newspapers and magazines were reluctant to print anything which could be construed as a violation of the Schriftleitergesetz (Act governing the Rules for Publication) of 4 October 1933, which banned the publication of any material which might 'undermine the strength of the Reich'.

One of the first foreign policy decisions of the Nazi government was to end Germany's membership of the League of Nations in October 1933. This had an adverse effect on the sale of Ditzen's books abroad, which in turn led to a reduction in his income. Otherwise, the Ditzens counted themselves fortunate in the idyllic Carwitz landscape with the produce of their farm, fish from the lakes and as many rabbits as they could eat. Ditzen declined all invitations to leave Carwitz, including one to read from his work in Copenhagen, and devoted himself to getting the farm in order and finishing 'Once a Jailbird'. He asked his brother-in-law, Fritz Bechert, for advice about the legal aspects of the novel. Bechert emphasized the importance of setting it in the period before 30 January 1933, since Kufalt would receive a much stiffer sentence under the current regime. Ditzen dispatched the final version of 'Once a Jailbird' to Rowohlt on 27 November.

At the beginning of December he finally found time to consider whether it might be necessary, in view of the political situation and current cultural policy, to make any changes to *Little Man – What Now?*, which was expected to go into a new edition in early 1934. Rowohlt had suggested cutting the reference to Lämmchen's Communist sympathies at the end of the chapter entitled 'Pinneberg walks through the Little Tiergarten, is afraid and cannot be happy' and had asked Ditzen for his views. Ditzen decided to make no changes to this passage or to his largely positive depiction of Jews in the novel. He did, however, remove the references to the SA and the Nazi Party, airbrushing the character of Lauterbach from a Nazi into a goalkeeper 'with violent tendencies'. It is a measure of Ditzen's meticulous approach that he made the changes in such a way that the number of words on each of the ten pages affected remained the same, so the typesetters only had to rearrange the text within the paragraphs concerned.

Ditzen's new surroundings and ordered lifestyle seemed to unleash new creative energies. The very day he finished his first version of 'Once a Jailbird', he started his next novel. He had first mentioned Once We Had a Child in August; in November he referred to this work as Der Salatgarten ('The Salad Garden') before reverting to the original title in the second week in December. He was enthusiastic about Once We Had a Child from the very beginning. He wrote to Rowohlt on 22 December: 'This book will be my best. It's a joy to write and quite different from my previous books. It's basically a number of individual stories (with very little dialogue) grouped around a very strong hero.' In the same letter he suggested another project: an anthology of stories for children based on the tales he devised to entertain Uli at meal times and on their long country walks. Rowohlt thought the 'Uli stories' a very good idea, not least, one presumes, on account of their unpolitical content.

The week before Christmas witnessed what was to become a regular ritual in the Ditzen household: the slaughtering of a pig. Frau Wendel, owner of the Deutsches Haus hotel in Feldberg, came to supervise the pickling and sausage-making which ensued. Ditzen confided to Rowohlt: 'Suse was astonished to learn that the traditional Mecklenburg sausages have a shot of rum or cognac in them. Sad to say, she has only bought the exact measure of alcohol required for the sausages.'

Ditzen's Christmas parcel from Leipzig contained the lead soldiers of his boyhood and his old edition of Robinson Crusoe, a particularly appropriate present at this time, for Carwitz represented Ditzen's attempt to reach a desert island after the storms of 1933 had almost wrecked his ship. By the end of the year this attempt looked most promising. He had stopped drinking, was enjoying his new novel and had a number of projects in the pipeline. The fresh air, regular meals and the tranquillity of Carwitz were doing all four Ditzens good. In addition, he had now fulfilled his twin ambitions to become a writer and to own a farm. There was indeed cause for celebration as the Ditzens and their guests – Dora Preisach, Heinz Dietrich Kenter's first wife, Marga, and Suse's mother – gathered round the Christmas tree in Carwitz in 1933.

6 1934–1938
Carwitz the Idyll

*People are challenged by the events, the dangers and the
opportunities of their age to adopt a position, actively to
participate or to oppose. Their conscience alone can tell
them how to act.*

– Reinhold Schneider[1]

On 8 January 1934, Ditzen set out for Berlin to discuss the publication of 'Once a Jailbird' and begin negotiating his new contract. Much
to the surprise and dismay of Rowohlt and Paul Mayer, he insisted on
including in his new novel a foreword aimed at placating the Nazi
literary authorities. In it he claimed that 'the ridiculous, grotesque and
pitiful consequences of the so-called humane justice system depicted
in these pages' were now a thing of the past thanks to the changes
which German society had undergone while the novel was being written. He was deaf to Mayer's plea to omit such an obvious concession
which could easily be construed as implying support for the Nazis,
insisting that he had no choice, that he could not emigrate because all
his money was tied up in the house in Carwitz, which would be difficult to sell, and that he would therefore have to 'swallow the bitter
pill'. When Rowohlt sent the final proofs of the foreword on 12 February, he included a note expressing his view that 'your formulation
does seem rather *too* ingratiating to me', but Ditzen was not to be
dissuaded. Mayer's prediction was borne out by the reaction of Thomas Mann, who read 'Once a Jailbird' in exile in Switzerland and
noted in his Diary on 14 March 1934: 'In order to be published in

Germany a book has to disown and deny its humane philosophy in an introduction.' Ditzen's assumption that such a concession would be sufficient to mollify his critics without alienating his supporters is further evidence of the political naivety demonstrated in his letter to Küthe the previous October. In the course of the year, he was to realize his mistake.

Dora Preisach arrived in Carwitz on 14 February, and the typing of *Once We Had a Child* began immediately. Although the submission date agreed with Rowohlt was not until 1 October, Ditzen drove himself at a frenetic pace and completed the novel by 27 February. His ostensible reason was to allow himself a long break in which to relax and enjoy Carwitz. Again, it seems likely that he wanted money – to renovate the house and outbuildings, as well as finally to pay off his debts to Hahn and Rohr.

There was, however, a price to be paid for putting himself under the degree of pressure required to complete a 580-page novel in just over three months. Rowohlt came to Carwitz at the end of February to read the manuscript. During his visit, Ditzen appears to have begun drinking again. He assured Dora Preisach on 6 March: 'A new regime is being established here. The last drop of alcohol has been consumed, tomorrow it is the turn of the last Gold Flake and an ordered life will begin.'[2]

Ditzen's nervous exhaustion was compounded by his apprehension about the reception of 'Once a Jailbird', due to be published in mid-March. Rowohlt, who clearly shared this apprehension, postponed a holiday in order to be in Berlin when the novel appeared in the shops, because he felt it judicious for the 'captain to be on board'. In addition, Ditzen suffered a recurrence of his gum disease at the beginning of March and both children contracted whooping cough in the course of the month. Ditzen became increasingly irritable: he postponed a visit from Martha Dodd and her friend the American teacher and translator Mildred Harnack arranged by Ledig; he refused to accompany Zingler and Rowohlt to Copenhagen to see a Danish dramatization of *Little Man – What Now?*; he complained that the complimentary copies of 'Once a Jailbird' which he received for signature had not been wrapped and stamped as he had requested; he sent Rowohlt a telephone bill for the trifling amount of 2.40 marks relating to a recent stay; and he declared himself jealous of Zingler's genuine and quite innocent affection for Suse.

Rowohlt's kindly advice to be careful with his money and not to start building in Carwitz until the success of 'Once a Jailbird' and *Once We Had a Child* was assured resulted in an angry exchange of letters. Ditzen finally admitted to Rowohlt on 22 March: 'My nerves are in shreds . . . I really don't want a repeat of the breakdown I had a year ago.'

Meanwhile, 'Once a Jailbird' had appeared in the shops on 12 March and the initial reaction was muted but positive. Besides the conciliatory foreword, each copy contained, at Ditzen's suggestion, a 'letter' from 'Fallada' to Rowohlt announcing his next novel, *Once We Had a Child*: 'But you won't forget, will you, to tell my readers as soon as possible that they can expect a quite different book from me – a more beautiful, more mature and richer one?!'

Given Ditzen's precarious psychological state, it is not surprising that he turned down an approach from the Deutsches Lichtspielsyndikat film company to work on a film starring Emil Jannings, 'similar to *Cavalcade*', the 1933 Hollywood box-office success based on the play by Noël Coward. The end of the month brought some good news: Rowohlt signed a contract with the *Berliner Illustrirte* for the serialization of *Once We Had a Child* which would bring in a much-needed 14,000 marks. The opportunities for pre-launch serializations were dwindling: the *Voßische Zeitung* closed on 1 April 1934, another victim of the growing Nazi stranglehold on every aspect of life in Germany, which was now a centralized state, already embarked on a programme of rearmament, with all 'non-Aryans' purged from the public service. The establishment of the Volksgerichtshof (People's Court) on 24 April to try cases of treason perfected the system of institutionalized terror in a country where party and state were one.

Ditzen had three gum operations in the spring of 1934. He determined at the beginning of May to avoid alcohol for twelve months, and wrote to Rowohlt on the day before his last stitches were due to be removed: 'This time I have proved conclusively that it all goes much more smoothly and painlessly if I don't drink.'

On the last Sunday in May, Ledig arrived in Carwitz with three visitors – Martha Dodd, Mildred Harnack and Boris Vinogradov – who were no doubt delighted to escape from Berlin, which was buzzing with rumours arising out of the tensions between the army and the SA, as well as between the SA and the party leadership.[3] Martha Dodd later recalled:

> Hans Fallada came out with his buxom, simple wife to meet us . . . He was a stockily built man with blondish hair and charming genial features; his wife plump, blonde, serene, with a pleasant face. They had two children, a young, bright-faced boy of four and an infant in arms. Their life seemed to be built around their family and their farm. He was isolated from life and happy in his isolation. There was some discussion and though I got the impression that he was not and could not be a Nazi – what artist is? – I felt a certain resignation in his attitude.

She concluded perceptively: '. . . he is the one remaining author of recognized talent writing in Germany and one can watch as time goes on what this intellectual and emotional passivity will do to his talent.'[4]

By the beginning of June, Ditzen was in sufficiently good spirits to be planning yet another novel. The *Berliner Illustrirte* carried photographs of the Ditzens in Carwitz prior to the serialization of *Once We Had a Child*, photographs which had been taken in March by a Herr Böker, who worked for Heinrich Hoffmann, Hitler's personal photographer. 'Once a Jailbird' was selling between three hundred and four hundred copies per week, and Ditzen was looking forward to receiving 19,100 marks from Rowohlt on 15 June with which he would finally clear his old debts. Building work in Carwitz was progressing well, too.

The calm of early June in Ditzen's life, as in Germany, was not to last. On the tenth, Hellmuth Langenbucher, editor of the official Book Trade Journal and in charge of 'all questions of cultural policy', published a review of 'Once a Jailbird' in the *Berliner Börsenzeitung* in which he remarked that 'Kufalt is one of those degenerate human beings for whom we have established protective custody nowadays'.[5] Langenbucher went on to recommend that the book trade should not promote such literature; his review was carried by a number of Nazi newspapers and journals. Further attacks followed: from the Nazi author Heinz Steguweit, who accused a bewildered Ditzen of using the name 'Steguweit' in 'Once a Jailbird' to take revenge for an unfavourable review which Steguweit claimed to have once written; from Will Vesper, editor of the Nazi journal *Die neue Literatur*, who described the novel as 'in many respects an embarrassing book, written badly and without conscience, produced on demand.' Ditzen, incensed by the injustice of many of these attacks, was only with great difficulty persuaded by Rowohlt not to respond.

The last weekend in June witnessed the unprecedented murder of over two hundred members of the SA, including its leader Ernst Röhm, as well as the assassination of General von Schleicher and two of Papen's aides. The power struggle between the SA and the army was resolved, at Hitler's instigation, in the army's favour. Hitler justified the execution without trial of many former colleagues and a number of completely innocent people in a speech to the Reichstag on 13 July which concluded with the warning: 'And let everyone be aware from now on that anyone who raises a hand to strike the State will face certain death.' That this applied to writers, too, was shown by the murder of Erich Mühsam in Oranienburg concentration camp on 11 July 1934. The playwright and critic Ehm Welk was also interned in Oranienburg in 1934 after publishing an article critical of Goebbels in the weekly *Die Grüne Post*. He was eventually released but not allowed to publish until 1937.

In mid-June, Ditzen had received a letter, signed by Gottfried Benn, from the Union of National Writers (the successor to the German PEN Centre), enquiring about his foreign contacts. Rowohlt advised Ditzen to answer this letter frankly and openly because 'Gottfried Benn is a thoroughly decent man.' Benn himself came under attack in the summer of 1934 when his Aryan credentials were questioned by the Nazi poet Börries von Münchhausen. In response, Benn wrote *Lebensweg eines Intellektualisten* ('The Life of an Intellectualist') to prove that the name Benn was not of Jewish origin. Soon afterwards, he retired from the literary scene and, claiming that 'the army is the aristocratic form of emigration,' resumed his career as an army doctor.[6] It was to be some eleven years before the paths of Ditzen and Benn would cross again.

The serialization of *Once We Had a Child*, nearly halted by the official attacks on Ditzen, began in the second week in June 1934. Ditzen had sustained his initial enthusiasm for the book and on its completion pronounced it his best work to date.[7]

Once We Had a Child tells the story of Johannes Gäntschow, the last in a long line of Rügen farmers, and opens with a description of the historical, geographical, economic, social and hereditary factors which have formed the protagonist. This first section is a masterpiece of narration, which appears to be written in an anecdotal and unstructured manner. However, a closer analysis shows how the narrator not only introduces Gäntschow but gradually draws the reader into the world of the novel. The narrator first describes the exterior of the Gäntschows' farmhouse, the Warderhof, then takes the reader on a guided tour of the interior, digressing freely on the adventures of Gäntschow's ancestors, before reaching the point where he can address the reader as '*wir*' (we) before finally using the familiar second-person singular form '*du*'.

Gäntschow, born in the same year as Ditzen, grows up on a remote farm with an alcoholic father. He learns about farming and spends many happy childhood hours with Christiane, daughter of Count von Fidde, a member of the local nobility. One of their pranks involves hiding a fugitive from justice who once saved their lives. When he is captured and shot, the count takes Christiane away and Gäntschow leaves the island. He trains as a mechanic in Greifswald and goes on to study engineering in Stettin. Then he abandons his studies, ends up in Holland, where he falls ill, and is brought home by his father, who subsequently finds him work as a farm manager. While working in eastern Pomerania, he marries a local schoolteacher, Elise Schütt, but their marriage is not a happy one. Following a miscarriage, they return to the Warderhof, which, since the deaths of Gäntschow's father and brother, has fallen into rack and ruin. Gäntschow restores the farm and meets Christiane again, who is now married to Herr Wendland. Gäntschow leaves Elise, wins Christiane's love and returns with her to the Warderhof, only to discover that his wife has laid waste to the farm. Once more, he builds it up, Christiane becomes pregnant, but their baby daughter dies shortly after birth. Christiane returns to her husband and Gäntschow is left alone.

This brief summary of the plot reveals Ditzen's delight in incorporating material based on his own life (the disastrous trip to Holland, his experience of farming, the death of his baby daughter) and that of his friends (Gäntschow owes much to Kagelmacher), as well his 'recycling' of stories: Elise's habit of leaving doors open originates in the short story *'Die offene Tür'* ('The Open Door'); Gäntschow's brother's love for the calf Blanka in *'Blanka, eine geraubte Prinzessin'* ('Blanka, A Stolen Princess').

Ditzen knew he was breaking new ground with this novel and was particularly proud of it for two reasons, one technical and one aesthetic. First, he had put behind him 'the never-ending dialogues, the little vignettes' of his previous three novels and had developed 'what I hope is a broader flow'; second, he felt as if he had returned to his 'intellectual forefathers' and mentions in particular the humorist Jean Paul and the realist Wilhelm Raabe, both of whom adopted a critical attitude in their writings and espoused universal, humanist values. There are indeed parallels between Raabe's *Stopfkuchen* and *Once We Had a Child*, both as regards their stubborn, non-conforming protagonists, who work inaccessible and inhospitable farms, as well as in the authors' skilful handling of narrative perspective.

Since its publication in 1934, *Once We Had a Child* has been a controversial work, often dismissed as an example of *Blut und Boden* literature, with a strong hero who is bound to the land and who rejects all things urban, including the labour movement. Ditzen's acknowledgement of the influence of Hamsun, whose complete works he had received for Christmas 1933, has only served to fuel this argument.[8]

Yet a comparison of *Once We Had a Child* with Hamsun's work, for example *Growth of the Soil* (1918) or *August* (1931), reveals very different authorial and narrative approaches. Gäntschow does share some characteristics with Hamsun's heroes Isak (in *Growth of the Soil*) and Ezra (in *August*): they are all extremely healthy, hardworking farmers who derive enormous satisfaction from working the land. Gäntschow's initial unwillingness to attend school and the later abandonment of his studies might be construed as evidence of the anti-intellectualism typical of 'blood and soil' literature. Such similarities are, however, superficial. It is inconceivable that Isak or Ezra would abandon their farms. Nor is Gäntschow a settler, carving out a living from the wilderness. Ditzen does not present the farmer and the land as the source of national renewal. Whereas Hamsun could remark through the character of Geissler to Isak, 'It's two-and-thirty thousand fellows of your stamp the country wants', no one – either inside or outside the world of the narrative – would dream of addressing such a remark to Gäntschow. Unlike Hamsun's heroes, Gäntschow develops in the course of the novel; he is ultimately shown to be, and indeed realizes himself to be, a failure.

Once We Had a Child is free of the racism so frequent in 'blood and soil' literature, nor does it contain an exemplary mother figure, a central feature of the genre. Hamsun's men of the soil invariably have a helpmate like Isak's wife Inger, who 'was in full flower and constantly with child'. Thirty-six hours after the birth of her first child (which came as a complete surprise to Isak), 'Inger was up, pottering about half-dressed – she had milked the cow and the goats, as if it might have been just an ordinary day.' No woman in Ditzen's novel bears any resemblance to this type of mother figure.

The fact that a German author writing in 1933–4 chose to set a novel in the countryside with a farmer as protagonist does not mean that the work in question is automatically of the *Blut und Boden* school. Ditzen's sister, Elisabeth Hörig, commented: 'It is really such a pity that novels about farmers are so fashionable at the moment. There is so much rubbish produced in this vein that it would melt a heart of stone . . . But your book is very different from all of that.'[9]

A crucial question in determining the nature of *Once We Had a Child* is the narrator's strategy and, in particular, his attitude towards Johannes Gäntschow. The narrator surrounds Gäntschow with a series of figures coming from all walks of life who, without exception, express criticism of him. The school inspector in Klein-Kirschbaum calls Gäntschow 'bloody-minded'; Frau von Brest refers to him as 'a barbarian'; Elise Schütt, who is totally devoted to Gäntschow, cannot satisfy him, and Christiane, who understands him perfectly, is unable to live with him. Wendland, the last character to speak to Gäntschow, tells him: 'Everyone is afraid of you. No one knows what you are going to do next.' Coming at the end of the novel, this opinion not only bears additional weight but also has the effect of a concluding statement.

The narrator's initial sympathy for the young Gäntschow who takes responsibility for his father's farm gradually gives way to an increasingly critical attitude: the narrator agrees with the workers' assessment of Gäntschow's refusal to involve himself in the labour movement; he criticizes Gäntschow's attitude towards his fiancée Elise; indeed, he is particularly sympathetic to Elise and Christiane, the victims of Gäntschow's moods and tantrums.

The narrator charts the change in Gäntschow from his return to Christiane until the moment of his great insight when she goes into labour: '. . . he understood everything. He had never loved her. He had never loved another human being on this earth, he had only ever loved himself – and now it was too late.' After the death of the baby, the narrator gradually abandons Gäntschow, confessing ignorance about his feelings. Gäntschow finally accepts the loss of his daughter as a punishment for his former way of life: 'For God's sake, it was just. If stupidity and coarseness were to go unpunished, what would become of this world, what sort of world would it be? There could be no doubt that he had been stupid and coarse. It had all turned out as it should. It was exactly right.'

It is not without significance that a German 'hero' should utter these views in 1934, for while they obviously refer to Gäntschow in the novel, the question 'If stupidity and coarseness were to go unpunished, what would become of this world, what sort of world would it be?' was an appropriate one in the context of the contemporary German scene. The importance of this final section for an understanding of the novel was underlined by Ditzen himself, who wrote to his sister Elisabeth on 16 May: 'There are few things I'm so proud of as these last few lines.'

An analysis of Ditzen's narrative strategy reveals a narrator who increasingly distances himself from his protagonist, whom he brings to a point of insight and then abandons. Gäntschow is presented as a man who recognizes his stupidity, selfishness and misanthropy too late to save his relationship with the woman he loves. If he is an example, then it is a negative one. This conclusion is supported by the analysis by the critic Jürgen Thöming, which views Gäntschow as 'a self-critical, cathartic self-portrait'.[10]

Once We Had a Child suffers, like *A Small Circus*, from narrative drift and a loss of momentum towards the end. Undoubtedly, stricter editing would have produced a better novel. In addition, Ditzen had difficulties managing a negative hero. Gäntschow has to appear attractive enough to capture and hold the reader's interest, yet has to be abandoned by narrator and reader in the end. Ditzen's love of story-telling also sometimes obscures his main narrative purpose – the novel is so bursting with tales that the narrator is in danger of forgetting his overall strategy.

While the official campaign against Ditzen in June did not have a major impact on the sales of either 'Once a Jailbird' or *Little Man – What Now?*, Ditzen could not help taking the attacks on his work personally. His thoughts began to turn to emigration and he confided to Kagelmacher: 'I cannot, like other heroes, go abroad and produce literature there, I'm so rooted in northern Germany that I cannot imagine being able to write anywhere else.'[11]

The arrival of a new housekeeper, Fräulein Kluge, on 1 July, as well as the presence of three nieces in the house, in addition to the children and the bustle of the soft-fruit picking season, made working in Carwitz very difficult. When Ditzen failed to make progress on a short story, '*Gute Krüseliner Wiese rechts*' ('Krüselin Meadow'), which he was writing to commission, he became: '. . . terribly depressed. I travelled around the country, wanted to, indeed was obliged to, write but could make no headway.'[12] By the end of the month, he was back in Carwitz, and 'Krüselin Meadow', which is set in a farming community and tells a tale of love, duty and marriage, was finished. Ditzen thought it one of his best short stories and it appeared in the weekend supplement of the *Berliner Morgenpost* on 27 October 1934.

Following the assassination of Dollfuss, the Austrian chancellor, in July 1934, Hitler consolidated his position in Germany after President Hindenburg died on 2 August by having himself declared head of state and commander-in-chief of the armed forces. With the support of the army secured and the presidency subsumed into the office of Führer and Reich Chancellor, the Nazi hold on power was now total.

Dora Preisach, fearing for her future as a Jew in Germany, decided to emigrate to Palestine with her father. The Ditzens were dismayed and wrote on 12 August offering her a full-time, live-in position in Carwitz as secretary, housekeeper, nanny and gardener – an invitation which she declined on account of her father. In the same letter Ditzen enclosed a circular from a committee set up by Rowohlt to collect money for Ringelnatz, whose work had been banned and who had been forbidden to appear on stage. Ditzen himself contributed 25 marks a month to the Ringelnatz fund.

Ringelnatz was not the only author in difficulties whom Rowohlt assisted. He continued to employ Franz Hessel, albeit in a more menial capacity: it was Hessel, for example, who wrote the publicity material for *Once We Had a Child*. Ditzen expressed his sympathy for him in a letter to his sister Elisabeth Hörig: 'It is a great shame, he is a real poet who makes no concessions; his readers have been scattered to the four corners of the earth and no one reads him here any more.'[13]

The Hörigs spent several weeks in Carwitz in August and September, where they met Kagelmacher and Dora Preisach. The attacks on Ditzen's work died down over the summer and in the last week of August he was invited to work on an official party film about the farming community to be directed by Carl Froelich, later president of the official Reich Film Chamber (*Reichsfilmkammer*). Rowohlt, who spent a long weekend with his wife in Carwitz in early September, advised Ditzen to decline this invitation, a piece of advice which he was only too happy to accept.

At the end of September the Ditzens set out for a holiday in Munich, where they visited their friends the Gundermanns. They left Fräulein Kluge in charge of Carwitz and their one remaining guest, Kagelmacher. In Munich they went to the beer festival and made several trips into the mountains 'with monastery beer and monastery cheese'. Ditzen's decision to forgo alcohol for a year had lasted less than five months. When they arrived back in Berlin, they went their separate ways – Suse to Carwitz and Ditzen to Hiddensee, where he 'did a lot of thinking and considered how to write a contemporary book without making it contemporary'.[14]

When she returned to Carwitz, Suse found a letter from the Ministry for Public Enlightenment and Propaganda drawing Ditzen's attention to the fact that his Swedish publisher, Bonnier, was in the forefront of 'anti-German agitation' and urging him 'to take this into consideration in future'. Suse forwarded the letter to Rowohlt, expressing the hope 'that this does not result in any unpleasantness, I really have had enough'.

Suse's health was beginning to suffer from the strain of Rudolf's nervous problems in February and March, the children's illnesses, the attacks on him in June, his renewed drinking and the constant stream of visitors over the summer. During a visit to Berlin in the second half of October, she underwent a series of tests, was diagnosed as 'mentally and physically exhausted' and was advised to have a complete rest for three months, preferably at a North Sea spa. Ditzen himself underwent extensive dental treatment in Berlin and also used his time there trying to interest publishers in a joint project he was planning with his sister Elisabeth: a picture book based on her photographs of the North Sea combined with one of his short stories. He hoped in this way to help his sister and brother-in-law, who was still out of work; however, he was unable to find a publisher.

It was from Berlin at the end of October 1934 that Ditzen took his wife and children to Leipzig to meet his parents for the first time. In the nine years since he had last seen his parents, Ditzen had become a successful author, a husband and a father. The tone of the correspondence with his parents had become warmer over the years; Wilhelm Ditzen's letter of forgiveness the previous July had removed all rancour from their relationship: the time had now come for reconciliation. While there was no doubt apprehension on all sides – Suse later recalled how her husband had tutored her in the type of behaviour expected in the daughter-in-law of a retired Supreme Court judge – the visit was a success. The Ditzens returned to Carwitz in early November and decided that Suse did not need to go to a spa; all the visitors had now left and the winter months would offer adequate opportunity for peace and rest.

Once We Had a Child had appeared on 11 October and by 8 November had sold 17,612 copies. The first reviews were quite positive: the critic and editor Felix Riemkasten praised the author's ability to tell a good story and captivate the reader; Karl Rauch, editor of

Das Deutsche Wort, also welcomed the novel and saw Gäntschow as a 'negative hero', an example of how not to conduct one's life. Then, on 11 November, the *Berliner Börsenzeitung* published a devastating review by Hellmuth Langenbucher which described the novel as not 'the kind of book we need nowadays'. The *Völkischer Beobachter* commented: 'A Berlin newspaper wrote sadly: "Once We Had a Fallada". He was never one of us.' One particularly zealous Nazi reviewer expressed the hope that *Once We Had a Child* would be consigned to the flames with the works of Mann and Brecht.[15]

When *Die Literatur* discussed the divergence of approach between Karl Rauch and Hellmuth Langenbucher, viewing it as proof of the 'continuing uncertainty in aesthetic matters' and suggesting that there might be 'another, third view' which would be 'more balanced and considered and less emotional', Langenbucher replied in the *Völkischer Beobachter* on 28 November 1934 that it was not a question of being right or wrong but 'a question of what is to the benefit of our nation and what is not! . . . people who are not able or willing to understand that should have the grace to leave the care of our culture to us!'

While Langenbucher dictated the official view that *Once We Had a Child* was not wholesome, positive and German, there was a small number of Nazi journalists who admired the work as a straight-forward 'blood and soil' novel and praised its 'feeling for race and blood'. Reviews in the English-speaking world were almost unanimously positive. The *New Statesman* compared Ditzen with Hardy and one Canadian reviewer declared: 'The ironist is here, the incorrigible iconoclast, playing havoc with the legend of the men of blood and iron.'[16] However, for Ditzen, in Germany in November 1934, it was the view of the *Völkischer Beobachter* that counted. After the Ministry for Public Enlightenment and Propaganda recommended the removal of *Little Man – What Now?* from all public libraries, Ditzen abandoned work on his new novel on the twelfth of that month. Instead he turned to writing children's stories, in response to a request he had received earlier in the year from the Reclam publishing house. He also ordered an English-language course in preparation for starting English lessons with his family – an indication that emigration was back on the agenda.

In the second week in November he attended his local branch meeting of the Writers' Union, where he was elected chairman: 'I simply stood up and just said they had better choose someone else, that my nomination would not be approved by the leadership, since I was a completely "undesirable writer".' His colleagues chose someone else without demur. Ditzen wrote to Heinz and Elisabeth Hörig on 22 November: 'I have nothing to hide and I am not going to keep my eyes shut. Nobody is forced to like my books and, anyway, Rowohlt is quite right: if you make concessions to those people, they'll really stick the knife in.' The experiences of 1934 had taught Ditzen the futility of the foreword he had written to 'Once a Jailbird'.

By the end of the month, Ditzen had resumed work on the novel after all; as he wrote to Rowohlt, 'you can only scratch where it itches.' Perhaps this would be the 'contemporary novel' which he had pondered on Hiddensee?

Rowohlt, who arrived with his wife in Carwitz on 1 December to witness another pig being slaughtered, urged Ditzen to take his time with his new work. The Rowohlts brought a piece of sad news: Joachim Ringelnatz had died on 27 November 1934, a mental and physical wreck.

The Ditzens went to Berlin in the second week in December to do their Christmas shopping and visit friends. One old friend Ditzen looked up was Lotte Fröhlich-Parsenow, whom he had met in Berlin during the First World War. She had now taken up sculpture again, and he bought two bronze figures from her as a Christmas present for Suse.

The year 1935, which was to bring much misery, started encouragingly. Ditzen, who had been off alcohol since mid-December, was making good progress with his new novel, which was provisionally entitled *Und wenn der letzte Schnee verbrennt* (literally: 'Even If the Last Drop of Snow is Burned'). He had received some requests for articles and short stories, and he was cheered by the news that Langenbucher had resigned from his post 'on grounds of ill-health'. From early January, English lessons were held on two evenings a week for Suse, Fräulein Kluge and Suse's niece Käti Blöcker. Ditzen wrote to his parents: 'I act as teacher, we read English fairy tales and do language work including dictation and grammar. We all knew a little English before and are now brushing it up and learning some more – we are all enjoying it a lot.'

After fifteen months in Carwitz, Ditzen was somewhat disenchanted with village life: 'They are all at war with each other, nobody has a good word to say about anyone else, and after a few not very pleasant experiences we have withdrawn from it all.' Ditzen modelled the squabbling and in-fighting in the fictional village of Unsadel in 'Even If the Last Drop of Snow is Burned' on his experience of Carwitz.

Throughout 1935, he was plagued by money worries. In the course of the year, he took out three loans – from the bank, from Rowohlt and from his parents – and was forced to suspend the quarterly payments he had been making via his parents to the Hörigs. His smallholding had required considerable investment in 1934 and had produced a 7,000 mark deficit for the year; the official campaign against his work was beginning to affect sales and the tax authorities calculated his tax bill for 1934 on the basis of his income in 1933. He would have done well to have heeded Rowohlt's advice about looking after his money.

Rowohlt had had a good year in 1934 and was confident that the Nazi government's first foreign policy coup – the plebiscite in January 1935 which returned the Saar to Germany after fifteen years under League of Nations administration – would usher in a period of 'great peace-making in Europe', which would be very good for business. With hindsight, it is only too obvious that the Saar's heavy industry, its coal and iron ore, were to fuel a very different business from the one Rowohlt had in mind.

By the end of February, Ditzen had finished the first draft of his novel and set about revising it. This proved more difficult than he had anticipated; then his typewriter broke down. A tax bill for 16,000 marks, which he was in no position to pay, added to his troubles. On 4 March, Rowohlt wrote suggesting that they should discuss Ditzen's new novel with Peter Suhrkamp, with a view to removing any politically sensitive material. He conveyed Suhrkamp's view that the title was too frivolous and that Ditzen could have saved himself a lot of bother if he had made a few judicious cuts to his previous two novels.

Rowohlt, who was only trying to be helpful, was completely unaware of Ditzen's antipathy towards Suhrkamp. In his '1944 Prison Memoirs', Ditzen identifies what irritated him so much about Peter Suhrkamp: 'All his life he remained a school master, an instructor, and he could be a real sourpuss and damned hurtful in this role.'[17] Ditzen did not take criticism easily, and Suhrkamp, although in principle extremely positive about Ditzen's work, nonetheless expressed some criticism: he had not approved of the Grosz illustration for *Little Man – What Now?* and he criticized the conclusion of *Once We Had a Child*, two aspects which, as we have seen, were particularly close to Ditzen's heart. In addition, Suhrkamp didn't hesitate to lecture Ditzen on his drinking or the negative effects of his behaviour on Suse, particularly in the summer of 1933.

The paranoia which had appeared the previous year in Ditzen's jealousy of Zingler now surfaced in the conviction that Suhrkamp was trying to drive a wedge between himself and Rowohlt. Ditzen replied to Rowohlt's suggestion, in a letter bristling with indignation, that he wanted nothing to do with Suhrkamp and that he did not want anyone to meddle with his work. He did, however, agree to change the rather unwieldy title of his current novel. By 16 March, Ditzen was suffering from 'a particularly nasty depression'.

Meanwhile, Rowohlt, still optimistic about the prospects for peace in Europe, had gone to Paris on 8 March and signed a contract with Jules Romains, the author of the comedy *Knock* and the 'roman fleuve' *Les hommes de bonne volonté*, the first volume of which had appeared in 1932. Romains, who was president of the German–French Friendship Society and enjoyed the favour of the Nazi authorities, insisted that Franz Hessel translate his work. Rowohlt saw a contract with Romains as a means of securing employment for the non-Aryan Hessel, who was finding it increasingly difficult to earn a living in Germany.

Göring's confirmation the next day of the existence of a German air force and Hitler's announcement a week later of the reintroduction of conscription – both in clear defiance of the Treaty of Versailles – dealt a severe blow to Rowohlt's international business. In addition, his marriage was in difficulties and he was also in the process of moving office. It was therefore a rather harassed Rowohlt who opened the door of his house in Grünheide on the evening of 16 March 1935 to a very irritable Ditzen, who was determined to start a row. After a heated exchange, Ditzen stormed out and caught the train to Munich, where the Gundermanns called a doctor and had him admitted to hospital. The diagnosis was 'manic depression, a recurrence of the illness of my youth'. He ascribed his depression in part to 'the ostracism to which I am subjected at the moment'. Suse arrived in Munich at the end of the month to bring him home. After an exhausting journey – a cancelled flight, a sleeper which broke down and then an overcrowded train – they eventually arrived back in Carwitz. Ditzen's depression, however, failed to lift completely.

Rowohlt declared himself willing to forgive and forget, urged Ditzen not to worry about his tax bill, assured him that there was no deadline for his novel and concluded: 'I am still of the opinion, dear Herr Ditzen, that the most important thing for you is to take a complete break from work as soon as possible and have a rest.'[18] Ditzen accepted Rowohlt's olive branch but insisted that Suhrkamp was trying to destroy their friendship. He could not help worrying about his declining income, and promised Rowohlt he would finish his novel as soon as possible. He had invited Dora Preisach for Easter with a view to dictating the novel, but for the whole of April he was in no condition to work. She was only too pleased to escape from Berlin: acts of terror against the German Jewish population had reached a new peak at the end of March.

Rowohlt wrote again on 11 April, reassuring Ditzen and telling him:

> What makes you, dear friend, so very worthwhile and fascinating is the fact that every nerve of your body and, even, your intellect, your mind, is constantly vibrating and trembling and always reacting to everything all the time. That is why you will never . . . be short of material. You will always have new ideas for new books, for your ideas come in quick succession. That is something quite magnificent.

Rowohlt sent an accountant to Carwitz on 24 April to advise Ditzen on his tax bill. However, by the end of the month Ditzen was still not eating well and was spending most of his time in bed. He wrote to his sister on 29 April: 'I can no longer write what I want. I really enjoy writing stories but you can only tell a good story by simply giving free rein to it, without thinking about the audience and so on. And so I can't write any more.'

Ditzen had been receiving treatment from the local doctor but, as this seemed to be having no effect, Suse took him to Berlin on 2 May to the clinic where he had been successfully treated in 1933. Here he suffered a complete nervous breakdown. The ensuing treatment included sleeping tablets, which turned out to be too strong and induced hallucinations. Suse later recalled: 'It was terrible. This time I really thought he was going insane.'

Rowohlt, who had been ordered by his doctor to take a twelve-day break, returned to Berlin on 12 May and was so shocked when he saw Ditzen that he contacted the leading psychiatrist in Berlin, Professor Bonhoeffer, at the Charité hospital, and had Ditzen transferred there immediately. Bonhoeffer stopped the treatment and Ditzen began to recover, although he retained no memory of the fourteen days when he had been so dangerously ill. A month later, he wrote to his sister that 'the terror which pursued me through all my hallucinations is still with me.'

Ditzen was very fortunate to have been placed under the care of Professor Karl Bonhoeffer. Not only was he leading in his field but, according to his daughter Christine: '. . . he had an exceptionally keen eye for all that was genuine, spontaneous and creative. He made us sense his respect for warm-hearted, unselfish, self-disciplined courses of action, and he took it for granted that we would side with the weaker party.'[19] Bonhoeffer's second son, Walter, had been killed on the Western Front in 1918; he was to lose another two sons, Klaus, a lawyer, and Dietrich, the resistance theologian, as well as two sons-in-law at the hands of the Nazi executioner.

Through Bonhoeffer, Ditzen was reunited with a schoolfriend from Leipzig, Willi Burlage, who had trained in psychiatric medicine under Bonhoeffer and worked a number of years as Bonhoeffer's registrar before taking over the Heidehaus clinic in Zepernick, near Berlin.

While Ditzen was in hospital, Suse called into Rowohlt's new office in Eislebener Strasse and asked Ledig to ensure that letters to Ditzen contained nothing that might upset him. She also took care of her sister, who had come to Carwitz for a rest. The question of Suse requiring a rest was, once more, deferred.

Ditzen was able to return to Carwitz at the beginning of June, determined to 'live more prudently. And completely without any kind of alcohol whatsoever.' For the first time since he had turned freelance in October 1931, he received no income from his writing in June 1935. In addition to the housekeeping and wages bills in Carwitz, there were now hospital accounts to be paid. The Ditzens were not entirely without income, however, for the produce of Suse's market garden brought in some 150 marks per month over the summer, but this was not enough to cover their outgoings. As soon as Ditzen felt sufficiently recovered, he sat down at his typewriter, for 'my main job is to finish the novel because our financial position is bad.'

Dora Preisach, who was waiting to emigrate to Haifa, arrived in Carwitz in the third week in June and was able to deliver the manuscript, now entitled *Altes Herz geht auf die Reise* (*Old Heart Goes on a Journey*) to Rowohlt on the last day of the month.[20]

This novel has been traditionally regarded as one of Ditzen's minor works and, indeed, the plot stretches the reader's credulity. A 66-year-old retired and somewhat unworldly teacher receives a letter from his 16-year-old orphaned god-daughter, whom he has never seen and who is being robbed of her inheritance by scheming foster-parents. As a result of this, he sets out to help her right a wrong. With the help of the young people of the village, he succeeds and they all live happily ever after. The novel even begins: 'Once upon a time there was an old teacher by the name of Gotthold Kittguß,' and the heading of the first chapter, 'Gotthold Kittguß is visited by an angel and sent to Unsadel', prepares the reader for a fairy tale.

However, given the difficulties Ditzen experienced in its writing and the trouble it was later to cause him, *Old Heart Goes on a Journey* deserves closer examination. The first striking aspect of the novel is the occupation of the hero – originally a teacher of religion and the classics, when the novel opens he is a New Testament scholar who has retired from the world into his study. This is an odd choice on two counts: firstly, because Ditzen, as we have seen, rejected Christianity in his adolescence and had hitherto only ever presented a very negative view of Christians in his work; secondly, Old and New Testament scholars were very much out of favour with the Nazis, on account of their supposed pacifism and consequent opposition to military service. Kittguß does not remain a New Testament scholar but in the course of the novel rejects biblical exegesis in favour of a much more active form of Christianity. Indeed, his position is identical to that of the Confessing Church (*Bekennende Kirche*) as articulated, for example, in Dietrich Bonhoeffer's view that the Church should 'not just bandage the victims under the wheel but put a spoke in the wheel itself'.[21] The good which Kittguß represents in the novel is based on the principles of non-violent Christian action. The heroine, Rosemarie, outlines her vision for the village of Unsadel: 'We want a different village ... What do we have now? Everyone is at war with everyone else ... we don't want that any more. Everyone should be friends, everyone should help everyone else.' Besides the biblical scholar, Rosemarie's allies include a mentally retarded youth and a doctor with a background in alternative medicine. This line-up was unlikely to find approval in Germany in 1935.

The forces of evil are personified in the Schliekers, Rosemarie's foster-parents who, as outsiders, have usurped the rightful owner and laid waste to Rosemarie's farm. While no one in the village likes them, no one is prepared to take action against them. The narrator explains, with a quotation from the writer Fritz Reuter, that the name Schlieker is a northern German form of 'Schleicher'. Among the Schliekers' many misdeeds are the abuse of innocent children and the burning of Rosemarie's father's books. The contemporary references to General von Schleicher, whose chancellorship paved the way for fascism, and the burning of valuable books, need little elaboration.

With *Old Heart Goes on a Journey*, Ditzen was attempting, as we have seen, to write 'a contemporary novel without making it contemporary'. He was not the only writer left in Germany in 1935 who was attempting to oppose the Nazi regime in his work. Werner Bergengruen conceived *Der Großtyrann und das Gericht* ('The Great Tyrant and the Court') as 'a weapon to be used on the front of intellectual resistance'. The novel describes a ruler's abuse of power and the vulnerability of his subjects, who are too frightened to resist. Bergengruen's approach is a conservative Christian one. In the end, the tyrant realizes his failings, and both he and his subjects are presented as being guilty in God's eyes. The Nazi cultural authorities welcomed this novel as a '"Führer" novel of the Renaissance age'. It remained to be seen how Ditzen's novel would be received.

In the course of the summer, the campaign against the Jews gathered momentum. Rowohlt received a letter in July from the Reich Literary Chamber instructing him to dismiss Paul Mayer by 1 January 1936. All contracts with foreign publishers now had to be approved by the chamber in advance. It is little wonder that Rowohlt fell ill.

On 27 July, all registry offices received instructions to conclude no more marriages between German Jews and non-Jews. In his farewell letter to Dora Preisach, written four days later, Ditzen wrote: 'We have been so worried about you in recent weeks that we almost prefer you to be far away.' They were going to miss Dora Preisach, for not only was she a good typist and a family friend but she had regularly gone shopping for them in Berlin and dispatched the kinds of groceries which it was impossible to buy in Feldberg.

At the end of July, Fräulein Kluge left their service, which meant a reduction in expenditure but also an increasing workload for Suse: 'Harvesting, planting, children, preserving, book-keeping and so on – she hardly has time to draw breath,' Ditzen wrote to Kagelmacher.

He had some good news at the beginning of August, when the *Berliner Illustrirte* offered 10,000 marks for the pre-launch serialization of *Old Heart Goes on a Journey*. Dr Palitzsch, one of the magazine's editors, arrived in Carwitz to work on the novel. At this point, it became clear that Ditzen's strategy of setting the novel in 1912 and presenting it as a fairy tale had not fooled anyone. If the novel was to be serialized and if he was to receive the much-needed 10,000 marks, changes were required: Kittguß was not to be religious, Rosemarie's young friend was not to be mentally retarded, Frau Schlieker was not to be an epileptic and each episode would have to contain something positive. Faced with the choice between his principles and his pocket, Ditzen declared: 'I cannot afford to be proud, I'll have to get down to work.'

This was the first of a number of occasions over the next nine years when Ditzen wrote humanist, clearly non-Nazi novels and then capitulated to the demands of the censor. As we have seen, he frequently wrote under great financial pressure, which continued to be an important factor. It also has to be said that his opposition to the Nazi regime was an instinctive, emotional one based on rather nebulous and individual concepts such as 'decency', not on a firm philosophical foundation such as Christianity or Marxism. This does not diminish his rejection of fascism in any way, but it does mean that his opposition remained isolated, individual and, like most opposition inside Germany, largely ineffective. All his life he had been a loner – an outsider at school, then a book-keeper and farm manager whose position lay between that of the farm labourers and the landowners, a prisoner in a regime which promoted the survival of the fittest, a newspaper man in a provincial town with the threat of dismissal hanging over him, and then a writer – by definition a solitary existence. It was not in his nature to seek out other opponents of fascism and join together in political action. He would help victims of fascism in an individual way where he could, he would never return the Nazi salute, he would attempt in his work to promote his concept of decency and humanity, but he could do no more. Moreover, in his attitude to fascism, we can also discern the lingering traces of an authoritarian upbringing in the Wilhelmine age.

So keen was Ditzen to earn money that he overcame his distaste for film work and spent the second half of August 1935 in Berlin working on a filmscript based on Jules Romains' *Donogoo Tonka*. For this he received 4,000 marks plus expenses. Suse and the children joined him when he was finished and they all paid a brief visit to Wilhelm and Elisabeth Ditzen in Leipzig, returning to Berlin by plane as a special treat for Uli.

On 2 September, Ledig submitted *Old Heart Goes on a Journey* to the Reich Literary Chamber to secure approval to publish abroad. Two days later, Ditzen finished abridging it for serialization and decided to take a four-week break. He told Rowohlt on 11 September that he was in 'excellent form, beginning to feel like working again' and that he was enjoying the good weather in Carwitz. The next day he received the chamber's response to *Old Heart Goes on a Journey*: he had been declared an 'undesirable author' (*unerwünschter Autor*), which meant that his work could not be published abroad, nor could translation rights be sold. Ditzen feared that this decision was a prelude to banning his work in Germany, too. Erich Kästner suffered a similar fate in the same year when all his books were included in the 'List of Harmful and Undesirable Writings'.[22]

On 15 September 1935, Hitler announced at the party congress in Nuremberg the infamous Law for the Protection of German Blood and German Honour, which stripped German Jews of their citizenship, prohibited marital and extra-marital relationships between German Jews and other Germans and prohibited German Jews from employing non-Jews in their households. This was followed up by a new Citizenship Law differentiating between Germans with proven Aryan credentials and the rest.

The day after the announcement of the Nuremberg Laws, the Ditzens went to Berlin to appeal against the chamber's decision regarding his 'undesirable' status. Everyone advised them 'to emigrate legally to London or Copenhagen'. Rowohlt was prepared to release Ditzen from all contractual obligations and help procure a new contract for him abroad. Ditzen wrote to his sister Elisabeth on 21 September: 'Suse and I are not keen on the idea of living in a country far away, because we are both so attached to Germany. I only really feel at home in northern Germany. Perhaps we will be able to avoid it after all. We do hope so.'

They were most reluctant to give up Carwitz, 'although on the other hand it is doubtful whether we'll be able to hold on to Carwitz if we stay' – as he admitted to Kagelmacher. While the preserving and sale of their fruit and vegetables had been very successful, and their pig farming kept them (as well as their wider family and friends) well supplied with meat, ham and sausage, Ditzen estimated that the smallholding would take another two years to make a profit. However, a big attraction of Carwitz was the amount of free food available – fish, rabbits, mushrooms, blackberries, sloes, and so on. In any case, they would only be allowed to emigrate if they paid the Reich emigration tax (*Reichsfluchtsteuer*) and, even if they could afford that, which was doubtful, they would have no resources left to start afresh in a new country.

Ditzen threw himself into work. He completed the collection of children's stories for Reclam on 28 September. At the beginning of October, he started a new novel, *Märchen vom Stadtschreiber, der aufs Land flog (Sparrow Farm)*, which he wrote in seventeen days.

An indication that he was feeling under pressure is the row he had in early October with Rowohlt, who, not unreasonably, suggested retaining 2,000 of the 9,000 marks fee due to Ditzen in October as partial repayment of a loan he had supplied earlier in the year. Ditzen flew off the handle, refused to come to the phone and accused Rowohlt of interrupting his writing. He eventually calmed down and apologized to his friend on 12 October, by which time he had negotiated a much-reduced tax bill. Ditzen assured Rowohlt that they were living as economically as possible, that Suse was in charge of all their financial affairs, and remarked: 'If I were a thrifty housekeeper and a sober businessman I would probably not write any books.'

Four days later, Rowohlt sent Heinz Kiwitz, whom he had engaged to illustrate *Sparrow Farm*, to Carwitz. Kiwitz had been active in the Association of Revolutionary Artists before the Nazis came to power, had been arrested by the Gestapo in September 1933 and been interned in Börgermoor concentration camp from January to March 1934. Since the beginning of 1935 he had been eking out a meagre existence in Berlin, where Rowohlt had come across him. If he did not know before, Ditzen learned from Kiwitz what could happen to opponents of the Nazi regime.

Fräulein Siebert, Rowohlt's personal secretary, started typing *Sparrow Farm* on 21 October in Carwitz. Five days later, the manuscript was ready and sent straight to the printers in Leipzig for publication in time for Christmas. Ditzen's work tempo did not let up. He woke on 30 October with an idea for another project, which he started immediately. He told his sister Elisabeth: 'I am not going to talk about it, not for a long time. It probably won't be possible to publish it.'

The question of publication was becoming acute. Rowohlt's business had been taken over by Ullstein, which itself had been swallowed by the huge Nazi Party publishing concern in Munich, Eher-Verlag, in 1934 – another indication of the general trend towards the centralization of economic and political life in Germany. Ditzen wrote 'in code' to Dora Preisach, now in Haifa, on 31 October: '[We] have been uncertain for the past four weeks whether to stay in Carwitz or take a trip, perhaps to see Hertha. Our little father is in poor shape and intends to resign on 1 April 1936.' 'Hertha' was Dora Preisach's second name and here indicates their indecision about emigration. 'Little father' is, of course, Rowohlt, who began to consider emigration in October 1935.

By 6 November, Ditzen was complaining that 'he was not in good form and not sleeping well'. The good news that the sale of the film rights to 'Once a Jailbird' would bring in 12,000 marks failed to raise his spirits. The decision of the Reich Literary Chamber regarding his 'undesirable' status, Rowohlt's situation, Kiwitz's experience and the question of emigration all pushed him further into depression. Two reviews of *Once We Had a Child* which appeared in November 1935 seem to have nudged him over the edge. After his depression worsened on Friday 22 November, Suse took him to Burlage's clinic, where he remained – apart from a short visit to Carwitz over Christmas – until the beginning of February 1936.

The news that Ditzen's 'undesirable' status was rescinded on 4 December no doubt contributed to the improvement Suse observed when she visited him the following weekend. Burlage and his colleague, Dr Wanda Oster, were able to reduce his medication shortly afterwards and, by the time *Sparrow Farm* appeared on 10 December, Ditzen was making slow but gradual progress.

Sparrow Farm is a sad illustration of Ditzen's response to Nazi intimidation in 1935: it is a fairy tale set in another century, with witches and sorcerers, black and white magic, which relates how the clerk Guntram Spatt comes into his inheritance and wins the hand of his cousin Monika.[23] Even this unpromising material permits glimpses of Ditzen's talent as a story-teller and his exploration of new narrative techniques. However, without Kiwitz's striking black and white woodcuts, the book would be of very little value.

Children's stories and harmless fairy tales with happy endings were two strategies for survival as a writer in Nazi Germany. While such work would earn Ditzen some money, it would undoubtedly arrest his development as a writer and, ultimately, not satisfy his own literary aspirations.

He returned to Carwitz at the beginning of February 1936, accompanied by Nurse Sophie Zickermann, whom he described as 'intelligent, witty and patient'. He was by now well recovered and sleeping without medication, although physically weak and irritable. Burlage had advised him to take a two-year break from writing and Ditzen seemed initially inclined to accept this advice. He turned his attention to his smallholding, had a boathouse built and an irrigation plant installed to use lake water to irrigate the garden during the spring and summer, when the sandy Carwitz soil frequently dried out, jeopardizing the fruit and vegetable harvest. He also determined not to read any more reviews of his work, citing the general reception of *Once We Had a Child* as an example of how wrong readers can be: '... all my dear women readers have completely misunderstood Gäntschow and think I actively support this way of treating women.'[24]

In the middle of February, the first episode of *Old Heart Goes on a Journey* appeared in the *Berliner Illustrirte*. A few days later, Rowohlt arrived in Carwitz to discuss Ditzen's future plans. As a result of their recent experiences, author and publisher agreed that an historical novel and translation work offered Ditzen two viable means of earning a living as a writer. Shortly after Rowohlt returned to Berlin, he sent Ditzen a copy of Clarence Day's *Life with Father*, which had enjoyed considerable success in the United States and Britain. Ditzen was enthusiastic and undertook to submit a German translation by 1 July for a fee of 800 marks. At the end of February he resumed work on the novel which he had begun the previous autumn, a medieval chronicle entitled *Wizzel Kien*. Historical novels became increasingly popular among non-Nazi writers such as Werner Bergengruen, Jochen Klepper and Reinhold Schneider. Klepper noted in his diary the popularity of history with authors and readers alike, and in particular 'the kind of history which does not justify or glorify the present but the kind which calls it into question', and wondered: 'Is this just the last refuge of impotent opposition?'[25]

The volume of seven children's stories which Ditzen had completed the previous September for Reclam appeared at the end of February 1936 under the title *Hoppelpoppel. Wo bist du?* ('Hoppelpoppel – Where are You?'). Hoppelpoppel was a pull-along toy dog which Elisabeth Ditzen had sent her grandson Uli in 1931 and to which he had become very attached. Ditzen had every reason to be satisfied with the book, apart from the paltry fee of 350 marks, because Reclam had engaged Felix Riemkasten, one of the few Fallada enthusiasts still tolerated by the Nazis, to write an appreciative postscript. Five of the seven stories had been published before. The two new ones – '*Häusliches Zwischenspiel*' ('Domestic Incident') and '*Die verlorenen Grünfinken*' ('The Lost Greenfinches') – are clearly based on family life in Carwitz and particularly on the relationship between the author and his son. Ditzen's children's stories are well observed and related in a gripping manner likely to hold a child's attention. They testify to Ditzen's own love of children and his delight in entering into their joys and sorrows. Such stories also provided him with an opportunity to depict a world based on the principles of humanity and decency where good inexorably triumphs over evil.

In the real world of 1936, it was the forces of evil which seemed to have gained the upper hand. On 7 March, the German government sent the army into the demilitarized zone of the Rhineland, thereby dealing a fatal blow to the Treaty of Versailles, and officially repudiated the Treaty of Locarno. This breach of international law resulted in a flurry of diplomatic activity but no action against German aggression. Ditzen feared that Germany's foreign policy would damage the sale of his books abroad. In the course of 1936, the German economy became increasingly geared towards war. Conscription was extended to two years and even Rowohlt was called up for four weeks' military training in April.

The health problems which had dogged Suse since the birth of the twins in 1933 came to a head in early 1936 and she was admitted to hospital on 16 March for a bladder operation which turned out to be more serious than expected. It was almost a month before she could return to Carwitz. The day before she went into hospital, Hubert Räder, a young man who had been engaged to take over the fruit and vegetable garden, arrived in Carwitz. Sophie Zickermann stayed on to look after the children, both of whom had contracted mumps. Ditzen went to Berlin on Saturday 28 March to visit Suse and spent the following day, when elections to the Reichstag recorded a 98.8 per cent vote of confidence in the Nazi regime, in the company of Rowohlt and Ledig in Grünheide.

Ditzen, Sophie and the children brought Suse home from hospital on Easter Saturday. A week later, on 17 April, he finished volume one of *Wizzel Kien*. That same evening, Uli was diagnosed as having meningitis; he was admitted to hospital in Berlin a few days later. Ditzen decided to take a break: 'My sensitivity to noise, which has become a sensitivity to the lightest sound, is getting worse and is a great source of annoyance both to myself and others.'[26] He confessed to Rowohlt on 17 April that he was 'not in good form'. Apart from the upset of Suse's absence and Uli's illness, he had been irritated by the comprehensive rewrite of his Jules Romains translation *Donogoo Tonka*. Then some craft guilds had objected to craftsmen being mentioned in the same context as poachers in *Old Heart Goes on a Journey*. The next blow came from an unexpected source: the *Volksgesundheit*, the official Nazi medical journal, concluded a review of *Old Heart Goes on a Journey* with an unmistakable threat: 'We are not willing to let someone whom we generously permit to continue to earn a living in Germany upset our reconstruction of the German nation. Herr Fallada would do well to note this for future reference.' The *Volksgesundheit* took exception to the positive role allotted to Dr Kimmknirsch, who had a background in alternative medicine and who was in the habit of telling his patients: 'I prescribe what I think is best – that's my affair. And you do with my prescriptions what you think is best – that's your affair.' The reviewer wrote that such a doctor 'in our National Socialist opinion has no longer any place in Germany'.

Rowohlt sent Ditzen this review from his army training camp near the Polish border in Frankfurt on the Oder on 26 April. For Ditzen, it was the last straw. He had made all the changes required to *Old Heart Goes on a Journey*; he had even agreed to change the title from 'Old Heart Goes on a Journey' to 'A Heart Goes on a Journey' to please the *Berliner Illustrirte*, and had not objected to a thoroughly objectionable introduction to the novel which had preceded the serialization. Even when every concession had been made, there was still no peace. Nor was there any hope of redress. With a heavy heart, he placed a notice in the newspaper advertising his property in Carwitz for sale. He wrote to his parents on 1 May: 'There is no point talking about these attacks. It feels as if it is open season on Hans Fallada. But now I must draw the logical conclusion from all of this. I see no possibility of ever writing again. So we are going to try – we have just taken the first steps – to sell Carwitz and then we'll see what we'll do.' The fact that the Ditzens were planning to emigrate is clear from the end of the letter: 'My dear parents, I am so sorry to have to write you this terrible letter. But it would be more terrible if I were suddenly to inform you of a fait accompli.'

By the time Elisabeth and Wilhelm Ditzen received their son's letter, he had been admitted to Burlage's clinic in Zepernick. The prospect of emigration had plunged him into another depression.

On 2 May, the day after his admission, Ditzen rang Suse to say he was feeling much better. Then he set out to visit Uli in hospital in Berlin. The sight of his son, who was still running a high temperature, greatly upset Ditzen and he suffered a relapse. Burlage diagnosed 'endogenous melancholia with attacks of depression' triggered by external events. He was confident that Ditzen's condition, while it might recur, was curable. Ditzen responded well to medication and was able to return home on 18 May. Sophie Zickermann returned to Carwitz with him and stayed on to nurse Uli, who had been discharged from hospital the previous week, and to keep an eye on Suse, who had developed a gall-bladder complaint.

By the end of June, Ditzen, Suse and Uli were all feeling better and Sophie Zickermann was able to leave. Ditzen wrote to the Hörigs on 28 June that his recent illness had taught him that 'the best sanatorium, the most caring doctor and the soundest sleep cannot help one solve life's more difficult problems.' They had received little response to their advertisement offering Carwitz for sale and decided 'to take things slowly and not make any hasty decisions'.

Faced with the prospect of not being allowed to publish the sort of books he wanted and the difficulty of selling the house and land in

Carwitz, Ditzen decided on a new strategy. He would take out a mortgage on the house to provide some financial security for a few years; he would economize by reducing the wages bill and renting out the land behind the house (retaining the market garden for their own use); and he would continue the *Wizzel Kien* project, which he intended to run to some eight volumes and which would not be published for three years. He was confident that he could negotiate a monthly fee with Rowohlt to cover this period. His strategy was based on the assumption, prevalent in Germany at the time, that the Nazi regime would run out of steam in a few years' time. The steps he was planning would guarantee some financial security and allow him to continue writing without actually publishing anything for the foreseeable future, thus avoiding the kind of attacks which were so detrimental to his health.

Ditzen submitted his translation of Clarence Day's *Life with Father*, entitled *Unser Herr Vater*, which he described as 'quite a nice, harmless bit of fun but really very slight', on 1 July. Two days later, Rowohlt arrived with the Burlages – now frequent visitors in Carwitz – and Burlage's colleague, Wanda Oster, for the weekend. When Ditzen explained his new strategy to Rowohlt, he was dismayed to discover that Rowohlt wanted him to keep writing the kind of book that could be serialized in the *Berliner Illustrirte* and turned into a film. Ditzen took the view that 'to become a successful writer of the most lightweight sort seems to me to be a great failure'.[27]

When Ditzen insisted that he wanted to continue with *Wizzel Kien*, Rowohlt offered him a mere 100 marks a month for three years. Ditzen promptly lost his temper, and relations between author and publisher remained cool for the next eight months.

The assumption that the Nazi regime would soon 'settle down' became increasingly untenable in the course of 1936. In June, Himmler, hitherto in charge of the SS, became in addition chief of police, thus bringing the police service firmly within the control of the Nazi Party. The Austro-German Agreement of 11 July further undermined Austria's independence and paved the way for its annexation some two years later. Germany's intervention on the side of Franco in the Spanish Civil War in July, and the appointment in September of

Göring as 'Plenipotentiary for the Four-Year Plan', with its barely concealed military objectives, indicated the Nazi government's priorities and its determination to stay in power.

Ditzen went ahead with his plans to take out a mortgage on his property, reduce his wage bill and rent out his land. The row with Rowohlt in July resulted in the abandonment of *Wizzel Kien*, but he did not abandon his determination to write serious novels. By the beginning of September, he informed the Hörigs that he had started a new novel but that he was 'working only for myself without any thought of publishing in the foreseeable future'. By the end of October he had written six hundred pages. A week before Christmas, he announced that his new novel 'is very similar to B.B.B. [*A Small Circus*] ... It is an advance on B.B.B. in so far as it has considerably fewer characters, the plot is much easier to follow and women play a much greater role.'

The new novel was titled *Wolf among Wolves*, and the main character, Wolfgang Pagel, was closely modelled on Wolfgang Parsenow, son of Lotte Fröhlich-Parsenow. The origin of this book may lie in a visit to Carwitz by the Fröhlichs in 1936 before they emigrated to the United States.[28]

Besides his new novel, Ditzen was also working on another book of children's stories. In September 1936 he wrote a foreword to a collection of woodcuts by Heinz Kiwitz which developed the story of Enak, one of the characters in *Sparrow Farm*. In this piece Ditzen praised Kiwitz's illustration of Enak, 'protector of the poor, friend of the whole world and always far removed from any sort of nastiness'. By the time this volume appeared, Kiwitz had left Germany to go into exile in Denmark.

In the third week in September, Ada Ditzen arrived in Carwitz. She had brought some translation work with her and had planned to stay some time. Ditzen had not seen his aunt for almost nineteen years. They had, however, corresponded and, as we have seen, she had supported him whenever she could. The Ditzens were therefore sorry to see her leave on 25 October, earlier than planned, when she received news that a close friend, a professor at the University of Marburg, had attempted suicide.

October also brought worrying news about Kagelmacher. His

unconventional lifestyle had attracted the attention of the authorities, who sent a welfare worker to investigate his circumstances. When he refused to cooperate, the Act for the Prevention of Hereditary Diseases of 1934 was invoked and he was informed that he was to be sterilized. This piece of legislation, originally a measure against the mentally handicapped, was increasingly used against people who did not conform to the Nazi ideal of the hard-working, patriotic German. When Kagelmacher refused to undergo voluntary sterilization, he was admitted to a psychiatric clinic for six weeks' observation. Ditzen asked Burlage for advice and admitted to having a bad conscience about not being able to do more for someone who for years had been 'a very loyal friend, and decent – unlike most of the others'.

In mid-October, Hubert Räder, who had been indispensable in the garden, was called up for military service. He had become a firm favourite with the children and endeared himself so much to the Ditzens that they invited him to spend his periods of leave in Carwitz, an offer he eagerly accepted. The signing of treaties with Italy and Japan in the autumn of 1936, which established the Berlin–Rome–Tokyo Axis, cast a long shadow over everyone's future, including young Germans like Hubert Räder.

By the end of 1936, Ditzen's household had shrunk to the immediate family, one maid and a gardener-cum-stockman. Their land had been rented out. The produce of their market garden would in future be for their own consumption, so they had no further use for the horse and cart, both of which were sold. They also planned to sell their cow once she had calved.

The Ditzens celebrated Christmas 1936 with Suse's mother and the Palitzsches, who had become friends as a result of Palitzsch's work on the serialization of *Old Heart Goes on a Journey*. Palitzsch had suffered a nervous breakdown in August and had convalesced in Feldberg and Carwitz. The New Year was welcomed 'quietly and completely without alcohol'. Ditzen asked Rowohlt not to tell him about bad reviews or attacks on his work and instructed Ledig not to forward any letters from admiring readers: 'I would like to withdraw into my shell like a snail and cut myself off from the world.'[29]

Yet even in a place as remote as Carwitz it was impossible to ignore 'the world' in 1937. On 14 February, the Ditzens' house was the target in an air-raid drill. A few days later, he received a letter from the military authorities informing him that he could be called up for eight weeks' training. Then the Palitzsches announced that they were going to divorce: Frau Palitzsch was, according to the Nuremberg Laws, a 'half-Jewess' and therefore an 'unsuitable' partner for her husband, who was a member of the Reich Cultural Chamber. In the first week in March, Kagelmacher arrived in Carwitz. He had now been diagnosed as schizophrenic and sentenced to compulsory sterilization. With Burlage's assistance, Ditzen organized a successful appeal and Kagelmacher eventually settled in Stralsund on the Baltic coast.

At the beginning of April, the Ministry for Education removed 'Hoppelpoppel – Where are You?' from all school libraries because the story '*Lüttenweihnachten*', which celebrated the banned pagan festival of 'Little Christmas', was considered unsuitable for children. Ditzen refused to accede to Reclam's request for a substitute story.

At this time, Ditzen had other, more serious matters on his mind. His father was terminally ill and died of cancer on Tuesday 14 April. Suse and Ditzen set out for Leipzig the same day and Rowohlt met them at the station in Berlin. This meeting marked an improvement in the relations between author and publisher. Rowohlt was delighted to hear about *Wolf among Wolves* and it was agreed that he should come to Carwitz after Wilhelm Ditzen's funeral. In Leipzig, Rudolf took charge of all the arrangements, looked after his mother and generally retained his composure during a very fraught seven days. It was little wonder that he fell ill as soon as he arrived home. He nonetheless managed to effect a reconciliation with Rowohlt and agreed a submission date for *Wolf among Wolves*.

Ditzen wrote to his mother on 1 May 1937, exactly a year after announcing his plan to sell Carwitz and possibly leave Germany: 'It is now so wonderful here that it makes my heart glad and dispels any thoughts we ever had of selling Carwitz: here we are and here we are going to stay.' One visitor, who was staying in Carwitz at the time, was coming to a different conclusion: Lore Soldin, a 'half-Jewess' according to the Nuremberg Laws, had lost her job and was seriously thinking of emigrating to England.

Ditzen finished *Wolf among Wolves* on 11 May. Rowohlt arrived with his wife a week later to read the manuscript and celebrate his fiftieth birthday in Carwitz. Rowohlt was now, in Ditzen's words, the government's 'Cultural Enemy Number One', on account of his espousal of 'non-Aryan' authors such as the Czech-German Urban Roedl (Bruno Adler) – author of a biography of Adalbert Stifter – and the Jewish poet Mascha Kaléko. It was therefore with some anticipation that Rowohlt sat down to read Ditzen's new work.

Wolf among Wolves opens at dawn on 26 July 1923 and comes to a close one night almost a year later.[30] It marks a further development of Ditzen's narrative technique and a return to the realism of *A Small Circus* and 'Once a Jailbird'. Its narrative sweep encompasses nearly every aspect of German society, from prostitutes to policemen, from drug addicts and gamblers to farm labourers and art dealers, from the landed gentry to scrap merchants, hoteliers to paramilitary activists. The narrator describes the effects of inflation on town and country: the poverty, the hunger, the unrest, the overcrowded prisons, the paramilitary activity, the despair. The novel tells the story of Petra Ledig and Wolfgang Pagel, lovers at the beginning of the novel, who must first mature as human beings before they can find true happiness together. Petra Ledig, like Lämmchen, discovers that she is pregnant at the beginning of the novel but, unlike Lämmchen, decides that Pagel 'must become a man before he can be a father'. Pagel spends four months working on the Neulohe estate east of the Elbe before returning to Berlin to marry Petra and take up the study of psychiatric medicine.

Ditzen drew on his memory of the period as well as his experience of agriculture, the landed gentry, alcoholism, police stations, prison cells, drug addiction and city life in drawing the many well-observed characters and situations depicted in the novel. Through it all runs his conviction that human beings are frequently the victims of circumstance – 'A desperate people in a desperate position; every despairing individual behaving desperately' – and his belief in human decency and human perfectibility. The narrator understands Petra Ledig's descent into prostitution, and believes in Wolfgang Pagel's ability to learn from his mistakes; he sympathizes with the estate workers in Neulohe who steal because they are hungry. The social criticism singles out the landed gentry, who treat their workers as less than human and squander the harvest at a time of food shortages. The paramilitary 'hero', Lieutenant Fritz, is condemned: 'this cold adventurer who was not concerned with the object of the struggle, but only with the struggle itself; this mercenary who would have fought for any party so long as there was unrest.'

Ditzen's depiction of the consequences of inflation ensured a favourable response from the Nazi cultural authorities, who approved of any critique of the Weimar Republic. The comparison of Captain von Prackwitz's tenancy agreement, imposed by his avaricious and cunning father-in-law, with the Treaty of Versailles under the motto 'To hell with the conquered!' could expect a warm reception from the Nazi press, as could critical remarks about the French occupation of the Ruhr. The depiction of the army's refusal to support the attempted right-wing coup on 1 October 1923 was viewed as realistic and in keeping with the period; it was not in fact until the year of the novel's publication that the German armed forces lost their independence and became integrated into the Nazi state. Like *A Small Circus* before it, *Wolf among Wolves* was seen by the Nazi press as an attack on the hated 'System Era' of the Weimar Republic. As Ditzen was concerned primarily to depict the results of inflation on German society and was not interested in, or indeed capable of, analysing the causes of the widespread misery, the Nazi reviewers, such as the critic of the *Völkischer Beobachter*, were content to read the novel as a reminder of how fascism had saved Germany from mass unemployment, hunger and chaos. Among Ditzen's most enthusiastic Nazi readers was Joseph Goebbels, who described *Wolf among Wolves* in his diary entry for 31 January 1938 as 'a super book' ('*ein tolles Buch*'). Goebbels went on to comment: 'That fellow has real talent.'[31]

In Part One of the novel, covering just over twenty-four hours in some 320 pages, Ditzen develops his narrative technique beyond the stage he achieved in the first part of *Once We Had a Child*. By dividing each chapter into short sub-sections, which initially seem to have little connection, the narrator captures the reader's attention and curiosity, which is then rewarded when the narrative returns to take up a story already begun. Reading becomes an intellectual game in which the reader is challenged to make connections and fit the various parts of the puzzle together. After all the characters have been introduced and the relationships between them established in Part One, the scene shifts from Berlin to Neulohe. The second part of the novel suffers from the kind of narrative drift identified in *Once We Had a Child*, resulting in an imbalance in the narrative, with too much space devoted to the last day in Lieutenant Fritz's life and too little to resolving the various narrative strands in the last chapter. Here the narrator rushes breathlessly from one sub-section to the next, frequently exclaiming, 'We're in a hurry!' as he relates the fate of the Pagels, the Prackwitzes and a whole host of minor characters in a hasty narrative shorthand.

In *Wolf among Wolves*, Ditzen continued his habit of re-using short stories and introducing the names of acquaintances, friends and employees: Ledig, Meier, Sophie, Räder, Liesbeth (a housemaid in Carwitz), Geyer and Wendt (a farm worker in Carwitz).

Rowohlt must have been delighted when he read *Wolf among Wolves* for, despite the features attractive to Nazi cultural practice, the novel is essentially a return to the realist, humanist literature which was Ditzen's strength. Unlike Adam Kuckhoff's *Der Deutsche von Bayencourt*, published by Rowohlt in the same year, *Wolf among Wolves* could not be described as a resistance novel. In it, however, Ditzen renewed his plea for decency and humanity. It is likely that, in 1937, Ditzen shared Wolfgang Pagel's definition of courage: 'I used to think that courage meant standing up straight when a shell exploded and taking your share of the shrapnel. Now I know that's mere stupidity and bravado; courage means keeping going when something becomes completely unbearable.' Five years later, Peter Suhrkamp was to formulate a similar definition of the writer's function in Nazi Germany: 'To give people courage, the courage to face life, is probably the best gift a writer can bestow. The courage to face life is different from the courage to face war. In the same way that to withstand an attack is more difficult than to launch one.'[32]

Rowohlt left Carwitz on 24 June, having promised Ditzen an advance of 10,000 marks. It was also agreed to give the job of proofreading to Franz Hessel. As Rowohlt was no longer allowed to employ the non-Aryan Hessel, he 'officially' paid Ditzen for proof-reading and Ditzen 'unofficially' paid Hessel.

A few hours after the Rowohlts' departure, Sophie Zickermann arrived to take care of Suse, who had developed a stomach ulcer and was to have six weeks' complete rest over the summer. Ditzen was able to secure ten days' 'harvest leave' from the army for Räder, and his niece Ilse Bechert provided additional help in the house. Thanks to the advance he received from Rowohlt, Ditzen was also able to employ a full-time housekeeper, Frau Ellenberg, from the middle of August.

Wolf among Wolves appeared in the shops in mid-September and sold seven thousand copies in four weeks; the first print run of ten thousand was sold out by mid-November. This unaccustomed success took Rowohlt by surprise; as a result, the next ten thousand copies were not available until 29 November. Although unable to match the performance of the top best-seller in Germany in 1937 – Margaret Mitchell's *Gone with the Wind* – *Wolf among Wolves* was a big success. The dearth of good contemporary German fiction undoubtedly accounted in part for the novel's sales figures. As has been shown, the best-selling novels in the period leading up to the Second World War in Germany tended to be nineteenth-century and early twentieth-century works such as Gustav Freytag's *Soll und Haben* (1855), Gustav Frenssen's *Jörn Uhl* (1901) and *Peter Moors Fahrt nach Südwest* (1906), as well as Hans Grimm's *Volk ohne Raum* (1926).[33]

Meanwhile, Ditzen had completed another volume of children's stories and undertaken to translate Clarence Day's *Life with Mother*. Franz Hessel spent a few days in Carwitz in mid-October. Ditzen described him as 'so calm and gentle, old Hessel, he won the children's hearts. He is the most patient person in the world . . . I called him "the last winter fly" for he buzzed so quietly and wistfully through our house.' Hessel's wife and children had already left Germany and he was living in straitened circumstances in Berlin. Ditzen visited him there in the third week in October and Hessel invited him to take any books he wanted from his substantial library. Hessel was another of Ditzen's 'non-Aryan' friends who was contemplating emigration.

At the beginning of November, the Ditzens' own Aryan credentials were questioned by the *Völkischer Beobachter*, as they had not yet procured their official 'Genealogical Identity Cards' (*Ahnenpass*). Ditzen turned to his sister Elisabeth, who had taken up genealogy as a means of earning a living, to undertake the necessary research and provide the documentation.

In the course of 1937, two features of Nazi Germany were becoming increasingly clear: the determination of the regime to remove 'destructive elements' and the setting of the whole economy on a course for war. 'Destructive elements' included not only German Jews (in the very wide definition of the Nuremberg Laws), Communists and Social Democrats, but also Christians who found National Socialism incompatible with their faith. Martin Niemöller, arrested in July 1937, was only one of some 130 clergymen who found themselves in detention camps in the autumn of that year.

Hitler's plans to annex Austria and Czechoslovakia as well as to march eastwards and possibly westwards to secure 'living-space' for the German nation caused consternation in the armed forces. Some generals, as well as the economics minister, Hjalmar Schacht, opposed the speed of rearmament; others feared the consequences of a war on two fronts and preferred to build alliances with the West in order to move against the East. In the course of the winter of 1937–8, many dissenting voices in the armed forces, as well as Schacht and the minister for foreign affairs, Constantin von Neurath, were removed and replaced by party members.

Hitler set this process in motion on 5 November 1937. That same evening, Ditzen had some good news: Mathias Wieman, a member of the Board of the Ufa Film Company, gave a glowing review of *Wolf among Wolves* on the radio. Wieman and his wife visited Carwitz in early December and he offered Ditzen some film work – an offer which Ditzen declined, not because he did not want film work (he could no longer afford the luxury of turning down work) but because he had received a much better offer. On 12 November, he signed a contract with the Tobis Film Company to write a novel 'dealing with the fate of a German family from 1914 until around 1933'. The project, to be submitted by 28 February 1938, had the approval of the Reich Minister for Public Enlightenment and Propaganda, Joseph Goebbels, who, as we have seen, had been impressed by *Wolf among*

Wolves. The star role was to be played by the renowned Emil Jannings, who had taken a personal interest in the negotiations with Ditzen.

Ditzen returned to Carwitz immediately after signing the film contract and got up the next morning at 3 a.m. to start work. By 28 November, he had written two hundred pages. This pace was impossible to sustain and, when the Burlages and the Rowohlts arrived on 8 December for the annual pig-slaughtering, Ditzen collapsed from nervous exhaustion. Burlage was able to treat him on the spot and, after a few days' rest, he resumed work on what was now known as *Iron Gustav*. Four days later he was in Berlin again, negotiating a film contract for *Old Heart Goes on a Journey*, which was finally signed on 20 December.

With contracts signed for a translation and two films, Ditzen could feel more secure at the end of 1937 than he had done for some years. Rowohlt had by now joined the Nazi Party, a step which he hoped would offer a degree of security and protection both to his business and to his authors. With Burlage's help, Ditzen was also becoming more confident about handling his continuing periodic bouts of depression. In fact, his wife and children's health was giving him more cause for concern than his own.

Both children were admitted to hospital in January 1938, Lore with a serious middle-ear infection and burst ear-drum, which required seven weeks' treatment in the Charité hospital in Berlin, and Uli with glandular fever, which required five weeks' hospitalization, followed by a five-month stay at the North Sea spa of St Peter. Suse, who had suffered a recurrence of her kidney complaint the previous autumn, fell ill again in early January. Meanwhile Ditzen continued working on *Iron Gustav*, which he finished on 30 January 1938. He had found it difficult writing a novel according to guidelines determined by the film company, and he described the result as 'hurried' and 'slipshod'.

A new typist, Else Marie Bakonyi, arrived on the evening of 31 January, and Ditzen began dictating the next day.[34] Work was interrupted on 3 February, when he had to report to the military authorities for an assessment of his fitness for duty. The year 1938 witnessed a stepping up of the preparations for war in Germany, and it is an indication of their urgency that someone with Ditzen's medical history was declared 'fit for limited military duties'. He returned to Carwitz and continued dictating at the astonishing rate of fifty pages per day. The worry about his children, the prospect of being called up for military service and the strain of dictation, especially since his new typist did not hide her political sympathies and criticized the novel's lack of patriotic fervour in the passages describing the outbreak of the First World War, all contributed to the onset of depression and the need for a few days' treatment in Burlage's clinic. Despite these setbacks, however, Ditzen managed to submit the manuscript on time, on 28 February.

Emil Jannings was pleased with Ditzen's novel, which offered him a first-class film role in the character of Gustav Hackendahl. Hackendahl was based on the Berlin coachman Gustav Hartmann, known as Iron Gustav on account of his total rejection of the motor car, who sprang to fame when he drove his coach and horse to Paris and back in 1928. Although the trip to Paris marks the climax of the novel, it accounts for only forty out of a total of some seven hundred pages and is very thin on geographical detail.[35] Ditzen's real interest lay in the depiction of the Hackendahl family and his elaboration of the epithet 'iron' beyond a mere refusal to move with the times:

> ... unrelenting, stubborn, obstinate but also upright and beyond reproach. Born late into a bourgeois world which seemed to him too soft, he tried to drum into his children those principles which – or so he thought – had led to his success: hard work, a sense of duty, absolute observance of the rules, subordination to the will of a higher authority – be it God, the Kaiser or the Law.

The novel follows the results of Hackendahl's authoritarian principles: his oldest son, Otto (born 1890), whom he beats and who is too afraid to tell his parents about his disabled girlfriend and their child, dies in the trenches in 1916; his older daughter, Sophie (born 1893), who is incapable of feeling affection, becomes matron of her own private clinic; his favourite son, Erich (born 1897), rebels and devotes his life to criminal activities; his favourite daughter, Eva (born 1896), escapes enslavement to her father only to become enslaved to a pimp; his youngest son, Heinz (born 1901), is the only one who develops into a decent human being, despite his experience of long-term unemployment. He marries one of Ditzen's strong working-class women and has a child. The novel spans the period from 29 June 1914 to the autumn of 1928.

Ditzen employs some of the narrative techniques he developed in *Wolf among Wolves*: the first chapter, subdivided into short sections, covers one day and introduces all the main characters. Fictional names are, again, based on friends, acquaintances and employees: Sophie, Frau Ellenberg, Lindemann, Eggebrecht and Simmichen (the schoolfriend who introduced Ditzen to Necker). Ditzen even allows himself an ironic aside on his own youth: his was 'a well-fed, aestheticizing generation with an inclination to flirt with suicide and beauty' who 'feasted on Hofmannsthal's verses'.

Ditzen also imbues the fictional Gustav's trip to Paris with a symbolic dimension. He not only describes it as a gesture of reconciliation towards the 'traditional enemy' but also as a triumph of the human spirit: '. . . we never give up hope. We may fall but we do not have to stay in the gutter. That is no reason to give up, we must keep on going!' Ditzen brought the story to a close on this note in 1928 and did not continue it, as stipulated in the contract, up to 1933. The critique of authoritarianism, the espousal of Franco–German entente and the promotion of human decency in the figure of Heinz Hackendahl, were clearly incompatible with an affirmation of the rise of National Socialism.

After submitting *Iron Gustav*, the Ditzens moved to Berlin to be near their daughter, Lore, and also to enable Suse to take driving lessons, for they planned to use some of the money from the novel to purchase a car. On Friday 4 March 1938, they became the proud owners of an eight-cylinder Ford. However, before Suse could take her driving test she was admitted to hospital with a serious attack of angina. The stresses and strains of the previous months had left her exhausted; her doctors therefore recommended a long course of treatment in a southern German spa.

The day after Suse entered hospital, the German army marched into Austria, which was soon declared a province of the German Reich. Ditzen spent that weekend visiting his wife and daughter in hospital and making arrangements for Lore Soldin to take charge of the household in Carwitz. He was able to bring his daughter home on 15 March, but it was not until 4 April that Suse was discharged from hospital.

When she arrived back in Carwitz, building had begun on a new woodshed, a smokehouse for curing their pork and a small flat for Hubert Räder, who was due to finish his military training in the autumn and would then make his home in Carwitz. As soon as Suse was sufficiently recovered, she took her driving test and, on 29 April, she and her husband set off for the spa town of Bad Mergentheim. They left Lore Soldin in charge in Carwitz, where she was safe from the increasingly virulent campaign against the Jews.

In Bad Mergentheim, Suse took the waters and Ditzen revised *Iron Gustav*, which he dispatched to Rowohlt on 30 May. He pronounced himself satisfied with the result but accepted the criticism of Friedo Lampe and Franz Hessel that the story of Heinz Hackendahl is not satisfactorily concluded. Ditzen wrote to Rowohlt that he was not capable of writing an alternative ending for Heinz because that would have required 'a quite different book (probably with a move towards party politics) and I had neither the strength nor the stomach for that'.[36]

Ditzen spent the beginning of June revising *Geschichten aus der Murkelei* ('Stories from a Childhood'), the anthology of children's stories he had completed the previous year, before leaving Bad Mergentheim on 13 June. The Ditzens visited Ada Ditzen and Ilse Bechert in Marburg before travelling on to Celle, now the home of both Elisabeth Ditzen and the Hörigs. They arrived back in Carwitz on 22 June, well rested and in time for the fruit harvest.

July 1938 brought two serious blows to Ditzen's future as a writer. On 1 July, Rowohlt was expelled from the Reich Literary Chamber and banned from publishing. All appeals against this decision proved fruitless – his Party membership was of no avail. His company – already in Nazi Party hands since Eher had taken over Ullstein – was handed over in an administrative move to the Deutsche Verlags-Anstalt in October, and he was retained as a consultant only until the end of the year. Ditzen's contract was due for renewal at the beginning of 1939, and he was thus faced for the first time in nineteen years with the prospect of negotiating with a new publisher. Rowohlt would not stay in Germany if he could not publish, and Ditzen viewed with apprehension a future without his friendship and support.

He completed the translation of Day's *Life with Mother* on 25 July and organized a 'non-alcoholic works outing' for family and staff to Kölpinsee the next day, largely to avoid the media attention which the filming of *Old Heart Goes on a Journey* in Carwitz had attracted.

The second blow fell two days later, on 28 July, when Ditzen and Rowohlt met Jannings and Fritzsche of the Tobis Film Company in the Kaiserhof Hotel in Berlin. There, Ditzen was told that Goebbels had approved the film project in principle and required only one major alteration: the continuation of the Hackendahls' story until 1933.[37] Ditzen, who, as we have seen, had tried to avoid describing the Nazis' rise to power, argued that he did not have the knowledge or experience of the Nazi Party to meet the minister's request and recommended entrusting one of the Party's writers with the task. Jannings suggested that Ditzen should tell Goebbels in person about his objections, especially since Goebbels had expressed a wish to meet him, an invitation which Ditzen declined. Goebbels refused to accept any excuses and insisted on the completion of the project: 'If Fallada still does not know his attitude to the Party, the Party has no doubts about its attitude to him!'[38]

Ditzen capitulated and spent the month of August writing the conclusion to *Iron Gustav* that Goebbels required. He persuaded himself that he had been dissatisfied with the fate of Heinz Hackendahl, in any case, and recast him as a convert to National Socialism; Gustav, too, became a Nazi sympathizer and Erich, the criminal, joined the Communists.

Ditzen later tried to justify his capitulation in the following terms: 'I do not like grand gestures, being slaughtered before the tyrant's throne, senselessly, to the benefit of no one and to the detriment of my children, that is not my way.'[39] He had, of course, been naive to sign a contract for a story whose narrative was to continue until 1933 and imagine that a Nazi film company and a Nazi minister for Public Enlightenment and Propaganda would not insist on a celebration of National Socialism. Having got himself into this situation, he felt that he had no alternative but to accede to Goebbels's request. His authoritarian upbringing had left deep traces. In the same way that Gustav Hackendahl had broken the will and extinguished the spirit of Otto, Eva and Erich, so Ditzen, when faced with an overbearing authority, caved in. In renouncing Heinz's commitment to decency, Ditzen was renouncing his own. By placing his talent in the service of the Nazi Party he was negating the humanist values he had consistently proclaimed since *A Small Circus*. It was one of Ditzen's strengths as a writer that he could portray with social and psychological accuracy the pressures of war, inflation, unemployment and authoritarianism on his contemporaries. It was one of his weaknesses as a human being that he could not withstand these pressures himself.

As he was writing the new conclusion to *Iron Gustav*, the Czech crisis was coming to a head. Margarete Bechert, who lived in Zittau on the Czech border, witnessed the events of the summer and autumn at first hand. Her daughter Ilse helped to look after the German refugees who had been fleeing from alleged persecution in Czechoslovakia all year, and the Becherts had German officers billeted in their home. As Germany stepped up its military manoeuvres along the Czech border, an increasing number of reservists became involved. Ditzen himself was called up in August but, with the support of the Tobis Film Company, lodged a successful appeal. After he submitted the manuscript of *Iron Gustav*, he and Suse set out on 10 September for the North Sea spa of St Peter to fetch Uli, who had been there since April, and to spend a few weeks' holiday at the Hörigs'. However, the political situation became so grave in mid-September that they cut short their stay and returned home early. In the event, international diplomacy forced the Czech government to cede the Sudetenland to Germany on 1 October, which did not prevent, but only postponed, the invasion of the rest of Czechoslovakia.

One author still writing in Germany in 1938 who made military aggression, expansionism and the ill treatment of subject peoples a theme of his work was Reinhold Schneider. In his *Las Casas vor Karl V* ('Las Casas before Charles V'), published in the same year as *Iron Gustav*, the sixteenth-century missionary Las Casas describes the Spanish conquest of Central and South America as 'illegal, tyrannical and hellish; worse and more cruel than anything perpetrated by the Turks and the Moors'. Schneider explores the conflict between the Christian belief in the equality of all human beings before God and the *realpolitik* of a Christian imperial power. This conflict is resolved in the novel by the intervention of the Emperor Charles V, a benevolent autocrat, who introduces reforms into the colonies. Thomas à Kempis is invoked towards the end of the novel to promise all Christians a reward in heaven for the suffering they have endured on earth. A conservative Christian writer was thus able to criticize sharply aspects of Nazi policy without calling into question the status quo. Ditzen, who had rejected Christianity, could only propose individual solutions and private idylls: the Pinnebergs, the Spatts, the Pagels. In a letter to Hermann Broch on 1 December 1937, he accepted Broch's criticism of the rather facile happy ending in *Wolf Among Wolves* and ascribed this to the fact:

> ... that I myself do not believe in the meaning of life. I have retreated to a position of simplicity, as you quite rightly say, but that is of course only a lazy compromise, not a real solution. But what else can I do?
> ... I have tried to console myself by saying: why should I do more than depict the way things are? Am I a reformer? A teacher? No, I am only a portrayer.
> But there is something missing ...

It is to Ditzen's credit that he recognized his shortcomings even if, in 1938, he was unable to do anything about them. He clearly believed Hitler's claim in the autumn of 1938 that the Sudetenland was 'the last territorial claim which I have to make in Europe'; he referred in a letter to his mother on 7 October to 'the relief that the threat of danger had once more passed; let us hope that we will have long and prosperous years of peace ahead.'

There was, however, to be little peace either in his life or in Germany. The *Iron Gustav* film project was dropped after Alfred Rosenberg, the Nazi Party's chief ideologue, objected to any film in which Ditzen was involved, an indication of the rivalry and in-fighting which characterized relations between the Nazi cultural bodies and often resulted in inconsistent treatment of writers and artists. Rosenberg's intervention unleashed a further round of official attacks on Ditzen's work. Then Ditzen began negotiations with his new publisher and discovered the difference between dealing with a purely commercial enterprise and his old friend Rowohlt. Gustav Kilpper of the Deutsche Verlags-Anstalt regarded Ditzen as a liability and not an author who could be promised long-term support. In a typical act of generosity, Rowohlt accompanied Kilpper to Carwitz one inhospitable November day in 1938 and ensured that Ditzen and Kilpper reached agreement.

Rowohlt may also have been involved in the contract which Ditzen signed with the Vier Falken Verlag for a new edition of *A Small Circus*.[40] As in the case of 'Once a Jailbird' four years previously, Ditzen once again wrote a foreword designed to placate the Nazi authorities which undermined the tenor of the work. Entitled 'Carwitz, November 1938', it describes the court case against the farmers in which 'many a witness was more guilty than those in the dock; the State Prosecutor was also guilty, as was the judge – everyone who tried to support this system was guilty, everyone who opposed it innocent.' It is unclear whether this strategy was suggested to Ditzen by the publisher or whether it was his own idea. In any case, it demonstrates the effect of Nazi intimidation on Ditzen in the summer and autumn of 1938.

By this stage, Rowohlt had plans to emigrate to his wife's family in Brazil. Lore Soldin was on her way to join her daughters in England, Franz Hessel was with his wife and children in Paris and Paul Mayer had left on a journey which would take him, ultimately, to Mexico. Horrified by the campaign against the Jews, which had culminated in the brutal pogrom of 9 November mockingly referred to by its perpetrators as the Reichskristallnacht (Night of Shattered Glass), the Ditzens, too, began to consider emigration again. Putnam, Ditzen's English publisher, arranged for a ship to pick up the whole family in Hamburg.[41] England was the destination of a number of refugees from Nazi-occupied Europe in 1938: John Heartfield, Kurt Hiller, Oskar Kokoschka, Monty Jacobs, the young Erich Fried, Elias Canetti and Elisabeth Castonier, among others, all arrived in London that year. Alfred Kerr, Stefan Zweig and Ernst Toller were already there. The Free German League of Culture (founded in December 1938) became 'one of the biggest exile organizations in the world, with a range of activities greater than any comparable association elsewhere'.[42] Ditzen could therefore expect to find some support for his writing in the English capital.

The family quietly made preparations for the journey, letting it be known in the village that they were going to visit Suse's relatives in Hamburg. When everything was packed and they were ready to go, Ditzen announced that he wanted to have one last walk over the Bohnenwerder and set off up the lane behind the house. When he returned some time later he declared that he could not leave Germany and that Suse should unpack. It is not difficult to imagine his feelings on that fateful walk: he felt bitterness at the thought of abandoning Carwitz, not only on account of its idyllic setting but also because it was his first real home and represented all he had achieved. He was apprehensive about writing in a non-German-speaking environment: 'What is an author who is not heard in his own language and cannot write in another?', as Kurt Pinthus commented in relation to Ernst Toller.[43] Looking back from the cell of a Nazi psychiatric prison in 1944, Ditzen defended his decision not to leave his native land: 'I am a German, I say that today with pride and sorrow, I love Germany, I don't want to live or work anywhere else in the world. I probably couldn't live or work anywhere else.'[44] The prospect of making a new start in a foreign country when his only experience of foreign travel had been the disastrous trip to Holland in his youth filled him with trepidation. When Gerhart Hauptmann was asked in 1938 why he stayed in Germany when he so obviously despised the Nazis, he retorted, 'Because I'm a coward, do you see? I'm a coward, do you see? I'm a coward.'[45] Ditzen was also concerned that his health would suffer as a result of the stresses and strains of the upheaval – at least in Germany he had a first-class doctor in his friend Willi Burlage.

Emigration was not an easy option: his fellow Rowohlt author Kurt Tucholsky had committed suicide in Sweden in 1935; Heinz Kiwitz went missing, presumed dead, in the Spanish Civil War; Franz Hessel died in France in 1941; Ernst Toller, Walter Benjamin, Stefan Zweig and Walter Hasenclever were all to take their lives in exile.

By the end of 1938, Ditzen knew that staying in Germany was not an easy option either. The deaths of Ringelnatz, Mühsam and, more recently, the journalist Carl von Ossietzky (the latter two both killed at the hands of the Nazis) and the sculptor Ernst Barlach demonstrated the fate of those who opposed the Nazi regime. His own experience told him that staying in Germany meant abandoning his serious literary ambitions. However, he convinced himself that he could survive if he concentrated on projects such as translation and children's stories (both Clarence Day's *Unsere Frau Mama* (*Life with Mother*) and his own 'Stories from a Childhood' had appeared in November 1938) as well as the 'little, big, light-hearted novel' which he had planned for the New Year. Ditzen was, of course, right: there was a huge demand for entertaining and undemanding literature as the shadows of war lengthened over Europe. Ledig, who had taken over as head of the Rowohlt division within the Deutsche Verlags-Anstalt, wrote to Ditzen just before Christmas 1938 that 'it is almost impossible to satisfy the hunger for light-hearted literature.' The question was not whether Ditzen could write such literature but whether he would be content to do so and what effect such prostitution of his talent would have on his literary development. It also remained to be seen whether the Nazi cultural authorities would permit him to pursue such a strategy. The decision not to emigrate in 1938 was bound to have far-reaching consequences.

7 1939–1944
Carwitz the Nightmare

I am a German, a Saxon from Dresden.
My homeland will not release me.
I'm like a tree – in Germany planted –
Which will wither there, too, if needs be.

– Erich Kästner[1]

From Ditzen's point of view, the most immediate and positive result of his decision not to emigrate was Suse's willingness to have another baby. As we have seen, Ditzen was very fond of children and enjoyed spending time with Uli, Lore and their friends. He described children as 'the only real riches' in a letter to Ada Ditzen's friend, Lili du Bois-Reymond. In 'Stories from a Childhood', published in 1938, the narrator, in a scarcely veiled reference to the author's own situation, begins the title story: 'Once upon a time there was a father who dreamed of having lots of children, preferably a dozen, six boys and six girls. But his dream was not fulfilled and he had only two: a boy he called 'der Murkel' (Shrimp) and a girl he called 'Mücke' (Midge).' Ditzen's desire for a large family was not unreservedly shared by his wife. Suse had taken a long time to recover from the birth of the twins in 1933. Her own poor health, her husband's illnesses and the general uncertainty of their situation had made her understandably reluctant to contemplate pregnancy again. Now that they had decided to stay in Germany and Ditzen's alcoholism was under control and his depressions more manageable, the 38-year-old Suse was prevailed upon to change her mind.

Although Ditzen's fee from the Deutsche Verlags-Anstalt had increased from 300 to 1,200 marks per month, relations with his publisher were strained and uneasy. He missed not only Rowohlt but Mayer and Hessel, whom he had known and worked with for twenty years. Ledig and the Rowohlt division of the Deutsche Verlags-Anstalt had moved to Stuttgart, which meant that Ditzen could no longer drop into the office on a regular basis. A further source of annoyance was the fact that he now received his accounts on a quarterly instead of, as previously, a monthly basis, an arrangement which did not suit him. Then, in early January, a short story he had written for Mathias Wieman was returned as 'unsuitable', and attacks on his work began appearing again in the press. In addition, the film of *Old Heart Goes on a Journey* had still not yet been approved for release. Ditzen became upset when he heard that Ledig had visited Rowohlt in Switzerland in the middle of the month without informing him – although it was highly unlikely that Ditzen would have wanted to accompany him. A visit to Berlin to consult the children's doctors seems to have aggravated his fragile state; by the last week in January he was hardly sleeping at all and Suse arranged for him to be admitted to a clinic in Berlin-Nikolassee recommended by Burlage, who had no beds available in Zepernick. After fourteen days' treatment, he was able to return to Carwitz on 10 February, determined 'to restrict myself totally to Carwitz, to see even fewer people and not even to travel to Berlin'.

By now, Rowohlt had left for Brazil and no new Rowohlt books appeared in the first three months of the year. *Iron Gustav*, despite its concessions to the Nazi censor, had not been well received and had disappeared from shop windows. The Reich Agency for the Promotion of German Literature described it as 'destructive' in tone, while admitting it was well written. In mid-March, more changes occurred at Rowohlt when Franz Moraller, who had been in charge of the Nazi Party's 'Cultural Office', was appointed joint managing director with Ledig. From this point on, Ledig signed all his letters with the Nazi '*Heil Hitler!*' – a greeting which Ditzen frequently returned and used increasingly in his correspondence with officialdom.

By the end of March 1939, the Nazi government's strategy was becoming clear: Hitler's claim to be acting solely on the principle of self-determination for all Germans was exposed as fraudulent by the invasion and dismemberment of Czechoslovakia. This afforded Germany access not only to the impressive Czech army stores but also to the Skoda arms works. This was followed by a show of strength which forced Lithuania to cede Memel. In addition, Romania agreed to provide Germany with much-needed oil and other natural resources. The success of German foreign policy was underlined by the celebrations on 1 April which accompanied the triumphant return of the 'Condor Legion' following Franco's victory in Spain.

The fact that not all Germans were enthusiastic about the policies being pursued by the Nazi regime was brought to Ditzen's attention that same day when a new typist, Frau Meisel, arrived in Carwitz to type *Kleiner Mann – großer Mann, alles vertauscht* ('Little Man – Big Man, Roles Reversed'), which Ditzen had dropped in November 1937 and resumed in January 1939. Frau Meisel, another unemployed woman, appears to have been involved in some form of oppositional activity, because Ditzen remarked in a letter to Ledig on 8 September 1939 that 'she wanted to keep me informed of her fate but did not write, probably because she did not want to involve me in anything.'

'Little Man – Big Man, Roles Reversed', whose title clearly echoes Ditzen's earlier best-seller, takes up the theme of the little man once more and relates the tale of an insurance clerk, Max Schreyvogel, and his wife, Karla, who inherit 7 million marks but who soon decide to rid themselves of their inheritance in order to save their marriage. The novel is narrated in the first person by Max Schreyvogel and addressed to his descendants as an 'explanation and justification' for the Schreyvogels' renunciation of such a fortune and their return to the modest existence of 'little people'.

After the experience of *Iron Gustav*, Ditzen was careful to set 'Little Man – Big Man, Roles Reversed' in an historical vacuum. The estate of Gaugarten, which the Schreyvogels inherit, may have been modelled on Baumgarten, where Ditzen spent the summer of 1919. The fictional village of Langleide shares some topographical features with Feldberg: both boast a Reiherberg hill and a Haussee lake. Ditzen continues to people his fiction with the names of friends, acquaintances and even family members: the Schreyvogels' housekeeper in Gaugarten is Fräulein Kluge; the fiancée of Max's friend Paulus is called 'Lilo', the name of Uli's nanny in St Peter who came to work in Carwitz; the Schreyvogels' daughter, like the Ditzens', is nicknamed 'Mücke'.

In this lightweight novel, with its facile moral that money does not necessarily bring happiness, Ditzen interweaves aspects of his own experience: his sudden wealth as a result of *Little Man – What Now?*; his tax problems (which both he and his protagonist solve by ignoring all financial advisers and dealing directly with the authorities); the alcoholism and womanizing which, as we shall see, were increasingly posing a threat to his marriage.[2]

Ditzen finished dictating 'Little Man – Big Man, Roles Reversed' on 26 April and decided to take a break before revising and submitting it. His general irritability is evident from his correspondence with Ledig, which culminated in the accusation in his letter of 27 April that Ernst Rowohlt 'would have spared me all the negative little reports which have arrived with almost every letter since January'.

The Ditzens had been planning to holiday in May in East Prussia, hoping to repeat the success of their trip in the same month of the previous year. However, the difficulty of securing visas for the Polish corridor and the tense relations between Germany and Poland, which resulted in Germany's renunciation of the Non-Aggression Pact with Poland on 28 April 1939, brought a change of plan, and they set off with Lore and one of their housemaids for Celle on 3 May. Uli was by now attending school in Berlin and living with the Burlages, who brought him home to Carwitz for Whitsun, when they had a much-needed break. Burlage's workload of up to 140 patients per day was very wearing and an indication not only of his professional commitment but also of the demand for psychiatric care in Berlin in 1939.

Ditzen submitted 'Little Man – Big Man, Roles Reversed' on 27 May. Kilpper and Ledig reacted enthusiastically and, by the beginning of July, Ledig had agreed a serialization deal with *Die Dame*, a fashion magazine with a significant literary section which sponsored an annual poetry prize and carried book reviews. The editor of *Die Dame* insisted on changing the title to *Himmel, wir erben ein Schloß* ('Heavens! We've Inherited a Castle').

In the summer of 1939, honey was added to the produce of the Ditzens' smallholding in Carwitz when Ditzen, on Hubert Räder's advice, acquired a beehive and a swarm of bees, mainly to pollinate the fruit trees which had been planted in the spring. When Suse was not involved in harvesting and preserving she was able to try out her new wooden punt, which she had bought at the Water Sports' Exhibition in Berlin in March. Summer no longer brought many visitors to the Ditzens' house in Carwitz – apart from Suse's sister and brother-in-law, Burlage's brother and a photographer from *Die Dame*. There was a successful day trip to Warnemünde for the Ditzen household, workers and their families on 11 July, then a visit to Elisabeth Ditzen in Celle at the end of the month. Celle had a Bee Research Centre and Ditzen used his visits to his mother to consult the experts on beekeeping. In the summer of 1939, on their trips to Berlin and Celle, the Ditzens would have driven past the newly opened concentration camp at Ravensbrück. Screened from the road by thick forest, there was no indication that this was anything more than the women's prison it purported to be.

In early August, the couple spent some time in Berlin settling Uli back into school and arranging treatment for Lore's tonsillitis. It was during this week in Berlin that Ditzen called into the Deutscher Verlag (formerly Ullstein) to see Palitzsch, Zingler and Erik Reger, who was now editor of the *Berliner Illustrirte*. They persuaded Ditzen to abandon his plan to write a novel about his schooldays before the First World War and to put his energies instead into the sort of work that could be serialized in the *Berliner Illustrirte* and which could earn him 40,000 marks. Ditzen was attracted by the security which such a sum could provide and announced his new project, entitled *Der ungeliebte Mann* ('The Unloved Man'), in a letter to Ledig on 15 August.

He spent the next nine days writing a short story, *Süßmilch spricht* ('Süßmilch Speaks'), which had been requested by the Stuttgart section of the Hitler Youth Movement.[3] 'Süßmilch Speaks' is a boys' adventure story which tells how Maxe Reichelt and his friend Murr, with Murr's dog, Beline, save the timber business of Maxe's father from the agitator and nihilist Süßmilch who claims to want to reorganize it along more egalitarian lines. The story proclaims the triumph of good (in the form of the lower-middle-class joiner Reichelt, who has painstakingly and with many sacrifices built up his modest business) over evil (in the form of a motiveless agitator who acts on a whim and mouths socialist phrases). It is a slight piece, which appears to endorse the Nazis' opposition to socialism through the character of Süßmilch, who turns out, however, to be more of a nihilist than a socialist. The boys succeed in persuading Süßmilch that 'there was enough destruction all around. What was still functioning should be preserved for the next generation.' In view of the story's lack of Nazi content, Ditzen sent it to Ledig for checking before its publication in the Hitler Youth Movement magazine *Rakete*.

The narrator in Ernst Jünger's *Auf den Marmorklippen* (*On the Marble Cliffs*), also written in 1939, describes how evil spreads through the land under the aegis of the 'Chief Ranger': 'Herein, above all, lay a masterly trait of the Chief Ranger: he administered fear in small doses which he gradually increased and which aimed at crippling resistance.'[4] Ditzen's decision to stay in Germany meant that he had to deal with these 'doses of fear'. One strategy was to write trivial novels such as his recently completed 'Little Man – Big Man, Roles Reversed' and his next project 'The Unloved Man'. When a commission arrived from a Nazi body, he was now prepared to fulfil it, but determined not to write fascist material. In 1939, it remained to be seen to what extent the 'Chief Ranger' would succeed in crippling Ditzen's resistance.

Ditzen dispatched 'Süßmilch Speaks' on 24 August, a few hours after the signing of the German–Soviet Non-Aggression Pact, which sealed the fate of Poland. The guarantees which Britain promised Poland the next day ushered in a flurry of diplomatic activity which was unable to stop the Nazi war machine. On 27 August, rationing was introduced in Germany as preparations for war entered their final stage. The Ditzens' smallholding cushioned them from the immediate effects of rationing – apart from coffee, which Ditzen considered indispensable to his writing. Nonetheless, he was able to begin 'The Unloved Man' on 28 August, expressing the hope in a letter to Ledig 'that I can achieve the ideal: an effect on one million readers and quality as well'.

At nine o'clock on the evening of Thursday 30 August 1939, Berlin radio broadcast the sixteen demands that the German government was making on Poland. The Ditzens, realizing that war was about to break out, used their remaining petrol to drive to Berlin the next day to bring Uli home. Hardly had they returned to Carwitz when Germany invaded Poland. As the German army swept all before it in a highly successful military operation, Ditzen and his family hurriedly brought in the hay and secured an air-raid shelter in the cellar for themselves and their neighbours. The car was put in the garage and Ditzen bought himself a bicycle.

Germany was officially at war with Britain and France from Sunday 3 September. German society was put on a war footing. Heydrich, Chief of the Security Police, threatened 'any person who expresses doubt about the victory of the German nation or questions the legality of the war' with arrest and detention. Yet, as the Western powers did not come to the aid of the Poles, and the conquest and partition of Poland was achieved within five weeks, there was much optimism in Germany that a full-scale war could be avoided. Uli's return to school in Berlin on 9 September is evidence of his parents' confidence that there was little risk of that.

The Terra Film Company, which had taken out an option to buy 'Little Man – Big Man, Roles Reversed' at the end of August, made Ditzen a firm offer on 6 September. Ten days later, he had an approach from Carl Froelich, the newly appointed president of the Reich Film Chamber, to write a filmscript about: 'a German who returns from America and is converted to the new Germany by an ordinary girl ... There is to be no mention of politics in the film. The people are to be National Socialists but are not to talk about National Socialism.' The 'ordinary girl' was to be played by Zarah Leander, a leading actress and heart-throb of the day. Ditzen wrote the piece, subsequently entitled *Dies Herz, das dir gehört* ('This Heart which Belongs to You'), in seventeen days and received a fee of 25,000 marks. He negotiated a further 5,000 marks for revising the script the following February. Filmscripts and serializations became an increasingly important source of income as the traditional outlets for his writing – literary journals and the literary supplements of daily newspapers – gradually closed down. Ledig managed to place only one of Ditzen's Christmas stories, '*Das versunkene Festge-schenk*' ('The Christmas Present at the Bottom of the Sea'), which appeared in *Die Woche*. Other writers who did not enjoy official patronage – such as Axel Eggebrecht, Jochen Klepper and Ernst von Salomon – also found filmscripts a lucrative source of income during the Nazi period.

Publishing abroad was becoming more difficult. This was particularly the case in Britain, where 'Hans Fallada' had been building up a considerable readership: by the end of 1938 Putnam had sold 22,079 copies of *Little Man – What Now? Once We Had a Child* had been selling well, too. The war not only brought Ditzen a reduction in income from foreign sales but severed the connection to his readers, especially in the English-speaking world, which was to lapse for seventy years – until the phenomenal success in 2009 of *Alone in Berlin*. In November 1939 he received two official invitations to undertake a lecture tour of Sweden, both of which he turned down.

With the advent of war, Carwitz became more remote than ever. The weekly grocery deliveries from Feldberg stopped and shopping had to be done by bicycle or on foot, a round trip of eight or nine miles. Räder and the other able-bodied men in the village were called up and, apart from the three weeks' harvest leave which he succeeded in securing for Räder in October, Ditzen had to manage his smallholding largely on his own. Self-sufficiency became even more important and Ditzen added poultry to his livestock.

By 8 November, he had completed 'The Unloved Man'. He lamented in a letter to his sister Elisabeth: 'It is a pity that everything has become routine and that I never experience now what I felt when I wrote *A Small Circus*. The last time I had that sort of experience was with *Once We Had a Child*. You get into a routine and that spoils everything, or at least almost everything.'[5] In addition, the strain of completing two prose works in such a short time had affected his sleeping. He wrote to Ledig on 1 December: '. . . when I work under time pressure, my daily work rate goes up and I don't sleep so well and when I don't sleep well I worry about being able to finish my work which makes me work more, so I sleep even less and in the end I hardly sleep at all – and then I collapse.'

Ditzen had other worries, too: Fritz Bechert had been called up and he feared a similar fate for himself; Suse was now pregnant and facing the possibility of another multiple birth; the additional domestic help they had hired in October turned out to be totally unsuitable and had to be asked to leave. He was once again admitted to Burlage's clinic in the third week in November, for eight days' treatment, and emerged improved at the beginning of December, determined to take at least a month's break before considering any new project.

Christmas was a quiet affair in Carwitz in 1939. Suse's mother was now too confused to make the journey from Hamburg. Marga Kenter, who had become a close friend after her first husband had worked on the dramatization of *A Small Circus*, joined the Ditzens for Christmas and the Burlages came for the New Year. The highlight of the first Christmas of the war was undoubtedly the chocolate and coffee extract which Ditzen received from his long-standing admirer in Switzerland, H. A. Wyss.[6]

The festivities were overshadowed by the news of Ada Ditzen's death on 25 December. Rudolf and Suse made the arduous journey to Marburg by train for the funeral. They decided to name the baby, if it turned out to be a girl, after this remarkable woman who had encouraged his literary beginnings and had supported him over the years.

They took Uli back to school in Berlin on 7 January 1940 and spent a few days with the Burlages. Ditzen consulted his dentist about a recurrence of his gum trouble and an optician about his deteriorating eyesight. He also discussed the changes Carl Froelich required to the manuscript of 'This Heart which Belongs to You'.[7] Ditzen was becoming concerned about his son's education. His school in Berlin had practically ceased to exist; the pupils simply reported every day to receive and submit homework. He found a more satisfactory alternative in a grammar school in Templin, fifteen miles east of Carwitz, which he had described in a letter to Kagelmacher the previous July: 'It is a boarding-school on the English model, set in a forest close to a large lake where the boys can swim and do sport.' When Ditzen and his wife went to Templin on 25 January 1940 to inspect the school, they had to travel by horse-drawn sledge, which took three and a half hours to complete the journey. The extremely cold winter, which lasted well into March, destroyed a number of their fruit trees and killed off some of the bees. The long winter was followed by a very dry period, which resulted in a poor fruit and vegetable harvest in 1940. Only their poultry farming flourished, producing a regular supply of meat and eggs.

Ditzen made good progress with his work in the first three months of 1940: he completed the revision of 'This Heart which Belongs to You' on 15 February, signed a contract for the filming of 'Little Man – Big Man, Roles Reversed' which netted him 17,500 marks at the beginning of March and finished 'The Unloved Man' two weeks later. Yet, as he confided to his mother, he was not happy: 'I am not satisfied with what I'm doing – and haven't been since *Wolf* . . . I cannot act as I want to – if I want to stay alive. And so a fool gives less than he has.'[8]

Relations with his publisher continued to deteriorate and reached a particularly low point when the Deutsche Verlags-Anstalt insisted in March on levying a fee for arranging film contracts and serializations, a clear departure from his contract. Kilpper rubbed salt in the wound by distinguishing between Ditzen and 'all our first-rate authors like Ina Seidel, Josef Ponten, Ernst Zahn, Waldemar Bonsels', who, he implied, did not need help in such matters.[9] Due to the paper shortage, only six thousand copies of 'Little Man – Big Man, Roles Reversed' could be printed for the launch in April, by which time orders for twelve thousand had been received. 'The Unloved Man' was adversely affected by new regulations for the allocation of paper which divided books into three categories. Those *promoted* by the party were automatically allocated paper, those *approved* by the party might or might not be allocated paper and those *rejected* by the party did not receive paper. As 'The Unloved Man' was in the second category, its fate was uncertain.

Ditzen's low spirits were exacerbated by his anxiety about Suse's confinement, which was now expected in April. She left Carwitz on 28 March to travel to Berlin and stay with the Burlages until the baby's birth.

Ditzen and Uli set out on 3 April on a horse and cart for Templin. Having settled his son into his new school, Ditzen travelled on by train to Berlin, where Suse had given birth to a baby boy. They chose the name Achim partly in memory of the Romantic writer and patriot

Achim von Arnim (1781–1831), who came from nearby Brandenburg and had attended the same school in Templin as Uli. It was only some two years later that they discovered that Achim was on an official list of 'names to be eradicated because they are Hebrew in origin'![10]

By June 1940, the German armies had established control not only of Poland but also of Norway, Belgium, Holland and France and seemed poised to invade England. The only grain of comfort Ditzen gleaned from these victories was the hope that the war would soon be over.

He moved into the guest-room when persistent toothache and the demands of a new baby began to adversely affect his sleep. His irritability was aggravated by the incompetence of his publisher, most probably due to Ledig being called up on 21 April. In his absence, the Deutsche Verlags-Anstalt transferred an incorrect and late payment for the first quarter of 1940 into Ditzen's account and then sent him reviews of 'Little Man – Big Man, Roles Reversed', when he had expressly forbidden this. He was further annoyed by the lack of response to 'The Unloved Man', which he had sent to Stuttgart on 24 May. By the end of June he was looking for another publisher.

Life in Carwitz, initially so idyllic, became increasingly less so as the Nazi regime strengthened its hold over German society. Without a car and with no friends locally and very few visitors, the Ditzens felt increasingly trapped. They had little in common with the villagers, who were envious of what they perceived to be an opulent lifestyle. Their experience in Berkenbrück of the nastiness encouraged by the Nazi authorities became an everyday occurrence in Carwitz. An extremely assiduous village mayor took pleasure in filing reports denouncing Ditzen for employing too many staff, buying too much wood, not handing over the required amounts of farm produce, and so on. Ditzen complained to his publisher, Gustav Kilpper, about 'the battles which you have to keep fighting against the obstructiveness all around, being robbed of all your friends, these times that wear you down – the end result is that you lose all enjoyment of life.'[11]

Ditzen was again admitted to Burlage's clinic in the first week of July 1940. When he emerged almost three weeks later, he was still 'wobbly'. He wrote to Dr Flint, one of Burlage's colleagues, on 27 July: '... things are just as bad as ever ... I long for the evenings and my sleeping pills ... I haven't drunk any alcohol, apart from three bottles of beer, and on that occasion my wife sat beside me and the bottles.' Suse's role in monitoring Ditzen's alcohol consumption and keeping the key to the medicine cabinet only exacerbated the problems in their marriage.

Meanwhile, Kilpper had responded positively to 'The Unloved Man' and Ledig had returned to Stuttgart, thanks to Kilpper's intervention with the War Ministry. Ditzen's assessment of this novel as 'a relatively weak book' is without doubt correct. It tells the tale of three 'unloved' men – the rich divorcee Peter Siebenhaar (who is blind), the young estate manager Siegfried Senden and the publican Fritz Bleesern – all of whom marry the women they deserve in the end. The hero, Fritz Bleesern, an apparently weak and ineffectual fellow – the very opposite of the contemporary Nazi ideal – proves himself to be a man of character and principle. The events are set in Berga (modelled on Feldberg) and Lenzen (modelled on Carwitz) and there are numerous references to places and buildings in the Feldberg lake district.[12]

In August 1940, Ditzen first mentioned their intention of selling the house in Carwitz after the war and moving closer to Berlin, not only because of their disenchantment with village life but because they were most reluctant to send the children away to boarding-school. The village school in Carwitz which Lore had started attending in March 1940 was proving most unsatisfactory. In his 1944 Memoir, Ditzen recalls two Nazi teachers. The first, Herr Ritzner, had to be removed from his post on account of the debts he accumulated – Ditzen, one of his creditors, lost 2,500 marks as a result. The second, Herr Schwoch (called 'Stork' in the memoirs), was a particularly ambitious and zealous party member who stopped at nothing to take control of the village, Schwoch had asked Uli where Hitler's portrait was hung in the Ditzens' house and whether his father greeted his family with '*Heil Hitler!*' every morning and evening. Frau Schwoch made a point of quizzing the Ditzens' farm workers and housemaids about any anti-Nazi sentiments which their employer expressed within his four walls. Schwoch's political activities gradually left less and less time for teaching and running the village school. By 1940, the school operated for only two hours a day on three days a week.

Ditzen did, however, recognize the advantages of country life during the war: a measure of the family's material well-being was the large number of food parcels dispatched to relatives and friends on a regular basis throughout the war.

In the course of the summer of 1940, the effects of the war reached Carwitz as the RAF bombing raids on Berlin resulted in air-raid alarms and some damage across northern Germany. The Ditzens had a fourteen-year-old evacuee from Duisburg, Bernhard Bickschäfer, to stay for five weeks, and Suse's sister and brother-in-law, Tilly and Peter Frerksen, arrived from Hamburg for an extended holiday in September.

At the beginning of September, the local employment exchange in Feldberg tried to remove a member of the Ditzens' domestic staff, 'probably as a result of someone in the village reporting us', as Rudolf commented in a letter to his mother on 17 September. He managed to postpone this for a month, until the bulk of the preserving and pickling was finished. In September, he and Suse spent four days in Berlin. He had an appointment with a potential new publisher, Goverts of Hamburg, but decided in the end to stay with the Deutsche Verlags-Anstalt. He also underwent tests in the Charité hospital because of his considerable weight loss and chronic insomnia. Towards the end of the month, the Ditzens set out for Lübeck and Hamburg, where they visited Suse's mother.

Ditzen's health continued to deteriorate. The serialization of 'The Unloved Man' in the *Wiener Illustrierte* brought him less money than he had hoped; he began negotiations with his publisher for a new contract and was disappointed to discover that his request for a longer-lasting contract and an increased quarterly payment was flatly rejected. On 15 October, the day after Hubert Räder arrived in Carwitz to spend three weeks' leave, Ditzen was admitted to Burlage's clinic once more. His depression was symptomatic of a wider unease which spread through Germany in the course of the late summer and autumn of 1940, as the victories of the spring failed to bring the war to an end.

Ditzen was not able to return to Carwitz until the third week in December, and then he was still weak and spent most of the Christmas period in bed. December brought a most welcome surprise: the return from Brazil of Ernst Rowohlt, who rang up on New Year's Eve from Berlin. Rowohlt later told Paul Mayer that he came back to Germany because he 'was convinced of the imminent collapse of the Hitler regime' and wanted to be on the spot 'to start publishing again'.[13] His dissatisfaction with life in Brazil and his impending divorce may also have been contributing factors. Rowohlt spent four days with the Ditzens in Carwitz in the middle of January 1941. By this time, Rudolf's nurse had left, and Suse had taken over the administration of his sleeping tablets. It is a measure of the fragile state of his health that Rowohlt's visit, while no doubt most welcome, contributed to a relapse. Another contributory factor was probably Kilpper's request to remove all references to Nazis, Communists and Jews in a new edition of *Kleiner Mann – was nun?* This Ditzen refused to do because, as he explained in a letter to Ledig on 23 January, 'the book, without wishing to overstate its importance, is an historical document and can only be understood in the context of the conflicts of the period.' The new edition of ten thousand copies went ahead with only one alteration: the typeface was changed to the now statutory Antiqua.[14] A further cause for concern were the restrictions on paper, which severely curtailed the number of Ditzen's books which could be published and, as a consequence, his income. Relations with his publisher continued to deteriorate and, by 25 February, Ditzen was asking Ledig to write to him as little as possible.

It is hardly surprising that his marriage suffered under these circumstances. In letters to people whom he considered true friends he adopts an increasingly bitter and sarcastic tone when referring to his wife. In January, in a letter to Wanda Oster, a former colleague of Burlage's, he describes how he received forty-eight books for Christmas, while 'Madam' (*'die Gnädige'*) received a fur coat. In a letter to his sister Elisabeth on 18 March he praises his wife's competence and efficiency and concludes '. . . soon she'll be able to write my books and I won't have to get out of bed at all.' Suse sought respite from her husband's depression, the unpleasantness of village life and the difficulties of running a farm and bringing up children in wartime by making regular trips to Berlin. She had found a friend and confidante in Evchen Burlage, who offered a sympathetic ear, organized trips to the theatre and generally helped her to relax. This friendship led to a deterioration in Ditzen's relations with Burlage, whom he increasingly regarded as being 'on Suse's side'. By June 1941, he was referring to his erstwhile doctor and friend as 'Fatso' ('*der Dicke*').

On 3 March, Ditzen began to feel better and emerged from what he referred to in a letter to Rowohlt as his '*Matratzengruft*' ('mattress-grave') – an allusion to the poet Heine's ironic name for the sickbed to which he was confined for the latter part of his life. Suse, much relieved, set out the next day for Berlin. On her return, however, she found her husband much worse and, on Burlage's advice, had him admitted to a sanatorium in Dresden. Ditzen discharged himself after three days, because the treatment was totally unsuitable, and he determined to treat himself at home. From this point onwards, his condition improved and, by the third week in March, he could manage without sleeping tablets.

Uli cycled over from Templin on 1 April and the children's delight in the Easter holidays contributed much to their father's recovery. By 14 April, he was expressing a desire to start writing again and a week later he had a short novel, *Zwei zarte Lämmchen weiß wie Schnee* ('Two Tender Lambs White as Snow'), ready for dispatch to Stuttgart. This insubstantial work tells the tale of the shy accounts clerk, Gerhard Grote, who falls in love with Rosa Täfelein and discovers in the process that 'it was much easier to fight than to obey without a murmur and then feel angry – with yourself! – for a long time.'[15]

Meanwhile, the German army had been pressing south-eastwards into the Balkans in an attempt to relieve the Italians, whose invasion of Greece the previous October had proved a military disaster. Bulgaria had joined the Tripartite Pact in February. Yugoslavia's signature on 25 March sparked off an attempted coup which was brutally quashed by the Germans, who proceeded to invade Greece on 5 April. Eighteen days later, Greece capitulated and German tanks rolled into Athens on 27 April. The German victories in the Balkans, which led Elisabeth Hörig to express the hope that the war would now soon be over, brought no rejoicing to Carwitz, for among the German dead was Hubert Räder. Ditzen wrote to his mother that Räder's death 'is a very great loss to us. We were very close to him. He was very loyal.'

Lore, in particular, missed her 'Uncle Räder', who always made time to play with her and who had taught her to ride her bicycle.

'Two Tender Lambs White as Snow', which Ditzen himself described as 'a complete failure', ushered in a new period of creativity. By the end of April, he was writing a volume of memoirs, although from the outset he insisted that 'I do not want to produce exact portraits but to let my imagination range freely over a number of topics such as parents, siblings, relatives.'[16]

Ditzen concluded in a letter to his sister Elisabeth on 2 June 1941 that his book, now entitled *Damals bei uns daheim* ('Our Home in Days Gone by'), would provide future generations of Ditzens with 'a totally confused picture of our forefathers!' He completed 'Our Home in Days Gone by', typed the manuscript himself, and dispatched it on 26 May so that Ledig would have time to read it before he returned to his regiment.

Eight days later, on 2 June 1941, he started work on a project designed for serialization in the *Berliner Illustrirte* and which he regarded solely as a money-making exercise. He wrote one episode at a time, kept it short, had the hero appear in each episode, omitted all sub-plots and did not allow any nasty situations to develop. The result, *Die Stunde, eh' du schlafen gehst* ('Before You Go to Sleep'), Ditzen himself described in a letter to Wanda Oster on 15 June as 'a completely idiotic novel as far as both plot and characterization are concerned'. Erik Reger, editor of the *Berliner Illustrirte*, who received the manuscript in the middle of July, apparently shared this view, for he refused to publish it.

The progress of the German armies was followed closely in Carwitz: the brother of one of the Ditzens' housemaids was killed during the capture of Crete in May; when the invasion of the Soviet Union began in June 1941 Ditzen wrote to his mother that 'we cannot help thinking of all the young blood that has flowed there again.' Tilly and Peter Frerksen, who spent three weeks in Carwitz in July, were particularly concerned about their only son, whose regiment was fighting on the Eastern Front.

Marga Kenter came to Carwitz during the first week in July. The summer of 1941 brought her much distress, for her partner, Alfred Schmidt (known as Sas), a music teacher and former Communist, was arrested on 10 August as part of a Gestapo round-up of members of the resistance group around Hanno Günther. He was first taken to police headquarters on Berlin's Alexanderplatz for questioning and then sent to Sachsenhausen concentration camp. This news greatly upset Ditzen, who had met Sas when he came to Carwitz at Easter 1937, and had admired what he later described as Schmidt's 'ethical-humanist' principles.[17]

Life in Carwitz did not become any easier as the war continued. In July, Ditzen was forced to have a dog put down after (unfounded) complaints from the villagers that it had been worrying livestock. Then there was a petty dispute about the collection of his milk which he took to the local branch of the Farmers' Union: he won his case, but the harassment continued. Ditzen became even more determined to leave Carwitz as soon as the war was over. He wrote to Kagel-macher on 22 July 1941: 'I am still plagued by a chronic depression which has been making life very difficult for me and my family for the past nine months.'

He complained to his old friend: 'I have been practically forbidden to depict shady characters. Only the Good, Pure and Decent – but that produces no problems that are worth depicting.' At the end of the letter he mentions his plans to spend the winter on something 'that I shall enjoy and so will my real readers'. This was the 'great project for which I need the cooperation of the Ministry of Justice', as he had told his mother on 9 July. In his next letter to her on 22 July he provided more details: 'I am planning a large-scale work, the story of a broker on the stock exchange, but obviously without any anti-Semitic content.'

He had applied to the Ministry of Justice for access to the Kutisker and Barmat files, a famous fraud case involving two Jewish financiers in the 1920s. This had been granted, thanks to the intervention of Kilp-per. Ditzen asked his mother to keep his plans secret because he was afraid that if the Propaganda Ministry got wind of the project Goeb-bels would intervene and access would immediately be withdrawn. As will be seen, his fears turned out to be justified – although in a very different way than he expected in July 1941.

After the harvest, which included mushrooms as well as beans, tomatoes, cucumbers and honey, Ditzen set out on 1 September for Berlin, to spend two weeks working on the Kutisker and Barmat files. He preferred a hotel room to the Burlages' flat in Kurfürsten Strasse – a further indication of the rift in their friendship. Hardly had he begun work than he had to set out for Hamburg for the funeral of his brother-in-law, Peter Frerksen, who had died suddenly of a heart attack at the Leipzig trade fair. The Ditzen children were very upset, particularly Lore, who found the loss of 'dear Uncle Räder and now this' hard to bear.

Ditzen found Berlin most uncongenial. Although he had excellent working conditions in the Ministry of Justice, the air raids only exacerbated his insomnia, and he returned to Carwitz on 21 September having obtained permission to take some material home with him.

He had secured a serialization deal for 'Before You Go to Sleep' with the *Münchner Illustrierte*, albeit for a much smaller sum than he had hoped. Otherwise, his prospects as a writer looked bleak: paper had not yet been approved for 'Our Home in Days Gone by', and he heard at the end of the month that the remaining copies of *Sparrow Farm* were to be destroyed, because Kiwitz's drawings were regarded as 'decadent art'.

Winter came early in 1941. On 6 October, snow fell on the German troops pushing towards Moscow and halted their advance. Snow took Carwitz by surprise as well: Ditzen was awakened at 4 a.m. on 28 October by a snowstorm. Suse and the women of the house ended up picking the remainder of the apples in snow and ice.

Ditzen had set aside his *Kutisker* project in the middle of October after an approach from the Wien-Film company to write a story 'for a great film about Berlin': 'What is envisaged is the tale of a young man from a small town in Brandenburg who comes to the city, is first crushed by it but then makes his home there. Period from 1910 until around 1930 with no mention of the war.'[18] Besides the attraction of the fee, Ditzen was excited by the prospect of writing about Berlin. He began work on 15 October and had finished Part One by the first week in December.

When the Soviet campaign had begun in the summer, Ditzen had foreseen that 'this fighting will cost many sacrifices and in thousands of homes people will be waiting in fear and worry.'[19] One of these homes was that of Suse's sister, the recently widowed Tilly Frerksen, who heard in early December that her only son had been killed in action on the Eastern Front. The experience of that first Russian winter had a serious impact on both the civilian population at home and on the military establishment. Following the enforced resignation of Field Marshal von Brauchitsch on 7 December, Hitler took over as commander-in-chief of the German army in the field: the Nazi Party's control of the armed forces was now complete.

Ditzen heard in the second week of December that official approval had been received to print 'Our Home in Days Gone by'. What he did not know was the reason for this sudden decision after months of prevarication. Karl Pagel, the Deutsche Verlags-Anstalt man in Berlin, regarded it as part of his job to maintain good relations with the Propaganda Ministry, and called on a regular basis to see a Dr Rudolf Erckmann there. On one such visit he happened to mention Ditzen's *Kutisker* project. Erckmann was not slow to see the propaganda opportunity offered by a combination of Ditzen's literary talent and this potentially anti-Semitic material. The immediate result was the approval of paper to print it.[20] Thus the Propaganda Ministry became involved in Ditzen's *Kutisker* project. For the present, however, he was unaware of official interest in his work and was so engrossed in the film project, provisionally entitled *Die Eroberung von Berlin* ('The Conquest of Berlin'), that he cut short his Christmas break and resumed writing on the afternoon of 26 December.

He finished 'The Conquest of Berlin' on 23 January 1942. The following week, Frau Klapper arrived to type the 850-page manuscript. Frau Klapper, whom Ditzen described as 'a pleasant house-guest', was another woman who had lost her job after the Nazis came to power and had taken up freelance secretarial work. Typing was completed on 25 February, and the manuscript was dispatched both to the Wien-Film company and the Deutsche Verlags-Anstalt the next day.

'The Conquest of Berlin' tells the story of Karl Siebrecht, born on the same day as Rudolf Ditzen, who is orphaned at the age of sixteen and sets out from a small provincial town to 'conquer Berlin'. From very small beginnings, he builds up a successful business transporting luggage between the main stations in the capital. The story spans the period from 1909 until the mid-thirties and becomes increasingly detached from its historical context as it approaches 1933. As the National Socialists, who are not mentioned in the novel, are tightening their grip on Germany, Siebrecht becomes increasingly involved in relationships with women, and the novel, which begins with some realistic scenes, typical of Ditzen at his best, ends on a note of crass sentimentality.

Three days after completing it, he received an official visit from the local police, who had been instructed by police headquarters in Schwerin to act on information received that he was a drug addict of many years' standing. Ditzen made a statement in which he confirmed that he had been cured of his morphine addiction in 1925. He listed the medication he received for his insomnia and the clinics where he had been treated, insisting that he did not abuse sleeping tablets, which he received only on prescription and which his wife kept in a safe place to which he had no access. Although not the first denunciation he experienced in Carwitz, this was the most pernicious so far, for it threatened to expose his criminal record as well as his history of alcoholism and mental illness to the Nazi authorities. He assumed that it had originated in the chemist's shop in Feldberg, where Suse had recently bought large quantities of Allional-Roche after the chemist advised her that this preparation would soon no longer be available.

A few weeks later, he was in trouble with the authorities again when he managed to buy enough wood to heat the house for two years. A disgruntled workman reported him for possessing illegal quantities and legal proceedings were threatened. In fact, Ditzen was guilty of many of the 'crimes' of which the authorities and, in particular, Mayor Schwoch, accused him. He explains in his '1944 Prison Memoirs':

> When this war began, my wife and I, who had both known starvation
> in the previous war, resolved to do all in our power in this war to ensure
> that we and our children had enough to eat, even if it meant breaking
> the law ... It wasn't my war, I didn't want Hitler and his armies to win

and I therefore had no reason to take the war into account . . . As far as I was concerned I was innocent, I was not bound by the laws passed by this criminal government.[21]

Ditzen was accused on eight counts of breaking the law relating to the misappropriation of wood, foodstuffs and seed – and was cleared on all counts. He concludes: 'I may be no great soldier on the battlefield, but I know how to wage my wars and fight my battles in my own way!'

He was still facing difficulties in his marriage as well. A reference in a letter to his mother in March 1942 to a 'minor source of contention' which had been 'resolved without divorce and splitting up the children' indicates the fragile state of the Ditzens' relationship. Rudolf had been sleeping in the guest-room since the end of April 1940 and in June 1942 was to move out of the house into the gardener's room across the yard. Suse's visits to Berlin became increasingly frequent in the course of 1942, and as his relationship with his wife deteriorated, Ditzen sought warmth and friendship with other women. The novelist Annemarie Steiner, whom Ditzen first met in 1938 and for whom he wrote the fairy tale 'Pechvogel und Glückskind' ('Unlucky Devil and Lucky Duck'), is but one example of many.[22]

'The Conquest of Berlin' provides instructive insights into his emotional life, for it is the first novel where a male protagonist rejects a working-class mother/wife. Karl Siebrecht divorces the plain, hard-working, submissive Rieke Busch, the mother of his child, and marries the glamorous, wealthy and capricious Hertha Eich who was 'a wonderful lover but never became a proper wife'. Siebrecht resolves his dilemma by remaining married to Hertha and adopting his son from his marriage to Rieke. As we shall see, Ditzen's own life was to follow an uncannily similar course.

The success of 'Our Home in Days Gone by', which appeared at the beginning of March, and a very reassuring visit to his publisher in Stuttgart later on in the month, did little to lift Ditzen's spirits. He felt he was running out of stories; he confided to Kilpper at the end of March: 'Since I've retired to this quiet place I feel increasingly empty – I repeat myself so often . . .' Indeed, 'The Conquest of Berlin' repeats motifs from *Iron Gustav*: the figure of Rieke Busch recalls Tutti Hack-endahl; Siebrecht's company bears many similarities to Gustav's business; both novels reflect Ditzen's fascination with Berlin.

At the beginning of April he started work on the second volume of his 'memoirs', 'Our Home Today'. Oscar Wilde's view that 'auto-biography is irresistible'[23] was certainly borne out by the success of Ditzen's memoirs. A further factor was the rosy glow of happiness-cum-nostalgia in which Ditzen enveloped his life, past and present. 'Our Home in Days Gone by' ended with the fictitious tale of 'Falla-da's' sexual initiation in Leipzig; 'Our Home Today' begins with a fulsome tribute to Suse. The intervening years in Ditzen's life – the courtrooms, clinics, sanatoria and prisons – are simply omitted. While 'Our Home Today' contains references to the war, the work is largely constructed around an idyllic family life in Mahlendorf (i.e. Carwitz) with chapters dedicated to members of the family and household (including a tribute to Hubert Räder) as well as to their animals, their car and 'Herr Fallada's' work routine.

The work's subtitle – *'Erlebtes, Erfahrenes und Erfundenes'* ('Things Experienced, Heard and Invented') – indicates the unreliabil-ity of the author's report. Ditzen himself confessed to Alfred Günther, Ledig's replacement at Deutsche Verlags-Anstalt: 'I tell some terrible lies in it.'[24] Indeed, the result is a greater work of fiction than some of his novels.

The two volumes of memoirs enabled Ditzen to concentrate on the personal to the almost complete exclusion of the political, thus repre-senting another strategy for survival in Nazi Germany.

Film work, serializations of undemanding, ahistorical novels and now highly fictionalized memoirs – all ensured his survival as a writer and brought in considerable sums of money. This kind of survival, however, not only failed to satisfy Ditzen's literary ambitions, it blocked his literary development. In Nazi Germany he could not develop his specific talent, which lay in the construction of large-scale narratives around the lives of ordinary men and women in contem-porary society, characterized by a commitment to humanist principles and a concern for social justice. The 'little man' was, after all, a spe-cific historical phenomenon. Ditzen's talent lay in exploring that 'little man' in his social environment. The attempt to write about 'little men' in an historical vacuum was doomed to failure. The strategy he adopted in 1939 of writing ahistorical and apolitical pieces had led him into a literary cul-de-sac by 1942. It was not only his health and his marriage which suffered under National Socialism. His development as a writer was stunted, too.

'Our Home Today' was completed on 14 May, and Else Marie Bakonyi, who had typed *Iron Gustav*, arrived next day to start typing. The manuscript was dispatched to Stuttgart two weeks later.

Throughout the spring and summer of 1942 the German army made little headway on the Eastern Front. Among the wounded in April 1942 was Ledig who sustained very serious injuries to his ribs and spine when a shell exploded close by. He then contracted pneumonia in an unheated ambulance on the way to the field hospital. He was sent back to Stuttgart for convalescence and was unable to return to his desk at Deutsche Verlags-Anstalt until the following year.

As the Nazi regime saw the tide of war beginning to turn against it on the battlefield, Hitler acquired total powers on the home front. A law was passed in the Reichstag on 26 April 1942 which effectively abolished any remaining civil rights and empowered the Führer to 'mete out punishment' to any German who failed 'to fulfil his duties', without 'being bound by existing legal regulations'.[25] One of the first victims of the ensuing round of repression was Alfred Schmidt-Sas, Marga Kenter's partner, who had been released from Sachsenhausen in March 1942 and was now re-arrested in June.

Ditzen had another experience of 'the envy and resentment and petty animosity which never dares to show itself openly but which is always hassling and hounding us'[26] in May when he injured his foot in a bicycle accident. The local doctor advised him to have an X-ray and provided him with a letter confirming that he needed an official car to take him to the nearest hospital in Neustrelitz. The authorities refused this request and told him to take the train. Ditzen decided to let nature take its course. Finally, when there was no sign of improvement, a local landowner gave him a lift to the hospital where it was discovered he had broken three bones, causing months of pain and discomfort.

In June, he was cheered by a visit from Ernst Rowohlt, who had reported for duty at the Air Ministry on his return from Brazil, and was initially posted to Stettin. At his own request Rowohlt was later transferred to Brussels and by the spring of 1942 was in Cape Sounion near Athens. The authorities had offered him the return of his business but he declined, preferring to wait until the war was over. It is likely that he discussed his future publishing plans with Ditzen in Carwitz in June 1942.

Meanwhile, Ditzen was not writing anything. After Goebbels's announcement on 1 June that, due to the chronic shortage of paper, only books 'important to the war effort' would be published, there seemed little point. In addition, his foot injury, the police enquiries into the allegations of drug addiction, as well as the circumstances of village life in Carwitz, contributed to his depression and loss of sleep. It is possible that it was in July 1942, during one of Suse's many absences, that he embarked on a relationship with Anneliese Benzin, a local girl who helped out in the Ditzens' household. She was young, lively and felt genuine sympathy for Ditzen's plight. Her boyfriend was in the army and on his return in 1944 they became engaged. This relationship therefore never posed any serious threat to the Ditzens' marriage. Ditzen later acknowledged the debt he owed to her: 'I shall never forget how you and your mother stood by me in very difficult times.'[27]

In July, Ditzen signed a contract with the *Berliner Illustrirte* for the serialization of 'The Conquest of Berlin' and a few weeks later sat down to cut the novel from 850 to 250 pages. The film company which had commissioned the work also required a thorough revision, and Ditzen had promised to revise the manuscript yet again for the book edition. In total he spent over a year on the various versions of this material and revised the filmscript four times. This was not calculated to improve his spirits.

As the summer progressed the bad news increased. The fiancé of Adelheid Hörig, Ditzen's favourite niece, was killed in July. Tilly Frerksen arrived in Carwitz at the end of July for three weeks' rest after the interrupted nights caused by the allied bombing raids on Hamburg. Tilly took charge of Achim while Suse took Lore to her new school in Potsdam. Rudolf's mother, sister and brother-in-law in Celle were suffering, too, from the raids on Hanover. Ditzen had advised the Hörigs to leave Celle in June, but they were loath to do so until some provision could be made for Elisabeth Ditzen who was house-bound and unable to manage on her own. Rowohlt's regiment was moved in August from the relative safety of Greece to the Caucasus. Although based at General Headquarters, Rowohlt saw active service on the Eastern Front. He wrote to Ditzen that he had enough to eat and drink but 'everything else is miserable, unrelentingly stupefying'.

Then, on 5 August, the Nazi war machine requested Ditzen's services. Captain Graff of the Army High Command wrote to him inviting him to visit the Front, read to the troops from his work and collect material for a book. Ditzen pleaded insomnia, irritability and a broken foot and asked to be excused. He knew that he could secure only a temporary reprieve.

On 5 October, he received a second visit from the police about his alleged drug addiction. The authorities had discovered that in his original statement he had omitted the short stay in a sanatorium in Dresden in 1941. He attributed this omission to the 'upset of my first interrogation' and emphatically rejected the allegations of drug abuse once more. Four days later Marga Kenter's partner, Alfred Schmidt-Sas, was condemned to death by the People's Court. A plea for mercy was lodged immediately, but the prospects were not good.

Ditzen's lethargy and depression continued throughout the autumn. Hardly had his foot healed than he had another accident: on 13 November he engaged a local man with a horse and cart to take him to the station in Feldberg to collect Suse on her return from visiting Elisabeth Ditzen in Celle and her own mother in Hamburg. On the way back to Carwitz the cart-seat broke, throwing them backwards onto the frozen road. The driver had gone some distance before he noticed the loss of his passengers. Then, on 23 November, the Deutsche Verlags-Anstalt building was damaged in an air raid and many books, manuscripts and papers were destroyed in extinguishing the fire. A further blow in November was the death of E. R. Weiss, the cover artist for many of Ditzen's books in the thirties. Ditzen wrote to Rowohlt that Weiss 'is unforgettably linked with my books. He was the one who did my best and most successful volumes'. Another source of irritation was the removal of Marcelin Riseau, a French prisoner-of-war allocated to the Ditzens in October and whom Ditzen found a good worker and congenial companion. Riseau's departure left him without any help at a time when he was not fully fit. He wrote to his mother at the end of November: 'I am quite disheartened. I have hardly slept at all for weeks now and I'm plagued by a constant depression. I'm seriously considering packing my bags and heading for a sanatorium in Berlin.' In the event he stayed in Carwitz but resolved to move house as soon as possible to escape what he described in a letter to Kagelmacher at the end of the month as 'the meanness of our dear fellow human beings'. On 7 December he was interrogated for two hours 'about my case'.

Ditzen was not the only writer to suffer from depression in 1942. The young Wolfgang Borchert, whose *The Man Outside* was to appear in the same year as Ditzen's last novel *Alone in Berlin*, wrote in August 1942: 'Often I get to the stage where I want to throw my life away – but then I tell myself: What for? It's not worth it. But this is no life at all!'[28] The novelist Jochen Klepper, another Deutsche Verlags-Anstalt author, drew a similar conclusion; he and his family committed suicide on 10 December 1942. As the tide of war began to turn against Germany, life became even more difficult for non-Nazi writers. 'Our Home Today' was the last book Ditzen published until after the war.

From then on, he sought solace from a hostile environment and his depression in alcohol. An admirer sent him a crate of Burgundy and this became his main sleeping-draught. He commented in a letter to Ernst Rowohlt on 2 January 1943 that 'it had a good effect on my sleep but the stuff makes me lazy, lazy and apathetic'.

Christmas 1942 was the first Christmas the Ditzens had no guests to stay in Carwitz. Marga Kenter had gone to spend the holiday with Alfred Schmidt-Sas's parents. It was also the first Christmas that Suse received no present from her husband. The following Monday, Rudolf drew up a list of New Year resolutions 'in order to shake off the apathy and depression': he resolved to move back into the guest-room in the house, to reduce his smoking and to stop drinking several bottles of red wine a day.

This resolution seems to have been somewhat short lived, for Ditzen commented after a trip to Berlin in January 1943 that 'it was astonishing how much drink there was to be had ... the first few days of abstinence afterwards were very difficult.'

In Berlin, Ditzen stayed with Else Marie Bakonyi. The discrepancy between his description of her as 'our friend' and Suse's reference to her as 'his typist' suggests that she may have been another of the women from whom Ditzen sought comfort in his distress.

Still smarting from Reger's refusal to publish 'Before You Go to Sleep', Ditzen negotiated a contract with a rival publisher, Hugenberg's Scherl Verlag, for the serialization of a new novel, which he started on 19 January.[29] He interpreted the lack of contact with the Deutsche Verlags-Anstalt as a lack of interest in his work, which, given the political difficulties involved in publishing 'Hans Fallada', may well have been the case. However, breakdowns in communication were also an inevitable consequence of war. In the course of 1943, Carwitz, which had hitherto escaped much of the hardship experienced by city-dwellers in wartime, began to be directly affected by the war effort. Growing vegetables became increasingly difficult. Smallholders were forbidden to buy seed and had to obtain plants from the larger nurseries, which often did not have a large enough supply.

The Allied and Soviet offensives in North Africa and around Stalingrad in the autumn of 1942 marked the turning point of the war. The sound of Allied war planes over Carwitz on their way to and from Berlin became a regular occurrence. The German defeats on the Eastern Front, which culminated in the surrender at Stalingrad, led the Nazi regime to redouble the war effort at home, by proclaiming 'total war'. All men between the ages of sixteen and sixty-five not already involved in the war effort were to be drafted into the munitions industry. This prospect plunged Ditzen into a deep depression and, at the end of January 1943, he was admitted to the Kuranstalt Westend in the Charlottenburg district of Berlin, a clinic run by Professor Zutt, a former colleague of Professor Bonhoeffer.

Total mobilization ushered in a new round of repression which

Carwitz bei Feldberg in Mecklenburg

7. The village of Carwitz ('Aerial photo from a height of some 100 m') *c.* 1935. The arrow indicates the Ditzens' smallholding.

18. In the new house in Carwitz on Suse's birthday, 12 March 1934.

9. With Uli in a motor boat on Carwitz Lake, August 1934.

Fun and games in the garden in Carwitz: Uli and Lore on top, their father on the ground (second from left), summer 1937.

21. At his desk in the study in Carwitz, leafing through the manuscript of *Once We had a Child*, 1934.

22. View of the study, 1934. The telephone number was Feldberg 76.

, *c.* 1935.

24. Visitors to Carwitz; (from left) Heinrich Maria Ledig, Martha Dodd and Mildred Harnack, 27 May 1934.

25. With friend and psychiatrist Willi Burlage.

5. With Peter Zingler, who was in charge of foreign rights at Rowohlt's, and Uli.

27. Sister and brother-in-law, Elisabeth and Heinz Hörig (extreme left), on holiday in St Peter on the North Sea.

28. Sophie Zickermann, nurse and long-standing family friend, summer 1936.

29. Publisher and friend, Ernst Rowohlt (press photo, undated).

Press photo, 8 July 1939.

31. Family boat trip, July 1939.

With Suse in Carwitz, July 1943.

33. First page of the 1944 Prison Diary.

34. Second wife, Ulla Ditzen.

35. Ulla Ditzen with her daughter from her first marriage, Jutta Losch.

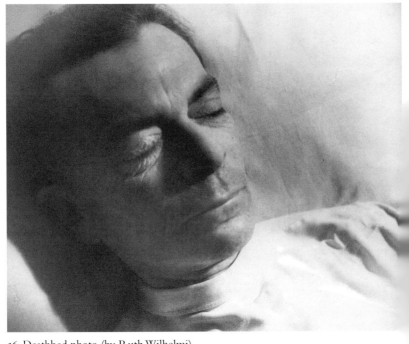

36. Deathbed photo (by Ruth Wilhelmi).

saw the executions of Mildred Harnack (who had visited Carwitz with Martha Dodd) and Alfred Schmidt-Sas. Three days after Schmidt-Sas's execution, on 8 April 1943, the Berlin couple Otto and Elise Hampel met their deaths in the same notorious Plötzensee prison. Although Ditzen was unaware of their existence at the time, their story was to form the basis of his last novel, *Alone in Berlin*. That April also saw the arrest of Professor Bonhoeffer's son, Dietrich, as well as his daughter and son-in-law, Christine and Hans von Dohnanyi.

Ditzen returned to Carwitz on 13 February and resumed work on yet another venture, *Der Jungherr von Strammin* ('The Master of Strammin'), closely modelled on Stevenson's *The Master of Ballantrae*. He told his sister that 'it is not very easy to concentrate on work because of what's going on in the East.'

At the end of the month, Ditzen had a further interview with the police in connection with drug-addiction allegations and was told informally that the case against him would most probably be dropped. He wrote to his mother on 15 March: 'The person who denounced me has turned out to be a thoroughly untrustworthy character and the State Prosecutor is reduced to clutching at straws in the shape of a completely ridiculous accusation made by our worthy mayor.'

He completed 'The Master of Strammin' on 7 March, and Else Marie Bakonyi arrived the following Saturday to start typing. Ditzen pronounced himself satisfied with the work, even if, as he confided to Ledig on 26 March, 'it's only a light read [*Unterhaltungsroman*]'.

In the meantime, he had been approached again by the army to undertake a tour of France to view German military options and meet the troops there. Realizing that he could not decline such an invitation if he valued his life, Ditzen seized this opportunity as the lesser of two evils, especially as it became clear that he would not have to wear a uniform, would have private accommodation and would not have to write anything. In addition, the destination of Bordeaux must have had a certain attraction. It was certainly preferable to working in an arms factory or running a large farm. Ditzen was also aware that it was only a matter of time before the end of the war; in a letter to Ledig on 12 May, he used the colloquial idiom 'we have managed to get over the dog, we'll manage the tail, too' ('*Wir sind über den Hund gekommen, werden wir auch den Schwanz schaffen!*'), in other words: the worst is over, the end is in sight. The end, however, did not come quickly.

Meanwhile, those writers who had gone into exile were involving themselves in the war effort on behalf of the Allies. Becher, Willi Bredel and Erich Weinert worked with the large number of German soldiers who had been taken prisoner in the Soviet Union to establish the National Committee for a Free Germany, which started to publish its own journal, *Freies Deutschland*, in July 1943. In the course of 1943, a series of such organizations sprang up in the United States, Great Britain, France and Sweden. In Mexico, the Free Germany Committee counted Paul Mayer among its members.

As the Allied bombing raids on Hanover increased, the position of the housebound Elisabeth Ditzen became increasingly precarious. Ditzen told his sister that he would be prepared to have his mother in Carwitz 'if there is absolutely no alternative', although he was only too aware of the difficulties for all concerned. His mother was used to her friends of similar outlook, class and tastes and would not adjust easily to life in the country; Suse was very busy and would have little time for her mother-in-law; Ditzen himself was 'difficult and not very patient', had not lived under the same roof as his mother for over thirty years and could not bear what he called his mother's 'droning on'. Suse's mother, too, was giving cause for concern: she had been admitted to a home, but in the spring of 1943 was moved to the geriatric unit of a hospital in Hamburg suffering from hardening of the arteries in the brain. She was in great danger both from the heavy bombing of Hamburg and from the Nazis' policy of euthanasia for the 'incurable'.

By mid-May, Ditzen had completed the book version of 'The Conquest of Berlin', which was to be called *Ein Mann will hinauf* ('A Man Wants to Get On'), and abridged 'The Master of Strammin' for serialization in Scherl's *Die Woche*, which netted him 15,000 marks.[30] On 14 May, he wrote to his mother, inviting her to move to Carwitz.

Three days later, he set out for Bordeaux, stopping briefly in Paris to visit one of his French publishers, Sorlot. By 1943, Ditzen had three French publishers (Sorlot, Albin Michel and Hachette), the German occupation of France having led to increased sales of his work. His tour of duty took him as far as Spain, from where he sent a card to Ledig at Whitsun. On his way back to Germany he visited Albin Michel in Paris and arrived home in the third week in June.

Although he had undertaken a punishing schedule, he arrived home in good spirits and was pleasantly surprised to discover that the authorities were now much better disposed towards him. Not only had all proceedings against him been dropped but he was inundated with requests for interviews, filmscripts and stories – all of which he declined. Among the letters awaiting him in Carwitz was one from Dr Erckmann in the Propaganda Ministry, the same Dr Erckmann whom Pagel of the Deutsche Verlags-Anstalt had informed of Ditzen's interest in the Barmat/Kutisker material. Now that a renewed campaign against the Jews was part of the 'total mobilization', Erckmann wrote to Ditzen offering him every support if he would make the *Kutisker* project a priority. Ditzen replied on 25 June that while he had completed all the research for the topic, he was very busy at the moment but would be able to start work at the beginning of 1944, no doubt hoping that Erckmann and his ilk would be gone by then. In response to a second letter from Erckmann in August, Ditzen outlined a plot, purporting to be based on the life of Kutisker but which bore very little resemblance to the historical facts. In his letter of 11 August he told Erckmann that he hoped to submit by the summer of 1944. On the same day, he wrote to Ledig expressing concern about 'the interest in high places' in the *Kutisker* project, 'which, as you know, has fascinated me for some time' and concluded: 'I fear that the novel in its basic approach will not turn out to be what the Ministry is expecting.'[31]

While Ditzen's star appeared to be rising, Ernst Rowohlt's was falling: he had been declared a German spy in Brazil, which had led to unpleasant consequences for his former wife, who had stayed on there; an operation for a stomach ulcer had involved a six-week stay in hospital; then he was discharged from the army with effect from 30 June as 'politically unreliable'. In addition, his second wife, Hilda Rowohlt, of whom he was very fond, had died tragically in a fire in mid-May. He wrote to Ditzen in mid-July that 'my nerves are completely shattered.'

Hardly had Ditzen returned to Carwitz than he was invited to undertake another tour, this time to Niemes in the Sudetenland to observe and report on the training of recruits. Ditzen expressed reluctance to be away from home during his children's summer holidays and secured agreement for Suse, Uli and Lore to accompany him. The date of departure was set for 2 August.

On 10 July 1943, the Allies landed in Sicily and, two days later, the Soviet army mounted a counter-offensive along the entire Eastern Front. The increased allied bombing resulted in an exodus from the German cities. Carwitz, a village of some 240 inhabitants, was allocated 60 refugees from the Rhineland. Two women and two small children from Mönchen-Gladbach were allocated to Ditzen, who gave them 'my lovely, quiet gardener's room-cum-study' and moved back into the guest-room in the house.

Besides the official evacuation, city dwellers had begun to make 'Hamsterfahrten', day trips into the country to obtain food – by barter or theft. The meat ration had been reduced from 350g to 100g per week on 31 May; bread, fat, sugar and potatoes were also rationed. Restaurants and all retail outlets not deemed vital to the war effort had been closed on 30 January and the purchase of clothes was restricted to children and victims of the Allied bombing. Ditzen was shocked to discover in January 1943 that Berlin's largest shoe shop had a total of four pairs of men's shoes for sale. The supply of luxury items from the Front – Ditzen's admirer, Herr Küthe, had sent 'Frau Fallada' silk stockings from France in 1940 – was a thing of the past.

Ditzen celebrated his fiftieth birthday quietly in Carwitz. He had issued strict instructions to Ledig that he wanted no official celebrations. He received a total of 173 books, which brought his library to four thousand volumes. In a letter to his mother in May 1941, Ditzen had described it as 'my big, almost my only hobby'; since 1939, he had stopped collecting contemporary literature and had been concentrating on rare first editions of the German classics. He still read some modern novels, but did not consider them worth keeping.

On 26 July 1943, he wrote to his sister Elisabeth: 'I do not think the times will soon become much easier but I do think the very hard times will not last much longer.'

Ditzen viewed his trip to Niemes as a much-needed family holiday. Arrangements were made for some friends of Else Marie Bakonyi to look after the smallholding in the family's absence; Tilly Frerksen took charge of Achim. Ditzen, Suse, Uli and Lore set out on 2 August. They passed through Berlin on the first day of the evacuation of the capital ordered by Goebbels: 'We arrived in the early stages of chaos and panic; our departure beggars all description, everybody fighting with everybody else.'[32] The Ditzens had rooms in the Hotel Ernst in Niemes and the children enjoyed horse-riding and swimming. Ditzen wrote to his mother on 11 August: 'I can't say I'm enjoying my work here yet, but I'm conscientiously making notes on everything I see.'

The proximity of Zittau made visits to Ditzen's sister Margarete possible, and much of their conversation revolved around their mother's move to Carwitz. On 24 August, Suse took the children back to Carwitz, got them ready for school then returned to Niemes, where Ditzen, who had moved out of the hotel and into army accommodation, had been leading a 'varied and often "wet" life'. Suse left for Zittau on 31 August, then continued to Berlin and Carwitz, where she sent packing-cases to Celle and arrived there herself at the end of the first week in September to organize her mother-in-law's move.

During this tour of duty in Czechoslovakia, Ditzen renewed his acquaintance with Annemarie Steiner. He spent a week at her family home and she accompanied him to his readings. She also took notes for the diary he was supposed to write – notes which he left with her and showed no interest in retrieving.

In early September Ditzen had set out for a second tour of France. The only indication of the reason for this trip is a rather enigmatic comment in a letter to Ledig on 16 August: 'I have very specific reasons for wanting to spend one or two weeks down there again.'

Whatever the reason, Ditzen did not much enjoy his second tour of France. He returned to Carwitz on 3 October, exhausted and suffering from a serious bout of influenza. He found his home occupied by four relatives: Suse's two sisters and a pregnant niece, who had been bombed out in Hamburg, as well as his aged and infirm mother.

Among his post was a letter from Ledig with the news that the paper supply for 'A Man Wants to Get On' had not yet arrived and a suggestion that they should meet and talk things over in person. Ditzen, fearing yet more bad news, refused to meet Ledig. However, he was not to remain in ignorance of his fate for long. Ledig wrote, in a private capacity, on 18 October, informing Ditzen that the Rowohlt division of the Deutsche Verlags-Anstalt was closing as a result of the war and that they would, therefore, have to meet. Five days later, Ditzen received official notification that Rowohlt would cease to exist after 31 December and that this was not primarily due to the war but to the 'restructuring of our Party firm'. Ditzen's period of apparent official approval had been short lived: it lasted little more than four months. Ledig made the arduous journey to Carwitz at the end of October to negotiate the winding up of Ditzen's 25-year association with Rowohlt.

Suddenly without a publisher, Ditzen was anxious to clarify his legal position and terminate his contract with Deutsche Verlags-Anstalt so that he could start to look for a new publisher. When Deutsche Verlags-Anstalt showed little sympathy for his plight and started a renegotiation of what had been agreed with Ledig, Ditzen put the matter in the hands of his solicitor on 17 November. Two days later, Suse took him to Dr Zutt's clinic in Berlin. There, Else Marie Bakonyi visited him on the twentieth, but he had to be brought home from Berlin on the twenty-second, after Zutt's clinic was damaged in an air raid. Between mid-November 1943 and mid-February 1944 the Allies dropped 22,000 tons of high explosive on Berlin. The same air raid that damaged Zutt's clinic claimed the life of Willi Burlage, who was conducting his evening surgery when a bomb demolished his apartment in Kurfürsten Strasse. His lodger, Ernst Rowohlt, had gone out for the evening and thus escaped certain death.

Suse took Ditzen to the university clinic in Greifswald on 10 December, but he was refused admission and forced to return to Carwitz. Eleven days later, Evchen Burlage arrived in Carwitz for an extended stay.

Ditzen described his situation in a letter to Kagelmacher the following July: 'And so I had anything up to twelve females in my house, with myself as the only man. My dear Kagelmacher, what I went through was sheer Strindbergian hell.'[33] The constant tensions at home and the loss of his publisher aggravated Ditzen's health. His only sources of consolation were alcohol and his friendship with Anneliese Benzin. Their affair was now common knowledge in Carwitz but Suse did not find out about it until the end of December. Ditzen told Kagelmacher in the same letter: 'Of course, it was really nothing new to her. Almost from the beginning of our marriage I had relationships on the side. Sometimes my wife knew about them, sometimes she suspected something, sometimes she had no idea.' Ditzen, however, insisted that 'they never seriously affected our good friendship and the deep respect which I had for her honesty and sincerity.'

Suse felt deeply hurt when she discovered that Ditzen had been carrying on an affair in their home, especially when she was the last to know about it. Burdened with responsibility for the children, the house, the smallholding, a difficult mother-in-law, a floating population of evacuees and a recently bereaved friend, this was simply too much to bear.

When Ditzen's depression had not lifted by the third week in January, he was readmitted to Dr Zutt's clinic. He was not to return to Carwitz until the end of March. In a letter to his sister Elisabeth on 2 March he described the weeks he spent in Berlin at the beginning of 1944 as: '. . . the worst I have ever known. A veritable mountain of unresolved and practically unresolvable problems inside me; then illness and lack of sleep – as well as the terrifying air raids which were the worst of all.' All the patients in the clinic had to be fully dressed by 5 p.m. each day in preparation for removal to the air-raid shelter; they were only allowed to put on their pyjamas and get into bed at 5 a.m. When his black-out blind was damaged by a bomb, Ditzen placed a tablecloth over his bedside lamp to enable him to read in the dark. His room had two external walls and a broken window, which made it very cold. Partly to get warm, he started going on long walks through Berlin in the afternoons with a nurse. He was devastated by what he saw and reported in a letter to his mother on

11 February: 'Sometimes you see houses which look completely unin-
habitable and ready to collapse and there are people squatting in
them.' He confided in Rowohlt: 'How many people will break down –
when this war is over and the tension which is keeping them going
now disappears?'

Despite the extreme discomfort of life in Berlin, he made a gradual
recovery and was able to manage 'almost without sleeping tablets' by
27 January. His recovery was greatly helped by his successful negotiations with a new publishing company, Wilhelm Heyne of Dresden,
on 26 January, in which he played his only negotiating card: the
Kutisker project, which enjoyed the support of the Ministry for Public
Enlightenment and Propaganda. He described this in a letter to Rowohlt as 'a novel which will never be completed but which is good
enough for an advance'. The advance in question amounted to 40,000
marks.

In Berlin, Ditzen had regular visits from Peter Zingler. Rowohlt,
too, dropped in when he was there; he spent 1944 planning the future
of his publishing business and making contacts with writers and other
publishers. His interest in Ditzen was not only that of a true friend –
'Hans Fallada' was high on his agenda for the future.

A visit from Suse at the end of January cheered Ditzen considerably and made him determined, as he wrote to his mother on the
thirtieth, 'to become reconciled with Suse again for it is only together
that we can overcome all our problems'.

By 22 February, he was well enough to leave the clinic and go to
Eisfeld in Thüringen to convalesce, staying with Margarete Norweg,
a former housemaid who was living with her parents and expecting
her second child. The week after Ditzen left, Berlin became an even
more dangerous place when the US air force commenced day-time
raids. On 6 March, German anti-aircraft fire prevented them from
completing their mission and so, forced to retreat, they dropped their
remaining bombs on Templin. Uli's school was not damaged but Suse
spent anxious hours before news of his safety reached Carwitz. Two
days later, Rowohlt's house in Grünheide was slightly damaged.
Ditzen and his wife became increasingly concerned about Lore's
safety in Potsdam and arranged for her to move school to Neustrelitz.

Long walks in the snow, good country air and plain food contributed to Ditzen's well-being. This was not adversely affected by a negative review of 'Our Home in Days Gone by' and 'Our Home Today' which marked Ditzen's return to official discredit. The lack of official sanction had held up his contract with Heyne, which was eventually signed in the second week in March. Three days later, Rowohlt wrote to Ditzen telling him of a contract he had negotiated on Ditzen's behalf with Hans Zehrer of the Stalling publishing house, temporarily located on Sylt. He urged Ditzen to go to Sylt as soon as possible. Ditzen, who by now had put on weight and was sleeping well, replied on 18 March that he had already signed a contract with Heyne and wanted to return to Carwitz, where he intended to write. Of his literary plans, he wrote: 'It's all too complicated to explain in a letter. But I have thought it all out carefully and I'm not going to do anything which would be damaging.' What he appears to have had in mind was a survival strategy: to use the protection of the Propaganda Ministry to secure the contract with Heyne (and a regular income), while writing the kind of novel he had originally intended, but delaying its completion until the war was over. In March 1944, with the western Allies in Italy and the Soviet army closing in, the war was expected to be over by the end of the year.

Ditzen returned to Carwitz on 29 March, fully recovered and, as he wrote to Uli before he left Eisfeld, 'ready to work hard. This year mostly out of doors, firstly because we don't have anyone to do the outdoor work and secondly because there is no great rush with my writing.'[34]

Five weeks later, he and his wife applied for a divorce. In a letter to Elisabeth and Heinz Hörig on 25 May, he blamed his wife's relations, Evchen Burlage and his own mother for turning Suse against him: 'I have made serious mistakes, I bear a heavy burden of guilt, but all this could have been worked out, could have been forgiven (as it had been forgiven before); a friendly relationship could have been established, for the sake of the children – if it had not been for my wife's dear relations and friends, and, sad to say, my own mother.'

A reunion with Anneliese Benzin, who had now moved away from Carwitz and was engaged to be married, had been the final straw.

Ditzen described Suse's reaction in a letter to Anneliese on 4 May: 'The village is of course full of the news that we have seen each other again. If the gossips knew how innocent our meeting was they would be sorely disappointed. I had a terrible reception at home.' Suse greeted him with the threat that she would do all in her power to prevent him marrying Anneliese. Ditzen's efforts to convince her that he had no intention of doing so were fruitless. He did not want to end his marriage to Suse, 'which, despite all its shortcomings, was still a pretty good marriage', and he insisted: 'I have a deep affection for her ... She will always remain for me the companion of difficult and not so difficult times. Despite all her efforts she cannot destroy the feelings I have for her.' Ditzen did not relish the prospect of divorce, which only seemed to compound his feelings of failure. He wrote to his sister Elisabeth on 25 May: 'I'm not enjoying my work any more ... I'm tired of life. What's the point of going on? ... My dream of becoming a great artist is shattered. I'm only a writer like so many others. Perhaps I was too interested in money and success, I don't know ... Everything is hopeless, everything is gloomy, nothing excites me any more.'

Acrimonious divorce proceedings did not improve relations in the household. By the time the divorce came through on 5 July, Ditzen had moved into the gardener's room across the yard, but he soon recognized this as a temporary solution. He was tempted by Rowohlt's invitation to Sylt but felt he was needed to work the smallholding, which Suse could not manage on her own.

Once the divorce was final, Ditzen's spirits improved. By 18 July he had started dictating the first part of the *Kutisker* novel. He described this project in a letter to his sister as 'a pretty tiresome job' and expressed the opinion that it would never be published. Else Marie Bakonyi had moved to Hanover, and the new typist turned out to be so unsatisfactory that, after a week, she was dismissed.

A further and more tangible reason for the improvement in Ditzen's spirits in the summer of 1944 was his friendship with Ursula (Ulla) Losch, a wealthy young widow. Following her husband's death in May, Ulla had moved with her mother and daughter to her country cottage on the outskirts of Feldberg.

In a letter to a colleague of Dr Zutt's on 12 July, Ditzen wrote that he intended 'to marry again as soon as possible, but not, of course, that little girl', in other words, Anneliese Benzin. On 8 August, he wrote to his sister Elisabeth: 'I may have found something to fill my days with joy again – let's see!'

Ulla Losch appeared to be the exact opposite to Suse, although both came from very humble origins. Suse, now forty-three years old, bore the marks of hard physical work on her hands and face. Her straight hair was streaked with grey, and although her open, honest face still retained some of the freshness of youth, it also showed the passing of the years. Ulla, on the other hand, was twenty-two and caused a sensation in Feldberg with her curls, make-up, nail varnish and jewellery. Yet, while Ditzen was no doubt flattered by the interest shown in him by such an attractive young woman, it is unlikely that it was a pretty face alone that won his heart. What drew him to Ulla Losch was her youthful exuberance, her affectionate nature, her sense of fun and her resourcefulness. While she gave the appearance of being a spoilt little rich girl, she had in fact known hard times before her employer, the soap manufacturer Kurt Losch, had picked her out on the shop-floor and married her. She combined the grit of a working-class girl with the chic of the bourgeoisie. While in Ditzen's novel 'A Man Wants to Get On' Siebrecht sought to reconcile the two types of women represented by Rieke Busch and Hertha Eich, Ditzen achieved that synthesis in the person of Ulla Losch.

Their relationship was cut short by the events of 28 August 1944. Ditzen, who had been drinking heavily, became involved in a row with Suse in the kitchen, in the course of which he fired a shot, although not directly at her. She seized his gun, hit him over the head with it, ran out and threw it into the lake. She then called the doctor, who could not come himself but sent the local policeman, who took Ditzen off to Feldberg to calm down. There the matter would have ended, had it not been for the excessive zeal of the authorities, in the person of a young lawyer from the state prosecutor's office, who happened to be in Feldberg. He insisted on initiating proceedings against Ditzen for threatening behaviour towards his wife. As a result, he was committed to the psychiatric prison in Neustrelitz-Strelitz for observation. As the doors of yet another institution closed behind him in September 1944, Ditzen was a man at the end of the road: an alcoholic, a writer unable to write, an emotional and physical wreck. It looked as if he was about to share the fate of the tree in Kästner's poem and wither and die with the Germany he had been unwilling to leave.

8 1944–1947
New Beginnings and Sentences of Death

> *A writer who gives us real insight into the hearts and minds*
> *of human beings, especially those considered ordinary and*
> *uninteresting, deserves the highest praise.*
>
> – Johannes R. Becher[1]

Ditzen's admission to the psychiatric prison in Neustrelitz-Strelitz at the end of August 1944 could be viewed as another example of what he often referred to as instances of 'good fortune in misfortune' (*'Glück im Unglück'*) in his life. As on previous occasions, institutionalization, by removing the availability of alcohol, guaranteed a successful detoxification programme. It also gave him the necessary geographical and emotional distance to tackle his personal problems. In the autumn of 1944, a psychiatric prison protected Ditzen from Goebbels's plans for total mobilization, including a directive of 25 September requiring all able-bodied men between the ages of sixteen and sixty not already in the armed forces to report for duty to the Volkssturm, a kind of Home Guard intended to form the last line of defence on the home front. As the Soviet army pressed westwards into Romania and Bulgaria, the British advanced eastwards into Belgium, and the US army reached Germany's western borders in September 1944, the campaign against opponents of the Nazi regime inside Germany intensified. Moreover, the failed attempt to assassinate Hitler on 20 July 1944 provided a pretext to get rid of not only the immediate conspirators but hundreds of others who had not been involved. Among the many victims of the Nazi executioner in the late summer of 1944 were Ulrich von

Hassell, the former German ambassador in Rome, Adam von Trott zu Solz, a member of the anti-fascist Kreisau circle, and Ernst Thälmann, the Communist leader who had been in prison since March 1933.

While Ditzen's situation in Neustrelitz-Strelitz was not without danger – he had been admitted 'for observation' and without a fixed term to a psychiatric prison which operated the Nazi policies of euthanasia and compulsory sterilization – he was, at least, removed from the major sources of his distress. It was only a matter of being a model patient, a role in which Ditzen was much practised, keeping a low profile and waiting for the end of the war, which could not now be far off.

Ditzen's request for writing materials as soon as he had settled in looked like a familiar prison survival strategy. Here he was able to use the officially sanctioned *Kutisker* project to good effect. Ditzen was not the only author incarcerated in a Nazi institution in 1944: the Communist writer Bruno Apitz was in Buchenwald, the Romance scholar and novelist Werner Krauss in Plötzensee prison in Berlin, the poet Paul Celan in Buzau work-camp in Romania, the dramatist Günther Weisenborn in Luckau gaol in Brandenburg, and the publisher Peter Suhrkamp was in Oranienburg. While many continued writing in the most difficult of circumstances, the manuscript which Ditzen began on 6 September 1944 is one of the most remarkable to have emerged from any Nazi institution. In it, Ditzen, far from keeping a low profile, eschewed all compromise and embarked on a collision course with the authorities.

The manuscript, known as the '*Trinker-Manuskript*', consists of 92 sheets of lined paper (i.e. 184 pages). It contains a number of short stories, the novel *The Drinker* and an account of Ditzen's experiences under the Nazi regime from January 1933 until the outbreak of war in 1939.[2] The manuscript falls into two parts. Pages 1 to 140 contain three short stories and the novel *The Drinker*; these are written on lined paper with twenty-four lines per page in Ditzen's tiny, compact, almost indecipherable hand. Pages 141 to 184 contain two short stories and his memoirs of life under the Nazi regime.

Ditzen proceeded as follows: he started writing on 6 September on page 1; by 21 September, he had finished the short story '*Der kleine*

Jü-Jü und der große Jü-Jü' ('Little Jü-Jü and Big Jü-Jü') and the novel *The Drinker* and had reached page 131. The next day he wrote *'Ich suche den Vater'* ('Looking for Father') and began *'Die Geschichte von der Kleinen und der Großen Mücke'* ('The Story of Little and Big Mücke'), which brought him to page 141. Then, on 23 September, he began on page 141 to record his recollections of the Nazi period and wrote on until page 184, continuing as before to write twenty-four lines per page. When he reached page 184, on 28 September, he turned the page upside down, numbered it 185 and wrote between the lines 'backwards' to page 141, which he reached on 5 October. By this stage, pages 141 to 184 had each at least forty-eight lines. He now turned page 141 around again and began to write page 229 of his manuscript in between the existing lines. He continued writing like this until he reached page 153 on 7 October, so that pages 141 to 153 were written on three times, producing seventy-two lines.

While this method produced a manuscript which appeared inde-cipherable, the risk he ran should not be underestimated. The novel *The Drinker*, written on twenty-four lines per foolscap page, could have been read with little difficulty. It had clearly nothing to do with the *Kutisker* project; its rogues' gallery of criminals and the mentally deranged, its depiction of homosexuality and its dark, sombre tone represented a flagrant breach of prevailing literary policy. The second major work in the manuscript, Ditzen's account of his experience of the Nazi regime, is a clearly anti-fascist piece and, while this section of the manuscript would be much more difficult to decipher, the dis-covery of its contents would have cost him his life.

The Drinker, which was not published until after Ditzen's death, marks a turning point in his literary development.[3] It was his first ser-ious novel since *Iron Gustav*; in it, he returned to the experimentation with narrative perspective and technique he had begun in the 1930s. The novel, which charts the decline of Erwin Sommer from a respect-able and successful businessman to an alcoholic, life-long inmate of a psychiatric hospital, is narrated in the first person by Sommer himself. This technique not only affords a fascinating insight into addiction and mental illness but also sets up a creative tension between the nar-rator's point of view and the reader's interpretation of the novel.

The narrator weaves a complex narrative in which Erwin Sommer, having infected himself with the mucus of tuberculosis patients, relates his story as he awaits death: the origins of his addiction, the decline of his business, the break-up of his marriage, his arrest and incarceration.

As in much of Ditzen's fiction, *The Drinker* has a strong autobiographical dimension. Sommer, like Ditzen, finds himself arrested for the attempted manslaughter of his wife. Ditzen's alcoholism, his experience of prisons, clinics and psychiatric hospitals, as well as his recent acrimonious divorce, all find expression in the novel. However, even in this most personal of works, there is a social dimension. As Max Schroeder pointed out in the postscript to the first Aufbau edition of 1953, 'society, including his unimpeachable wife, does not help [Sommer] in the least but propels him further into decline, until he has only one goal in mind, death in a state of intoxication.' In its author's concern with the causes and effects of institutionalization, *The Drinker* can be seen as a companion piece to 'Once a Jailbird'.

The influence of Dickens, one of Ditzen's favourite novelists, may be seen in the figure of Polakowski, the fawning swindler, with his reddish hair and habit of cracking his finger joints, who bears more than a passing resemblance to Uriah Heep in *David Copperfield*.

The Drinker has no happy ending. Sommer's wife, who bears a certain resemblance to Anna Ditzen, is unable to tolerate her husband's behaviour and divorces him. She remarries and finds happiness with her second husband, with whom she has two children. Sommer commits suicide.

The endings of Ditzen's novels often provide insights into his thoughts and emotions, into his response to the question 'What now?' As we have seen, the idyll at the end of *Little Man – What Now?* became increasingly problematic throughout the 1930s, until, by 1942, in 'A Man Wants to Get On', there was no longer a happy young couple to carry the author's hopes for the future. A comparison of the endings of *The Drinker* and *Little Man – What Now?*, some twelve years previously, indicates the change in Ditzen's approach. In *Little Man – What Now?* stars signify the happiness of the young couple and their optimism that love conquers all:

And suddenly the cold had gone, an immeasurably gentle green wave lifted her up and him with her. They glided up together; the stars glittered very near; she whispered: 'But you can look at me! Always, always! You're with me, we're together . . .'

The wave rose and rose. It was the beach at night between Lensahn and Wiek, the other time when the stars had been so near. It was the old joy, it was the old love.

In *The Drinker*, Erwin Sommer stands alone at the window of his cell: 'spinning the web of my revenge ever tighter and more tangled, in the cold glitter of the stars.' While in *Little Man – What Now?* it is the Pinnebergs' love that transports them away from the 'tarnished earth' ('*befleckte Erde*'), at the end of *The Drinker* only suicide can offer an escape from this 'soiled earth' ('*beschmutzte Erde*').

Despite the autobiographical dimension of *The Drinker*, there is one obvious difference between Erwin Sommer and Rudolf Ditzen: Sommer becomes an alcoholic, is divorced, declared insane and dies by his own hand; Ditzen recovers from his alcoholism, is released from psychiatric prison and effects a reconciliation of sorts with his former wife. The act of writing *The Drinker* enabled Ditzen to escape Sommer's fate. The real autobiographical dimension of *The Drinker* lies in the vehicle it provided for Ditzen's rehabilitation.

After the cathartic experience of *The Drinker*, Ditzen embarked on his account of life under the Nazi regime. It was almost as if he first had to deal with the problems in his personal life before turning to the wider, political scene. His experience of writing *The Drinker* had also demonstrated that the prison authorities did not scrutinize his work very closely, although he interrupts his memoir on 24 September to record: 'Every ten minutes or so a guard comes into my cell, looks curiously at my scribblings and asks me what I am writing. I reply, "A children's story" and continue writing. I dismiss from my mind all thoughts of what would happen to me if anyone reads these lines.' This is one of three *Sonderblätter* [special pages] in the manuscript in which Ditzen reflects on his situation in the institution and on the act of writing in which he is engaged.

Ditzen's account of his life since 1933 consists of a series of episodes relating to his own experiences and those of his friends and acquaint-ances. He had no access to reference works or other aids, which accounts for some of the factual errors in the work, such as placing the Reichstag fire in January (not February) 1933. Following his description of the evening of the fire, which – as we have seen – the Ditzens spent with the Rowohlts in one of Berlin's top restaurants, he ranges over a number of topics: Rowohlt's problems with the Nazi regime; his own arrest and detention in 1933 and the Berkenbrück affair; the guests in Pension Stössinger; the publication of *Wolf among Wolves*; his friendships with Paul Mayer, Leopold Ullstein and Peter Suhrkamp; village life in Carwitz during the 1930s and 1940s under the Nazi regime; Rowohlt's emigration and return; the story of Alfred Schmidt-Sas; his encounter with the cartoonist e.o. plauen and the actor Mathias Wieman; his experience with Jannings, Goebbels and the *Gustav* project; the *Kutisker* novel; and, finally, the outbreak of the Second World War.

Ditzen again defends his decision to stay in Germany: 'I am a Ger-man and I prefer to go under with this accursed and blessed nation than enjoy an illusory happiness in a foreign country.' (24 September 1944). He concludes his account with the assertion that a great bur-den had been lifted from him. There is indeed no doubt that the desire to give vent to his emotions by recording his experiences was a major motivation in writing this piece. Ditzen, however, also uses it to justify his behaviour since 1933 and, on occasion, is at pains to underline his oppositional stance: he allies himself with Rowohlt as a fearless opponent of the Nazis and denies being a member of the Reich Literary Chamber.[4] He glosses over his compliance with Goebbels's instruc-tions about the conclusion of *Iron Gustav* and claims that those, like himself, who stayed in Germany and did not get involved in 'ridicu-lous enterprises such as conspiracies or coups d'état' were 'the salt of the earth'.

Ditzen also allows his personal animosity towards Peter Suhrkamp, whom he (unjustly) suspected of trying to come between himself and Rowohlt, to spill over into his account.

This document, which is a heady mixture of fact, fiction, self-justification, contradictions, political naivety and malicious gossip, leaves no doubt about Ditzen's hatred of the Nazi regime. It also reveals a slightly guilty conscience about not having done more to oppose it. In addition, it illustrates that Ditzen's approach to politics had remained largely emotional and instinctive.

Ditzen's next problem was how to smuggle the manuscript out of prison. Here, again, the *Kutisker* project came to his aid, and he was allowed home to Carwitz for the day on Sunday 8 October 1944 to collect the material he needed to finish the novel. He left Neustrelitz-Strelitz with the '*Trinker-Manuskript*' under his shirt.

Another reason for returning to Carwitz was to attempt a reconciliation with Suse. On 27 September, he had made a will designating her as his sole heir. Ten days after his visit, Suse wrote that she was willing to give their relationship another chance if he would provide more money, stop drinking and sever all relations with the Benzin family. His response was to make the house and smallholding over to her 'as the first visible sign of my firm intention to make amends'.[5]

Meanwhile, Rowohlt, who had spent the summer on Sylt with his friend the printer and publisher Hans Zehrer making plans for a new publishing house, had been forced to abandon these when Albert Speer – now minister for armaments and war production – injected new life into the German war effort. Zehrer was called up and Rowohlt ordered to report to the Volkssturm in the Grünheide suburb of Berlin. Rowohlt was, however, determined to sign up Ditzen for his new venture, and made the difficult journey to visit him in Neustrelitz-Strelitz in the last week in November. He found his friend in good spirits, for Ditzen had just been informed that his prison sentence had been set at three months and two weeks, which meant that he would be released on 13 December. They discussed how Ditzen could withdraw from his contracts with Heyne and the Deutsche Verlags-Anstalt. Ditzen undertook to send his contracts to Rowohlt as soon as he was released so that Rowohlt could take legal advice.

On 30 November, Ditzen wrote to Suse to say that he had finished writing the *Kutisker* novel two days before. It is not known whether this had been a topic of conversation during Rowohlt's visit.

He spent the first nine days of December writing *Fridolin der freche Dachs* (*That Rascal, Fridolin*), a children's story about the antics of a badger, for his daughter, Lore. He was released on 13 December 1944 after what must count as one of the most productive periods of his writing life. As soon as he arrived in Carwitz he wrote to the typist Gertrud Kramer, who had typed the first part of *Kutisker* the previous summer, and asked her to come on 10 January for two to three months to type the remainder.[6] Then he spent a week typing *That Rascal, Fridolin*.

Relations with Suse improved. He wrote to Rowohlt on 27 December: 'I have effected a reconciliation with her, but there are still some problems – I'll tell you all about it when I see you.' Rowohlt was due to come to Carwitz on 2 January 1945 to discuss Ditzen's contracts and read three unpublished novels.[7] It is not recorded whether he did in fact keep this appointment. If he did, Ditzen had even more startling news for him than he could ever have imagined. The day after writing to Rowohlt, Ditzen persuaded Suse that he was honour bound to inform Ulla Losch of their reconciliation and to end his relationship with her. On 28 December 1944 he thus left Carwitz to go to Feldberg to perform this painful duty. He did not return that evening, and the next day he and Ulla Losch became engaged.

A few days later, he wrote to his sister Elisabeth announcing his engagement. He described Ulla as 'strikingly pretty, a woman of the world, who goes in for make-up and nail varnish and seems anything but a competent housewife – all in all, then, the complete opposite of Suse. But perhaps that's where the attraction lies.' He describes himself as 'in high spirits' and adds: '... and even if I'm almost certain that the whole affair will come unstuck one fine day, at the moment I think it's wonderful.' He added that Ulla, who had a third share in the Losch soap manufacturing company, was 'filthy rich' and that one of her brothers-in-law had already accused him of being a bounty hunter.

Ulla Losch represented youth, vitality and fun to a man whose life had been singularly lacking in these ingredients in recent years. She was not only physically attractive but sexually available. There is no doubt that she was genuinely fond of Ditzen. In addition to mutual attraction, they were living in uncertain times. The old order was crumbling, the future was unclear. In January, the Red Army had arrived on German soil in East Prussia and was advancing through Poland. The main topic of debate in Feldberg was whether the Americans or the Russians would arrive there first. By now, rumours of the SS atrocities in the Soviet Union had reached Germany and the population was in dread of Soviet reprisals. With chaos and disintegration all around, Ulla Losch and Rudolf Ditzen were eager to grasp whatever chance of happiness presented itself. Both had suffered during the war: Ulla had been widowed at twenty-two with a young daughter. He had sought solace in alcohol; she had found relief in morphine. One of the ironies of Ditzen's life is that, while surviving both world wars, he came into contact with morphine in the closing months of each of them. In January 1945, he had not touched morphine for twenty years and did not foresee any danger.

Ditzen moved into Ulla's house in Klinkecken on the edge of Feldberg, which she shared with her mother and daughter, in the middle of January. They were married on 1 February 1945 in Berlin. According to Rowohlt, the ceremony was a modest affair and the celebrations afterwards were interrupted by an air raid. Rowohlt took advantage of this interruption to absent himself from the remainder of the proceedings.[8] Air raids, particularly carpet-bombing, were now a regular occurrence over German cities, and the new couple, deciding that Ulla's flat in Berlin was no longer safe, returned to Klinkecken in Feldberg. On her marriage, Ulla was allowed to retain her two residences but under the terms of her first husband's will was required to sell her shareholding in the Losch company to her two brothers-in-law, which she did, for 450,000 marks.

Ditzen went to Berlin in March to check up on Ulla's flat and was shocked by the scenes of devastation and deprivation all around. Despite the imminent collapse of the Nazi regime, Martin Bormann, the extremely influential head of the Party Chancellery, and Wilhelm Keitel, Chief of Staff to the High Command, were issuing orders that every village, town and city was to be defended to the last man, on pain of death. Soldiers were being forced into battle at gunpoint, deserters were being shot, as was anyone who hoisted a white flag, and the retreating German army was pursuing a scorched-earth policy in the eastern part of the country. So distressed was Ditzen by what he saw and heard that he fell ill, causing a recurrence of his old heart condition.

He was hospitalized in mid-April but was back in Klinkecken ten days later. On 27 April he went to Carwitz to visit his mother, Suse and the children. Next day, without any resistance, Feldberg fell to the Soviet army. A wave of suicides followed, including the deputy mayor, and the local chemist, who first killed his children.

On Sunday 29 April, the Red Army reached Carwitz and searched every house for valuables. Elisabeth Ditzen recorded in her diary: 'I cannot write about what else happened. Poor Suse suffered a lot ... We thought things might be bad, but not this bad.'9 Rape was clearly not official Soviet policy, but the Soviet authorities had great difficulty in controlling their men, many of whose mothers, wives, sisters and daughters had suffered a similar, and indeed worse, fate at the hands of the SS. Almost forty years later, in conversation with the present author, Suse described how former Nazis in Carwitz told Soviet soldiers where unprotected women could be found. While she understood why the rapes happened, she could not cope either physically or emotionally with the experience and became ill. She described how she managed to hide Lore, then eleven, from the soldiers and recalled that it was thanks to Evchen Burlage that she was able to obtain medication from Berlin and receive treatment in Feldberg.10

Meanwhile, the Red Flag had been hoisted over the Reichstag and the first ten exiles, led by Walter Ulbricht, had returned to Germany from Moscow. In the light of later developments, it is easily forgotten that these men did not initially intend to set about establishing the first socialist, let alone communist, state on German soil. Rather, their immediate aim was to: 'root out Nazism and militarism, re-educate the German people and carry out democratic reforms. These would include the trial of Nazi war criminals, measures against monopolies, and reforms in agriculture and education.'11

While, in the longer term, Soviet global objectives were a decisive factor in Russian policy towards Germany, in the spring and summer of 1945, 'official' policy envisaged the development of a democratic and demilitarized Germany, united within its pre-Nazi borders. Such an objective required the involvement of all anti-fascists and non-fascists in a broad democratic alliance. It is within this context that the course of the remainder of Rudolf Ditzen's life should be seen.

After the Soviets arrived in Feldberg, they put the population to work to revive the local economy. Rudolf and Ulla were enlisted, too, in fetching and carrying as well as working on the land. Some time in the first week in May, the local commandant, Major Sidelnikoff, got to know Ditzen.[12] Whether he made himself known to the commandant – possibly to protest about the rapes in Carwitz, which he heard about during his visit on 2 May – or whether, as the Soviet writer Grigorij Weiss asserts, a former Russian prisoner of war told the commandant about Ditzen's kindness to her,[13] is unclear. In any case, by 8 May, the commandant was sufficiently convinced of his non-Nazi credentials to involve him in the ceremony to mark the end of the war. Ditzen's role was to deliver a speech to the assembled population of Feldberg. The only part of his speech which has survived is the sentence 'The Russians come as your friends,' recorded in Elisabeth Ditzen's diary. This, no doubt, fell on sceptical ears, not only after years of anti-Soviet propaganda but also in view of the excesses of the Red Army locally. Ditzen's speech was not well received. After all, he was known in Feldberg as a drunk and a womanizer who had deserted his family and taken up with a woman under half his age. Local sympathies were firmly on Suse's side.

He told the commandant about the memoirs he had written in Neustrelitz-Strelitz and was promptly instructed to type them, since the manuscript, as we have seen, was largely illegible. He started this job on 9 May. While typing, he added a few embellishments, which, although relatively minor, served to emphasize his opposition to fascism, to justify aspects of his behaviour between 1933 and 1945 and to curry favour with the Soviet authorities.[14] The most striking addition is a foreword in which he claims: 'Twelve years long, through twelve unending dismal years during Nazi rule, I was unable to write one word I wanted to.' This is an exaggeration, as is his claim that the Nazi authorities locked him up in July 1944 and attempted to have him certified in order to silence him for ever. While the handwritten version refers to Germany as 'this accursed and blessed nation', the typed manuscript reads only 'this accursed nation', which probably reflects Ditzen's view of his fellow Germans in the spring of 1945.

The typed manuscript is incomplete. It is unclear whether Ditzen did not finish typing it or whether the remaining section has been lost. According to Elisabeth Ditzen's diary, her son continued to do physically exhausting work in the next few weeks, although by 13 May Ulla was no longer required to. He would therefore have had to type the manuscript in his spare time. On Friday 25 May, a rumour reached Carwitz that Ditzen had been made mayor of Feldberg and the outlying villages. Fifteen-year-old Uli set out for Feldberg with some asparagus for his father and stepmother and returned on Sunday with confirmation: Ditzen had been appointed mayor for eighteen months, after which elections would be held. Ditzen and Ulla, with Ulla's mother and daughter, were moving out of Klinkecken and into a house in the centre of the town which had become vacant after the suicide of the former inhabitants. This change in status may have been responsible for the unfinished typed manuscript.

Ditzen's appointment as mayor was part of the Soviet strategy of involving all non-fascists in the construction of a democratic, unified and neutral Germany. Nor was he the only writer who had remained in Germany and was subsequently appointed mayor by the Soviet authorities: Günther Weisenborn, who had been active in the resistance, was briefly mayor of Luckau in Brandenburg in the spring of 1945.

A key figure in the development of this policy was Johannes R. Becher, who returned from exile in the Soviet Union in early June 1945. During his ten years there he had made regular radio broadcasts to Germany, edited the journal *Internationale Literatur*, involved himself in the 'Free Germany' Committee, and spent considerable time doing propaganda work with German prisoners of war. Becher became convinced that cultural policy would have a strategic role to play in undoing fascist indoctrination, the extent of which had become evident in the fanaticism with which the war had been prosecuted to the last. No sooner had Becher arrived in Berlin than he established the *Kulturbund zur demokratischen Erneuerung Deutschlands* (The Cultural Association for the Democratic Renewal of Germany) which drew together artists and writers with non-fascist credentials and involved them in the creation of a democratic cultural policy. In the spring and summer of 1945 Becher sought out Bernhard Kellermann, Günther Weisenborn and even made a long and difficult journey into Poland to win the support of the ailing Gerhart Hauptmann in Silesia, who had made his name as a naturalist dramatist over fifty years before with *The Weavers* and *Before Sunrise*:

> There can have been few periods in contemporary European history when so many writers, artists and intellectuals committed themselves so indefatigably to the construction of a new society as happened in the GDR after 1945. Indeed never before had the rulers of any previous German state fostered the integration and sought the cooperation of its cultural intelligentsia so assiduously as did the authorities in the Soviet zone of occupation from 1945.[15]

This commitment to an anti-fascist, democratic Germany had been evident in the programme of the German Communist Party on 11 June 1945 (written by Anton Ackermann in Moscow):

> We take the view that to impose the Soviet system on Germany would be wrong, for this path would not be in accordance with the present situation in Germany. We are rather of the view that the crucial interests of the German nation at present require a different strategy for Germany, namely, the establishment of an anti-fascist, democratic regime, a parliamentary democracy, a republic with all democratic rights and freedoms for the people.[16]

The programme published by the Social Democratic Party four days later was imbued with the same spirit, so that closer cooperation between the two parties on the left seemed a natural development. By now, the first theatre had reopened in Berlin, the *Berliner Rundfunk* radio station was broadcasting again and a daily, non-party newspaper, the *Berliner Zeitung*, was in circulation.

While the struggle to shape the future of Germany was being waged in Berlin, Ditzen was struggling in Feldberg against the legacy of the past. A contemporary description of him records: 'In no way did the Mayor look like a writer. He looked more like a stiff, German civil servant, carefully shaven and combed, wearing a worn but well-ironed grey suit with a silver watch chain in his waistcoat.'[17]

Despite the efforts of the Soviet authorities to curb their troops' excesses, the plundering and rapes in the outlying villages continued. When Ditzen and his wife visited Carwitz on 10 June, they took Lore back to Feldberg with them and invited Suse, Elisabeth Ditzen and the two boys to join them in the large house they had been allocated in Feldberg's Prenzlauer Strasse – an invitation which was readily accepted. This in itself is an indication that relations between the various members of the extended Ditzen family were tolerable. Ulla Ditzen's charm and genuine concern no doubt played an important role in keeping the household running smoothly. Elisabeth Ditzen was favourably impressed by her new daughter-in-law and commented in her diary on 12 June: 'I like Ulla, a pretty girl, kind and always thoughtful towards me. I have the impression that she and Rudolf are very happy together. May it remain so.' She noted, too, that young Uli appeared to have a crush on his stepmother.

In Suse's absence from Carwitz, the hens and bees were stolen, as were most of her bottled vegetables and preserves. Indeed, theft was one of the major problems Ditzen had to deal with as mayor. He justified dealing harshly with a woman who had helped herself to two leather chairs from the town hall by referring to 'the ever escalating problem of stealing'.[18] The other matters that Mayor Ditzen had to cope with included domestic disputes, arms finds, people who refused to work and the wilful destruction of property. An instance of the uncooperative and destructive attitude widespread at the time was the removal of doors in the former swimming pool, which reopened as a kindergarten in the summer of 1945; they were subsequently fished out of the Haussee lake.

Mecklenburg, due to its geographical position, also experienced the largest influx of refugees of any region in the Soviet zone, a total of 631,000 by the end of 1945. Feldberg saw large numbers in the summer of 1945. Those on these refugee treks were given overnight accommodation in a former hotel, the Stieglitzenkrug, before being chaperoned on their way the next day.

Ditzen's job was a very difficult one. His mother recorded in her diary in the middle of June: 'Rudolf is not well. He has too much work and too many difficulties. He says he's the most hated man in Feldberg.' Ditzen found his work deeply depressing, for fascism had left deep traces: people refused to hand over fascist literature, they tried everything to avoid having to work, they thought only of themselves and their own advantage. His initial relief and optimism when the war eventually ended turned gradually, in the course of the summer, to pessimism about ever eradicating the legacy of fascism. He confided in a letter to Paul Bruse, mayor of Neustrelitz: 'I never fail to be deeply disturbed by how the Germans show themselves to be so wretched in defeat; with very few exceptions they prove that the world is quite right to despise the German nation.'[19] He and Ulla had hoped to have children, but this dream, too, remained elusive. Despite a minor gynaecological operation in June, Ulla was unable to conceive.

By early August, Ditzen could no longer bear the 'dung beetles . . . crawling around me'.[20] In these circumstances of pessimism and hopelessness, he took his new wife's advice and began to seek solace in morphine. It was not long before he suffered a complete collapse and, on 14 August, he was admitted to Neustrelitz hospital. Ulla Ditzen, after a suicide attempt, was admitted along with him.

He and Ulla were not the only ones whose physical and psychological health suffered in the aftermath of the war. Two days later, Dr Rischer, who worked closely with Ditzen in Feldberg and who may well have been one source of morphine, was admitted to Neustrelitz hospital. In September 1945, Ditzen's niece Ilse Bechert was undergoing treatment in a psychiatric hospital and another niece, Adelheid Hörig, was critically ill.

On the day Rudolf and Ulla were discharged from hospital, one of the most popular measures in the Soviet zone, the Democratic Land Reform, was announced under the slogan '*Junkerland in Bauernhand*' (literally: 'the Junker lands into the farmers' hands'). Large estates of over 247 acres were split into 12-acre plots and handed over to some 504,000 small farmers. Ditzen, however, had no intention of returning to the land. He had had enough of Feldberg, which he later described as 'a thoroughly disgusting hole' ('*ein völlig ekelhaftes Nest*').[21] He was determined to go to Berlin, a decision which, in view of the massive population movements at the time, required official approval. Ditzen and Ulla, fearing that their application would not be successful, simply set out for Berlin without seeking permission. They found Ulla's six-room flat in Meraner Strasse in the Schoeneberg district of the capital severely damaged and occupied. They were eventually able to take possession of three and a half rooms, although only one of these was habitable and it had 'no heating and the window was boarded up'.[22] As they had moved to Berlin illegally, they had no ration cards and lived off the black market for the first six weeks – an extremely expensive business, which used up most of Ulla's remaining money and jewellery. The stay in Neustrelitz hospital had not been long enough to cure their morphine addiction, and this, too, added to their expenses. When Ditzen went to fetch the nearest doctor to administer morphine to Ulla, who was the more seriously addicted, he found himself talking to the poet Gottfried Benn, who had recently opened a surgery in nearby Bozener Strasse. Benn, another survivor of the Nazi regime, whose wife had committed suicide, was sympathetic to Rudolf and Ulla and tried to help.

By September 1945, the postal service had been resumed and the provisions of the Potsdam Agreement with respect to demilitarization, denazification and reparations were being implemented. Cultural life was reawakening. The Deutsches Theater, in the Soviet sector of Berlin, had reopened with a production of Lessing's *Nathan the Wise*, in keeping with the Soviet commitment to fostering the German humanist tradition. Lessing was considered to be an appropriate choice because of his commitment to the principles of the Enlightenment and his struggle against the irrationality and backwardness of his times. The radical and Jewish poet Heinrich Heine was also rediscovered; his satirical *Deutschland – Ein Wintermärchen* (*Germany – A Winter's Tale*) was published by the newly founded Aufbau publishing house in 1945.

Despite problems of illness and illegality, Ditzen began to make contacts with other writers and editors. He was in correspondence with Ledig in Stuttgart, who obtained a licence to publish in the American sector in November, and with Rowohlt in Hamburg, who had applied to the British authorities for a licence. He met Peter

Suhrkamp, who, as a victim of fascism, was one of the first publishers to receive permission to publish, as well as Erik Reger, Mathias Wieman and Paul Wiegler, a former editor with Ullstein. It was through Wiegler that Ditzen came to the attention of Becher, who, as we have seen, was anxious to involve all non-Nazi writers in the reconstruction of Germany. Ditzen met Becher in the second week of October. Becher immediately offered assistance, material and intellectual. Ditzen was issued with a Category 1 ration card, normally reserved for manual workers in heavy industry; Ulla's ration card was a standard manual worker's one. In addition, Becher promised to arrange for a lorry to collect Ditzen's books and their belongings from Feldberg and to find them more suitable accommodation.

Becher's patronage of Ditzen should be viewed not only in the context of Soviet cultural policy in the immediate post-war period but also in the light of Becher's own experience. As we have seen, he, too came from a legal family, rebelled against Wilhelmine authoritarianism, was involved in a duel with a tragic outcome in his youth and spent some time in Binswanger's clinic in Jena during the First World War. While Becher's rebellion led him into the Communist Party and then into exile in Paris and Moscow, Ditzen's led to drug addiction and alcoholism. Both men suffered from recurrent bouts of depression. In Becher's short essay '*Lob der Schwermut*' ('In Praise of Melancholy'), written in January 1950, he argues that people who do not suffer from melancholy are the ones who are really ill:

> In a state of melancholy we experience ourselves as the 'other people' who we could have become and did not. The meaninglessness of our existence oppresses us and we have lost hope of giving our lives a meaning. But melancholy itself is that hope. The burden of the life we have not lived shows us that there is something alive in us – that we have not become hopelessly dehumanized and reified. Melancholy is a curable illness because what causes our illness is what causes the illness of humanity and the illnesses of the world – and those people who do not suffer melancholy are in their healthiness the most ill, they are the terminally ill with no hope of recovery, because they remain unaware of their illness.

He rejects the idea that melancholy is a medical condition which requires psychiatric treatment: 'In view of the abnormality of our human-inhuman condition, nothing is as normal as melancholy.'[23] Becher thus had very personal as well as political reasons for supporting Ditzen. He also admired Ditzen's talent as a story-teller and his ability to tap into popular sentiment, to create characters with whom readers could identify. In his role as head of the *Kulturbund*, Becher was anxious to break down traditional divisions between 'high' and 'popular' culture, seen by Marxists such as he as a legacy of capitalism, and develop a truly popular, democratic cultural life. Ditzen, for his part, was happy to endorse the anti-fascist, democratic aims of Becher's *Kulturbund*, and the *Deutsche Volkszeitung* printed a letter from him to this effect on 18 October.

Becher sent Roman Peresvetov, editor of the cultural section of the *Tägliche Rundschau*, the daily published by the Soviet military administration, to Meraner Strasse to elicit contributions from Ditzen and persuaded Peresvetov to pay him as large a fee as possible.[24]

Becher had other, larger plans for Ditzen and passed on to him a Gestapo file relating to the case of a working-class couple, Otto and Elise Hampel, who had been executed in 1943 for distributing anti-fascist material. Becher, who clearly knew Ditzen's interests as a novelist, shrewdly chose a tale of two ordinary people who had no links to the Resistance and who carried on their hopeless struggle in isolation and with heroic single-mindedness. However, Ditzen did not receive the complete Gestapo file: he appears not to have seen the final volume, which contains the documents after sentencing in which the Hampels, who had not expected a death sentence, break down and accuse each other of instigating the campaign against Hitler in a fruitless attempt to escape execution. Ditzen was thus able to portray the Hampels as heroic to the end. The reason why the Gestapo file was incomplete is unclear.[25]

Ditzen was initially reluctant to use this material. He told Heinz Willmann, secretary of the *Kulturbund*, that he had not been a member of the Resistance and did not want to give the impression that he had. However, Willmann managed to persuade him that the Hampels had not been members of the Resistance either but were simply the kind of ordinary people whom Ditzen excelled in portraying in his novels. He signed a contract with Aufbau on 18 October which stipulated a submission date of 1 January 1946. Next day, he signed a serialization deal with the *Neue Berliner Illustrierte*. The November issue of the journal *Aufbau* carried an essay by 'Hans Fallada' entitled *'Über den doch vorhandenen Widerstand der Deutschen gegen den Hitlerterror'* ('The Resistance which Did Exist inside Germany to Hitler's Terror'), in which Ditzen announced his plans for the novel.[26]

After almost a year without a publisher, Ditzen was suddenly overwhelmed with commissions for short stories, essays and reviews. The first book which Aufbau was going to reissue was his 'Once a Jailbird'. In December 1945, the *Tägliche Rundschau* carried his short story *'Oma überdauert den Krieg'* ('Grandma Survives the War'), as well as an excerpt from the memoirs he had written in Neustrelitz-Strelitz entitled *'Osterfest 1933 mit der SA'* ('Easter 1933 with the SA'). For the first time in months, Ditzen was earning money again. Ulla sold her house in Feldberg to her brother-in-law, Ewald Losch, at the end of October, for 12,000 marks, which enabled them to repay the debts they had incurred during their first weeks in Berlin.

By the middle of November, he and Ulla had moved into a spacious house, with garage and garden, in Eisenmenger Weg, Pankow, just around the corner from the Bechers' house. This part of Pankow was a prime residential area reserved for Russian officers and the new cultural elite, with a guard at the entrance to monitor visitors. Ulla had brought her daughter Jutta from Feldberg at the end of September; Suse had been to Berlin in mid-October to discuss the future of the two elder children, Uli and Lore. She had satisfied herself that her former husband and his second wife were no longer taking morphine and that their home was a suitable one in which to place Uli.

All that Ditzen required to start working again was to have one room in the house furnished with his books and belongings. Leo Scholz, a friend of Ulla's in the removal business, to whom she had left her flat in Meraner Strasse, promised to organize a lorry to collect their things from Feldberg and Carwitz. After a delay of six weeks, during which time Ulla had obtained permission and engaged a Soviet officer to accompany them, it turned out that Scholz was unable to arrange the removal. Ulla went to Feldberg at the beginning of December and again on 13 December, when she brought Uli back to Berlin.

A new departure for the otherwise publicity-shy Ditzen was public speaking and reading from his work. He accompanied Becher to Schwerin on Saturday 8 December 1945 to speak to a packed house about the Nuremberg Trials. Ditzen saw the Trials as drawing a line under the 'horrors of yesterday' and preparing the ground for 'a brighter tomorrow'. He expressed his conviction that, despite the widespread breakdown of moral values in Germany, 'a seed of decency has survived. It is our duty to preserve this seed of decency, to pass it on, to sow a whole field from this one seed.'[27] Thus, his concept of 'decency' found political expression for the first time in the anti-fascist, democratic policies pursued in the Soviet zone in the immediate post-war period. He also spoke in Halle and made a number of radio broadcasts about his work as a writer. For Becher, literature was a social phenomenon and the writer had an important social role; Ditzen may not have fully shared this view but he was willing to overcome his natural reticence and appear in public.

Christmas 1945 was a time for moderate rejoicing in the Ditzen household in Berlin. He had found work, was earning money and was surrounded by his new wife and children. Uli improvised a Christmas tree, Becher turned up with a toy shop for Jutta, and there was a goose on the table for Christmas dinner. Besides the minor irritant of an unconnected gas-cooker, Ditzen was frustrated by the lack of a proper study to begin work on the novel he had promised to submit by 1 January. He was also concerned about his wife's inability to manage without morphine. In addition, he was profoundly pessimistic about the future of Germany and did not share Becher's optimism about the possibility of reforming the German nation into a democratic and peace-loving people. At a Christmas party in the Bechers' house, Ditzen, who had had too much to drink, almost came to blows with Wilhelm Pieck, the chairman of the Communist Party, over what Ditzen viewed as Pieck's hopeless idealism. The Russian writer, Konstantin Fedin, an observer at the Nuremberg Trials who happened to be in Berlin at the time, witnessed Ditzen's impatient response to Pieck's rosy view of the future, and reported him as saying: 'Germans today only recognize the reality they see with their own eyes, not what they are told. It is the politicians' job to subordinate themselves to reality. It is the artists' job to describe that reality the way it is.'[28]

On the last day of 1945, a newspaper in Hanover published an article which was to do Ditzen much damage. In an open letter to the *Neuer Hannoverischer Kurier*, the former typist, Else Marie Bakonyi, questioned 'Fallada's' anti-fascist credentials. She quoted passages from letters which Ditzen had written to her in 1943 after his first tour of France and during his second one, in which he expressed confidence in a German victory and declared: 'We are the masters of the world.' She accused him of opportunism and a desire to 'once again make your peace with the powers that be'. This letter was taken up by other newspapers and a women's magazine, and Ditzen found himself once more the object of attacks in the press.

He dismissed Bakonyi's accusations as 'the revenge of a spurned woman'[29] but, in view of the growing rift between the Soviet Union and the Western Allies, the affair had much wider ramifications. Ditzen was called to account by the Soviet authorities and insisted that his letters to Bakonyi should be read in the light of the strict censorship in operation during the war years and that anyone reading them in 1943 could not fail to recognize their ironic tone.[30] The 'Fallada' case was investigated by the Control Commission for Germany; the (British) investigating officer, Captain Wallach, concluded that it would be impossible officially to blacklist 'Fallada', since the USA was opposed to blacklisting in principle and the Soviet Union had 'publicized F. before the real facts about him became known, too much to allow them to drop him at short notice'.[31]

The campaign against Ditzen in the Western press came at a particularly crucial time. By the beginning of 1946, he was publishing again. Not only was he writing for radio, newspapers and journals in the Soviet zone, he was also in regular contact with Ledig in Stuttgart and Rowohlt in Hamburg, who was still awaiting a licence from the British authorities. Rowohlt was hopeful about cooperating with Becher, whom he remembered as 'an exceptionally nice man' with 'unusual charm and charisma'.[32] As Rowohlt had been a member of the Nazi Party, he was required to undergo a 'rehabilitation process' before he could be permitted to set up in business again. Part of this process involved providing letters from friends and colleagues confirming that he had never subscribed to the aims or methods of the Nazi Party. Rowohlt asked Ditzen if he could write such a letter on his behalf – and Ditzen was only too happy to do so.

The attacks on Ditzen affected his sleep; his intake of sleeping pills increased daily and it seems likely that he took morphine again. By the end of January he was undergoing treatment in Professor Zutt's clinic in what was now the British sector of Berlin. As a result of the Soviets' denazification campaign, Zutt had been released from his duties at the Charité hospital in the Soviet sector and was concentrating on his private clinic, the Kuranstalt Neu-Westend. Ulla was admitted to the same clinic on 10 February.

In mid-February, Ditzen found himself in the firing line again, this time on account of *Wolf among Wolves*, which was denounced as a fascist novel by the journalist Hans Habe in the Munich newspaper the *Neue Zeitung*. He wrote immediately to Carwitz and begged Suse to send any English or American reviews that she could find to enable him to mount a counter-campaign. Ditzen was careful to conceal from Suse his treatment in Zutt's clinic, which continued until 22 March. He knew that, if she found out, she would insist on Uli's return to Carwitz and would refuse to permit any of the children to move to Berlin again. Uli, who was equally keen to remain with Ulla and his father, was only too happy to collude in this deception.

When Ditzen returned home on 22 March, he found a letter waiting for him from Becher requesting the repayment by the end of the month of 3,300 marks which Ulla had borrowed. Ulla's debts, which strained Ditzen's resources to the limit, became an increasing bone of contention during the spring of 1946. His earnings were well above average for the times[33] but were not sufficient to finance the couple's morphine addiction. His precious and extensive library, most of which Ulla had managed to transport to Berlin by July 1946, was therefore sold off to pay their debts.

Besides his personal problems, Ditzen faced considerable insecurity. Aufbau's new edition of 'Once a Jailbird', published at the end of March, quickly sold out. At the same time, however, the Soviet authorities removed all copies of *A Small Circus* from public libraries because of its criticism of the Social Democrats – a particularly sensitive issue in view of the increasingly promoted cooperation in the Soviet sector between Communists and Social Democrats which resulted in the merging of the two parties in April 1946.

When Ditzen suffered another breakdown in May, Becher took charge of the situation and engaged Dr Kupke, who had both Rudolf and Ulla admitted to a clinic in nearby Martha Strasse. Not only was Zutt's clinic too expensive but, as relations between the Western Allies and the Soviet Union deteriorated, it was becoming increasingly difficult to move between the Soviet and the other zones in Berlin. Ditzen found himself the only male patient in the Martha Strasse clinic, which primarily treated sexually transmitted diseases.

Ditzen's illnesses did not stop him writing. In February, he had begun a novel based on his experience of the collapse of the Nazi regime and its aftermath, provisionally entitled '*Fallada sucht einen Weg*' ('Fallada Seeks a Way'). He wrote to Kurt Wilhelm of Aufbau on 13 February: 'I long to write a decent novel again. I long to get involved, to play my part and not just stand half-heartedly on the sidelines.'[34] In March, he outlined a plan for a novel entitled *Das Volk hat Raum* ('The Nation Does Have Space'), envisaged as a response to Hans Grimm's *Volk ohne Raum* ('Nation without Space') of 1926, which had been a Nazi favourite.

In early June, while still in the Martha Strasse clinic, he completed a piece on Alfred Schmidt-Sas and sent Uli with it to Marga Kenter for her approval. He also wrote a short story '*Pfingstgruß an Achim*' ('A Whit Greeting to Achim'), which was published on 9 June in the *Tägliche Rundschau* and dispatched to Carwitz for his youngest son. On the twenty-seventh, the *Tägliche Rundschau* published the first of a series of nine '*Kalendergeschichten*' ('Fables'), clearly influenced by the spirit of Johann Peter Hebel's *Schatzkästlein* (*Treasure Chest*), which are among the best of the twenty-one short stories which appeared during Ditzen's last period in Berlin.

On one of his regular visits home in the middle of June 1946, Ditzen found that Ulla had run up more debts. In reply to one solicitor's demand, he wrote: 'I'm afraid my wife is addicted to morphine and is undergoing treatment at the moment in hospital. In fact, I'm considering a divorce because of her addiction and the debts she continually incurs.'[35] Ditzen understood his wife's predicament only too well. He was also very fond of her. He loved her youthfulness, her vitality, the laughter she brought to his life; he also recognized her untiring efforts to make a home for them all, her success in negotiating with the authorities and the arduous trips she made to Feldberg and Carwitz. She was also very keen to fulfil his wish for more children. In the course of the summer of 1946, it was, however, becoming increasingly clear to him that she could not provide the ordered lifestyle he required for his writing.

By the end of July, he was discharged from the clinic. He had a meeting with a Major Reginald Colby of British Intelligence on 30 July to discuss the resumption of his links with his London publisher. Also present that evening was Günther Weisenborn, who was in contact with Schneekluth of Heyne Verlag, Ditzen's former publishers in Dresden.

On 11 August 1946, Ditzen finished Der Alpdruck ('The Nightmare'). Begun in February as 'Fallada Seeks a Way', and described by him as 'half fact, half fiction', it draws on his experiences from April 1945 to July 1946. In the Preface he describes the novel as a '*document humain*, a report, as true to the facts as possible, of how Germans felt, suffered and acted from April 1945 into the summer of 1946'.[36] As Günter Caspar points out in a postscript to the 1987 Aufbau edition, 'The Nightmare' is full of contradictions and has a rather unconvincing storyline. The inconsistencies are due largely to Ditzen's inability to resolve the conflicts arising from his recent and current situation. Thus Doll, Ditzen's protagonist and alter ego, feels at the same time both detached from and implicated in the fate of the German nation. Ditzen's characterization of the novel as 'a medical report' applies as much to the author as to the German nation. The book comes to life in sections where he describes either places with which he is familiar, like the sanatorium where Doll goes to be cured of his morphine addiction, or characters such as the vet 'Farken-Willem'. Gottfried Benn makes an appearance as Dr Pernies, Becher as Granzow.[37] The novel ends on a positive note, with Doll's discharge from hospital and his optimism that 'the nations will get their houses in order again, even Germany, this beloved, this wretched Germany, this ailing heart of Europe will become well again.' It is unlikely that Ditzen shared this optimism.

Ditzen was no doubt pleased that his daughter Lore would be joining Uli in Berlin at the beginning of September, but Ulla continued to be a source of concern. After two gynaecological operations and a course of hormone injections, she became pregnant in the latter half of August. However, she suffered severe morning sickness and had to be admitted to the University Women's Hospital, where she soon afterwards had a miscarriage. Realizing that 'I would lose all my strength and enthusiasm for work if I stayed with Ulla,'[38] Ditzen told his second wife that he intended to leave her. Ulla's reaction was an indication of her devotion to him, for she said that she would only agree to a divorce if Suse would remarry him. Suse's response to this suggestion was an unequivocal 'No' – too much bitterness had passed between them for a second marriage to be successful. She did, however, offer the hand of friendship and promise any help she could give. Suse had by now established a new life for herself. The smallholding was thriving, she was taking in paying guests and had enough produce spare to send apples and pears to Rudolf and Ulla in Berlin in October 1946.

Meanwhile, Ditzen had patched up his relationship with Ulla and had turned his attention to the Hampel portfolio given him by Becher. After four weeks' intensive work, he finished the novel *Jeder stirbt für sich allein* (*Alone in Berlin*) on 26 October and declared: 'I think it's the first proper Fallada since *Wolf among Wolves*, even though I didn't really like the material to start off with.'[39]

Fallada's 1946 manuscript tells the story of Otto and Anna Quangel, a middle-aged, working-class couple who are typical of their time. Otto Quangel's carpentry business has folded in the economic turmoil of 1930 and, after four years of unemployment, he obtains a job as a foreman in a furniture factory. The Quangels attribute this stroke of good fortune to Nazi economic policy and are initially impressed by Hitler's 'greatness and good intentions'.[40] However, they refuse to join the Nazi Party – partly because of their thriftiness, which prohibits an unnecessary expense such as membership dues, and partly because they do not approve of the unfair advantages which party members enjoy over the rest of the population. Otto Quangel had been forced to join the German Labour Front, a Nazi umbrella organization which had replaced the free trade unions in 1933, and he held a minor office in it. Anna Quangel had chosen to join the NS-Frauenschaft, the Nazi women's organization, where she, too, had a small post of responsibility.

Their lives are changed forever by their son's death in France in 1940. They both resign their posts in the Nazi organizations and embark on a campaign of writing anti-Nazi postcards and letters, which they leave in public buildings. Over a period of more than two years, they produce almost three hundred cards and nine letters. Their campaign gradually becomes the main purpose of their lives and they imagine its effects are widespread. In fact, most of the cards and eight of the letters are handed in to the Gestapo – an indication of the widespread conformity and/or intimidation at the time. Eventually, through a series of coincidences, they are caught, charged and sentenced to death. The narrator does not leave his story there but, addressing the reader directly for the first time, begins the final chapter: 'But we don't want to end this book with death, dedicated as it is to life, invincible life, life always triumphing over humiliation and tears, over misery and death.' Besides changing the name Hampel to Quangel, Ditzen changed the motive for the postcard campaign. In the Hampel case, it was the death of Elise's brother that triggered the couple's resistance. In *Alone in Berlin*, it is the death of the Quangels' son which has such a devastating effect.

This fictional representation of the death of a son clearly echoes the death of Ditzen's younger brother in France in 1918. Twenty-eight years later, Ulrich Ditzen's memory was still very much alive in the family. After finishing the novel, Rudolf wrote to his mother in December 1946: 'On the 15th our Uli would have celebrated his birthday, he would no longer be a young man now, and it would perhaps – no, it is much better for him and for us that we can think of him as he was when he left us. For me he is always very young, very idealistic – and so serious, so decent.'

The novel contains other allusions to Ditzen's family and friends. Pastor Lorenz, who remains true to his Christian principles in his work in a Nazi prison, recalls Ditzen's maternal grandfather of the same name, who was also a prison chaplain and who, like his literary counterpart, also died of tuberculosis.

Frau Lore Rosenthal, the Jewish woman who lives in the same building as the Quangels, shares some biographical details with Lore Soldin: both have a daughter called Eva and a granddaughter called Harriet living in Ilford, England. Ditzen had just received the first letter for many years from Lore Soldin in September 1946. The musician and conductor Dr Reichhardt, from whose words the title of the novel is taken, bears a striking similarity to Alfred Schmidt-Sas, Marga Kenter's partner.[41]

The retired judge, Herr Fromm, with his love of reading and his absolute commitment to justice, may well be a reference to Ditzen's father. Two of the very positive women figures in the novel, Anna Quangel, who supports her husband through thick and thin, and Anna Schönlein, who hides fugitives from fascism, are given the first name of Ditzen's first wife. Dr Stark, the Nazi lawyer who was supposed to defend Otto Quangel, shares a name with the lawyer who advised Ditzen in 1933 against taking the Sponars in Berkenbrück to court. The village schoolteacher in Carwitz, Herr Schwoch, known for his pronounced Nazi sympathies, appears in the novel as a teacher and 'a rampant Nazi, a cowardly little yapper and denouncer'. There are even similarities between Ditzen himself and Otto Quangel, a taciturn carpenter who 'keeps himself to himself', has no time for books and would seem at first glance to have little in common with the author. Yet Quangel's individual type of resistance, his refusal to get involved with any resistance group and the conclusion he drew from his experience reflect Ditzen's view of his own behaviour in 1946: 'My crime was thinking I was so clever, wanting to act alone, when I know that the individual is ineffectual. No, what I did was nothing to be ashamed of, but the way I did it was wrong ... I had to fight and I would do so again and again. Only differently, quite differently.' Otto Quangel utters these words at the age of fifty-three, Ditzen's age when he was writing the novel.

The profound pessimism of 'The Nightmare' had by the autumn of 1946 given way to a more balanced view. The picture of Germany from 1940 to 1943 painted in *Alone in Berlin* shows not only the widespread intimidation, which made resistance very difficult, and the gangster aspects of the Nazi regime, it also pays tribute to the courage of individuals who risked their lives in everyday acts of resistance and opposition which testify to the survival of the 'seed of decency' even in the darkest days of Nazi Germany.

In this, his last, novel, Ditzen returns to the narrative techniques of *Iron Gustav* and *Wolf among Wolves*. The narrative revolves around 55 Jablonski Strasse in Berlin's north inner city. The narrator begins the tale with the postwoman Eva Kluge entering the building which houses the Quangels, Frau Rosenthal, Justice Fromm, the Persickes – a Nazi family – as well as Emil Barkhausen, a petty criminal and Gestapo informer. The narrative interweaves the lives of these characters and radiates outwards to related characters and events: Eva's estranged, work-shy, ne'er-do-well husband Enno, who is murdered by the Gestapo, and her sons in the SS, who are guilty of atrocities in the Soviet Union; Trudel Hergesell, fiancée of the Quangels' son, who is a member of a Communist resistance cell in the factory where she works; and Commissar Escherich of the Gestapo, who is in charge of the hunt for the postcard-writer and who describes himself in the end as 'probably the only man Otto Quangel converted with his postcard campaign'.

An important tool in the production of credible characters is Ditzen's skilful use of inner monologue, appropriate in each case to the age, sex and class of the character. Eva Kluge's thoughts, relayed on the second page of the novel, not only provide an exposition but give an insight into a character who has the courage to leave the Nazi Party and make a fresh start. The differing attitudes of Quangel's workmates to him are conveyed by 'indirect' speech, as are the thoughts of the men on death row in Plötzensee prison. The author's mastery of dialect and dialogue are evident in the portrayal of the speech of a wide range of characters from many different sections of society.

The novel reads like a thriller. The reader is quickly drawn into the lives of these ordinary people and is anxious to know how the Quangels will extricate themselves from the Nazi organizations to which they belong, and what the outcome of their postcard campaign will be. What will happen to Eva Kluge when she officially announces her intention to leave the Party? Will Enno Kluge be able to turn over a new leaf? Will Frau Rosenthal be saved? Will Persicke drink himself into an early grave? And his son Baldur – will he make a career in the SS? Will Pastor Lorenz be able to effect a change of doctor in the prison? How will the Quangels bear up in court?

As we have seen, Ditzen concluded his novels set in the 1930s and early '40s with happy endings which took the form of romantic idylls. *Alone in Berlin* also concludes on a positive note but, by 1946, Ditzen's view of a happy ending had changed dramatically. No longer do a young married couple starting a family stand as a symbol of hope. Indeed, the young couple in this novel, the Hergesells, lose their baby and die in a fascist prison. At the end of *Alone in Berlin* the symbol of hope is Kuno Kienschäper, a young man who has turned his back on the spiritual and emotional deprivation of his biological family and is on the threshold of a new life in the country where his adoptive parents, Eva Kluge and her second husband, have been given land as a result of the Democratic Land Reform. By 1946 Ditzen's response to the question 'What now?' was no longer romantic love; nor was it the suicide chosen by Erwin Sommer in *The Drinker*; instead it was the determination of a young man to find personal fulfilment in becoming a useful member of a new society.

And so Becher's encouragement and the Hampel case enabled Ditzen to achieve the literary potential that had lain dormant for so long. With *Alone in Berlin*, Ditzen wrote the first anti-fascist novel of the post-war period and made an early contribution to the process of coming to terms with the past (*Vergangenheitsbewältigung*), for the moral of the story is clearly that every act of resistance is significant. When Quangel despairs of having achieved anything with his postcard campaign, Dr Reichhardt replies: 'Who can say? At least you opposed evil. You weren't corrupted. You and I and the many locked up here, and many more in other places of detention, and tens of thousands in concentration camps – they're all resisting, today, tomorrow . . .'

While Ditzen was writing about two victims of fascism, the International Military Tribunal in Nuremberg was calling those responsible for these and many other crimes against humanity to account. The shape of the new Germany was also becoming clearer. In the local and regional elections on 20 October 1946, the merged Communist and Social Democratic Party polled the largest share of the vote in the Soviet zone and the Soviet sector of Berlin. In Berlin as a whole, however, the (unmerged) Social Democrats attracted more than twice the votes of the new, merged party. Berlin was set to become one of the first sites of conflict in the Cold War.

Gertrud Kramer arrived in Eisenmengerweg in early November to start typing Ditzen's manuscript, which he submitted on the twenty-fourth of the month. Ditzen did not live to see the publication of his last novel, and it seems unlikely that he had any input into the editing process. The text which was published posthumously in 1947 and which, until 2011, formed the basis for all subsequent German editions of the novel, as well as the 2009 English translation, differs in a number of ways from the manuscript which Ditzen submitted in November 1946.

The editor in 1947, Paul Wiegler, undertook a number of stylistic improvements, such as the elimination of repetition, and he also made corrections: in the final chapter of Ditzen's manuscript, for example, the name of the Kienschäpers' adopted son appears as Toni instead of Kuno. For reasons which are quite unclear, Wiegler changed the name of one of the characters from Barkhausen to Borkhausen. He was not always consistent in his approach: he removed the description 'Communist' from the resistance cell to which Trudel and Karl Hergesell belonged on its first mention but left it in place when it appears a second time. He also deleted the reference on the first page of the novel to the fact that Eva Kluge was a member of the Nazi Party but then had to add it later because her decision to leave the party is a key factor in the development of the plot.

Wiegler reduces the number of swear words, expletives and other colourful terms of abuse significantly. He seems averse to superlatives of all kinds and reduces some descriptions of violence, such as the account of Escherich's suicide.

His changes affect the characterization of two figures in the novel: the retired judge, Herr Fromm, and Anna Quangel. In the case of Fromm, he cuts information about his past, when he was known as a hanging judge on account of the twenty-one death sentences he had passed in the course of his career, which had led to attempts on his life and threatening letters. The complexity in Ditzen's portrayal of Fromm is thus significantly reduced in the 1947 edition.

The major change which Wiegler made concerns the characterization of Anna Quangel. In the 1947 edition, she is not a member of the Nazi women's organization. She is a housewife and mother. This change means that there are no references to Anna Quangel's courage and initiative in leaving the women's organization, to her plan to leave a postcard in the building which houses the organization, to the line of questioning relating to her membership of the organization during her trial, or to the witnesses from the organization at her trial. As a result of this cut, Anna Quangel is reduced to a one-dimensional figure and her assertiveness during her trial comes as a surprise to the reader.

Wiegler's editorial decisions seem to have been motivated by a number of factors: an editor's normal attention to style and correctness, his own aversion to linguistic excess of any kind, and political considerations. It was presumably not considered appropriate for a 'heroine' such as Anna Quangel to have voluntarily joined a Nazi organization. Similarly, a positive character such as Eva Kluge could not be portrayed as having once been a member of the Nazi Party, even though it was highly likely that a job in the post office was dependent on party membership. Fromm, who is the embodiment of justice in the novel, could not be tainted by an association with death sentences.

Wiegler also deleted an aside by the narrator in chapter twenty-one of Ditzen's manuscript to the effect that the Quangels, like most Germans, 'were deep down no friends of the Jews'. Again, the 'heroes' had to be above reproach – even though casual anti-Semitism was widespread in pre-war Germany, as Ditzen knew only too well.

Wiegler's changes do not have a major impact on the plot or on most of the characterization. Their major effect is to make the 1947 edition less colourful, less complex and, to some extent, less realistic – or, in the words of Almut Giesecke, editor of the 2011 unexpurgated German edition, the original is 'rawer and coarser, but more intensive'.[42]

Ditzen described himself in good spirits and full of plans at the end of October 1946. The book, film and pre-launch serialization rights of *Alone in Berlin* were all sold. A new edition of his children's stories, 'Stories from a Childhood', was due to appear in time for Christmas. Aufbau had even agreed to publish 'The Nightmare', a novel which did not fit into the cultural policy enunciated by Pieck earlier in the year, which prioritized the German humanist literary tradition, followed by twentieth-century socialist classics.

Uli and Lore were making good progress at school and there was time for family trips to the theatre and cinema. Ditzen's Swedish publishers made contact and sent parcels of chocolate and coffee. Old friends, too, got in touch: Lore Soldin wrote from England, Dora Preisach from Palestine. The long-running saga of the Ditzens' gas connection was also resolved at the end of October. In the third week in November, Suse paid a visit to Eisenmengerweg which passed off amicably.

Less than ten days later, Rudolf and Ulla Ditzen were admitted to the Charité hospital after 'a complete breakdown, abuse of sleeping-pills – always the same old story'.[43] The pressure of completing *Alone in Berlin* in record time no doubt contributed to this breakdown. The presence of Gertrud Kramer in the house was a bone of contention between Ditzen and his wife, as was what Ditzen perceived to be Ulla's too close relationship with Becher.[44] As it became clear that a longer stay in hospital would be necessary, the children were sent home to Carwitz for Christmas.

Ditzen wrote to his sister Elisabeth on 27 December from the Charité hospital: 'I have not much appetite for life any more and even the pleasure of finishing a successful novel does not last very long when you are in urgent need of five pairs of shoes and there's no coal left to heat the house.' He agreed to talk to medical students about his history of addiction to morphine, cocaine, sleeping-pills and alcohol and, according to one eye-witness account, made a lasting impression on his audience.[45] He was kept strictly separate from his wife, whom the doctors considered to be a serious morphine addict.

On 21 December 1946, in a letter to Kurt Wilhelm, Ditzen described himself as 'quite well mended' and mentioned his plans for a young person's novel once *Alone in Berlin* was out of the way. Six days later, he wrote what was to be his last letter to his mother, in which he also referred to his plans for the future – 'I must get on my feet again' – and accepting his temporary separation from Ulla: 'I am the guilty one, I am the man, I should have given her a lead and helped her instead of stupidly giving in to her every wish ... She is such a good child, has a really good heart and she loves me very much.' He wrote that he was feeling much better although not yet well enough to start working.

Ulla, who was profoundly unhappy at their separation, appears to have lobbied for their removal to a small wartime hospital in a former school at 21–3 Blankenburger Strasse in the Niederschönhausen district of Berlin, near their home in Eisenmengerweg. She was eventually successful, and they moved in early January 1947.

Ditzen did not recover sufficiently to realize his intentions of making a new start and, here, on the evening of Wednesday 5 February 1947, he died. In his last letter to his mother he had written:

> Some part of me has never been completely finished, something is missing, with the result that I'm not a proper man, only a human being who has aged, an old grammar-school-boy ['*ein altgewordener Gymnasiast*'], as Erich Kästner once said of me ... I know I'm weak, but not bad, never bad. But that's no excuse, it's poor enough at fifty-three to have become nothing more than a weak man, to have learned so little from my mistakes.

Rudolf Ditzen's redeeming feature was his awareness of his own weaknesses. It was the source of his literary inspiration as well as the cause of his mental torment. He lived more lives than one, clawing his way back each time – in 1913, 1921, 1928, 1944, 1946 – until his body was no longer able. He died more deaths than one – he called his periods of addiction his 'little deaths' and viewed the relationship between the 'little deaths' and the 'big death' as one between brothers. His literary work is uneven. He wrote too much, and even some of his best novels could have been improved by more rigorous editing. And yet his depiction of ordinary men and women and his ability to tell a good story touched a chord in his readers and secured him a devoted following in Germany which continues to the present day. His love of literature was reflected not only in his extensive library but in his own writing – in its allusions to Dickens, Stevenson, Raabe, Hamsun, Dostoyevsky and Flaubert, as well as in the quality of his best work.

Paul Mayer, Ditzen's best editor, was still in Mexico when he learned of the author's death. He summed up Ditzen's contribution to German literature in the German-language *Demokratische Post* on 1 March 1947:

> German literature has not many realistic writers. Hans Fallada is one of them. His work, mutilated by political terror, is even as a torso important enough not to be forgotten.

Notes

INTRODUCTION

All unpublished material referred to in this and subsequent chapters is in the Hans Fallada Archive, Carwitz and Neubrandenburg, unless stated otherwise. All English translations are by the author, unless otherwise indicated.

1. 'The Ballad of Reading Gaol', in *The Works of Oscar Wilde*, edited by G. F. Maine (London: Collins, 1948), pp. 822ff.
2. Hans Fallada, *Kleiner Man – was nun?* (Reinbek: Rowohlt, 1978). *Little Man – What Now?*, translated by Susan Bennett, introduced by Philip Brady (London: Libris, 1996; New York: Melville House, 2009).
3. Hans Fallada, *Jeder stirbt für sich allein* (Berlin and Weimar: Aufbau, 1981); new, unabridged edition (Berlin: Aufbau, 2011). *Alone in Berlin*, translated by Michael Hofmann with an Afterword by Geoff Wilkes (London: Penguin, 2009). For a discussion of the differences between the two German editions, see chapter 8 below.
4. Hans Fallada, '*Wie ich Schriftsteller wurde*' ('How I Became a Writer'), in Hans Fallada, *Lieschens Sieg und andere Erzählungen* (Reinbek: Rowohlt, 1973), pp. 189–230 (211).
5. Thomas Mann in a letter to Walter von Molo on 7 September 1945, in Thomas Mann, *Briefe*, edited by E. Mann (Frankfurt/Main: Fischer, 1979), p. 443.
6. Johannes R. Becher, *Über Hans Fallada* (Berlin: Kinderbuchverlag, 1965) [unpaginated].
7. Alfred Geßler, *Hans Fallada. Sein Leben und Werk* (Berlin: Volk und Wissen, 1972).
8. Tom Crepon, *Leben und Tode des Hans Fallada* (Halle/Leipzig: Mitteldeutscher Verlag, 1978).
9. Werner Liersch, *Hans Fallada. Sein großes kleines Leben* (Berlin: Verlag Neues Leben, 1981).

10. See also Günter Caspar, *Fallada-Studien* (Berlin/Weimar: Aufbau, 1988) and Hans Fallada, *Drei Jahre kein Mensch*, edited by Günter Caspar (Berlin: Aufbau, 1997).

11. For a comprehensive account of films about Ditzen/Fallada as well as films based on his work, see Hans Haupt, *Filmographie* (Feldberg: Hans Fallada Archive, 1996).

12. Jürgen Manthey, *Hans Fallada* (Reinbek: Rowohlt, 1963).

13. Ibid., p. 173.

14. Dieter Mayer (ed.), *Hans Fallada: Kleiner Mann – was nun?* (Frankfurt/Main: Diesterweg, 1978). Hans Jürgen Frotscher, *Hans Fallada: Kleiner Mann – was nun?* (Munich: Oldenbourg, 1983).

15. Roy Reardon (ed.), *Hans Fallada, Kleiner Mann – was nun?* (London: Methuen, 1987).

16. The Simon and Schuster edition was substantially shorter than Putnam's, which was also incomplete. Ditzen was consulted about the proposed cuts in September 1932 and gave his approval – he even suggested additional cuts 'since the American publishers seem especially keen to produce a shorter version'. The reason for this policy is unclear.

17. *Who Once Eats out of the Tin Bowl*, the title of the first English translation of *Wer einmal aus dem Blechnapf frißt*, fails to convey either the idiom of the German title or the major theme of the novel – the failure of the criminal justice system to prevent re-offending. The US title, *The World Outside*, certainly makes more sense, but it, too, fails to convey adequately the meaning of the German. For these reasons, the title 'Once a Jailbird' – the English equivalent of *Wer einmal aus dem Blechnapf frißt* – will be adopted here.

18. Hans Fallada, *The Drinker*, translated by Charlotte and A. L. Lloyd (London: Libris, 1989); *Little Man – What Now?*, translated by Susan Bennett.

19. Rudolf Ditzen to Dr Gawronski, 6 April 1936.

20. Werner Liersch, *Hans Fallada. Sein großes kleines Leben* (expanded new edition) (Hildesheim: Claassen, 1993).

21. Klaus Farin, *Hans Fallada. 'Welche sind, die haben kein Glück'* (Munich: Thomas Tilsner, 1993).

22. Hans Fallada, *Das Frühwerk*, 2 vols. (Berlin/Weimar: Aufbau, 1993).

23. Proceedings of the following conferences have been published: the 1993 conference in Greifswald (Rostock: Hinstorff, 1995), the 2004 Fallada Forum conference in Berlin (Berlin: Individuell, 2005), the 2006 Fallada Forum conference in Saskatchewan (Regina: University of Regina, 2008), the 2007 Fallada Forum conference in Berlin (Göttingen: V&R unipress, 2008), the 2008 Fallada Forum conference in Berlin (Göttingen: V&R

unipress, 2009), and the 2008 Fallada Forum conference in Tennessee (Göttingen: V&R unipress, 2009). See Bibliography for details.

Papers presented at the second Greifswald conference in 1997 and two conferences organized by the Hans Fallada Society since 2002 in Carwitz have been published in the *Hans Fallada Jahrbuch*; the 2009 Carwitz conference papers were published as a monograph in 2011 (Berlin: De Gruyter). For details, see note 25 below and Bibliography.

24. federchen in Neubrandenburg has been publishing monographs on aspects of Fallada's life and work since 1988: for details, see entries in the Bibliography under Heinrich, Knüppel, Kuhnke, Lange and Witzke.

25. To date, five volumes of the Yearbook (*Hans Fallada Jahrbuch*) have appeared: 1995, 1997, 2000, 2003 and 2006. Number 2 contains the papers from the 1995 Greifswald conference, numbers 4 and 5 papers from Hans Fallada Society conferences held in Carwitz in 2002 and 2005.

26. *Hans Fallada. Sein Leben in Bildern und Briefen*, compiled by Gunnar Müller-Waldeck and Roland Ulrich with Ulrich Ditzen (Berlin: Aufbau, 1997).

27. Cecilia von Studnitz (ed.), *Ich bin nicht der, den Du liebst. Die frühen Jahre des Hans Fallada in Berlin* (Neubrandenburg: federchen, 2007). Michael Töteberg and Sabine Buck (eds.), *Hans Fallada. Ewig auf der Rutschbahn. Briefwechsel mit dem Rowohlt Verlag* (Reinbek: Rowohlt, 2008). Uli Ditzen (ed.), *Hans Fallada – Anna Ditzen. Wenn du fort bist, ist alles nur halb. Briefe einer Ehe* (Berlin: Aufbau, 2007). Uli Ditzen (ed.), *Hans Fallada – Uli Ditzen. Mein Vater und sein Sohn* (Berlin: Aufbau, 2004).

28. Cecilia von Studnitz, *Es war wie ein Rausch. Fallada und sein Leben* (Düsseldorf: Droste, 1997).

29. Hans Fallada, *Damals bei uns daheim/Heute bei uns zu Haus* (Berlin/ Weimar: Aufbau, 1982).

30. Rudolf Ditzen to Elisabeth Hörig, 26 April 1941.

31. Rudolf Ditzen to Wanda Oster, 26 April 1941.

32. Rudolf Ditzen to Elisabeth Hörig, 26 April 1941.

CHAPTER 1: THE SEARCH FOR SELF

1. Oscar Wilde, *The Portrait of Dorian Gray* in *The Works of Oscar Wilde*, pp. 112ff.

2. Elisabeth Hörig to Rudolf Ditzen, 19 July 1937.

3. Elisabeth Ditzen, '*Erinnerungen*' (p. 141), Hans Fallada Archive. The memoirs of Elisabeth and Wilhelm Ditzen as well as those of their daughter Elisabeth Hörig are available in manuscript form in the Hans Fallada Archive: Elisabeth Ditzen, '*Erinnerungen*'; Wilhelm Ditzen, '*Erinnerungen*'; Elisabeth Hörig, '*Szenen aus dem Familienleben, Erinnerungen an die Berliner Jahre, 1900–1910*'.

4. Eda Sagarra, 'Malwida von Meysenbug (1816–1903): A Biographical Essay', in *Neglected German Progressives* 2, Galway Colloquium 1985, German Department, University College Galway, Ireland, pp. 15–26 (p. 23). After fleeing Germany, Malwida von Meysenbug worked as a German teacher in London and then as a governess and translator in Paris before finally settling in Rome. She counted Nietzsche and Wagner among her close friends. In addition to her German translation of Alexander Herzen's memoirs (Hamburg: Hoffmann and Campe, 1855–9), she is best known for her *Mémoires d'une idéaliste entre deux révolutions 1830–1848* (Geneva/Basel: Georg, 1869) and her short stories.

5. Elisabeth Ditzen, '*Erinnerungen*', p. 185.

6. Wilhelm Ditzen, '*Erinnerungen*', p. 89.

7. Elisabeth Hörig to Rudolf Ditzen, 10 July 1941.

8. Elisabeth Hörig, '*Szenen*', p. 19.

9. Testimony of Adelaide Ditzen, *Rudolstädter Akte* (124–7), Hans Fallada Archive.

10. Manthey, *Hans Fallada*, p. 13.

11. Heinz and Elisabeth Hörig to Rudolf Ditzen, 3 January 1934.

12. Elisabeth Ditzen, '*Erinnerungen*', p. 181.

13. Rudolf Ditzen, '*Gedanken über den Glauben*' (1910/1911), Hans Fallada Archive.

14. Ibid. Rudolf's father had come to similar conclusions at around the same age. His memoirs recall the philosophical discussions on the existence of God which he had with his schoolfriend Theobald von Bethmann-Hollweg, later to become Imperial Chancellor: 'We came to the conclusion that the existence of God is not proven. But in the radical manner typical of youth we were not content with half measures. We went further: from "not proven" to "not provable" and from there to the final conclusion: "God does not exist."'

15. Paul Vogel, '*Jahresbericht des Königin-Carola-Gymnasiums in Leipzig für das Schuljahr Ostern 1910 bis Ostern 1911*', Hans Fallada Archive.

16. Testimony of Adelaide Ditzen, *Rudolstädter Akte*. The account given here of the events of 1910 and 1911 is based on the statements and writings of Rudolf Ditzen, his family, friends and doctors as well as his

landlords and teachers in Rudolstadt, which are collected in the *Rudol-städter Akte* in the Hans Fallada Archive.

17. See Ditzen's account of this event in the 'Autobiography' ('*Lebenslauf*') which he wrote for Professor Binswanger in 1911 during his stay in the psychiatric hospital in Jena, reproduced in Daniel Börner (ed.) '*Wenn Ihr überhaupt nur ahntet, was ich für einen Lebenshunger habe!*' *Fallada in Thüringen* (Weimar and Jena: Hain, 2010), pp. 17–67 (32–3).

18. Karl Pinthus, 'Leipzig and Early Expressionism', in *The Era of Expressionism*, edited by P. Raabe, translated by J. M. Ritchie (London: Calder and Boyars, 1974), p. 68.

19. *Rudolstädter Akte*, Hans Fallada Archive:

> *Sind wir nicht zur Trauer hier geboren?*
> *ich hatte einstmals Freude,*
> *nun ist sie ganz vorbei,*
> *– und einmal ist genug …*

> Are we not born to sorrow here?
> Once I knew joy,
> But now that's all past,
> - And once is enough …

20. The Commission set up in 1906 to revise the Criminal Code, which counted Wilhelm Ditzen among its members, had issued a draft report in 1909. After widespread debate, a new draft Criminal Code was published in 1913 but, because of pressure of other parliamentary business in the months before the outbreak of the First World War, it never came before the Reichstag (see Richard J. Evans, *Rituals of Retribution. Capital Punishment in German Politics and Society since the Seventeenth Century* (Harmondsworth: Penguin, 1997), pp. 462–6).

CHAPTER 2: RUDOLF DITZEN AND HANS FALLADA

1. Rudolf Ditzen, '*Gestalten und Bilder*' ('Shapes and Images'), pp. 18–19. Unpublished manuscript.

2. Max Krell, 'Expressionism – Glory and Decline', in *The Era of Expressionism*, p. 303.

3. 'Shapes and Images', p. 38.

4. See Jean Full, '*Hans Fallada et Romain Rolland. Trois lettres inédites de Fallada (1912)*', *Recherches Germaniques*, 3 (1973), pp. 223–34. The letter of 28 October 1912 indicates that Adelaide Ditzen was still in

contact with Malwida von Meysenbug's protégées, Olga and Natalie Herzen (the daughters of Alexander Herzen) some nine years after von Meysenbug's death.

5. Eugen Diederichs Verlag to Rudolf Ditzen, 9 December 1912.

6. Rudolf Ditzen, '*Deutschland in der heutigen französischen Litteratur* [sic]', December 1912. Unpublished manuscript.

7. Certificate of the Ersatz-Commission des Aushebungsbezirks Ronneburg, 10 April 1913.

8. Report by Dr Tecklenburg, October 1913.

9. 'Shapes and Images', p. 39:

> *Am Morgen, als der Himmel matt erst blaute,*
> *Ging er froh sinnend zwischen Feldern hin,*
> *Er strich mit seiner Hand das Korn, das hell betaute,*
> *Und lachte froh aus unbeschwertem Sinn.*
> *Dann sah er eines Pfluges Furchen-ziehen*
> *Und riss die Zügel harsch in seine Hand,*
> *Er trieb die Pferde und in heissem Mühen*
> *Beackert er das früh gemähte Land.*
> *Am Mittag liegt er müd in kühlem Schatten*
> *Und trinkt aus einem irdenen Kruge Bier*
> *Doch schon vergass er, was das ist, Ermatten*
> *Und stürmt beschwingten Fusses weit von hier.*

> In the morning as the sky turned weakly blue,
> Between the fields he strode to meet the day,
> He touched the corn ears shining in the dew,
> And laughed in a carefree, happy way.
> Then the aimless furrows of a plough he spied
> And roughly seized the reins into his hand,
> He drove the horses, heaved and sighed
> And soon ploughs all the new-mown land.
> At midday he lies coolly in the shade
> And from a pitcher drinks his beer,
> And soon forgets the weariness he felt
> And storms off with new vigour far from here.

10. See *Germany. A Companion to German Studies*, edited by Michael Pasley (London/New York: Methuen, 1982), p. 310.

11. Thomas Mann, '*Gedanken im Kriege*', *Die neue Rundschau* 25 (1914) vol. 10, pp. 1474–5.

12. Hans Fallada, *Strafgefangener Zelle 32, Tagebuch* (Prison Diary, 1924) (Berlin: Aufbau, 1998), p. 39.

13. Hans Fallada, 'How I Became a Writer', pp. 191–2.

14. Elisabeth Ditzen to Rudolf Ditzen, 7 October 1931.

15. Hans Fallada, 'How I Became a Writer', p. 194.

16. Richard Huelsenbeck, '*Die dadaistische Bewegung*', *Die neue Rundschau*, 31 (1920), pp. 972–9.

17. Sylvia von Harden, '*Erinnerungen an einst ...*', *Imprimatur*, 3 (1961/62), pp. 219–22.

18. Verse 4:

> *Ewig fühl ich Seewind um die Wangen wehen,*
> *Ewig zupft am Mantel mich Verstehen,*
> *Doch will ich ihm in die Augen sehen,*
> *Lacht es laut und ist nur Scherz, nur Scherz.*

> Sea breezes blow continually round my face,
> Perception tugs continually at my coat,
> But if I try to look into its face,
> It laughs aloud and it's all a joke, a joke.

Verse 7:

> *Doch da das Licht und Bild der Welt verging,*
> *Stieg aus dem Augendunkel das helle Ziel,*
> *Er sah die Weite, weggesprengt den Ring,*
> *Da er nicht suchte, fiel der Schleier, fiel.*

> But as this world's brightness faded fast,
> From out the darkness rose the sea so clear,
> He looked into the distance, the spell destroyed at last.
> Now he'd stopped searching, his goal was near.

19. Verse 4:

> *Die Hirne treiben tausend bunte Blasen –*
> *Die Hände schlagen A und schlagen N –*
> *'Blassrote Rosen stehen trüb in Vasen' –*
> *'Ob ich ihn heute wiederum nicht seh?'*

> Their minds blow thousands of bright bubbles –
> Their hands beat out A and beat out N –
> 'Pale pink roses droop in vases' –
> 'Will I not see him today again?'

20. Adelaide Ditzen to Dr Tecklenburg, 6 January 1918.

21. Rudolf Ditzen to Anne Marie Seyerlen, 8 January 1918. C. von Studnitz (ed.), *Ich bin nicht der, den Du liebst*, pp. 124–6. All subsequent references to Ditzen's letters to Anne Marie Seyerlen are to be found in this edition.

22. Adelaide Ditzen to Dr Tecklenburg (undated).

23. Adelaide Ditzen to Dr Tecklenburg, 6 January 1918.

24. Adelaide Ditzen to Dr Tecklenburg, 3 March 1918.

25. Wilhelm Ditzen to Dr Tecklenburg, 14 May 1918.

26. Karl Jakob Hirsch, *Heimkehr zu Gott. Briefe an meinen Sohn* (Munich: Desch, 1946), pp. 64–9.

27. Hans Fallada, '*Sachlicher Bericht über das Glück, ein Morphinist zu sein*' in *Drei Jahre kein Mensch*, pp. 5–24. Hans Fallada, *Short Treatise on the Joys of Morphinism*, translated by Michael Hofmann (London: Penguin, 2011).

28. Eric Hobsbawm, *Age of Extremes: The Short Twentieth Century* 1914–91 (London: Michael Joseph, 1994), p. 128.

29. Hans Fallada, *Der junge Goedeschal*, in *Frühe Prosa*, vol. 1, pp. 1–280.

30. Testimony of Bernhard Hübner, *Rudolstädter Akte*.

31. For an overview of adolescent novels in Germany around the turn of the twentieth century as well as a (comparative) assessment of the literary merit of 'Young Goedeschal', see Carsten Gansel '"*Es war eine verdammte Zeit*" – *Moderne Adoleszenzkrisen als traumatische Erinnerung. Neue Überlegungen zu Hans Falladas Frühwerk 'Der arme Goedeschal'*, in Carsten Gansel and Werner Liersch (eds.) *Zeit vergessen, Zeit erinnern. Hans Fallada und das kulturelle Gedächtnis* (Göttingen: V&R unipress, 2008), pp. 95–111.

CHAPTER 3: 'THAT LITTLE TENT OF BLUE'

1. Entry for 27 January 1922, in *The Diaries of Franz Kafka* 1910–23, edited by Max Brod, translated by M. Greenberg with H. Arendt (Harmondsworth: Penguin, 1964), pp. 406–7.

2. Ernst Toller, *Gesammelte Werke* (Munich: Hanser, 1987), vol. 5, p. 85.

3. Johannes R. Becher, Letter to Katharina Kippenberg, 7 March 1921, in *Briefe* 1909–58 and *Briefe an Johannes R. Becher* 1910–58, edited by Rolf Harder (Berlin and Weimar: Aufbau, 1993), 2 vols., I, p. 102.

4. Hans Fallada, *Die Kuh, der Schuh, dann du*, in Fallada, *Frühe Prosa*, vol. 2, pp. 7–111.

5. Rudolf Ditzen to Johannes Kagelmacher, 24 November 1938.
6. Hans Fallada, *Anton und Gerda*, in Fallada, *Frühe Prosa*, vol. 1, pp. 283–542.
7. See Günter Caspar's Afterword to Hans Fallada, *Märchen und Geschichten* (Berlin und Weimar: Aufbau, 1985), pp. 674–5.
8. Hans Fallada, *Strafgefangener Zelle 32*, pp. 10–11.
9. Ernst von Salomon, *Der Fragebogen* (Reinbek: Rowohlt, 1997), p. 21.
10. Hans Fallada, *Im Blinzeln der großen Katze*, in Fallada, *Frühe Prosa*, vol. 2, pp. 283–420.
11. Hans Fallada, *Die große Liebe*, in Fallada, *Frühe Prosa*, vol. 2, pp. 115–74.
12. According to Günter Caspar, Afterword to Fallada, *Frühe Prosa*, vol. 2, p. 522.
13. Hans Fallada, *Der Apparat der Liebe*, in Fallada, *Frühe Prosa*, vol. 2, pp. 177–280.
14. Bertolt Brecht, *Bertolt Brechts Hauspostille/Manual of Piety*, bilingual edition, translated by Eric Bentley (New York: Grove Press, 1966).
15. Tom Crepon and Marianne Dwars, *An der Schwale liegt (k)ein Märchen* (Neumünster: Karl Wachholz, 1993), pp. 22–3.

CHAPTER 4: BREAKTHROUGH

1. '*Umzug nach Berlin 1930*', in *Ringelnatz in kleiner Auswahl als Taschenbuch* (Berlin: Karl K. Henssel, 1964), p. 105.
2. Fallada. *Ewig auf der Rutschbahn*, p. 50.
3. The short stories mentioned in this chapter are to be found in Hans Fallada, *Märchen und Geschichten*.
4. Rudolf Ditzen to Johannes Kagelmacher, 21 October 1928.
5. Rudolf Ditzen to Wilhelm and Elisabeth Ditzen, 20 December 1928.
6. Rudolf Ditzen to Wilhelm and Elisabeth Ditzen, 6 March 1929.
7. Rudolf Ditzen to Johannes Kagelmacher, 8 March 1929.
8. Rudolf Ditzen to Margarete Bechert, 10 February 1929.
9. Johannes Kagelmacher to Rudolf Ditzen, 5 April 1929.
10. Rudolf Ditzen to Wilhelm and Elisabeth Ditzen, 12 August 1929.
11. Rudolf Ditzen to Wilhelm and Elisabeth Ditzen, 31 August 1933.
12. Caspar, *Fallada-Studien*, Chapter 1.
13. Ernst Rowohlt, '*Die Geschichte einer Wieder-Entdeckung*' (1930), Hans Fallada Archive.
14. '*Lebensabriss von Hans Fallada*', *Frankfurter Illustrierte*, 7 September 1932.

15. Rudolf Ditzen to Johannes Kagelmacher, 5 October 1929.
16. Rudolf Ditzen to Ernst Rowohlt, 14 August 1929.
17. Rudolf Ditzen to Wilhelm and Elisabeth Ditzen, 3 November 1929.
18. Rudolf Ditzen to Wilhelm and Elisabeth Ditzen, 12 August 1929.
19. Rudolf Ditzen, '*Bauern-Krieg wider Neumünster*', *Das Tage-Buch* 10 (1929), 37 (14 September 1929), pp. 1516–19.
20. Rudolf Ditzen, '*Landvolkprozess*', *Die Weltbühne* 25 (1929), 49 (3 December 1929), pp. 832–5.
21. Martha Dodd, *My Years in Germany* (London: Gollancz, 1939), p. 74.
22. Thomas Wolfe, *You Can't Go Home Again* (New York: Harper and Brothers, 1940), p. 661.
23. See Crepon/Dwars, *An der Schwale*, pp. 92–106, for a discussion of the relationship between the fictional characters in *A Small Circus* and their factual counterparts in Neumünster.
24. See Ernst von Salomon, *Der Fragebogen*, p. 329.
25. Rudolf Ditzen to Margarete Bechert, 12 November 1930.
26. Rudolf Ditzen to Johannes Kagelmacher, 1 November 1930.
27. Rudolf Ditzen to Wilhelm and Elisabeth Ditzen, 25 November 1930.
28. Rudolf Ditzen to Elisabeth Ditzen, 8 February 1931.
29. Rudolf Ditzen to Elisabeth Ditzen, 29 March 1931.
30. Axel Eggebrecht's review appeared in the July 1931 edition of *Die Literarische Welt*.
31. Peter Suhrkamp's review was published in the January 1932 edition of the journal *Uhu*; Caspar, *Fallada-Studien*, p. 50.
32. Rudolf Ditzen to Wilhelm and Elisabeth Ditzen, 19 April 1931.
33. Rudolf Ditzen to Wilhelm and Elisabeth Ditzen, 21 June 1931.
34. Ibid.
35. Reinhard Kühnl (ed.), *Der deutsche Faschismus in Quellen und Dokumenten* (Cologne: Pahl-Rugenstein, 1975), p. 145.

CHAPTER 5: SUCCESS

1. Siegfried Kracauer, *Die Angestellten* (first published, 1930; Frankfurt am Main: Suhrkamp, 1971). This translation is from the Introduction by Philip Brady to Fallada, *Little Man – What Now?*, p. xviii. All quotations are from this edition.
2. Hans Fallada to Herr Hünich, 17 October 1932.
3. Hans Fallada to Johannes Boysen, 7 January 1933.
4. Rudolf Ditzen to Elisabeth Ditzen, 14 February 1932.

5. Rudolf Ditzen to Suse Issel, 17 February 1929. Fallada/Ditzen, *Wenn du fort bist*, p. 73.

6. Conversation with Frau Anna Ditzen, 4 May 1984.

7. Hans Fallada to Herr Zellner, 27 November 1932.

8. Hans Fallada to Herr Benda, 3 November 1932.

9. Kühnl, *Der deutsche Faschismus*, p. 146.

10. Rudolf Ditzen to Wilhelm and Elisabeth Ditzen, 1 November 1931.

11. Rudolf Ditzen to Wilhelm and Elisabeth Ditzen, 29 November 1931.

12. Rudolf Ditzen to Wilhelm and Elisabeth Ditzen, 19 December 1931.

13. Rudolf Ditzen to Wilhelm and Elisabeth Ditzen, 25 January 1932.

14. Ibid.

15. Rudolf Ditzen to Wilhelm and Elisabeth Ditzen, 6 February 1932.

16. Kühnl, *Der deutsche Faschismus*, p. 138.

17. Eric Hobsbawm, *Age of Extremes*, p. 119.

18. Siegfried Kracauer, *Die Angestellten*, p. 91.

19. Ernst Bloch, *Heritage of Our Time*, translated by Neville and Stephen Plaice (Berkeley/Los Angeles: University of California Press, 1990), pp. 24–6.

20. Rudolf Ditzen to Wilhelm and Elisabeth Ditzen, 18 December 1932.

21. Paul Mayer, *Ernst Rowohlt* (Reinbek, 1968), p. 82.

22. Rudolf Ditzen to Ernst Rowohlt, 24 May 1932.

23. Peter Suhrkamp to Rudolf Ditzen, 14 July 1932. Fallada, *Ewig auf der Rutschbahn*, p. 86.

24. Clara Viebig, '*Lämmchen und Ihr Junge*', undated review.

25. Rudolf Ditzen to Wilhelm and Elisabeth Ditzen, (early) September 1932.

26. Rudolf Ditzen to Peter Zingler, 9 July 1932.

27. Rudolf Ditzen to Wilhelm and Elisabeth Ditzen, 16 July 1932.

28. Rudolf Ditzen to Wilhelm and Elisabeth Ditzen, 25 July 1932.

29. Ernst Rowohlt to Rudolf Ditzen, 8 July 1932.

30. Rudolf Ditzen to Wilhelm and Elisabeth Ditzen, 8 January 1933.

31. Ibid.

32. Rudolf Ditzen to Ernst Rowohlt, 27 July 1933.

33. Symonette, Lys and K. H. Kowalke (eds.), *Speak Low (When You Speak Love): The Letters of Kurt Weill and Lotte Lenya* (London: Hamish Hamilton, 1996), p. 73.

34. Symonette and Kowalke claim that after the Reichstag fire the publisher Walter Steinthal, a close friend of Weill's, 'telephoned Weill on behalf of Fallada, who had already been arrested, warning that Weill should leave Berlin' (*Speak Low*, p. 77). In fact, Fallada was not arrested after the

Reichstag fire, and while it is, of course, possible that he contacted Steinthal, the absence of any reference to the source for this information in Symonette and Kowalke's account makes their claim impossible to verify.

35. Victor Klemperer, *Ich will Zeugnis ablegen bis zum letzten. Tagebücher 1933–44* (Berlin: Aufbau, 1995), 2 vols., I, p. 15.

36. Hans Fallada, *In meinem fremden Land. Gefängnistagebuch 1944*, edited by Jenny Williams and Sabine Lange (Berlin: Aufbau, 2009), p. 60. This will be referred to in the body of the text as the '1944 Prison Memoirs'.

37. Fallada, *In meinem fremden Land*, p. 72.

38. Jürgen C. Thöming, '*Hans Fallada. Seismograph gesellschaftlicher Krisen*', in *Zeitkritische Romane des 20. Jahrhunderts. Die Gesellschaft in der Kritik der deutschen Literatur*, edited by H. Wagener (Stuttgart: Reclam, 1975), pp. 97–123.

39. Rudolf Ditzen to Margarete Bechert, 5 August 1933.

40. Hans Fallada to Herr Benda, 3 November 1932.

41. Conversation with Frau Anna Ditzen, 9 September 1983.

42. Symonette/Kowalke, *Speak Low*, p. 96.

43. Ernst Rowohlt to Rudolf Ditzen, 4 October 1933.

44. As a result of the success of *Little Man – What Now?* in the USA, Universal Pictures acquired the film rights and engaged Frank Borzage to direct the film, which starred Margaret Sullavan as Lämmchen and Douglas Montgomery as Pinneberg. After the première on 31 May 1934, Universal sent Ditzen some stills, which he found 'disgusting': 'Lämmchen in an evening gown in the attic, Lämmchen with a new dress in every scene – and no scene which would give you the slightest idea of the social circumstances of the unemployed.' See Caspar, *Fallada Studien*, pp. 284–333; also reprinted in Haupt, *Filmographie*, p. 5.

45. Hans Fallada to F. H. Küthe, 21 October 1933. In '*Briefwechsel mit F. Hermann Küthe*', Stiftung Archiv der Akademie der Künste, Berlin: 137/44.

46. Rudolf Ditzen to Ernst Rowohlt, 20 October 1933.

CHAPTER 6: CARWITZ THE IDYLL

1. Reinhold Schneider, *Gesammelte Werke*, edited by Edwin Maria Landau (Frankfurt: Insel, 1978), vol. III, p. 462.

2. Rudolf Ditzen to Dora Preisach, 6 March 1934.

3. Ledig's three companions were committed opponents of the Nazi regime. Martha Dodd, as we have seen, was the daughter of William

E. Dodd, the US ambassador to Berlin from 1933 to 1937, and was instrumental in helping victims of fascism to escape from Germany. Her fellow American, Mildred Fish, a writer, teacher and translator, had married Arvid Harnack and moved to Germany in 1929. She was later to become actively, and fatally, involved in the Resistance through her friendship with Greta and Adam Kuckhoff and Harro and Libertas Schulze-Boysen. Boris Vinogradov was the First Secretary at the Soviet Embassy in Berlin from September 1930 until November 1934. During this time he fell in love with Martha Dodd; it is possible that his official request for permission to marry her contributed to his execution in 1938 after his return to the Soviet Union. For a detailed discussion of Ditzen's visitors on 27 May 1934, see Manfred Kuhnke, *Besuch bei Fallada: Sonntag, der 27. Mai 1934 – ein besonderer Tag im sonderbaren Leben des Hans Fallada* (Neubrandenburg: federchen, 1996).

4. Dodd, *My Years in Germany*, p. 76.

5. For a description of Langenbucher's leading role in formulating and implementing cultural policy in Nazi Germany, see Jan-Pieter Barbian, *Literaturpolitik im 'Dritten Reich'. Institutionen, Kompetenzen, Betätigungsfelder* (Munich: dtv, 1995), p. 272, n. 11.

6. Reinhold Grimm, '*Im Dickicht der inneren Emigration*', in *Die deutsche Literatur im Dritten Reich*, edited by Horst Denkler and Karl Prümm (Stuttgart: Reclam, 1976), p. 408.

7. Hans Fallada, *Wir hatten mal ein Kind* (Reinbek: Rowohlt, 1980).

8. Hamsun's work was held in high esteem by the National Socialist cultural elite. Langenbucher's *Volkhafte Dichtung der Zeit* (1935), a standard Nazi literary work, praises in particular his *Growth of the Soil* as a fine example of a 'settler story' (p. 95). Hamsun greatly admired Adolf Hitler and counted himself among 'his close supporters' (see Harald Naess, 'Who was Hamsun's Hero?', in *The Hero in Scandinavian Literature*, edited by J. M. Weinstock and R. T. Rovinsky (Austin and London: University of Texas Press, 1975), pp. 63–86).

9. Elisabeth Hörig to Rudolf Ditzen, 14 May 1934.

10. Jürgen C. Thöming, '*Hans Fallada als verlorener Sohn Johannes Gäntschow*' in *Hans Fallada. Beiträge zu Leben und Werk*, Müller-Waldeck, G. and R. Ulrich (eds.), pp. 183–210.

11. Rudolf Ditzen to Johannes Kagelmacher, 17 June 1934.

12. Rudolf Ditzen to Johannes Kagelmacher, 31 July 1934.

13. Rudolf Ditzen to Elisabeth Hörig, 20 December 1933.

14. Rudolf Ditzen to Elisabeth and Heinz Hörig, 12 October 1934.

15. Theodor Jacobs, 'Verdorrte Schrift', Der Student in Mecklenburg-Lübeck (Rostock), 5 February 1935.

16. L.R.H, 'Novelist Plays Havoc with Legend of Men of Iron', Winnipeg Free Press, 28 December 1935.

17. Fallada, In meinem fremden Land, p. 113. Rowohlt shared this view of Suhrkamp as an 'eternal schoolmaster': see his letter to Ditzen of 14 November 1945 (Fallada, Ewig auf der Rutschbahn, p. 389).

18. Ernst Rowohlt to Rudolf Ditzen, 6 April 1935.

19. Eberhard Bethge, Dietrich Bonhoeffer. Theologe, Christ, Zeitgenosse (Munich: C.H. Beck, 1968). Translation by John Brownjohn in Love Letters from Cell 92. Dietrich Bonhoeffer and Maria von Wedemeyer (London: Collins, 1994), p. 266.

20. Altes Herz geht auf die Reise (Berlin: Aufbau, 1995).

21. Dietrich Bonhoeffer, No Rusty Swords, translated by Edwin Robertson and John Bowden (London and New York: Collins, 1965), p. 225.

22. Kästner, however, was allowed to publish abroad. The total ban on his work in Germany was lifted temporarily in July 1942 to enable him to work on the film Baron Münchhausen, only to be reinstated six months later at Hitler's personal instigation.

23. Hans Fallada, Märchen vom Stadtschreiber, der aufs Land flog (Berlin: Aufbau, 1991).

24. Rudolf Ditzen to Elisabeth and Heinz Hörig, 10 February 1936.

25. Jochen Klepper, Unter dem Schatten deiner Flügel. Aus den Tagebüchern der Jahre 1932 bis 1942, edited by Hildegard Klepper (Berlin: Union, 1970), p. 241.

26. Rudolf Ditzen to Wilhelm and Elisabeth Ditzen, 18 April 1936.

27. Rudolf Ditzen to Elisabeth and Heinz Hörig, 15 July 1936.

28. This visit is mentioned by Günter Caspar in his Afterword to Hans Fallada, Märchen und Geschichten, p. 668.

29. Rudolf Ditzen to Ernst Rowohlt, 9 January 1937. Fallada, Ewig auf der Rutschbahn, p. 219.

30. Hans Fallada, Wolf unter Wölfen (Reinbek: Rowohlt, 1991). Wolf among Wolves, translated by Phillip Owens. Restored, and with additional translations by Thorsten Carstensen and Nicholas Jacobs. (New York: Melville House, 2010). All quotations are from this edition.

31. Joseph Goebbels, Tagebücher 1924–45, edited by Ralf Georg Reuth (Munich: Piper, 1992), vol. 3, p. 1192.

32. Peter Suhrkamp, 'Der Zuschauer', Die neue Rundschau, 11 (1942), p. 525. Die neue Rundschau, edited by Peter Suhrkamp from 1933 to

1936 and then published by him when he took over the Fischer Verlag in 1937, pursued a policy of making minimal concessions to the Nazi regime in order to create a space for the voices of inner emigration. The journal was closed down in the autumn of 1944 following Suhrkamp's arrest on a charge of high treason.

33. Eda Sagarra, '*Blut und Boden* Fiction and the Tradition of Popular Reading Culture in Germany', in *The Burden of German History, 1919–45*, edited by M. Laffan (London: Methuen, 1988), pp. 31–47.

34. Else Marie Bakonyi, like most of the typists who came to Carwitz, had become unemployed after the Nazis had come to power. The wife of a Hungarian Jew, she had lost her job as a journalist on the liberal *Berliner Tageblatt* newspaper in 1933 and had worked variously as a screenwriter, translator and typist since then.

35. The version of *Der eiserne Gustav* discussed here is based on Caspar's reconstruction of the original: Hans Fallada, *Der eiserne Gustav, Ausgewählte Werke in Einzelausgaben*, vol. vi (Berlin and Weimar: Aufbau, 1984).

36. Rudolf Ditzen to Ernst Rowohlt, 30 May 1938.

37. Goebbels had discussed the novel on 23 July during a visit to Jannings's country seat in Austria. Jannings was initially reluctant to make any changes but eventually accepted Goebbels's directive that 'the end is to be completely rewritten and presented in a more positive light.' In a diary entry for 23 July Goebbels records his intention 'to dictate a new conclusion myself'.

38. Fallada, *In meinem fremden Land*, p. 170.

39. Ibid.

40. Hans Fallada, *Bauern, Bonzen und Bomben* (Berlin: Vier Falken Verlag, 1938).

41. The following description of Ditzen's emigration plans is based on Anna Ditzen's account as told to the author in September 1983. See also the account in Fallada, *In meinem fremden Land*, p. 17.

42. J. M. Ritchie, 'Literary Exile in Great Britain' in *German Writers and Politics* 1918–39, edited by Richard Dove and Stephen Lamb (London: Macmillan, 1992), p. 154.

43. Karl Pinthus, 'Life and Death of Ernst Toller', *Books Abroad* 14 (1939), p. 7.

44. Fallada, *In meinem fremden Land*, p. 17.

45. Ferenc Körmendi, '*Warum ich Deutschland nicht verlasse*', *Die Welt* (10 November 1962).

CHAPTER 7: CARWITZ THE NIGHTMARE

1. Erich Kästner, 'Notwendige Antworten auf überflüssige Fragen', in Das Erich Kästner-Buch, edited by Rolf Hochhuth (Zürich: Atrium, 1959), p. 155.

2. Hans Fallada, Kleiner Mann – großer Mann, alles vertauscht (Reinbek: Rowohlt, 1970).

3. Hans Fallada, Süßmilch spricht (Olten and Freiburg: Walter-Verlag, 1983).

4. Ernst Jünger, On the Marble Cliffs, translated by Stuart Hood (London: New Direction, 1947), p. 41.

5. Rudolf Ditzen to Elisabeth Hörig, 25 August 1939.

6. Wyss, a Swiss journalist, was one of the few literary critics to publish an interview with Ditzen, whom he had visited in Berlin in February 1933 during the filming of Little Man – What Now? The interview appeared on 16 April 1933 in the Neue Zürcher Zeitung. Wyss also published reviews of Ditzen's work in the Schweizerische Monatshefte and sent parcels to Carwitz on a regular basis during the war years.

7. In the event, this film was never made. Dies Herz, das dir gehört was first published in 1994 by Aufbau Verlag, Berlin.

8. Rudolf Ditzen to Elisabeth Ditzen, 17 September 1940.

9. Gustav Kilpper to Rudolf Ditzen, 29 March 1940. Ina Seidel (1885–1974) was one of the eighty-eight writers who signed the 'oath of most loyal obedience' to Hitler in October 1933. Her novel Lennacker, of 1938, is a family saga relating the history of a family of Protestant clergymen who are guided by the principle of complete obedience to the powers that be. Her poem 'Lichtdom' ('Cathedral of Light') is a song of praise to Hitler. Josef Ponten (1883–1940), who also signed the oath of obedience to Hitler in 1933, was a nationalist author and travel-writer. The fifth volume of his Volk auf dem Wege ('Nation on the Move') cycle appeared in 1940. Ernst Zahn (1867–1952) was a conservative Swiss novelist who specialized in lightweight, popular fiction. Waldemar Bonsels (1881–1952) was a popular writer of the 1920s. His Indienfahrt ('Indian Journey') was one of the most widely read books of 1922, and his Die Biene Maja ('The Bee Maja') was the sixth most published novel between 1915 and 1940. The Nazis were initially uncertain how to categorize a writer who was conservative but not fascist. It was largely his popularity as well as his willingness not to antagonize the authorities that eventually secured him official approval.

10. Rudolf Ditzen to Elisabeth Ditzen, 15 December 1942.

11. Rudolf Ditzen to Gustav Kilpper, 21 July 1940. Fallada, *Ewig auf der Rutschbahn*, p. 315.

12. Hans Fallada, *Der ungeliebte Mann* (Munich: Heyne, 1980). This completely innocuous book caused Ditzen more problems than he could have anticipated. First, he had to emphasize that Peter Siebenhaar's blindness was the result of a war wound, because Nazi legislation prohibited the congenitally blind from marrying. Then, after the novel was published, Hans Schmalfuß of the War Veterans' Association lodged a formal complaint about the depiction of the war-blind in the person of the 'selfish and tyrannical' Peter Siebenhaar. Ditzen replied to Schmalfuß on 20 February 1942: 'In Siebenhaar I was only portraying a pathetic man, who tries to exploit his disability to elicit sympathy and love from those around him.' Schmalfuß was eventually persuaded to drop the affair by Ditzen's lawyer, Carl Haensel.

13. Mayer, *Ernst Rowohlt*, p. 136. Mayer quotes Erich Kästner as saying on Rowohlt's return: 'The rats are boarding the sinking ship' (ibid., p. 137). (If true, Kästner was repeating Karl Kraus's alleged greetings to Bertolt Brecht and his family on their arrival in Vienna in March 1933.)

14. Antiqua is a Roman typeface. Until 1940, the Nazis had promoted and used Gothic typefaces as being traditionally German. In March 1940, however, assuming that they were about to found an international empire in which the use of Gothic print would be impractical, the Nazi authorities abandoned it and reverted to Roman typefaces.

15. Hans Fallada, *Zwei zarte Lämmchen weiß wie Schnee* (Reinbek: Rowohlt, 1967), p. 81.

16. Rudolf Ditzen to Elisabeth Hörig, 26 April 1941.

17. '*Das Todeshaus formt einen Dichter*': draft outline of a novel Ditzen planned to write about Schmidt-Sas in 1946. For an overview of the life of Alfred Schmidt-Sas, see Volker Hoffmann, *Der Dienstälteste von Plötzensee. Das zerrissene Leben des Musikerziehers Alfred Schmidt-Sas (1895–1943)* (Berlin: Trafo, 2000). See also Manfred Kuhnke, *Falladas letzter Roman. Die wahre Geschichte* (Friedland: Steffen, 2011) as well as Ditzen's account in Fallada, *In meinem fremden Land*, pp. 134–42.

18. Rudolf Ditzen to Alfred Günther (Deutsche Verlags-Anstalt), 12 October 1941. *Ewig auf der Rutschbahn*, p. 343.

19. Rudolf Ditzen to Elisabeth Ditzen, 22 July 1941.

20. See Ledig's letter to Ditzen of 11 August 1943 for an account of the background to the approval of paper for *Damals bei uns daheim*.

21. Fallada, *In meinem fremden Land*, pp. 240–1.

22. See Gunnar Müller-Waldeck, '"*Er war ein Ermunterer.*" *Gespräch mit Annemarie Steiner*', *Hans-Fallada-Jahrbuch* 3 (2000), pp. 64-81.

23. Oscar Wilde, 'The Critic as Artist' in *Intentions* (London: Methuen, 1934), p. 97.

24. Rudolf Ditzen to Alfred Günther, 21 April 1942.

25. Alan Bullock, *Hitler: A Study in Tyranny* (Harmondsworth: Penguin, 1962), p. 675.

26. Rudolf Ditzen to Adelheid Hörig, 18 December 1942.

27. Rudolf Ditzen to Anneliese Benzin, 7 January 1945.

28. Aline Bußmann, *Erinnerungen an Wolfgang Borchert. Zur zehnten Wiederkehr seines Todestages am 20. November 1957* (Hamburg: Rowohlt, 1957), p. 8.

29. *Die Stunde, eh du schlafen gehst* was first published in 1954 by Goldmann, Munich.

30. *Ein Mann will hinauf* was first published in 1953 by Südverlag, Munich. Since 1970, it has appeared under the title *Ein Mann will nach oben*. *Der Jungherr von Strammin* was first published under the title *Junger Herr – ganz groß* in 1952 by Ullstein, Berlin.

31. Rudolf Ditzen to Heinrich Maria Ledig, 11 August 1943.

32. Rudolf Ditzen to Elisabeth and Heinz Hörig, 5 August 1943.

33. Rudolf Ditzen to Johannes Kagelmacher, 23 July 1944.

34. Rudolf Ditzen to Uli Ditzen, 27 March 1944. Fallada/Ditzen, *Mein Vater und sein Sohn*, p. 169.

CHAPTER 8: NEW BEGINNINGS AND SENTENCES OF DEATH

1. Johannes R. Becher, *Der Aufstand im Menschen*, edited by Ilse Siebert (Berlin and Weimar: Aufbau, 1986), p. 5.

2. The texts in the '*Trinker-Manuskript*' have been published as follows:
   i. Short stories: Hans Fallada, *Drei Jahre kein Mensch*, edited by Günter Caspar (Berlin: Aufbau, 1997).
   ii. Novel: *Der Trinker* in Hans Fallada, *Der Trinker/Der Alpdruck*, edited by Günter Caspar (Berlin and Weimar: Aufbau, 1987). English translation: *The Drinker*, translated by Charlotte and A. L. Lloyd (London: Libris, 1989). Published in the US in 2009 (New York: Melville House).
   iii. Memoirs: Hans Fallada, *In meinem fremden Land*, edited by Jenny Williams and Sabine Lange (Berlin: Aufbau, 2009).

3. *Der Trinker* was first published by Rowohlt in 1950 because Erich Wendt, director of Aufbau in East Germany, and Becher did not wish to publish what they viewed as a nihilistic and bleak novel at that time. The English quotations in the following discussion are taken from Hans Fallada, *The Drinker*.

4. From 1934, any writer who wanted their work published in Germany had to be a member of the Reich Literary Chamber, part of the institutional apparatus established by Goebbels in November 1933 to ensure Nazi control of all cultural activities. Ditzen's claim that he was not a member of the Reich Literary Chamber is simply not true. On 11 July 1934, he was issued with Membership Card no. 841 (see *Hans Fallada. Sein Leben in Bildern und Briefen*, p. 125).

5. Rudolf Ditzen to Anna Ditzen, 25 October 1944. Fallada/Ditzen, *Wenn du fort bist*, p. 415.

6. It appears likely that Gertrud Kramer did go to Carwitz in January 1945; Werner Hütter visited Ditzen on 19 January and reports that he was dictating a manuscript to a typist in his study. See Werner Hütter, 'Besuch bei Hans Fallada', *Hans Fallada Jahrbuch*, I (1995), pp. 147–54.

7. It seems likely that Ditzen wanted to show Rowohlt the three novels the Deutsche Verlags-Anstalt had returned unpublished: 'Before You Go to Sleep', 'A Man Wants to Get On' and 'The Master of Strammin'. There is no evidence that Rowohlt was aware of *The Drinker* in December 1944. Even if he was, it is unlikely that he would have been able to read it in manuscript form.

8. See Mayer, *Ernst Rowohlt*, p. 142.

9. Elisabeth Ditzen, 'Tagebuch 1945', Hans Fallada Archive.

10. Conversation with Anna Ditzen, 9 September 1983, Feldberg.

11. Jonathan Steele, *Socialism with a German Face* (London: Cape, 1977), p. 34.

12. For information regarding the day-to-day events in Feldberg during Ditzen's period of office I am grateful to Herr Heinrich Kardel of Feldberg, who kindly provided me with a number of documents relating to this time.

13. Grigorij Weiss, *Am Morgen nach dem Kriege* (Berlin: Verlag der Nation, 1981), pp. 85–9.

14. The typed manuscript is entitled '*Der unerwünschte Autor: Meine Erlebnisse während zwölf Jahre Naziterror*', Hans Fallada Archive. For a detailed discussion of the differences between the handwritten and

typed manuscripts, see Fallada, *In meinem fremden Land*, pp. 281–4, 296–7, 303–4, 308–9.

15. *Culture and Society in the GDR*, edited by G. Bartram and A. Waine, GDR Monitor Special Series, No. 2 (1983), p. 7.

16. *Deutsche Geschichte 3: Von 1917 bis zur Gegenwart*, edited by Hans-Joachim Bartmuss et al (Berlin: Deutscher Verlag der Wissenschaften, 1968), pp. 398–9.

17. Weiss, *Am Morgen nach dem Kriege*, p. 91.

18. Heinrich Kardel, '*Hans Fallada, Kleiner Mann – nun?, Dokumentation über den Bürgermeister "Hans Fallada"*' (unpublished manuscript).

19. Rudolf Ditzen to Paul Bruse, 30 November 1945.

20. Chief among these was Major Mjasnik, the Soviet commander in Feldberg, 'who made life almost unbearable', as Ditzen wrote to Paul Bruse on 30 November 1945.

21. Rudolf Ditzen to Harro Stowe, 20 August 1946.

22. Rudolf Ditzen to Anna Ditzen, 16 October 1945. Fallada/Ditzen, *Wenn du fort bist*, p. 435.

23. '*Lob der Schwermut*', in Becher, *Der Aufstand im Menschen*, pp. 38–9.

24. *Erinnerungen an Johannes R. Becher*, edited by the Johannes R. Becher Archive (Leipzig: Reclam, 1974), pp. 243–7.

25. For a detailed discussion of the background to the novel, see Manfred Kuhnke, *Die Hampels und die Quangels. Authentisches und Erfundenes in Hans Falladas letztem Roman* (Neubrandenburg: federchen, 2001) and *Falladas letzter Roman. Die wahre Geschichte* (Friedland: Steffen, 2011).

26. Hans Fallada, '*Über den doch vorhandenen Widerstand der Deutschen gegen den Hitlerterror*', in Sabine Lange, *. . . wir haben nicht nur das Chaos, sondern wir stehen an einem Beginn . . . Hans Fallada 1945–7* (Neubrandenburg: federchen, 1988), pp. 45–56.

27. Hans Fallada, '"*Meine Damen und Herren!" Rede, gehalten in Schwerin am 8 December 1945*', in Lange, ibid., pp. 57–63.

28. Konstantin Fedin, '*Ein Sohn des deutschen Volkes. Zum 84. Geburtstag von Wilhelm Pieck*', in *Fedin und Deutschland. Aus dem Werk. Alte und neue Begegnungen. Stimmen der Freunde* (Berlin: Aufbau, 1962), p. 249.

29. Rudolf Ditzen to Elisabeth and Heinz Hörig, 15 February 1946.

30. All that has survived of the letters which Ditzen sent to Bakonyi from France in 1943 are the extracts she quotes in her letter to the *Neuer Hannoverischer Kurier* on 31 December 1945. The full text of Ditzen's letter of 27 September 1943 as quoted by Bakonyi is as follows:

I have just completed a three-day tour in which I viewed a French town which has been beautifully and routinely destroyed by the British. Nonetheless, the French are still insisting on waiting for the British to arrive and make no secret of their hatred of us. Wandering through French towns and villages, unarmed and in civilian clothes, you see and hear a lot. Sometimes I think that things will turn out badly after all, but then things have never turned out badly before. I have never been as optimistic as now after Italy's treachery and our steady retreat on the Eastern Front. I have heard and seen a lot. I know that it will take only two or three months before we are ready for a quite different war. Then England will collapse in four days and America will discover the true meaning of war. These are words which you have never heard from me before, or ever expected to hear from me, but we must believe in victory otherwise nothing has any meaning. I have spent time with our young men on military airfields and I have sat nearly every night in an air raid shelter, all of that cannot be in vain. We are the masters of the world, definitely the masters of Europe. It won't be long now.

31. I am indebted to Wolf-Rüdiger Dähnrich for the information about the investigation of the Fallada case by the Control Commission for Germany. Wallach's words come from the Control Commission's papers lodged in the Document Centre, Berlin.

32. Ernst Rowohlt to Rudolf Ditzen, 2 January 1946. Fallada, *Ewig auf der Rutschbahn*, p. 399.

33. Caspar has estimated that Ditzen received around 3,000 marks per month from Aufbau, in addition to his income from short stories, reviews, and so on, from November 1945 to February 1946 (personal communication).

34. The correspondence with Kurt Wilhelm is published in: *Allein mit Lebensmittelkarten ist es nicht auszuhalten ... Autoren und Verlegerbriefe 1945–9*, edited by Elmar Faber and Carsten Wurm (Berlin: Aufbau, 1991), pp. 71–83.

35. Rudolf Ditzen to Dr Selzer, 21 June 1946.

36. Hans Fallada, *Der Alpdruck*, in Hans Fallada, *Der Trinker/Der Alpdruck*, edited by Günter Caspar.

37. The name 'Granzow' belonged to the owner of a transport and removal business in Feldberg with whom Ditzen had dealings during his period as mayor.

38. Rudolf Ditzen to Anna Ditzen, 16 September 1946. Fallada/Ditzen, *Wenn du fort bist*, p. 462.

39. Rudolf Ditzen to Anna Ditzen, 27 October 1946. Fallada/Ditzen, ibid., p. 466.

40. All English quotations in the following discussion are taken from Hans Fallada, *Alone in Berlin*, translated by Michael Hofmann (London: Penguin, 2009).

41. See Kuhnke, *Die Hampels und die Quangels*, pp. 99–121.

42. *Jeder stirbt für sich allein* (2011), p. 697.

43. Rudolf Ditzen to Elisabeth Ditzen, 22 December 1946.

44. An undated note in Ulla's handwriting in the Archive protests that '. . . Becher, of all people, can never break up our relationship'. Ulla goes on to insist that she loves Ditzen and his children and that she would be willing to have them all, including Suse ('which would indeed be a sacrifice'), come to live in Eisenmengerweg. The only person she refuses to have under her roof is a certain 'Gertrud' (presumably Gertrud Kramer).

45. Kuhnke has shown that the hospital scene depicted in the biographies of Manthey and Liersch, as well as in the film *Fallada, Letztes Kapitel*, is based on incorrect information. See Manfred Kuhnke, '*Szene im Hörsaal*', *Neue Deutsche Literatur*, 39 (1991), pp. 167–72.

Bibliography

I WORKS BY HANS FALLADA
1. Bibliography

For a comprehensive bibliography in German of Fallada's published novels, short stories, newspaper articles, literary criticism, translations, speeches and letters from 1920 to 1992, see *Hans Fallada 1893–1947. Eine Bibliographie*, compiled and annotated by E. Dünnebier (Neubrandenburg: federchen, 1993).

2. Fallada's published novels, diaries and essays quoted in this biography, presented in the order in which they were written

Das Frühwerk, 2 vols. (Berlin and Weimar: Aufbau, 1993)
Strafgefangener Zelle 32, Tagebuch 22. Juni–2. September 1924 (Berlin: Aufbau, 1998)
'*Stimme aus den Gefängnissen*', *Das Tage-Buch*, 6, (1925) 1, pp. 9–15
'*Tscheka-Impressionen*', *Das Tage-Buch*, 6 (1925), 15, pp. 522–6
'*Stahlhelm-Nachtübung*', *Das Tage-Buch*, 6 (1925), 33, pp. 1227–9
'*Was liest man eigentlich in Hinterpommern?*' *Die Literarische Welt*, 1 (1925), 1, pp. 4–5
'*Bauern-Krieg wider Neumünster*', *Das Tage-Buch*, 10 (1929), 37, pp. 1516–19
'*Landvolkprozeß*', *Die Weltbühne* 25 (1929), 49, pp. 832–5
'*Sachlicher Bericht über das Glück, ein Morphinist zu sein*', in Hans Fallada, *Drei Jahre kein Mensch* (Berlin: Aufbau, 1997), pp. 5–24; *Short Treatise on the Joys of Morphinism* (London: Penguin, 2011)

Bauern, Bonzen, Bomben (Berlin and Weimar: Aufbau, 1981); *A Small Circus* (London: Penguin, 2012)

Kleiner Mann – was nun? (Reinbek: Rowohlt, 1978); *Little Man – What Now?* (London: Libris, 1996; New York: Melville House, 2009)

Wer einmal aus dem Blechnapf frißt (Reinbek: Rowohlt, 1980)

Wir hatten mal ein Kind (Reinbek: Rowohlt, 1980)

Märchen vom Stadtschreiber, der aufs Land flog (Berlin: Aufbau, 1991)

Altes Herz geht auf die Reise (Berlin: Aufbau, 1995)

Wolf unter Wölfen (Reinbek: Rowohlt, 1991); *Wolf among Wolves* (New York: Melville House, 2010)

Der eiserne Gustav (Berlin and Weimar: Aufbau, 1984)

Kleiner Mann – großer Mann, alles vertauscht (Reinbek: Rowohlt, 1970)

Süßmilch spricht (Olten: Walter, 1983)

Dies Herz, das dir gehört (Berlin: Aufbau, 1994)

Der ungeliebte Mann (Munich: Heyne, 1980)

Zwei zarte Lämmchen weiß wie Schnee (Reinbek: Rowohlt, 1967)

Die Stunde, eh' du schlafen gehst (Munich: Goldmann, 1954)

Damals bei uns daheim/Heute bei uns zu Haus (Berlin and Weimar: Aufbau, 1982)

Ein Mann will nach oben (Reinbek: Rowohlt, 1970)

Der Jungherr von Strammin (Munich: Heyne, 1984)

Pechvogel und Glückskind (Greifswald: Steinbecker, 1998)

In meinem fremden Land. Gefängnistagebuch 1944 (Berlin: Aufbau, 2009)

'Osterfest 1933 mit der SA', *Tägliche Rundschau*, 28 November–4 December 1945

'Wie ich Schriftsteller wurde', in Hans Fallada, *Lieschens Sieg und andere Erzählungen* (Reinbek: Rowohlt, 1973), pp. 189–230

Der Trinker/Der Alpdruck (Berlin and Weimar: Aufbau, 1987); *The Drinker* (London: Libris, 1989; New York: Melville House, 2010)

Jeder stirbt für sich allein (Berlin and Weimar: Aufbau, 1981); new, unabridged edition (Berlin: Aufbau, 2011): *Alone in Berlin* (London: Penguin, 2009)

3. Collections of Fallada's short stories

Hoppelpoppel. Wo bist du? (Stuttgart: Reclam, 1955)

Gesammelte Erzählungen (Reinbek: Rowohlt, 1967)

Lieschens Sieg und andere Erzählungen (Reinbek: Rowohlt, 1973)
Märchen und Geschichten (Berlin and Weimar: Aufbau, 1985)
Geschichten aus der Murkelei (Berlin: Aufbau, 1995)
Drei Jahre kein Mensch (Berlin: Aufbau, 1997)

4. Published correspondence and other archival material

Hans Fallada. Sein Leben in Bildern und Briefen, compiled by Gunnar Müller-Waldeck and Roland Ulrich with Ulrich Ditzen (Berlin: Aufbau, 1997)

Hans Fallada–Uli Ditzen. *Mein Vater und sein Sohn. Briefwechsel*, edited by Uli Ditzen (Berlin: Aufbau, 2004)

Hans Fallada–Anna Ditzen. *Wenn du fort bist, ist alles nur halb. Briefe einer Ehe*, edited by Uli Ditzen (Berlin: Aufbau, 2007)

Ich bin nicht der, den Du liebst. Die frühen Jahre des Hans Fallada in Berlin, edited by Cecilia von Studnitz (Neubrandenburg: federchen, 2007)

Hans Fallada. *Ewig auf der Rutschbahn. Briefwechsel mit dem Rowohlt Verlag*, edited by Michael Töteberg and Sabine Buck (Reinbek: Rowohlt, 2008)

5. Unpublished works

Ditzen, R. *'Gedanken über den Glauben'* (1910/1911), Hans Fallada Archive

— *'Deutschland in der heutigen französischen Litterature'* (1912), Hans Fallada Archive

— *'Gestalten und Bilder'* (1917), Hans Fallada Archive

Ditzen, E. *'Erinnerungen'*, Hans Fallada Archive

— *'Tagebuch 1945'*, Hans Fallada Archive

Fallada, H. *'Briefwechsel mit F. Hermann Küthe'*, Akademie der Künste, Berlin: 137/44

Fallada, H. *'Der unerwünschte Autor: Meine Erlebnisse während zwölf Jahre Naziterror'*, Hans Fallada Archive

Hörig, E. *'Szenen aus dem Familienleben, Erinnerungen an die Berliner Jahre, 1900–10'*, Hans Fallada Archive

Kardel, H. *'Hans Fallada, Kleiner Mann – nun?'*, Dokumentation über den Bürgermeister Hans Fallada' (unpublished manuscript).

II WORKS BY OTHER WRITERS

Becher, J. R., *Der Aufstand im Menschen*, edited by Ilse Siebert (Berlin and Weimar: Aufbau, 1986)

— *Briefe 1909–58* and *Briefe an J. R. Becher 1910–58*, 2 vols., edited by Rolf Harder (Berlin and Weimar: Aufbau, 1993).

Becher-Archiv (ed.), *Erinnerungen an Johannes R. Becher* (Leipzig: Philipp Reclam jun., 1974)

Benjamin, W., *Berlin Childhood around 1900*, translated by Howard Eiland (Cambridge, Mass., and London: Belknap, 2006)

Bergengruen, W., *Schreibtischerinnerungen* (Zurich: Die Arche, 1961)

Brecht, B., *Gesammelte Werke in 20 Bänden* (Frankfurt am Main: Suhrkamp, 1967)

Dodd, M., *My Years in Germany* (London: Gollancz, 1939)

Fedin, K., '*Ein Sohn des deutschen Volkes. Zum 84. Geburtstag von Wilhelm Pieck*', in Fedin, K., *Fedin und Deutschland. Aus dem Werk. Alte und neue Begegnungen. Stimmen der Freunde* (Berlin: Aufbau, 1962), pp. 245–50

Hamsun, K., *Growth of the Soil* (New York: Vintage, 1972)

Harden, S., von, '*Erinnerungen an einst . . .*', *Imprimatur* 3 (1961/62), pp. 219–22

Hirsch, K. J., *Heimkehr zu Gott. Briefe an meinen Sohn* (Munich: Desch, 1946)

Huelsenbeck, R., '*Die dadaistische Bewegung*', *Die neue Rundschau* 31 (1920), pp. 972–9

Jünger, E., *On the Marble Cliffs*, translated by Stuart Hood (London: New Direction, 1947)

Hochhuth R. (ed.), *Das Erich Kästner-Buch* (Zurich: Atrium, 1959)

Kafka, F., *Tagebücher 1910–23*, edited by M. Brod (Frankfurt am Main: Fischer, 1954)

Klepper, J., *Unter dem Schatten deiner Flügel. Aus den Tagebüchern der Jahre 1932 bis 1942*, edited by H. Klepper (Berlin: Union, 1970)

Krell, M., *Das alles gab es einmal* (Frankfurt am Main: Suhrkamp, 1961)

Mann, T., *The Magic Mountain*, translated by H. T. Lowe-Porter (Harmondsworth: Penguin, 1964)

— *Briefe*, edited by E. Mann (Frankfurt am Main: Fischer, 1979)

— '*Gedanken im Kriege*', in *Die neue Rundschau*, 25 (1914), 10, pp. 1474–5

— *Tagebücher 1933–4*, edited by P. de Mendelssohn (Frankfurt am Main: Fischer, 1977)

Ringelnatz, J., *Ringelnatz in kleiner Auswahl als Taschenbuch* (Berlin: Karl H. Henssel, 1964)

Salomon, E. von, *Der Fragebogen* (Reinbek: Rowohlt, 1997)

Schneider, R., *Gesammelte Werke*, 10 vols., edited by H. M. Landau (Frankfurt am Main: Insel, 1977–82)

Toller, E., *Gesammelte Werke*, 5 vols., edited by W. Frühwald and J. M. Spalek (Munich: Hanser, 1987)

Wilde, O., *The Works of Oscar Wilde*, edited by G. F. Maine (London: Collins, 1948)

Wolfe T., *You Can't Go Home Again* (New York: Harper and Brothers, 1940)

III WORKS ABOUT FALLADA
1. Bibliography

For a comprehensive bibliography in German of secondary literature relating to Fallada published during the period 1931 to 1995 see *Hans Fallada 1893–1947. Bibliographie zur Sekundärliteratur*, compiled and annotated by R. K. Zachau (Neubrandenburg, 1998).

2. Monographs, conference proceedings and journal articles

Becher, J. R., *Über Hans Fallada* (Berlin: Kinderbuchverlag, 1965)

Börner, D., *'Wenn Ihr überhaupt nur ahntet, was ich für einen Lebenshunger habe!' Hans Fallada in Thüringen* (Weimar and Jena: Hain, 2010)

Bredohl, T. and J. Williams (eds.), *Die Provinz im Leben und Werk von Hans Fallada* (Berlin: Individuell, 2005)

Bredohl, T. and M. Zimmermann (eds.), *Berlin's Culturescape in the Twentieth Century* (Regina: University of Regina, 2008)

Caspar, G., *Fallada-Studien* (Berlin and Weimar: Aufbau, 1988)

Crepon, T., *Leben und Tode des Hans Fallada* (Halle/Leipzig: Mitteldeutscher Verlag, 1978)

— *Kurzes Leben – langes Sterben. Hans Fallada in Mecklenburg* (Rostock: Hinstorff, 1998)

Crepon, T. and M. Dwars, *An der Schwale liegt (k)ein Märchen* (Neumünster: Karl Wachholz, 1993)

Faber, E. and C. Wurm, *Allein mit Lebensmittelkarten ist es nicht auszuhalten ... Autoren und Verlegerbriefe 1945–49* (Berlin: Aufbau, 1991)

Farin, K., *Hans Fallada. 'Welche sind, die haben kein Glück'* (Munich: Thomas Tilsner, 1993)

Fritsch-Lange, P. and L. Hagestedt (eds.), *Hans Fallada und das Literatursystem der Moderne* (Berlin: de Gruyter, 2011)

Frotscher, H. J., *Hans Fallada: Kleiner Mann – was nun?* (Munich: Oldenbourg, 1983)

Gansel, C. and W. Liersch (eds.), *Zeit vergessen, Zeit erinnern. Hans Fallada und das kulturelle Gedächtnis* (Göttingen: V&R unipress, 2008)

Gansel, C. and W. Liersch (eds.), *Hans Fallada und die literarische Moderne* (Göttingen: V&R unipress, 2009)

Geßler, A., *Hans Fallada. Sein Leben und Werk* (Berlin: Volk und Wissen, 1972)

Hans Fallada Jahrbuch 1, edited by R. Ortner and G. Müller-Waldeck (Neubrandenburg: federchen, 1995)

Hans Fallada Jahrbuch 2, edited by R. Ortner and G. Müller-Waldeck (Neubrandenburg: federchen, 1997)

Hans Fallada Jahrbuch 3, edited by P. Fritsch and R. Ulrich (Neubrandenburg: federchen, 2000)

Hans Fallada Jahrbuch 4, edited by P. Fritsch-Lange (Neubrandenburg: federchen, 2003)

Hans Fallada Jahrbuch 5, edited by P. Fritsch-Lange (Neubrandenburg: federchen, 2006)

Haupt, H., *Filmographie* (Feldberg: Hans Fallada Archive, 1996)

Heinrich, B., *Du bist doch bei mir, aber wir sterben allein. Studien zu Hans Falladas Frauenbild* (Neubrandenburg: federchen, 2007)

Hoffmann, V., *Der Dienstälteste von Plötzensee. Das zerrissene Leben des Musikerziehers Alfred Schmidt-Sas (1895–1943)* (Berlin: trafo, 2000)

Knüppel, S., *Falladas Gesichter. Literarische Physiognomien in Romanwerk Hans Falladas* (Neubrandenburg: federchen, 2009)

Kuhnke, M., 'Szene im Hörsaal', *Neue Deutsche Literatur*, 39 (1991), pp. 167–72.

— ... *daß ihr Tod nicht umsonst war! Authentisches und Erfundenes in Hans Falladas letztem Roman* (Neubrandenburg: federchen, 1991); revised edition entitled *Die Hampels und die Quangels* (Neubrandenburg: federchen, 2001); updated edition entitled *Falladas letzter Roman. Die wahre Geschichte* (Friedland: Steffen, 2011)

— *Besuch bei Hans Fallada* (Neubrandenburg: federchen, 1996)

— *Verstrickt in die Zeiten. Anmerkungen zu den verwobenen Lebenslinien von Johannes R. Becher und Hans Fallada* (Neubrandenburg: federchen, 1999)

— *Der traurige Clown und der Elefant auf dem Seil. Hans Fallada und e.o. plauen* (Neubrandenburg: federchen, 2003)
— *Väterchen Rowohlt, Freund Franz, die unselige Miss Dodd. Hans Falladas Besucher in Carwitz* (Neubrandenburg: federchen, 2006)
Lamp, H., *Fallada unter Wölfen. Schreiben im Dritten Reich. Die Geschichte des Inflationsromans 'Wolf unter Wölfen'* (Friedland: Steffen, 2002)
Lange, S., *. . . wir haben nicht nur das Chaos, sondern wir stehen an einem Beginn . . . Hans Fallada, 1945–7* (Neubrandenburg: federchen, 1988)
— *Im Mäckelnbörgischen, in der Welteinsamkeit. Hans Fallada in Carwitz und Feldberg 1933–45* (Neubrandenburg: federchen, 1995)
Liersch, W., *Hans Fallada. Sein großes kleines Leben* (first edition, Berlin: Neues Leben, 1981; expanded new edition, Hildesheim: Claassen, 1993)
Loohuis, W. J., *Hans Fallada in der Literaturkritik. Ein Forschungsbericht* (Bad Honnef: Keimer, 1979)
Manthey, J., *Hans Fallada* (Reinbek: Rowohlt, 1963)
Mayer, D. (ed.), *Hans Fallada: Kleiner Mann – was nun?* (Frankfurt/Main: Diesterweg, 1978)
Müller-Waldeck, G. '"*Er war ein Ermunterer." Gespräch mit Annemarie Steiner*', *Hans Fallada Jahrbuch* 3 (2000), pp. 64–81
Müller-Waldeck, G. and R. Ulrich (eds.), *Hans Fallada. Beiträge zu Leben und Werk* (Rostock: Hinstorff, 1995)
— *Neues von Daheim und Zuhaus* (Frankfurt am Main/ Berlin: Ullstein, 1993)
Studnitz, C. von, *Es war wie ein Rausch. Fallada und sein Leben* (Düsseldorf: Droste, 1997)
Thöming, J., '*Hans Fallada. Seismograph gesellschaftlicher Krisen*', in *Zeitkritische Romane des 20. Jahrhunderts. Die Gesellschaft in der Kritik der deutschen Literatur*, edited by H. Wagener (Stuttgart: Reclam, 1975), pp. 97–123
Weiss, G., *Am Morgen nach dem Kriege* (Berlin: Verlag der Nation, 1981)
Wenzel-Orff. H., *Hans Fallada – Lebensorte. Ein Fotokatalog.* (Feldberg: Hans Fallada Gesellschaft, 1997)
Williams, J., 'Some Thoughts on the Success of Hans Fallada's *Kleiner Mann – was nun?*'. *German Life and Letters* 49 (1987), pp. 306–18
— 'Hans Fallada's Literary Breakthrough: *Bauern, Bonzen und Bomben* and *Kleiner Mann – was nun?*' in K. Leydecker (ed.), *German Novelists of the Weimar Republic. Intersections of Literature and Politics* (Rochester, New York: Camden House, 2006), pp. 253–68
Wolff, R. (ed.), *Hans Fallada. Werk und Wirkung* (Bonn: Bouvier, 1983)
Zachau, R. K. (ed.), *Typography and Literature. Berlin and Modernism*, (Göttingen: V&R unipress, 2009)

IV GENERAL

Artz, J., *Sehen was bleibt. Der Maler und sein Werk: Kurt Dietrich Losch 1889–1994* (Berlin: Sammlung Artz, 1994)

Barbian, J.-P., *Literaturpolitik im 'Dritten Reich'. Institutionen, Kompetenzen, Betätigungsfelder* (Munich: dtv, 1995)

Bartram, G. and A. Wayne (eds.), *Culture and Society in the GDR*, GDR Monitor Special Series No. 2 (1983)

Bergschicker, H., *Deutsche Chronik 1933–45* (Berlin: Elefanten, 1981)

Bismarck, Ruth-Alice von and Ulrich Kabitz (eds.), *Brautbriefe Zelle 92. Dietrich Bonhoeffer. Maria von Wedemeyer. 1943–5*, with an Afterword by Eberhard Bethge (Munich: C. H. Beck, 1992). Translation by John Brownjohn: *Love Letters from Cell 92. Dietrich Bonhoeffer and Maria von Wedemeyer* (London: Collins, 1994)

Bloch, E., *Heritage of Our Time*, translated by Neville and Stephen Plaice (Berkeley and Los Angeles: University of California Press, 1990)

Bonhoeffer, D., *No Rusty Swords. Letters, Lectures and Notes from the Collected Works of Dietrich Bonhoeffer*, edited and introduced by Edwin H. Robertson, translated by Edwin H. Robertson and John Bowden (London: Collins, 1965)

Bullivant, K. (ed.), *Culture and Society in the Weimar Republic* (Manchester: Manchester University Press, 1977)

Bullock, A., *Hitler. A Study in Tyranny* (Harmondsworth: Penguin, 1962)

Bußmann, A., *Erinnerungen an Wolfgang Borchert. Zur zehnten Wiederkehr seines Todestages am 20. November 1957* (Hamburg: Rowohlt, 1957)

Denkler, H. and K. Prümm (eds.), *Die deutsche Literatur im Dritten Reich* (Stuttgart: Reclam, 1976)

Dove, R. and S. Lamb (eds.) *German Writers and Politics 1918–39* (London: Macmillan, 1992)

Evans, R. J., *Rituals of Retribution. Capital Punishment in German Politics and Society since the Seventeenth Century* (Harmondsworth: Penguin, 1997)

Gaevernitz, G. v. S. (ed.), *Revolt against Hitler: The Personal Account of Fabian von Schlabrendorff* (London: Eyre and Spottiswoode, 1948)

Goebbels, J., *Tagebücher 1924–45*, 5 vols. (Munich: Piper, 1992)

Hobsbawm, E., *Age of Extremes: The Short Twentieth Century 1914–91* (London: Michael Joseph, 1994)

Kiaulehn, W., *Mein Freund der Verleger – Ernst Rowohlt und seine Zeit* (Reinbek: Rowohlt, 1967)

Klemperer, V., *Ich will Zeugnis ablegen bis zum letzten. Tagebücher* 1933–45, 2 vols. (Berlin: Aufbau, 1995)

Körmendi, F., 'Warum ich Deutschland nicht verlasse', *Die Welt*, 10 November 1962

Kracauer, S., *Die Angestellten* (Frankfurt am Main: Suhrkamp, 1971)

Kühnl, R., *Der deutsche Faschismus in Quellen und Dokumenten* (Cologne: Pahl-Rugenstein, 1975)

Laffan, M. (ed.), *The Burden of German History* (London: Methuen, 1989)

Langenbucher, H., *Volkhafte Dichtung der Zeit* (Berlin: Junker & Dünnhaupt, 1935)

Loewy, E., *Literatur unterm Hakenkreuz* (Frankfurt am Main: Fischer, 1969)

Mayer, P., *Ernst Rowohlt* (Reinbek: Rowohlt, 1968)

Naimark, N. N., *The Russians in Germany. A History of the Soviet Zone of Occupation*, 1945–9 (Cambridge, Mass., and London: Harvard University Press, 1995)

Pasley, M. (ed.), *Germany. A Companion to German Studies* (London/New York: Methuen, 1982)

Pike, D., *The Politics of Culture in Soviet-occupied Germany*, 1945–9 (Stanford, California: Stanford University Press, 1992)

Pinthus, K., 'Life and Death of Ernst Toller', *Books Abroad* 14 (1939), pp. 4–11

Raabe, P. (ed.), *The Era of Expressionism*, translated by J. M. Ritchie (London: Calder and Boyars, 1974)

Ritchie, J. M., *German Literature under National Socialism* (London: Croom Helm, 1983)

Smail, D., *White-Collar Workers, Mass Culture and 'Neue Sachlichkeit' in Weimar Berlin* (Bern: Peter Lang, 1999)

Steele, J., *Socialism with a German Face* (London: Jonathan Cape, 1977)

Suhrkamp, P., 'Der Zuschauer', *Die neue Rundschau* 11 (1942), 523–5

Symonette, L. and K. H. Kowalke (eds.), *Speak Low (When You Speak Love): The Letters of Kurt Weill and Lotte Lenya* (London: Hamish Hamilton, 1996)

Weinstock, J. M. and R. T. Rovinsky (eds.), *The Hero in Scandinavian Literature from Peer Gynt to the Present* (Austen: University of Texas Press, 1975)

Willett, J., *The New Sobriety. Art and Politics in the Weimar Period* (London: Thames and Hudson, 1978)

Witzke, C., *Domjüch. Erinnerungen an eine Heil- und Pflegeanstalt in Mecklenburg-Strelitz* (Neubrandenburg: federchen, 2001)

Wulf, J., *Literatur und Dichtung im Dritten Reich* (Frankfurt/Berlin/Wien: Ullstein, 1983)

Index

Fallada's works are indexed under Fallada, Hans (Rudolf Ditzen). Titles of short-story collections are included, but not the titles of individual short stories, though non-fiction or short autobiographical pieces have been included. Italic numbers refer to illustrations.

PENGUIN MODERN CLASSICS

ALONE IN BERLIN
HANS FALLADA

'A truly great book .. an utterly gripping thriller' Justin Cartwright, *Sunday Telegraph*

Berlin, 1940, and the city is filled with fear. At the house on 55 Jablonski Strasse, its various occupants try to live under Nazi rule in their different ways: the bullying Hitler loyalists the Persickes, the retired judge Fromm and the unassuming couple Otto and Anna Quangel. Then the Quangels receive the news that their beloved son has been killed fighting in France. Shocked out of their quiet existence, they begin a silent campaign of defiance, and a deadly game of cat and mouse develops between the Quangels and the ambitious Gestapo inspector Escherich. When petty criminals Kluge and Borkhausen also become involved, deception, betrayal and murder ensue, tightening the noose around the Quangels' necks ...

'Fallada's great novel, beautifully translated by the poet Michael Hofmann, evokes the daily horror of life under the Third Reich, where the venom of Nazism seeped into the very pores of society, poisoning every aspect of existence. It is a story of resistence, sly humour and hope' Ben Macintyre, *The Times*

'[*Alone in Berlin*] has something of the horror of Conrad, the madness of Dostoyevsky and the chilling menace of Capote's *In Cold Blood*' Roger Cohen, *New York Times*

He just wanted a decent book to read ...

Not too much to ask, is it? It was in 1935 when Allen Lane, Managing Director of Bodley Head Publishers, stood on a platform at Exeter railway station looking for something good to read on his journey back to London. His choice was limited to popular magazines and poor-quality paperbacks – the same choice faced every day by the vast majority of readers, few of whom could afford hardbacks. Lane's disappointment and subsequent anger at the range of books generally available led him to found a company – and change the world.

'We believed in the existence in this country of a vast reading public for intelligent books at a low price, and staked everything on it'
Sir Allen Lane, 1902–1970, founder of Penguin Books

The quality paperback had arrived – and not just in bookshops. Lane was adamant that his Penguins should appear in chain stores and tobacconists, and should cost no more than a packet of cigarettes.

Reading habits (and cigarette prices) have changed since 1935, but Penguin still believes in publishing the best books for everybody to enjoy. We still believe that good design costs no more than bad design, and we still believe that quality books published passionately and responsibly make the world a better place.

So wherever you see the little bird – whether it's on a piece of prize-winning literary fiction or a celebrity autobiography, political tour de force or historical masterpiece, a serial-killer thriller, reference book, world classic or a piece of pure escapism – you can bet that it represents the very best that the genre has to offer.

Whatever you like to read – trust Penguin.